RENEWALS 458
DUE

D0337602

Secularism and State Policies toward Religion
The United States, France, and Turkey

Why do secular states pursue different policies toward religion? This book provides a generalizable argument about the impact of ideological struggles on the public policy-making process, as well as a state-religion regimes index of 197 countries. More specifically, it analyzes why American state policies are largely tolerant of religion, whereas French and Turkish policies generally prohibit its public visibility, as seen in their bans on Muslim headscarves. In the United States, the dominant ideology is "passive secularism," which requires the state to play a passive role by allowing the public visibility of religion. The dominant ideology in France and Turkey is "assertive secularism," which demands that the state play an assertive role in excluding religion from the public sphere. Passive and assertive secularism became dominant in these cases through certain historical processes, particularly the presence or absence of an *ancien régime* based on the marriage between monarchy and hegemonic religion during state-building periods.

Ahmet T. Kuru is Assistant Professor of Political Science at San Diego State University. He is currently a Postdoctoral Research Scholar at and Assistant Director of the Center for the Study of Democracy, Toleration, and Religion at the School of International and Public Affairs, Columbia University. His dissertation, on which this book is based, received the Aaron Wildavsky Award for the best dissertation from the Religion and Politics Section of the American Political Science Association. He is the author of several articles that have appeared in journals such as *World Politics*, *Comparative Politics*, and *Political Science Quarterly*.

Cambridge Studies in Social Theory, Religion, and Politics

Editors

David C. Leege, *University of Notre Dame*
Kenneth D. Wald, *University of Florida, Gainesville*

The most enduring and illuminating bodies of late-nineteenth-century social theory – by Marx, Weber, Durkheim, and others – emphasized the integration of religion, polity, and economy through time and place. Once a staple of classic social theory, however, religion gradually lost the interest of many social scientists during the twentieth century. The recent emergence of phenomena such as Solidarity in Poland; the dissolution of the Soviet empire; various South American, Southern African, and South Asian liberation movements; the Christian Right in the United States; and Al Qaeda have reawakened scholarly interest in religiously based political conflict. At the same time, fundamental questions are once again being asked about the role of religion in stable political regimes, public policies, and constitutional orders. The series Cambridge Studies in Social Theory, Religion, and Politics will produce volumes that study religion and politics by drawing on classic social theory and more recent social scientific research traditions. Books in the series offer theoretically grounded, comparative, empirical studies that raise "big" questions about a timely subject that has long engaged the best minds in social science.

Titles in the series:

Joel S. Fetzer and J. Christopher Soper, *Muslims and the State in Britain, France, and Germany*
Jonathan Fox, *A World Survey of Religion and the State*
Anthony Gill, *The Political Origins of Religious Liberty*
Pippa Norris and Ronald Inglehart, *Sacred and Secular: Religion and Politics Worldwide*

Library
University of Texas
at San Antonio

Secularism and State Policies toward Religion

The United States, France, and Turkey

AHMET T. KURU

CAMBRIDGE
UNIVERSITY PRESS

Library
University of Texas
at San Antonio

CAMBRIDGE UNIVERSITY PRESS
Cambridge, New York, Melbourne, Madrid, Cape Town, Singapore, São Paulo, Delhi

Cambridge University Press
32 Avenue of the Americas, New York, NY 10013-2473, USA

www.cambridge.org
Information on this title: www.cambridge.org/9780521741347

© Ahmet T. Kuru 2009

This publication is in copyright. Subject to statutory exception
and to the provisions of relevant collective licensing agreements,
no reproduction of any part may take place without the written
permission of Cambridge University Press.

First published 2009

Printed in the United States of America

A catalog record for this publication is available from the British Library.

Library of Congress Cataloging in Publication data
Kuru, Ahmet T.
Secularism and State policies toward religion : the United States, France, and
Turkey / Ahmet T. Kuru.
p. cm. – (Cambridge studies in social theory, religion, and politics)
Includes bibliographical references and index.
ISBN 978-0-521-51780-5 (hardback) – ISBN 978-0-521-74134-7 (pbk.)
1. Religion and state. 2. Religion and state–United States. 3. Religion and state–
France. 4. Religion and state–Turkey. I. Title. II. Series.
BL65.S8K87 2008
322'.109–dc22   2008034153

ISBN 978-0-521-51780-5 hardback
ISBN 978-0-521-74134-7 paperback

Cambridge University Press has no responsibility for the persistence or
accuracy of URLs for external or third-party Internet Web sites referred to in
this publication and does not guarantee that any content on such Web sites is,
or will remain, accurate or appropriate. Information regarding prices, travel
timetables, and other factual information given in this work are correct at
the time of first printing, but Cambridge University Press does not guarantee
the accuracy of such information thereafter.

To

Uğur and Çiçek, who were with me at the beginning of my life,
and Zeynep, who, I hope, will be with me at the end of it.

Contents

Figures and Tables

Glossary of Abbreviations

AMERICAN ORGANIZATIONS

AA   American Atheists
ACLJ   American Center for Law and Justice
ACLU   American Civil Liberties Union
ADL   Anti-Defamation League
AJC   American Jewish Congress
AU   Americans United for Separation of Church and State
NEA   National Education Association
PFAW   People for the American Way

FRENCH ORGANIZATIONS

CFCM   French Council of the Muslim Faith
CLR   Committee on Secularism and the Republic
FNMF   National Federation of Muslims of France
PCF   French Communist Party
PS   Socialist Party
UDF   Union for French Democracy
UMP   Union for a Popular Movement
UOIF   Union of Islamic Organizations of France

TURKISH ORGANIZATIONS

AK Party	Justice and Development Party
ANAP	Motherland Party
AP	Justice Party
CHP	Republican People's Party
CUP	Committee of Union and Progress
Diyanet	Directorate of Religious Affairs
DP	Democratic Party
DSP	Democratic Left Party
DYP	True Path Party
FP	Virtue Party
MGK	National Security Council
MHP	Nationalist Action Party
MNP	National Order Party
MSP	National Salvation Party
PKK	Kurdistan Workers' Party
RP	Welfare Party
SP	Felicity Party
TESEV	Turkish Economic and Social Studies Foundation
TÜSİAD	Association of Turkish Industrialists and Businessmen
YÖK	Council for Higher Education

Acknowledgments

I would like to thank several individuals and institutions for their support in the course of writing this book, which is based on my PhD dissertation. At the University of Washington, I have worked with a fascinating group of advisors. Reşat Kasaba was helpful in sharpening my knowledge of and arguments on Turkish politics and history. Steve Hanson inspired me to take the ideas and ideologies seriously in a social scientific analysis. Tony Gill contributed to my analysis of religion and politics through a comparative and global perspective. Tony also continually reminded me of the importance of human actors' rational calculations and strategic behaviors. Joel Migdal deserves the most credit because for the last six years he spent many hours reading, editing, and criticizing drafts of this book with a real respect, critical thinking, and intellectual creativity. Joel encouraged me to see the complexity of political phenomena and to have a process-oriented perspective. Additionally, Turan Kayaoğlu, my officemate for five years, contributed to this work through his hard-to-please scientific perspective and criticisms.

Two institutions played crucial roles in the subsequent parts of the writing process. At San Diego State University's Department of Political Science, I found insightful colleagues. Ron King was particularly encouraging and supportive. The postdoctoral fellowship provided by the Center for the Study of Democracy, Toleration, and Religion (CDTR) at the School of International and Public Affairs, Columbia University, was a great opportunity to make the final revisions.

Al Stepan, the director of CDTR, played a key role with his ongoing support and inspiring thoughts. Also at Columbia, Ira Katznelson and Philip Hamburger provided significant comments on chapters on the theoretical framework and the United States. Denis Lacorne, who was a visiting scholar from Sciences-Po, commented on my analysis of both American and French cases.

The field research for this study was financially supported by the University of Washington, Institute for Humane Studies, and Acton Institute for the Study of Religion and Liberty. During my research in France, Kamil Karaoğlu and his family showed unforgettable hospitality and helped me contact Muslims in France. Hamit Bozarslan maintained institutional support at the École des Hautes Études en Sciences Sociales. Semih Vaner kindly invited me to present my project to a French audience in his panel. I received the most detailed feedback in France from Valentine Zuber. For my research in Turkey, I am primarily indebted to my parents-in-law, Ziyaeddin and Adviye Akbulut, who helped me contact politicians. During my research in the United States, Christopher Soper and Jeremy Gunn made the greatest contribution. I substantially benefited from the comments of these two rare experts on both American and French cases. The bibliography contains a list of American, Turkish, and French academics with whom I had valuable conversations and interviewees who shared their opinions with me. I am thankful to all of them.

I also thank the editors at Cambridge University Press, Lewis Bateman, Kenneth Wald, and David Leege, for their encouraging guidance throughout the review and production processes and the two anonymous referees for their useful recommendations. Other individuals who kindly contributed to this project with their critical comments include Juan Linz, Joan Scott, Nilüfer Göle, Karen Barkey, John Bowen, Andrew Arato, Ted Jelen, Rajeev Bhargava, Gary Jacobsohn, Daniel Philpott, Charles Kurzman, Jamie Mayerfeld, Farid Abdel-Nour, Mark Hall, John Eastman, Katherine Stenger, Madhavi McCall, Ronnee Schreiber, Van Tarpley, Farhad Khosrokhavar, Rossella Bottoni, Jan Erk, Ali Ihsan Aydın, Jonathan Laurence, Emmet Kennedy, Metin Heper, Zehra Arat, Berna Turam, Ergun Özbudun, Kemal Karpat, Kemal Kirişçi, Hasan Kayalı, Hakan Yavuz, Benjamin Fortna, Cihan Tuğal, Zühtü Arslan, Ed Webb, Bekim Agai, Elise Massicard, George Gavrilis, Nader Hashemi, Birol Başkan, Şaban Kardaş, Ceren Belge, Ramazan Kılınç, Senem Aslan, Etga Uğur,

Işık Özel, Arda İbikoğlu, Mustafa Gökçek, Murat Somer, Mehmet Ali Doğan, Zeynep Şahin, Hatem Ete, and Ahmet Yükleyen. I also want to thank those who provided inspiring comments on different parts of this project presented at several conferences and universities, including Yale; Princeton; Columbia; Cornell; Arizona State; the New School; San Diego State; Villanova; Dickinson; Iowa State; Brigham Young; SOAS (London); Sciences-Po (Paris); and the Universities of California (San Diego), Washington (Seattle), Wisconsin (Madison), Illinois (Urbana-Champaign), Ottawa, Arizona, Utah, and Portland.

Some portions of this book have appeared in the following essays previously, and I am grateful to the publishers for allowing me to use them: "Passive and Assertive Secularism: Historical Conditions, Ideological Struggles, and State Policies towards Religion," *World Politics* vol. 59, no. 4 (2007): 568–94; "Secularism, State Policies, and Muslims in Europe: Analyzing French Exceptionalism," *Comparative Politics* vol. 41, no. 1 (2008): 1–19; "Reinterpretation of Secularism in Turkey: The Case of the Justice and Development Party," in *The Emergence of a New Turkey: Democracy and the AK Parti*, ed. M. Hakan Yavuz (Salt Lake City: University of Utah Press, 2006).

Last but not least, I want to thank several family members and friends for their encouragement and support. My wife, Zeynep Akbulut Kuru, critically read the entire manuscript, though she was busy writing her PhD dissertation. I dedicate this book to three persons for their unconditional love – Zeynep and my parents, Uğur (1935–2004) and Çiçek Kuru.

Secularism and State Policies toward Religion
The United States, France, and Turkey

Introduction

In the aftermath of the cold war, religion is playing an increasing role in politics across the globe. This trend has been a serious challenge to political scientists, who have generally left studies on religion and politics to legal scholars, philosophers, and historians.[1] Especially in the United States, this issue is often confined to the "true meaning" of the First Amendment or the correlation between religious affiliations and voting preferences. Recently, a group of political scientists have conducted comparative analyses of state-religion relations, although their number is still limited.[2] In addition to religion's rising importance in world politics, the decline of two old impediments has been influential in this change.

The first impediment that distracted many political scientists from taking religion seriously was secularization theory. According to this theory, religion is a "traditional" phenomenon, which will eventually be marginalized by the modernization process, including industrialization, urbanization, and mass education.[3] Pippa Norris and Ronald

---

[1] Kenneth Wald and Clyde Wilcox analyzed the flagship journal of political science, *American Political Science Review (APSR)*. From 1906 to 2006, the *APSR* published only twenty-one articles "with a religious term in the title" and "strongly concerned with religion." Public law and political philosophy were the subfields that supplied about 80% of these articles. Wald and Wilcox 2006, 523–5.

[2] Rare examples of comparative political analysis include Gill 1998; Monsma and Soper 1997; Fetzer and Soper 2005; Jacobsohn 2003.

[3] Bruce 2002.

Inglehart argue that economic growth, socioeconomic equality, and human development result in long-term changes in existential security, leading to the erosion of religious values, beliefs, and practices. In short, religion is doomed to wither away in developed societies.[4] The number of secularization theory's critics, however, is increasing. A competing theory is the religious market approach of Rodney Stark, Laurence Iannacconne, and Anthony Gill. They stress that individuals' religious demands do not decline in response to the so-called secularization process. Instead, religious participation changes by the quality of the supply of "churches."[5] Other critics give credit to the valid parts of secularization theory. Jose Casanova stresses that the theory has failed in its predictions of (1) the decline of religion in terms of loss of faith and a decrease in religious participation and (2) the individualization of religion, with its waning public importance. The only valid part is its emphasis on the declining dominance of religion over other spheres, such as the political, economic, and scientific.[6] According to Peter Berger, secularization theory has only two valid explanations. One concerns the secularization of European societies regarding their declining religious beliefs and participation. The other details the emergence of a global secular elite, who share a worldwide secular way of life, removed from local traditions.[7] In sum, social scientists have become less bound by the secularization theory and more aware of religion's significant public role.

The second source of distraction was the normative argument that religion should not play a substantial public role in a modern democratic polity. Philosophers such as John Rawls and Jürgen Habermas initially required that a public discourse be secular.[8] They argued that people should participate in democratic deliberation by putting aside their religious doctrines, which impeded consensus due to their

---

[4] Norris and Inglehart 2004. See Kuru 2005b.

[5] According to this approach, state regulation of religion makes religious markets inefficient and decreases religious participation (e.g., in Western Europe), whereas deregulation promotes pluralistic and competitive religious markets that efficiently satisfy diverse religious tastes and increase religious participation (e.g., in the United States). Stark and Finke 2000; Stark and Iannacconne 1994; Gill 1999; Young 1996. For a significant critique, see Norris and Inglehart 2004.

[6] Casanova 1994.

[7] Berger 1999, 10–12.

[8] Rawls 1971; Habermas 1999; Habermas 1998.

dogmatic aspects. Some of these philosophers later rethought the role of religion in the public sphere. Rawls stressed that political liberalism should not be a comprehensive doctrine that challenged secular or religious worldviews.[9] He developed the concept of "overlapping consensus," which may open spaces to religious views in public debates.[10] Charles Taylor went beyond Rawls by reinterpreting "overlapping consensus" as a way of coexistence for secular and religious discourses.[11]

Other thinkers have emphasized that religious discourses are not different from ideological arguments and, therefore, welcome the public sphere. Alfred Stepan emphasizes that all religions are "multivocal"; they may have both democratic and authoritarian interpretations. For Stepan, the *sine qua non* for democracy is not secularism but "twin tolerations" between the state and religions, as indicated by the presence of established churches in several Western European democracies.[12] Casanova points out how religions have positively contributed to the public life by defending traditional values, questioning states and markets, and protecting the common good against individualist theories.[13] The exclusion of religion from public debates is particularly problematic for political theorists, such as Nancy Fraser, who criticize the idea of a monolithic public sphere, which would become exclusionary at the expense of various religious, ethnic, and social groups. For Fraser, a truly democratic society should have room for multiple, alternative, and competing public spheres, which allow for cultural diversity.[14] In sum, these scholars emphasize that it is normal for religion and politics to interact. Therefore, the proper question for the political scientists is "*how* religion and politics interact, not *whether* they should."[15]

Even if certain political scientists are not influenced by secularization theory or by a normative view against public religion, they may still avoid making a comparative analysis of state-religion relations for two reasons. First, such an analysis is more difficult than, for example, a comparative economic study because of the lack of consistent

[9] Rawls 1996. See also Habermas 2006; Habermas 2004.
[10] Dombrowski 2001; March 2007.
[11] Taylor 1999.
[12] Stepan 2001.
[13] Casanova 1994, 228–9.
[14] Fraser 1997, 69–98.
[15] Cochran 1998, xiv (emphasis in original).

terminology. Among the three cases that I picked, the United States, France, and Turkey, only France is unanimously defined as a secular state. A major reason for the disagreement over the United States is its constitution, which does not literally include the concepts of "secular state" or "separation [of church and state]." Turkey's problem of definition is the state's control over Islam, which sounds odd for a secular state. I explain these puzzles throughout the book.

The second hurdle is the idea that each country has its unique conditions of state-religion relations, which makes a comparative analysis difficult.[16] This problem is particularly valid for my cases because the United States, France, and Turkey are largely viewed as exceptional countries. America is perceived as "exceptional" because it is the only "Western" society with constantly vibrant church participation. It would be redundant to say that France is seen as exceptional. One could even say that "French" is synonymous with "exceptional."[17] France is the only Western European country that explicitly uses the term *secular republic* in its constitution. Finally, Turkey is regarded as an exception by being both Muslim and Western – a "torn country" à la Huntington.[18] Despite these so-called exceptions, there are important similarities among the three cases to warrant comparison.[19] The term *secularism* as defined in this book captures these similarities, while still highlighting the differences among them. Such a comparison has significant, generalizable consequences for the study of religion and politics. With its comparative politics perspective, the book differs from sociological works on societal and individual religiosity,[20] philosophical works on secularism as a worldview,[21] critical works on the deconstruction of secularism as a discourse and as power relations,[22] and anthropological works on secularism as an everyday practice.[23]

[16] Mardin 1995.
[17] "L'exception française: mythe ou réalité?" *Sciences humaines*, no. 46, September–November 2004.
[18] Huntington 1993, 42–3.
[19] The French Council of State issued a report on secularism in 2004. The only two non-EU countries analyzed in the report are the United States and Turkey. Conseil d'Etat 2004, 377–82.
[20] Casanova 1994; Norris and Inglehart 2004.
[21] Taylor 2007.
[22] Asad 2003; Scott 2007; Hurd 2007.
[23] Navaro-Yashin 2002; Özyürek 2006.

The following theoretical chapter summarizes main puzzles and arguments, discusses case selection, explores the theoretical framework and its alternatives, explains the methodological tools and data sources, and defines relevant terminology. Then, two chapters focus on each of the three cases. One chapter is devoted to (1) current state policies toward religion, particularly in education, and (2) how ideological struggles shape the policy-making process. The second chapter in each set examines the historical origin and trajectory of current ideological conflicts. I counterintuitively chose to put the contemporary chapters before the historical ones because they explain both the dependent variables (policy trends toward religion) and explanatory variables (ideological dominance and struggles). The historical chapters then trace the genealogy of ideological dominance using an historical variable (*ancien régime* based on the marriage between monarchy and hegemonic religion). The conclusion includes a comparative review of the empirical chapters and their generalizable results.

I

Analyzing Secularism

History, Ideology, and Policy

On December 11, 2003, the Stasi Commission, including twenty French academics and social activists, submitted a report on secularism to President Jacques Chirac. The French executive and legislators embraced the commission's recommendation of a law to prohibit students' religious symbols in public schools. Although the primary target of the law was Muslim headscarves, it also included "large" Christian crosses, Jewish kippa, and Sikh turbans. A week after the Stasi Report, the U.S. Department of State released its "2003 Report on International Religious Freedom." At the accompanying press conference, Ambassador John Hanford answered the following questions:

Question: What was your reaction to President Chirac's headscarf ban...?
Ambassador: [A] fundamental principle of religious freedom that we work for in many countries of the world, including on this very issue of headscarves, is that all persons should be able to practice their religion and their beliefs peacefully without government interference.... President Chirac is concerned to maintain France's principle of secularism and he wants that, as I think he said, not to be negotiable. Well, of course, our hope is religious freedom will be a non-negotiable as well. One Muslim leader said this is a secularism that excludes too much.... [A] number of countries ... restrict headscarves ... where people are wearing these with no provocation, simply as a manifestation of their own heartfelt beliefs, that we don't see where this causes division among peoples.

Question: You're referring to Turkey, yes?
Ambassador: Turkey would be another country, yes.[1]

As the ambassador stresses, there is a sharp policy distinction among the United States, which allows students to display religious symbols; France, which bans such symbols in public schools; and Turkey, which prohibits them in all educational institutions, both public and private, schools and universities. What is puzzling about these three states is that although each has a different policy on student displays of religious symbols, they all are "secular states" regarding two main characteristics: (1) their legislative and judicial processes are secular in the sense of being out of institutional religious control, and (2) they constitutionally declare neutrality toward religions; they establish neither an official religion nor atheism.[2] Other states have established religious laws and courts as the basis of their legislative and judicial systems ("religious states"), recognized an official religion ("states with an established religion"), or shown an official hostility toward religions generally by establishing atheism ("antireligious states").[3] Table 1 differentiates among these four sorts of states in terms of their relationships to religion.[4]

Although they are secular states, the United States, France, and Turkey have been deeply concerned with religion and have engaged it on many fronts. The rules of these three states regarding the wearing of headscarves reflect a broad array of policy differences among them.[5] Historical and contemporary debates on secularism in all these three

---

[1] "Release of the 2003 Annual Report on International Religious Freedom," December 18, 2003, http://www.state.gov/s/d/rm/27404pf.htm.
[2] While defining a secular state, some scholars emphasize (1) separation of church/ mosque and state, and (2) religious freedom. See Smith 1999, esp. 178–83. A complete separation is neither constitutionally declared nor a practical issue in many secular states. Religious freedom is both constitutionally declared and practical; yet, it is not necessary or sufficient to be secular for a state to provide religious freedom.
[3] By religion, I imply a set of beliefs and practices that refer to a supernatural being, generally God. In this definition, neither atheism nor ideologies like Marxism are a religion.
[4] For similar typologies, see Wood 1998, 81–8; Madeley 2003a; Durham 1996, 36.
[5] Several terms are used to define particular Muslim-woman dress. The following are English words and their French and Turkish equivalents, respectively. *Headscarf (foulard*; *başörtüsü* or *türban*) implies a cloth worn around the head, while *veil (voile*; *peçe*) covers the face. *Veil* may also be used interchangeably with *hijab (hijab*; *tesettür*) to mean dressing modestly in general. *Chador (tchador*; *çarşaf*) is a black robe that covers the entire body from head to toe. See also Liederman 2000, 373–5, 380n16.

TABLE I. *Types of State-Religion Regimes*

	Religious State	State with an Established Religion	Secular State	Antireligious State
Legislature and Judiciary	Religion-based	Secular	Secular	Secular
The State toward Religions	Officially Favors One	Officially Favors One	Officially Favors None	Officially Hostile to All or Many
Examples	*Iran Saudi Arabia Vatican*	*Greece Denmark England*	*United States France Turkey*	*North Korea China Cuba*
Number in the World	12	60	120	5

Source: Appendix A.

cases have pointed to education as the main battlefield. State policies toward religion in schools are controversial because struggling groups try to shape the young generation's worldview and lifestyle. This study, therefore, focuses on six of the most publicly debated state policies on (1) student religious dress and symbols in public schools, (2) pledges recited in public schools, (3) private religious education, (4) religious instruction in public schools, (5) public funding of private religious schools, and (6) organized prayer in public schools.

Despite the dynamism of the policy formation process, states still follow distinct and relatively stable trajectories in their general policies toward religion. There is a sharp qualitative distinction between state policies toward religion in the United States and those in France and Turkey. In America, students are allowed to display religious symbols and recite the Pledge of Allegiance, which includes the statement "one nation, under God." In France and Turkey, however, the state pursues totally opposite policies on these two points. Even regarding other policy issues, there is a positive tone toward religion in the United States, in contrast to two other cases. Religious instruction in Turkish schools is directly related to the state's desire to control religion and the fact that private religious education is prohibited. Similarly, in France, the state funds religious private schools as long as these schools sign

TABLE 2. *State Policies toward Religion in Schools*

	Ban on Students' Religious Symbols in Public Schools	A Pledge Referring to God Recited in Public Schools	Ban on Private Religious Education	Religious Instruction in Public Schools	State Funding of Religious Private Schools	Ban on Organized Prayer in Public Schools
United States	No	Yes	No	No	No	Yes
France	Yes	No	No	No	Yes	Yes
Turkey	Yes	No	Yes	Yes	No	Yes

a contract to accept certain state control over them. On the surface, the ban on the organized school prayer seems similar. Yet an in-depth analysis reveals a distinction. In France and Turkey, the main justification of the ban would be that the prayer contradicts the principle of secularism and the secular character of the public school. In the United States, however, an important rationale is that school prayer implies a "psychological coercion" over students with minority religious beliefs.[6] Table 2 compares my three cases regarding these six policies.

Beyond these specific policies in schools, the three cases also show two opposite attitudes toward religion in their public spheres. In the United States, there is clear, official, public visibility of religion, which is not the case in France or Turkey. "In God We Trust" appears on all American currency. Many official oaths, including the swearing-in of the president, customarily contain the statement "so help me God" and are often made by placing the left hand on a Bible. Sessions of the U.S. Congress begin with a prayer by a chaplain, and the sessions of the Supreme Court start with the invocation "God save the United States and this Honorable Court." Such public religious discourses do not exist in Turkey or France.

These differences point to my central question: why are American state policies inclusionary toward public visibility of religion while policies in France and Turkey are largely exclusionary? Stated differently, the main dependent variable of this work is the variation of

---

[6] *Lee v. Weisman*, 505 U.S. 577 (1992); *Santa Fe v. Doe*, 530 U.S. 290 (2000).

policies on religion, particularly the two opposite policy tendencies of three secular states.

STRUGGLING IDEOLOGIES: PASSIVE SECULARISM AND ASSERTIVE SECULARISM

I argue that state policies toward religion are the result of ideological struggles.[7] The main source of public policy making on religion in almost all antireligious states (such as North Korea, China, and Cuba) is diverse interpretations of the communist ideology, whereas in many religious states (such as Iran and Saudi Arabia) it is various understandings of Islamism.[8] Many states with established churches (such as Greece, Denmark, and England) lack the totalitarian ideologies like communism and Islamism. Yet they experience certain struggles between leftist and rightist groups to shape state policies on issues such as the elimination of religion from state identity cards, multiculturalism, and state neutrality toward all religions.[9]

Because the dominant ideology plays a crucial role in the formation of state policies, its change implies a substantial policy transformation. Two recent examples are post-Shah Iran and postcommunist Russia. Although the Iranian Revolution and the collapse of the Soviet Union had multiple causes,[10] ideological transformation marked their results, in terms of new patterns of policy orientations. In the aftermath of the Iranian Revolution, Shia Islamism replaced the Shah's secularist ideology. This ideological rupture caused extensive policy repercussions on state-religion relations.[11] Similarly, the elimination of the communist ideology in former Soviet republics led to major

---

[7] I deliberately use the term *ideology*, rather than the term *culture*. Culture is practical and habitual, which makes it more inconsistent and fuzzier than ideology. Ideology is a set of ideas related to consistent utopias, which makes it easier to recognize, categorize, and analyze. As Stephen Hanson emphasizes, ideologies are "formal, explicit, and relatively consistent" and "articulated by political elites," whereas cultures are "informal, implicit, and relatively inconsistent" and "held by people within a given institutional setting." Hanson 2003, 356. See also Scott 1999.

[8] U.S. Department of State 2007; Kindopp and Hamrin 2004; Hefner 2005; Al-Rasheed 2002.

[9] Liederman 2003, 296–7; Mouritsen 2006; Fetzer and Soper 2005, 33.

[10] Skocpol 1982; Solnick 1999.

[11] Arjomand 1988.

policy transformations.[12] Today the Russian state is no longer anti-religious; instead, it is a secular state that has affirmative relations with the Orthodox Church.[13] It also tries to please Muslims with particular policies, such as being an observant member of the Organization for the Islamic Conference.

In secular states, ideological struggles to shape state policies generally take place between two different notions of secularism – what I call "assertive secularism" and "passive secularism."[14] Assertive secularism requires the state to play an "assertive" role to exclude religion from the public sphere[15] and confine it to the private domain. Passive secularism demands that the state play a "passive" role by allowing the public visibility of religion. Assertive secularism is a "comprehensive doctrine,"[16] whereas passive secularism mainly prioritizes state neutrality toward such doctrines.

In Mexico, assertive secularism has been the dominant ideology despite the challenge of the conservatives, who want more public visibility of religion. State policies reflected assertive secularism with strong anticlericalism in the early twentieth century, whereas

---

[12] Ramet 1999. For the Soviet Union's Marxist and atheistic policies toward Islam, see Bennigsen and Lemercier-Quelquejay 1981. For Marxist ideology's impact on Soviet policies in general, see Hanson 1997.

[13] Papkov 2006; Anderson 2007; Krindatch 2006.

[14] Two scholars have already discussed distinct meanings of secularism in their insightful but short philosophical essays. Charles Taylor defines the first mode of secularism, which existed in American history, as secularism based on a "religious common ground." The second mode, for him, depends on a "political ethic independent of religion." The first mode is slightly different from passive secularism, while the second mode is similar to assertive secularism in my terminology. Taylor 1999. Wilfred McClay uses the terms *negative* and *positive* conceptions of secularism. Negative secularism is similar to my passive secularism because it "is a minimal, even 'negative' understanding of secularism, as a freedom 'from' establishmentarian imposition." It "is merely a provisional lingua franca that serves to facilitate commerce among different kinds of belief, rather than establish some new 'absolute' language, an Esperanto of postreligious truth." Positive secularism is similar to my assertive secularism, because it is a "more robust, more assertive, more 'positive' understanding of secularism ... the one that affirms secularism as an ultimate faith...." McClay 2002, 63–4.

[15] "The public sphere is a common space in which the members of society are deemed to meet through a variety of media: print, electronic, and also face-to-face encounters; to discuss matters of common interest; and thus to be able to form a common mind about these." Taylor 2004, 83. See also Habermas 1999.

[16] For comprehensive doctrines, see Rawls 1996.

they became relatively moderated in the 1990s.[17] India is a country where passive secularism has been dominant. Although there are ongoing academic and political debates about different interpretations of passive secularism, state policies constantly accommodate religions in the public sphere.[18] The challenge to passive secularism did not come from assertive secularism in India, but it has come from Hindu nationalism.[19] The Netherlands is another case where passive secularism is dominant. Despite the fall of the "pillarization model," all four main "pillars" – Protestants, Catholics, socialists, and liberals – still have strong public roles. Until the recent debates about the Muslim immigrants, the Netherlands was regarded as a stable model of state-religion relations that accommodated all religious groups.[20]

Passive and assertive secularist ideologies are particularly important for my three cases. In France, the supporters of assertive secularism (*laïcité de combat*) are dominant, while those of passive secularism (*laïcité plurielle*) are in opposition. Similarly, in Turkey, there is a conflict between the dominant assertive secularists (the Kemalists) and the resisting passive secularists (mainly the pro-Islamic conservatives). The United States is the only one among the three where passive secularism is dominant. Yet it faces a struggle between two interpretations of passive secularism (accommodationism and separationism).

The constitutions of these three states indicate the dominance of these two types of secularism. Both the French and Turkish constitutions identify their particular state as "secular": "France is an indivisible, secular, democratic, and social Republic" (Art. 2), and "The Republic of Turkey is a democratic, secular and social State" (Art. 2). However, neither defines the limits of state intervention in the religious realm. In other words, the French and Turkish constitutions point to secularism as an official ideology and as an identity of the state rather than as a functional legal principle delineating the relationship of the state to religion. In the United States, by contrast, the

---

[17] Marshall 2000, 216–20; Blancarte 2005, 250–4.
[18] Bhargava 1999; Pantham 1999.
[19] Sahu 2002.
[20] Knippenberg 2006; Dekker and Ester 1996; Monsma and Soper 1997, 51–86.

First Amendment to the Constitution does not identify the state as secular. It simply states "Congress shall make no law respecting an establishment of religion, or prohibiting the free exercise thereof." Both the first part (the Establishment Clause) and the second part (the Free Exercise Clause) require state neutrality toward religions. Moreover, the First Amendment is a part of what is known as the Bill of Rights. This implies that secularism in the United States is primarily an issue of individual rights, rather than an established comprehensive doctrine that defines the good life.

The ideological distinction and its policy implications can easily be observed in the public spheres of the three countries. In the words of Nilüfer Göle, Turkey "suffers from an excess of secularism ... which involves the forced secularization of the public sphere [and] ... a total repression of any symbols or organizations of faith....Today we see how the public sphere was really under the tutorship of state, which through authoritarian means imposed a secular way of life."[21] French philosopher Regis Debray stresses the same issue by comparing France and the United States in an exaggerated manner:

Above the nation, in France, there is humanity. Above the society, in America, there is God. The President in Paris takes an oath on the constitution voted by the people from the world, and in Washington on the Bible, which came from the heavens. The first one, after saying, "Long live the Republic, long live France," will be painted in his library with the *Essays* of Montaigne in his hands. The other will end his discourse on "God Bless America" and will be photographed in front of the starred flag.[22]

From a Marxist point of view, dominant ideology is a mere reflection of the economic structure and a means for the dominant economic class to exert power.[23] In my analysis, however, ideology is neither a superstructure nor a simple instrument of power. Ideology and material conditions are separate but interrelated. I attach importance to

[21] Göle 2004, 93.
[22] Debray 1992, 22–3.
[23] In the words of Karl Marx and Frederick Engels, "In every epoch the ideas of the ruling class are the ruling ideas [which] ... are nothing more than the ideal expression of the dominant material relationships." Marx 1994, 129. Antonio Gramsci, a neo-Marxist, however, rightly challenges this perspective by emphasizing the independent role of ideology for the establishment of hegemony. Gramsci 1991. See also Billings 1990, 4–6; Williams 1996, 373–4.

struggles between two secular ideologies within a country, rather than take countries as monolithically passive or assertive secularist. Dominant ideologies in my three cases always face ideological resistance. They are in a constant struggle with opposing ideologies. Due to this struggle, state policies toward religion experience several exceptions, contradictions, and changes. In some empirical chapters, I use the metaphor of a "swinging pendulum" to stress the recurring shifts of state relations to religion, which move back and forth along the spectrum of diverse policies based on the balance of power between struggling ideological groups.

In sum, ideological struggles between the supporters of passive and assertive secularism shape the two opposite policy tendencies in my three cases. Passive and assertive secularism became dominant in these cases as a result of particular historical conditions during their secular state-building periods. In France and Turkey the presence of an *ancien régime* based on the alliance of monarchy and hegemonic religion was a crucial reason for the emergence of anticlericalism among the republican elite. The antagonistic relations between the republicans and the religious institutions underlay the historical dominance of assertive secularism. America, however, was a relatively new country of immigrants that lacked an *ancien régime*. Therefore secular and religious elites sought and achieved an overlapping consensus on the separation of church and state at the federal level. The result was the dominance of passive secularism. This historical explanation completes my argument summarized in Figure 1.

The chapter proceeds as follows. First, I examine three alternative theories that would explain this policy divergence differently. I then elaborate my historical explanation based on the presence or absence of an *ancien régime*. The next section discusses the conceptual categories. The final section focuses on methodology.

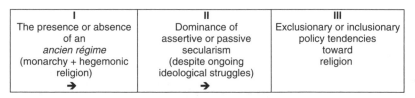

I	II	III
The presence or absence of an *ancien régime* (monarchy + hegemonic religion) ➔	Dominance of assertive or passive secularism (despite ongoing ideological struggles) ➔	Exclusionary or inclusionary policy tendencies toward religion

FIGURE 1. Dependent and Independent Variables

ALTERNATIVE THEORIES: MODERNIZATION, CIVILIZATION, AND RATIONAL CHOICE

Modernization theory, civilizational approach, and rational-choice theory are three important theories that scholars refer to while analyzing religion and politics. Modernization theory has different versions. Some scholars emphasize the epochal impact of modernization to explain the transformation of medieval sociopolitical systems to modern ones.[24] They offer important insights for the analysis of the historical ruptures in the United States, France, and Turkey through secular state building. However, their broad perspectives do not provide parsimonious explanations for particular state-religion relations. I focus therefore on the parsimonious version of modernization theory, which emphasizes economic development as the determining factor.

Modernization theory predicts the decline of religion's political role through economic development.[25] According to Norris and Inglehart, the process of modernization includes "[t]he division of church and state, and the rise of secular-rational bureaucratic states."[26] Modernization theory would explain the variation in different states' policies toward religion regarding their various levels of modernization, which are generally measured by three criteria of human development: GDP per capita, literacy rate, and life expectancy.

According to the United Nations Development Programme's (UNDP) "Human Development Index for 2007–2008," the United States and France have close scores and rankings of development: the United States (0.951/12th) and France (0.952/10th). Turkey, however, has a much lower score and ranking of development (0.775/84th).[27] The first two cases are located among the countries of high development whereas Turkey is among the ones of medium development. Modernization theory, therefore, would not successfully explain why a highly developed country (France) differs from another highly developed country (the United States) while being relatively similar to a moderately developing case (Turkey) in terms of state policies toward religion.

---

[24] Anderson 1998; Gellner 1983a; Taylor 2001; Taylor 2004.
[25] Inglehart 1997; Inkeles and Smith 1976.
[26] Norris and Inglehart 2004, 8; also 208–10.
[27] UNDP, "Human Development Reports," http://hdr.undp.org/en/statistics/, accessed on May 19, 2008.

TABLE 3. *Human Development and Official Religion*

	States with Official Religions	States without Official Religions	TOTAL
High Development	30 (43%)	39 (57%)	69 (100%)
Medium Development	35 (41%)	50 (59%)	85 (100%)
Low Development	1 (5%)	21 (95%)	22 (100%)
TOTAL	66 (36%)	110 (64%)	176 (100%)

Source: Appendix B

Modernization theorists would respond by saying that they provide a general explanation of an international trend of state-religion relations, rather than of specific state policies in a few cases. I analyzed 176 countries in terms of their levels of development and official religion, using UNDP's "Human Development Index" and my own dataset for state-religion regimes. Table 3 summarizes the results. Countries with high development have a much higher percentage (43%) of having official religions than countries with medium (41%) and low development (5%). Such a result is the opposite of what modernization theory would predict.

Other large-N analyses also provide similar results. Robert Barro and Rachel McCleary examine 188 states and conclude that although "[t]he standard view is that richer countries are less likely to have state religions ... per capita GDP has an ambiguous effect on the probability of state religion."[28] By analyzing 175 states, Jonathan Fox also notes that "economically developed states have lower levels of separation of religion and state."[29] In sum, although modernization is an important factor in the analysis of state-religion relations, its mono-causal and linear perspective does not explain diverse state-religion regimes, let alone specific secular state policies.

The second theory is the civilizational approach, which is generally called "essentialism" by its critics.[30] This approach focuses on text-based religious essentials to explain religion's impact on sociopolitical

[28] Barro and McCleary 2005, 1348.
[29] Fox 2006, 560; Fox 2008, 99.
[30] Bulliet 1996; Yavuz 2003, 16–18; Stepan 2001; Roy 2007, 15, 43. A particular version of civilizationalism has also been called "Orientalism." Said 1979; Said 1997,

life. According to this approach, for example, "Islam is the blueprint of a social order. It holds that a set of rules exists, eternal, divinely ordained, and independent of the will of men, which defines the proper ordering of society.... These rules are to be implemented throughout social life."[31]

Civilizational approach mainly argues (1) inherent distinctions between certain religions and religious communities and (2) direct causal impacts of these religious differences on politics.[32] According to Bernard Lewis, Islam and Judaism are similar to each other and different from Christianity in the sense that these two do not have clear and distinct conceptions of "clergy" versus "laity," or "sacred law" versus "secular law." Therefore, he defines state-religion struggles as a "Christian disease" and secularism as a "Christian remedy."[33] Lewis claims clearly divergent stands for Christianity and Islam toward state-religion relations: "The distinction between church and state, so deeply rooted in Christendom, did not exist in Islam."[34] Lewis and other defenders of civilizationalism often refer to a well-known verse of the Bible to prove the compatibility of Christianity and secularism: "Render therefore unto Caesar the things which be Caesar's, and unto God the things which be God's."[35] Samuel Huntington expands Lewis's thesis to other religions and cultures: "In Islam, God is Caesar; in China and Japan, Caesar is God; in Orthodoxy, God is Caesar's junior partner. The separation and recurring clashes between church and state that typify Western civilization have existed in no other civilization."[36]

Civilizational approach rightly alerts us to the importance of religion in post–cold war world politics. It focuses our attention on key theological differences, which can have impacts on individuals' political preferences. Beyond this general concern, however, it has few specific things to say about state-religion relations. Civilizationalism would explain various state policies toward religion through the diverse

---

esp. 36–68. Civilizational approach is not always critical of Islam. For a pro-Islamic civilizational perspective, see Davutoğlu 1994.

[31] Gellner 1983b, 1. See also Gellner 1992, 5–7. For a critique of Ernest Gellner's civilizationalism, see Varisco 2005, 53–80; Sunar 2004, 175–86.

[32] Lewis 1990; Lewis 2003; Huntington 1993; Smith 1999, 185–91.

[33] Lewis 1991b, 10–12, 26; also Lewis 1996, 62.

[34] Lewis 1991a, 2–3.

[35] Luke 20:25, quoted by Lewis 1991b, 15.

[36] Huntington 1996, 70.

TABLE 4. *State-Religion Regimes in Forty-Six Muslim Countries*

Religious (Islamic) States	States with an Established Religion (Islam)	Secular States	Antireligious States
11	15	20	0

Sources: Appendices A and C.

religious backgrounds of particular states. Because it overemphasizes the similarities within the West and the differences between
Western and Muslim countries, civilizationalism cannot explain why a
"Western" country (France) pursues policies toward religion that are
different from those of another "Western" country (the United States)
and similar to those of a "Muslim" country (Turkey).

Civilizationalists would reply that Turkey is an exception in the
Muslim world with its secular state. A general survey of the Muslim
world, however, also challenges their claims. Ira Lapidus stresses that
there have existed separate religious and political authorities in the
Muslim world since the eighth century. At that time, independent
Sunni schools of law, Shia sects, and Sufi tariqas, in addition to secular
military and administrative rulers, challenged and replaced the institution of the caliphate, which claimed to represent both political and
religious authorities.[37] Recently, the U.S. Commission on International
Religious Freedom issued a report on the constitutions of forty-four
Muslim-majority countries. The commission, referring also to countries
where Muslims are minority, concludes that "More than half of the
world's Muslim population (estimated at over 1.3 billion) lives in
countries ... that either proclaim the state to be secular, or that make
no pronouncements concerning Islam to be the official state religion."[38]
My state-religion regimes index includes data very similar to this textual analysis as summarized in Table 4.[39] This disproves the alleged
political unity in the Muslim world.[40]

[37] Lapidus 1975.
[38] Stahnke and Blitt 2005a, 2; Stahnke and Blitt 2005b, 951.
[39] As explained in Appendices A and C, my index is based on the U.S. Department of State's "Reports on International Religious Freedom."
[40] Fox indicates that states with majority Muslim population, in general, have fewer sep-
arationist policies toward religion than "Western" states. Beyond this generalization,

Critics of civilizationalism also stress that this approach has difficulty explaining not only the Muslim world but also Christian societies. The civilizational argument about the inherent church-state separation in Christianity overly romanticizes Christian societies by ignoring their (1) historical religious wars and church-state struggles, (2) substantially diverse state-religion regimes at present, and (3) current experience of religiously driven debates on political and legal issues, such as divorce, abortion, gay rights, and evolutionism, which cannot be simply explained by rendering these things onto Caesar.[41]

A more refined version of civilizationalism admits the diversity among Christian societies but argues an essential difference between the Catholics and Protestants.[42] According to this perspective, Protestantism is compatible with secularism, while Catholicism is not. As Casanova emphasizes, this approach is unable to explain the complex relations between the Catholic Church and the states, changing Catholic views toward democracy, and persistent established churches in Protestant countries.[43] Gill points out the strategic flexibility of the Catholic Church. It seeks state intervention in order to restrict Protestant proselytism in Latin America where Catholicism is a dominant religion, while it asks for more church-state separation and religious freedom in post-Soviet Russia where Catholicism remains in the minority.[44] He shows elsewhere that the Catholic Church implemented various political strategies even in different Latin American countries with regard to diverse political and religious competitions.[45] The civilizational approach, in short, ignores the contextual conditions that shape political attitudes of Catholics and Protestants. In the words of Stathis Kalyvas, "The dissimilar political behavior of Catholics and Protestants does not appear to be culturally driven: when challenged by anticlerical legislation, Protestants in the Netherlands reacted the same way Catholics did,

---

his dataset shows the variation of state-religion relations in both groups. Fox 2008; Fox 2006.

[41] Arslan 1999, 120–31.
[42] Madeley 2003b; Debray 1992, 23.
[43] Casanova 2001.
[44] Gill 2005, 13–15.
[45] Gill 1998.

whereas when no anticlerical attack took place, Irish Catholics did not organize politically on the basis of religion."[46]

Civilizationalism generally underestimates human agency,[47] while rightly stressing that religion has an impact on politics. This impact, however, depends on diverse human interpretations of religion. Some Christians may defend church-state separation referring to the previously mentioned verse of the Bible. Others may interpret Christianity as a total blueprint for life by referring to another verse: "No one can serve two masters.... You cannot serve both God and money."[48] Likewise, Muslims interpret Islamic principles in terms of their political context. Mumtaz Ahmad stresses the diverse strategies of an Islamic movement, Jamaat-i Islami, on secularism. It defends an Islamic state in Pakistan where Muslims are majority, while supporting the secular state in India where they are minority.[49] Some Muslims embrace the idea of an Islamic state, while others, such as Abdullahi An-Naim, defend the necessity of a secular state to fully live Islam as a free individual.[50] For these reasons, I do not take religion per se as a determining factor. Instead, I focus on interpretations of religions linked with various political ideologies.

The third and final theory is rational choice, which differs from modernization and civilizationalism by not maintaining a deterministic explanation. It attaches importance to individual preferences, rational calculation, and structural constraints,[51] and provides significant insights for the analysis of actors' strategies in political struggles. This theory is also valuable for examining contextual human interpretations of religion. I agree with rational-choice theorists' critique of civilizationalism cited in the preceding text. I still have major reservations about this theory's explanation of state-religion relations.

---

[46] Kalyvas 1996, 3n6.

[47] Dale Eickelman and James Piscatori use the term *Muslim Politics*, instead of *Islamic Politics*, to emphasize that politics in Muslim societies is based on complex practices of Muslim agents, rather than so-called Islamic essentials. Eickelman and Piscatori 1996.

[48] Matthew 6:24.

[49] "While the Jamaat in Pakistan denounces secularism and the secular state as 'an evil force,' the Jamaat in India is equally vigorous in defending secularism as a 'blessing' and a 'guarantee for a safe future for Islam.'" Ahmad 1991, 505. See also El Fadl 2003; Messick 1988; Yılmaz 2005.

[50] An-Na'im 2008.

[51] Olson 1984; Hirschman 1972; Bates 1981; Gill 1998; Waldner 1999.

Gill is one of the few rational-choice theorists who examine the causes of state policies toward religion.[52] He argues that these policies differ due to the political rulers' varying calculations of opportunity costs based on their preferences for (1) sustaining political survival, (2) minimizing the cost of ruling, and (3) succeeding in economic growth, in addition to maximizing government revenue and minimizing civil unrest.[53] Gill would argue that in France and Turkey, state rulers pursue more restrictive policies toward religion than do rulers in the United States because these policies help them minimize the opportunity costs.

The strength of Gill's argument is its capacity to explain political rulers' strategic flexibility. However, it is unable to explicate the decisions of an important set of actors, the members of supreme/constitutional courts, who do not primarily care about political survival, the cost of ruling, or economic development, while deciding cases on state-religion relations.[54] Moreover, Gill's approach sounds state-centric because it focuses on rulers at the expense of societal actors in the formation of state policies. It also disregards the ideological divisions between rulers arguing standard preferences for them. This approach would have problems regarding my cases. The ban on students' headscarves in Turkey and France has been politically risky (in the former) and has created huge ruling costs, while not helping economic development at all.

The main weakness of rational-choice theory (or, at least, its "thin" version) is that it largely takes individual preferences as given.[55] For this theory, a ruler and a farmer have distinct preferences shaped by their socioeconomic status regardless of their ideology. This book tries to go beyond rational choice by unpacking individuals' preferences through the analysis of their ideologies. It shows that a ruler and a farmer may have shared preferences if they embrace the same ideology.[56] A related

---

[52] See also Finke 1990; Gill and Keshavarzian 1999.
[53] Gill 2007, esp. 232.
[54] As elaborated in the empirical chapters, I explain judges' decisions on secularism through their ideological positions.
[55] See Opp 1999; Green and Shapiro 1996. Ira Katznelson and Barry Weingast's volume includes essays that try to fix this problem of rational choice by combining it with historical institutionalism. Katznelson and Weingast 2005.
[56] Rational-choice theorists generally claim to be methodologically individualist. Yet because they take preferences as given and underestimate ideas, they explain change

problem is that rational-choice analyses generally undermine ideas as either justifications for already decided behaviors or as instruments for material interests. I take ideas as genuinely important factors in the construction of preferences and interests. In the words of Max Weber: "Not ideas, but material and ideal interests, directly govern men's conduct. Yet very frequently the 'world images' that have been created by 'ideas' have, like switchmen, determined the tracks along which action has been pushed by the dynamic of interest."[57]

To conclude, neither economic determinism of modernization theory, nor religious determinism of civilizationalism, nor standard preferences of rational-choice theory are able to successfully explain state policies toward religion. This book claims to explain them through the analysis of ideological struggles. It keeps a balance between civilizationalism (which overemphasizes the role of ideas at the expense of human agency) and rational choice (which undermines the role of ideas in actors' preference formations and behaviors). On the one hand, it takes ideologies and religions seriously. On the other, it stresses that neither secularism, nor Islam, nor Christianity is monolithic. Instead, all three are open to interpretations. Even if one accepts the book's argument about the importance of ideologies, there is still a question to be answered: why is passive secularism dominant in the United States, whereas assertive secularism is dominant in France and Turkey? To answer that requires an historical analysis.

HISTORICAL FORMATION AND DOMINANCE OF ASSERTIVE AND PASSIVE SECULARISM

The emergence and dominance of ideologies on state-religion relations is a complex process that requires a qualitative analysis of historical trajectory for each case. It is hard to provide a deterministic causal explanation about them. My general argument is that political relations of and perceptions about religions cause particular formations of ideologies and state-religion regimes. A religion's close

primarily through structural transformations. One rational-choice theorist stresses, "Behavioral changes (over time) are the consequences of changed constraints; behavioral differences (across individuals) are the consequences of differing constraints." Iannacconne 1996, 28.

[57] Weber 1946, 280. See also Hall 2005, esp. 152–4; Bleich 2002.

relations with political authority create certain negative perceptions against it among the authority's discontents. In the words of Alexis de Tocqueville: "There have been religions intimately linked to earthly governments, ... but when a religion makes such an alliance ... it sacrifices the future for the present.... Hence religion cannot share the material strength of the rulers without being burdened with some of the animosity roused against them."[58]

I specify this broad point by examining religions' political relations during the state-building period, which is generally the critical juncture that creates a path dependence concerning state-religion interactions. In certain cases, modern state building defines an *ancien régime* based on the marriage between the old monarchy and religious hegemony, which is perceived by the progressive elite as a barrier against the new republican regime. The main product of an *ancien régime* is the anticlerical (or antireligious) movement against it. The anticlericals perceive the hegemonic religion as the source of justification for the declining monarchy and the potential supporter of its reestablishment. Religious conservatives oppose the disestablishment of their religion because they want to keep the hegemony. In short, the *ancien régime* becomes the basis of the polarization between the anticlericals and conservatives.

In addition to their different levels of hostility against religion, anticlerical movements also have various results, contingent on their organization, popular support, and timing. They may create either an antireligious state, or a secular state where assertive secularism is dominant. These results are also changeable as seen in the previously discussed transformations from antireligious Soviet Union to secular Russia. The following examples of Spain and Portugal indicate change from assertive secularism to passive secularism as dominant ideology.

The Soviet Union was an example of the first result (the antireligious state). The Orthodox Church in Russia faced an antagonism from the antireligious Bolsheviks mainly due to its fusion with the Russian monarchy.[59] In the *ancien régime*, "the Russian Orthodox Church was

---

[58] Tocqueville 2000 [1835], 297. Such a close state-religion relation is more likely to make "secularity as a symbol of opposition." Chaves 1992, 276.
[59] Krindatch 2006, 271.

the established church of the Russian Empire, and the Tsar was its head."[60] That was one of the main reasons why Lenin and other leaders of the 1917 Revolution were hostile to the church. Their atheism was much more antagonistic toward religion than Marx's philosophical atheism.[61] As a result of Soviet antireligious policies, the number of the Russian Orthodox Church's parishes, which was around fifty thousand in 1917, decreased to two hundred to three hundred in 1939.[62]

Mexico is a clear example of the second result (the dominance of assertive secularist ideology). During the nineteenth century, the liberal republicans regarded the Catholic Church as the ally of conservative authoritarian rulers. Whenever they got power, the liberals pursued anticlerical policies, such as confiscating church properties and making legal marriage a civil, not religious, act. The conservatives succeeded in establishing a monarchy in 1864, but it lasted only three years. Having an ambivalent *ancien régime* in their minds, the liberals led the state (re)building in 1910 and adopted the Constitution of 1917, which established the ideological dominance of assertive secularism, in general, and secular, compulsory, and free education, in particular (Art. 3). In response, conservative forces staged the Cristero Rebellion from 1926 to 1929.[63] The failure of the rebellion led the liberals to implement assertive secularist policies, and some policies sounded antireligious. Although the "Catholic Church did not *legally* exist in Mexico" following the Constitution of 1917, governments de facto accommodated the Catholic Church by allowing it to use church buildings. The constitutional amendment in 1992 maintained basic religious freedoms and provided legality to the Catholic Church.[64]

Spain and Portugal are examples where the second result temporarily existed. In both countries anticlericalism emerged as the republicans' reaction to the Catholic Church's cooperation with monarchies. In the words of Paul Manuel: "Absolute political power and legitimacy in Portugal and Spain until ... the modern era were in the hands of the monarch.... The Roman Catholic Church legitimized the monarch's claim to divine authority, and, in turn, typically

---

[60] Berman 1996, 287.
[61] Ibid., 289.
[62] Ramet 1999, 231.
[63] Bailey 1974.
[64] Gill 2007, 116 (emphasis in original).

received royal grants of land, among other goods."[65] In the nineteenth century, the republican elite challenged this "Iberian *ancien régime.*" As a result of the Catholic Church's continuing support to the crown and aristocracy, "the Republicans became staunchly anticlerical."[66] In both countries, the anticlericals founded assertive secularist republics with oppressive policies against the church in the early twentieth century. Yet the conservatives fought back and established "pro-clerical fascist and corporatist regimes in the 1930s."[67] Finally, both Spain and Portugal became democracies in the 1970s and 1980s, where the Catholic Church is disestablished but keeps certain privileges through concordats.

In countries where there is no *ancien régime*, the anticlerical movement does not exist or is marginal. The existence or absence of an *ancien régime* has four components as seen in the preceding cases: (1) monarchy, (2) hegemonic religion, (3) an alliance between the two, and (4) a successful republican movement. In cases where *ancien régimes* exist, such as Russia, Mexico, Spain, and Portugal, all four components are historically present. In countries where there is no *ancien régime*, some components are missing. That may lead to a religious state, a state with established religion, or a secular state with the dominance of passive secularism. Iran today is an example of the first result. During the Revolution of 1979, the first, second, and fourth components existed. Yet the hegemonic religion did not ally with the monarchy. On the contrary, the Shia clergy gained popularity by challenging the Shah and led the revolution. Another religious state, Saudi Arabia, has not experienced a republican transformation since its independence in 1926; therefore, it does not have an *ancien régime*. If a republican movement emerges and succeeds, then the current regime, which is based on the alliance between the Saudi monarchy and Wahhabi leaders, will become an *ancien régime*.

In certain European countries that have established churches, there is no *ancien régime* due to an absence of a republican transformation. Although it is symbolic, the monarchy-church alliance still persists; it is therefore a modern, at least contemporary, not ancient, regime.

---

[65] Manuel 2002, 74.
[66] Ibid., 76.
[67] Ibid., 77. See also Casanova 1994, 75–81.

Britain is relatively different from Scandinavian monarchies because the Anglican dominance was weaker than the Lutheran hegemony. The Anglican establishment was contested by several alternative religions, from Catholicism to various Protestant denominations. Similarly, it "had much less social or political power than the Catholic Church in some countries. Hence there was no reason for a radical attack."[68] In Britain, there "was no need to overthrow religion itself, because there was no pope ... , no monopolistic priesthood."[69] As a result, a clash did not take place between religious and secularist forces: "there was no 'conflict of two Great Britains' resembling the 'conflict of two Frances.'"[70] Greece is unique in Europe: it had a republican transformation but has kept the established religion. There is no such thing as a "Greek *ancien régime*," because the Greek Orthodox Church was not a strong supporter of monarchy against the republicans. The church generally obeyed any political authority as a result of its Caesaropapist tradition, which accepted the superiority of the state power.[71] Therefore, the church "as an institution has been used by conservative, reformist fascist and socialist regimes alike."[72]

Among the secular states, those that lack an *ancien régime* experience the dominance of passive secularism. Ireland and Poland historically had a hegemonic religion but not a monarchy versus republic division. Therefore, the Catholic hegemony was not perceived as an antirepublican force. Instead, the Catholic Church historically was a symbol of resistance against "English colonization" in Ireland[73] and foreign "invasions, partitions, and occupations" in Poland.[74] Germany had a monarchy and republican transformation but not a religious hegemony. During the *Kulturkampf*, the conflict was not between religion and secularism; it was mainly between the Protestant state authority and Catholicism.[75] The Netherlands has had a monarchy but has not had a hegemonic religion. The "formation of the Dutch state

[68] Modood and Kastoryano 2006, 163.
[69] Himmelfarb 2003, 51.
[70] Baubérot and Mathieu 2002, 33.
[71] Mavrogordatos 2003.
[72] Kokosalakis 1987, 231.
[73] Dillon 2002, 48.
[74] Byrnes 2002, 27.
[75] Henkel 2006, 309; Fetzer and Soper 2005, 106; Gould 1999, 83.

and the building of the Dutch nation have been dominated by the religious cleavage of Calvinists and Roman Catholics."[76] Its church-state disputes included multiple actors, rather than two opposite (religious and secular) forces. That led to a passive secularist regime, the Dutch "pillarization system."[77]

Colonized India historically lacked both a local monarchy and hegemonic religion. The founders of modern India adopted passive secularism to maintain both the political autonomy of the state and the peaceful coexistence of majority Hindus with a large Muslim minority.[78] Canada and Australia also experienced the absence of monarchy (as two other former British colonies) and religious diversity (of several Protestant denominations and Catholics). That explains the absence of an *ancien régime* and dominance of passive secularism in these cases.[79]

The existence or absence of an *ancien régime* is a crucial factor in my three cases. Passive and assertive secularism, which had largely been formulated in the minds and writings of intellectuals for decades, became dominant ideologies during the periods of secular state building in the United States (1776–1791: from the Declaration of Independence to the First Amendment); in France (1875–1905: from the Constitutional Laws of 1875 to the 1905 law separating church and state); and in Turkey (1923–1937: from the foundation of the republic to the constitutional amendment enshrining secularism as a constitutional principle).

These periods are critical junctures when the secular state replaced the old types of state-religion regimes and left an ideological and institutional legacy that has persisted ever since. A critical juncture, in general, is a moment when both agency and structural conditions are available for a systematic change. It is a period when "choices close off alternative options and lead to the establishment of institutions that generate self-reinforcing path-dependent processes."[80] In my three cases, the critical junctures followed structural crises caused by wars: the American War of Independence (1775–1783), the Franco-Prussian

---

[76] Knippenberg 2006, 328.
[77] Dekker and Ester 1996.
[78] Bhargava 2007; Jacobsohn 2003.
[79] Lyon and Die 2000; Monsma and Soper 1997, 87–120.
[80] Capoccia and Kelemen 2007, 341.

War (1870–1871), and the Turkish War of Independence (1919–1922). Moreover, in all cases, there existed powerful agents, ideological groups, that were willing and able to form the new order during the structural crisis. When the new system becomes consolidated, it creates a path dependence. In the aftermath of this transformation, a new change becomes difficult and requires a new critical juncture.[81] The length of critical junctures may vary, as long as it is shorter than the "duration of the path-dependent process it initiates."[82] In the words of Ruth Collier and David Collier, it "may range from relatively quick transitions – for example, '*moments* of significant structural change' – to an extended period that might correspond to one or more presidential administrations, a long 'policy period,' or a prolonged 'regime period.'" In their work, critical junctures range from nine to twenty-three years.[83] In my analysis they range from one and a half decades in the United States and Turkey to three decades in France.

In France and Turkey, the *ancien régime* deeply affected the ideological backgrounds of secular and religious movements, as well as their relations. In both countries, religion was an important pillar of the monarchy, which made the republican elite anticlerical; in a sense they opposed religion's influence over society and polity. Moreover, Catholicism in France and Islam in Turkey were hegemonic religions. Therefore, conservative Catholics and Islamists sought to preserve religious establishments. It was difficult to find a religious justification of state-religion separation, and there was almost no ideational bridge between secular and religious movements. Severe conflict between the two was foreseeable. The dominance of assertive secularism, in a nutshell, meant the victory of the secular movement over its religious rival.

America, however, was a relatively new country of immigrants. It had neither a local monarchy nor a hegemonic religion. Hence, the

---

[81] According to James Mahoney, critical junctures "are moments of relative structural indeterminism when willful actors shape outcomes in a more voluntary fashion than normal circumstances permit.... Before a critical juncture, a broad range of outcomes is possible; after a critical juncture, enduring institutions and structures are created, and the range of possible outcomes is narrowed considerably." Mahoney 2001, 7.

[82] Capoccia and Kelemen 2007, 350.

[83] Collier and Collier 1991, 32.

TABLE 5. *Historical Conditions and Relations during Secular State Building*

	I→	II→	III→	IV
United States	The absence of an *ancien régime* (no local monarchy and diversity of Protestant denominations)	Secular groups were not against religion's public role; religious groups were open to church-state separation	Overlapping consensus between secular and religious groups	Dominance of *passive secularism*
France and Turkey	The presence of an *ancien régime* based on monarchy and hegemony of Catholicism and Islam	Secular groups were against religion's public role; religious groups were seeking to preserve the establishment of Catholicism and Islam	Severe conflict between secular and religious groups	Dominance of *assertive secularism*

republican elite did not perceive religion as an ally of an old monarchy. Instead, there was a diversity of competing Protestant denominations, none of which could claim a bare majority. Because of the intense religious diversity, many religious groups saw the church-state separation as a second-best choice and a guarantee to their religious freedom. Secular and religious elites had an ideational common ground based on John Locke's liberalism. The dominance of passive secularism depended on an "overlapping consensus" – an agreement that secular and religious movements reached for different purposes. Table 5 summarizes this historical argument.

The facts that secularism chronologically and world-historically took place in France before it did in Turkey, and that the Turkish framers were inspired by the French model, did not weaken the argument based on the *ancien régime*. First, Turkish framers preferred the French model to other alternatives because the historical conditions in both countries were relatively similar. Second, the Turkish model is not a simple imitation of the French one; the two had several differences. Finally, Turkey took initiative earlier than France on several issues, such as putting secularism into the constitution (1937 in Turkey and 1948 in France), banning students' headscarves, and creating an umbrella organization to control Islam (Turkish Diyanet in 1924 and the French Council of the Muslim Faith in 2003).[84]

Since the secular state building, passive and assertive secularism have preserved their dominance in the three cases through ideological indoctrination, institutional socialization, and public education, despite certain challenging forces and conceptual transformations. This path dependence is a crucial dimension of ideological struggles in the public-policy formation process in these three cases. These complex relations and processes require nuanced conceptual tools.

CONCEPT FORMATION, TYPOLOGY, AND CONTINUUM

Typologies and continua, which help us understand abstract phenomena and evaluate concrete cases, are complementary, not mutually exclusive, conceptual tools. The choice of one or the other is based on the depth of the analysis. Regarding religion's institutional control over legislature and judiciary, there are only two types – religious states (e.g., Iran) and nonreligious states (e.g., the United States). To increase the conceptual precision, one needs to descend in the "ladder of abstraction," in the words of Giovanni Sartori.[85] A simple way of descending is to add another criterion, such as state neutrality toward religions. That increases the number of types to four: religious states (e.g., Iran), states with established religion (e.g., England), secular states (e.g., the United States), and antireligious states (e.g., China). Obviously these are Weberian "ideal types."[86] Some cases may perfectly fit these types, although many exist through a continuum

---

[84] According to Pierre-Jean Luizard, the model for French and Turkish state policies toward Islam is the French colonial rule in Algeria, which implemented the principle of state control over Islam, rather than state-Islam separation. Luizard's interview with Ali İhsan Aydın, "Türkiye'de Sömürge Modeli Laiklik Uygulanıyor," *Zaman*, March 14, 2008. See also Luizard 2006.

[85] Sartori 1970. See also Goertz 2006; Collier and Mahon 1993; Collier and Levitsky 1997.

[86] In the words of Max Weber, "An ideal type is ... a unified *analytical* construct. In its conceptual purity, this mental construct cannot be found empirically anywhere in reality. It is a *utopia*. Historical research faces the task of determining in each

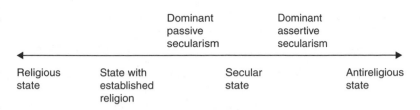

FIGURE 2. Continuum of State-Religion Regimes and Secularism

between them. Germany, for example, is a secular state regarding the typology, but the fact that the German state is collecting church tax (mainly for Catholic and certain Protestant churches) puts it in a continuum between the secular state and the state with established religion.[87] Spain, Portugal, and Poland are also cases that deviate from ideal types. On the one hand, they do not have constitutionally established religions; on the other hand, they provide privileges to the Catholic Church through concordats. Israel and Egypt are states with established religions with regard to the general typology. Yet, as Yüksel Sezgin convincingly points out, religious laws and courts are ruling on the issues of personal status (e.g., marriage, divorce, maintenance, and inheritance) in both cases.[88] Based on that, one may put them in a continuum between states with established religions and religious states.

This book continues descending in the ladder of abstraction by examining the diversity of secular states. Therefore, it adds another variable – whether a secular state pursues exclusionary or inclusionary policies toward religion in the public sphere. That leads the development of the two types (assertive and passive) of secularism. Figure 2 locates the typologies of state-religion regimes and secularism in a continuum.

Assertive and passive secularist ideologies can be defined as *dichotomous types*. State policies, however, are more complex and less consistent than ideologies. The two types of secularism imply ideal types, while the real state policies exist through the continuum between them. States are neither completely assertive secularist (excluding religion

individual case, the extent to which this ideal-construct approximates to or diverges from reality." Weber 1949, 90 (emphasis in original).

[87] Monsma and Soper 1997.

[88] Sezgin 2007. For ideological struggles between proreligious and prosecular groups to shape Israeli state policies toward religion, see Wald 2002; Sezgin 2003.

FIGURE 3. Continuum of Passive and Assertive Secularism

entirely from the public sphere) nor purely passive secularist (allowing any sort of public visibility of religion). Even the dominance of assertive or passive secularism in a country is a *matter of degree*. France and Turkey, despite their ideological similarity, still differ from each other with regard to the levels of the exclusion of religion from the public sphere. Certain policies, such as the ban on private religious education and the prohibition on wearing headscarves at universities and in private schools, indicates that the Turkish state has a more exclusionary attitude toward religion than does the French state, as Figure 3 demonstrates.

I explain the differences between the French and Turkish cases with diverse impacts of democracy and authoritarianism.[89] From the secular state building in the late nineteenth century to the present, assertive secularism in France has coexisted with a multiparty democracy and has gained substantial popular support. It was challenged by Catholic movements that supported the reestablishment of monarchy and the authoritarian rules, such as the Vichy regime (1940–1944). Due to the French democracy, the opponents of assertive secularism have had the political means to criticize certain policies, and the assertive secularists have made compromises from their utopian ideological views (see Chapters 4 and 5). In Turkey, by contrast, assertive secularism was established by an authoritarian single-party rule in the early twentieth century and has been defended since 1960 by several military *coup d'états* against democratically elected governments. In the Turkish elections, assertive secularist politicians have always received fewer votes than the conservatives. That reflects the tension between assertive secularism and democracy in

---

[89] Zana Çıtak argues that state policies toward religion have been more exclusionary in Turkey than in France because the historical formation of nationalism in Turkey was independent of, if not against, Islam, whereas that of France had both anti-Catholic and pro-Catholic trajectories. Çıtak 2004. This argument ignores the historical and contemporary existence of pro-Islamic nationalism in Turkey. Chapter 7 explains that a founder of Turkish nationalism, Ziya Gökalp, was pro-Islamic, at least not anti-Islamic.

Turkey. Under the shadow of the authoritarian military and judiciary, it has been much more difficult to oppose assertive secularist policies. The assertive secularists, therefore, have rarely accepted policy compromises. Yet democratization has also caused relative moderation of assertive secularist policies in Turkey (see Chapters 6 and 7).[90]

Diverse characteristics of French and Turkish *ancien régimes* contributed to the different impulses of democracy and authoritarianism in the two cases. In France, the Catholic Church represented a hierarchical organization relatively isolated from the French society, due to its certain features, such as the pope's supranational authority and the clergy's celibacy. There was a tension between several segments of the French society and the church regarding issues, such as the church's large properties, since the time of feudalism.

In Turkey, however, the role of religion in the *ancien régime* was relatively different. Islamic institutions, from the ulema in Istanbul to Sufi tariqas in local areas, were very diverse. These institutions were comparatively more deeply embedded to the society because there was not an extraterritorial pope or isolated clergy with celibacy. In this regard, there was no monolithic polarization between the "mosque" and certain segments of the "people." The pious foundations, for example, were seen as a shared value of the society, not the property of the ulema. The tension happened between the Westernist elite and Islamic leaders in the late Ottoman and the early Republican period. Moreover, the Islamists in Turkey, unlike the Catholic Church in France, did not try to reestablish the monarchy. Yet the Turkish republican elite still saw the Islamists as the representative of the *ancien régime*, in terms of the hegemony of Islamic way of life.

As a result, assertive secularism was largely imposed as a top-down elite project in Turkey, while it has been established through a relatively more bottom-up process in France. Assertive secularism in Turkey was the pillar of the Westernization project, which alienated the traditional culture of the masses by importing a new European way of life. In France, assertive secularism was more indigenous. That is a reason why the assertive secularists became successful under multiparty democracy in France, whereas they have needed authoritarian means in Turkey. In short, despite their similar historical background

---

[90] See Bauberot 2000, 36–40; Burdy and Marcou 1995, 29; Massignon 2000, 362.

TABLE 6. *Groups in a Continuum between Passive and*
Assertive Secularism

	Nonsecularist Groups	Passive Secularists	Assertive Secularists
United States	Christian Right	Accommodationists, Separationists	Strict separationists
France	Far-Right	Pluralistic secularists	Combative secularists
Turkey	Islamists	Conservatives	Kemalists

(*ancien régime*) and dominant ideology (assertive secularism), France and Turkey are still different with regard to certain characteristics of their *ancien régimes*, which impacted their diverse levels of democratization. That explains why Turkey has more restrictive state policies toward religion than France does.

Throughout the book, I avoid defining my cases as assertive or passive secularist states. Instead, I define them as countries where one of the two secularist ideologies has domination, which is still resisted by alternative ideologies. This book also problematizes the monolithic view of the state by stressing that state actors are divided through ideological lines.[91] Therefore, the final conceptual attempt of the book to descend in the ladder of abstraction is to unpack countries as arenas of struggle for ideological groups. I just summarize these groups in Table 6 and leave explanations to the empirical chapters.

METHODOLOGY

This study primarily analyzes three countries and enlarges the number of cases and units of observation by comparing different periods of time (e.g., historical and contemporary) and various cases (e.g., movements and parties) within countries. I chose the United States, France, and Turkey because they allow me to conduct a cross-regional and cross-cultural comparison. These cases also provide variations in dependent and explanatory variables.[92] They direct to generalizable results

---

[91] Migdal 2001.
[92] King, Keohane, and Verba 1994, 128–32.

on secularism, which is an important state-religion regime embraced by a majority of the states as noted in Table 1. The United States and France are the two founders of secularism, which have been imitated by other secular states worldwide. Turkey, for its own part, is the first secular state in the Muslim world. As An-Na'im stresses, its ability to balance Islam and secularism will

play an important role in informing this debate throughout the Muslim world. If Turkey is able to show that a secular regime can still find a place for religious discourse and human rights for all, then it will go a long way toward rehabilitating the term "secular" among Muslims everywhere. Likewise, if Turkey is able to show that it can allow an Islamic political voice to be heard while maintaining a secular government and constitutional rights for all, it will reassure secularists throughout the world that Islam has a place in political discourse.[93]

In order to test alternative theoretical explanations, I primarily use Mill's methods of difference and agreement as summarized in Tables 7 and 8.[94] The method of difference searches for the causes of diverse results in similar cases. The United States and France are similar in terms of levels of economic development and civilizational identity. The difference of dominant secularist ideologies explains their opposite policies toward religion. The method of agreement examines similar results in different cases. France and Turkey are different regarding economic development and civilization. Yet they share a similar dominant ideology, which explains their similar policies.

The methods of difference and agreement, however, are not sufficient in themselves to test theories because they only show correlation and omit certain variables.[95] Therefore, I analyze the causal processes through the method of process tracing.[96] Process tracing divides a narrative into systematic parts and closely evaluates microdynamics of change from one part to the other in order to reveal the interaction between explanatory and dependent variables. Using this method, I explore step by step the processes in which (1) historical conditions and relations lead to ideological dominance and (2) contemporary ideological struggles shape state policies.

---

[93] An-Na'im 2008, 222.
[94] Mill 1961; George and Bennett 2005, 151–60.
[95] Lieberson 1992.
[96] Mahoney 2000b; George and Bennett 2005, 205–32.

TABLE 7. *The United States and France: Method of Difference*

	Alternative Explanatory Variables			Dependent Variable
	Economic Development	Civilization	Dominant Ideology	State Policies toward Religion
United States	High	Western	Passive secularism	Inclusionary
France	High	Western	Assertive secularism	Exclusionary

TABLE 8. *France and Turkey: Method of Similarity*

	Alternative Explanatory Variables			Dependent Variable
	Economic Development	Civilization	Dominant Ideology	State Policies toward Religion
France	High	Western	Assertive secularism	Exclusionary
Turkey	Moderate	Islamic	Assertive secularism	Exclusionary

This study employs a comparative historical methodology.[97] It analyzes how ideological path dependence formed in a country's historical critical juncture has a persistent impact on contemporary public policies. The beginning of a path dependence is not always an arbitrary, accidental event.[98] On the contrary, in my cases, the path dependence of passive and assertive secularism began through purposeful political struggles. Once the ideological and institutional path dependence emerges, it endures for a long time, even though it becomes relatively inefficient.[99] As Kathleen Thelen rightly emphasizes,[100] path dependence does not necessarily mean an inevitable historical determinism.[101]

[97] Mahoney and Rueschemeyer 2003; Brady and Collier 2004; Collier 1991.
[98] Mahoney 2000a; Putnam 1994.
[99] Pierson 2000a; Pierson 2000b; Page 2005.
[100] Thelen 2000; Thelen 2003.
[101] Mahoney 2000a; Putnam 1994.

What it stresses is that ideological and institutional change is possible, but it remains very difficult. Such a change requires a new critical juncture with institutional flux and deliberate political action.

This book uses data gathered from three main sources. First, it depends on primary sources, such as legal and political documents. I analyzed historical and contemporary decisions of the U.S. Supreme Court, the French Council of State, and Turkey's three highest courts. In addition, I explored the discussions on and the contents of certain bills passed by the U.S. Congress, French Parliament, and Turkish Parliament. The research is also extended to the memorandums and speeches of politicians, particularly presidents, prime ministers, and ministers (or secretary) of education. I gathered this data through archival research (e.g., in the Library of Turkish Parliament), online sources (e.g., the Web site of the French National Assembly), and anthologies (e.g., Miller and Flowers 1996, a collection of U.S. Supreme Court decisions). I also surveyed newspapers and magazines, both print and online versions. All translations from Turkish and French are mine, unless otherwise noted.

The second data source is the elite interviews that I conducted during my field research in Turkey (Ankara and Istanbul, July–September 2004), France (Paris and Auxerre, October–December 2004), and the United States (Washington, D.C., Salt Lake City, Seattle, and San Diego, 2005–2007) with politicians, bureaucrats, academics, and religious leaders listed in the bibliography. The third source, needless to say, is books and articles on the history of and current debates on the state-religion relations in the three primarily analyzed cases, twenty-five briefly examined countries, and several others of the 197 coded countries in the index.

PART I

THE UNITED STATES

2

Passive Secularism and the Christian Right's Challenge (1981–2008)

During the presidential campaign in August 1980, the Republican presidential nominee, Ronald Reagan (1911–2004), unlike his rival Jimmy Carter, accepted an invitation to address evangelical Christians in Dallas. To the audience of "10,000 conservative Christians, including 2,500 pastors," Reagan said, "I know this group can't endorse me, but I want you to know that I endorse you and what you are doing."[1] That event was an important step forward in Reagan's alliance with the Christian Right led by evangelical leaders, such as Jerry Falwell and Pat Robertson. The Christian Right was based on a decade-long activism as a reaction to several court decisions on issues such as the prohibition of Bible reading and organized prayer in schools, the legalization of abortion, and the removal of tax-exempt status of schools that practiced racial discrimination.

Reagan's presidential inauguration in 1981 meant the beginning of a new era in state-religion relations in the United States. The conservatives, in general, and the Christian Right, in particular, gained a powerful ally at the White House,[2] though some of them would later be

---

[1] Quoted by Smith 2006, 318. See also Balmer 2008, 119.
[2] In 1976, Jimmy Carter was elected as the first evangelical president. Two of Carter's four successors, William Clinton and George W. Bush, were also evangelicals, while two others, Ronald Reagan and George H. W. Bush, were conservative but not evangelicals. Mary Seger defines evangelicals with regard to three criteria: "belief in the absolute authority of the Scripture, a born-again or conversion experience, and an eagerness to evangelize others." Segers 1998, 110. See also Smith 2002, esp. 15–17.

disappointed by Reagan's lack of sufficient support for school prayer amendments and appointment of moderate conservative Sandra Day O'Connor to the Supreme Court.[3] Reagan's presidency consolidated the alliance between the Christian Right and the Republican Party. Recently, former President Carter pointed out this turning point and criticized the increasing politicization of the evangelical Protestants through their relationship with the GOP:

> When I was younger, almost all Baptists were strongly committed on a theological basis to the separation of church and state. It was only 25 years ago when there began to be a melding of the Republican Party with fundamentalist Christianity, particularly with the Southern Baptist Convention. This is a fairly new development, and I think it was brought about by the abandonment of some basic principles of Christianity.[4]

The Democratic Party has been very cautious about not losing religious voters totally to the GOP. In the recent "under God" debate, for example, it took a position similar to that of the Republicans. In March 2000, Michael Newdow, an avowed atheist and parent of a student at a public elementary school in California, filed a lawsuit in a federal district court. He sued the teacher-led daily recitation of the Pledge of Allegiance, which included the phrase "one nation, under God." Although students were not compelled to participate, Newdow argued that his daughter would be harmed by the state-run ritual that proclaimed the existence of God. When the district court dismissed the case, Newdow appealed to the Ninth Circuit Court of Appeals. In June 2002, the court ruled with a 2–1 vote that the phrase "under God" in the Pledge of Allegiance, as well as the California requirement that teachers lead the recitation of the pledge, violated the Establishment Clause of the First Amendment.[5]

The decision sparked immediate and emotional comments by politicians.[6] White House Press Secretary Ari Fleischer announced that President George W. Bush defined the ruling as "ridiculous."[7] Senate

---

[3] Balmer 2008, 108–24; Jelen 2000, 72–3; Kobylka 1995, 97, 105, 109; Kengor 2004.
[4] Carter's interview with Ayelish McGarvey, "Carter's Crusade," *American Prospect*, April 9, 2004.
[5] *Newdow v. U.S. Congress*, no. 00–16423.
[6] Gunn 2004, esp. 423–4, 496.
[7] "White House Reaction to Circuit Court Ruling," June 26, 2002, http://www.whitehouse.gov/news/releases/2002/06/20020626–8.html.

minority leader Thomas Daschle called the decision "just nuts."[8] Senator Robert Byrd, the only remaining senator who voted for the statute on adding "under God" to the pledge in 1954 (as a member of the House), said that the judge who made the decision was "stupid."[9] Beyond these personal remarks, Congress took a bipartisan stand against the decision. The Senate and the House of Representatives reaffirmed the words "under God" in the pledge by voting 99–0 and 416–3, respectively. Moreover, Congress enacted a new bill to keep "under God" in the pledge and "In God We Trust" as the national motto, which was signed by President Bush into law in November 2002.[10] Seven months later, all fifty state attorneys general filed a petition to urge the U.S. Supreme Court to reverse the judgment.[11] In June 2004, the Court ruled that Newdow lacked standing to sue, because he did not have sufficient custody over his daughter.[12] Because the Court avoided directly addressing the constitutionality of the reference to God in the pledge, the debate did not end.[13]

The discussion regarding the pledge shows the enthusiasm with which the executive and legislative branches promote religious expressions in American public life. Both Republican and Democratic politicians have followed the popular mood on this issue. According to a survey in 2002, nine of ten Americans think that the phrase "under God" should remain in the pledge.[14] This phrase is one of the religious discourses that make the American public sphere different from its

---

[8] "Flap after Court Rules Pledge of Allegiance Unconstitutional," June 27, 2002, http://www.foxnews.com/story/0,2933,56310,00.html.

[9] "Is The Pledge of Allegiance Unconstitutional?" June 26, 2002, http://transcripts.cnn.com/TRANSCRIPTS/0206/26/asb.00.html.

[10] Public law 107–293, November 13, 2002.

[11] "State Attorneys General Unanimously Seek Supreme Court Review of Pledge of Allegiance Case," June 10, 2003, http://www.naag.org/news/pr-20030610-pledge.php.

[12] *Elk Grove Unified School District v. Newdow*, 542 U.S. 1 (2004). The child's mother, Sandra Banning, had the legal custody of her daughter. She declared that her daughter was a Christian who believed in God and had no objection either to personally reciting or hearing others recite the pledge, including the reference to God.

[13] Newdow filed a new case on behalf of three parents and their children. In September 2005, a federal judge in Sacramento ruled that it was unconstitutional to require public school children to recite the pledge including the phrase "under God." The school districts appealed the ruling. "Pledge of Allegiance Resources," http://pewforum.org/religion-schools/pledge/, accessed on June 2, 2008. Newdow also sued regarding the use of the motto "In God We Trust" on currencies. In 2006, the federal judge affirmed the motto's constitutionality.

[14] "Vast majority in U.S. support 'under God,'" June 30, 2002, http://archives.cnn.com/2002/US/06/29/poll.pledge/.

French and Turkish counterparts. Chapter 1 explained this difference among the three cases with regard to their opposite secularist ideologies (passive and assertive). Nevertheless, state-religion relations in the United States are too complex to be explained simply by a single dominant ideology. The financial separation of the state and religious institutions in the United States, for example, is more rigid than it is in France and Turkey.[15] Taxpayer money cannot be used directly to fund religious schools in the United States, whereas the French state finances Catholic schools and the Turkish state runs Islamic Imam-Hatip schools (see Chapters 4 and 6).[16] Moreover, the United States, like France and unlike Turkey, is one of the rare countries where there is no religious instruction in public schools.[17] Additionally, school prayers – even a student-initiated and student-led prayer at a high school football game – are prohibited in America.[18]

Why do state policies toward religion in the United States have these two seemingly opposite dimensions (i.e., monotheistic public discourse and separationist policies), especially in public schools? This puzzle cannot be solved without analyzing passive secularism's two different and struggling interpretations in the United States – accommodationism and separationism. The accommodationists regard close state-religion entanglements, including official monotheistic references and public funding of religious schools, as compatible with secularism, as long as the state does not favor one particular religion at the expense of others. The separationists, however, see close relations between the state and religion as contrary to secularism. The ideal principle of relation for them is absolute separation symbolized by the metaphor "wall

---

[15] Stephen Monsma and Christopher Soper compare the United States with four other Western democracies (the United Kingdom, Germany, the Netherlands, and Australia) and conclude that the United States is the only one, among these five, that strictly prohibits state funding of religious schools. Monsma and Soper 1997.

[16] As a result, private religious schools have expensive tuitions in the United States, whereas many of them are almost free in France. Lacorne 2003, 79.

[17] Mathieu 2005, 276.

[18] According to Fox, the U.S. policies toward religion are much more separationist (score: 0) than those of France (score: 22.92) and Turkey (score: 47.21). The score of "0," which makes America the only country with absolute state-religion separation, is an exaggeration. The reason is that Fox's dataset picked only specific policies while ignoring the political role of religion in the United States at symbolic and discursive levels. Fox 2008, 108, 219.

of separation." This struggle results in the Janus-faced image of state-religion relations in the United States.

I will begin with the main dependent variable of the book: six state policies toward religion that show the American state's inclusionary stand toward religion in comparison to the French and Turkish states. Then, I will analyze the ideological struggles on state-religion relations in the United States. I conclude by tracing the impact of these struggles on public-policy formation toward three highly controversial issues on schools – school prayer, freedom of religious speech, and school vouchers.

THE U.S. POLICIES TOWARD RELIGION IN SCHOOLS

U.S. policies are largely tolerant toward public visibility of religion in schools. Among the six following policies, students' freedom to display religious symbols and reciting a pledge referring to God particularly emphasize America's difference from France and Turkey. The ban on state funding of religious private schools, as well as on organized school prayer and religious instruction in public schools, emphasizes the complexity of U.S. policies, which need to be taken as a field of constant ideological struggles.

The Pledge

Since 1892, the Pledge of Allegiance has been recited in certain public gatherings as an oath of allegiance to the American Republic and its national flag. Currently, it is read in public schools as a daily morning ritual. Its official form is the following: "I pledge allegiance to the flag of the United States of America, and to the Republic for which it stands, one Nation under God, indivisible, with liberty and justice for all."

The phrase "under God" was added into the pledge in 1954. There are three conflicting views on this phrase. For some defenders, it is constitutional in spite of being religious because it does not establish a particular religion.[19] Others argue that it is constitutional because of

---

[19] Justice Clarence Thomas's concurring opinion, *Elk Grove Unified School District v. Newdow*, 542 U.S. 1 (2004).

being a historical, patriotic, and ceremonial statement.[20] The critics, however, take it as a religious statement that discriminates against atheists and any followers of nonmonotheistic religions.[21]

Students' Religious Symbols

There is no general restriction against student display of religious symbols in the United States. An exceptional headscarf case happened in 2004 due to the dress code policy of a public school, Benjamin Franklin Science Academy in Muskogee, Oklahoma. The school banned a sixth-grade Muslim girl, Nashala Heam, from wearing a headscarf. In April 2004, the U.S. Justice Department intervened on the side of the student. Assistant Attorney General Alexander Acosta announced it and said: "No student should be forced to choose between following her faith and enjoying the benefits of a public education." Islamic organizations applauded this action as a "message to ... [France that] banned hijabs in schools."[22] A more well-known but less relevant case is *Goldman v. Weinberger* of 1986, where the U.S. Supreme Court decided by 5–4 that the Air Force had the right to ban an officer from wearing religious headgear (a yarmulke, in this case). The Court stressed that the armed forces were different from civil institutions, and that the "purpose of the military and its need to foster cohesiveness were regarded as appropriate justifications to restrict the religious rights of individuals."[23] Nevertheless, in the following year, Congress passed legislation that reversed this decision by allowing the members of the armed forces to wear religious apparel.[24]

The general principle in the U.S. legal system is that religious practices cannot be prohibited by being singled out. In this regard, the French ban on religious symbols or the Turkish ban on headscarves has no legal standing in the American system. The controversial issue

---

[20] Chief Justice William H. Rehnquist's and Justice O'Connor's concurring opinions, *Elk Grove Unified School District v. Newdow*, 542 U.S. 1 (2004).
[21] Gunn 2004; The Ninth Circuit Court of Appeals' majority opinion, *Newdow v. U.S. Congress*, no. 00–16423.
[22] Brian Knowlton, "U.S. Takes Opposite Tack from France," *International Herald Tribune*, April 3, 2004.
[23] *Goldman v. Weinberger*, 475 U.S. 503 (1986).
[24] Public Law 100–180, section 508 (reference (c)).

in the United States is whether an individual can be excused from a general ban because of his or her religious beliefs. In some cases, the regulation stresses such an exception. The U.S. Department of State, for example, specifies in its guideline for passports that "*Unless worn daily for religious reasons*, all hats or headgear should be removed for the photo."[25] For cases without such an exception, there are two arguments. This debate is important for understanding the possibility of a future headscarf ban in the United States.

The first argument is that religious practices have a unique right to be exempt from general regulations because they are protected by the Free Exercise Clause. The rationale of this approach is that religious practices are beyond personal choices; they are perceived as obligations by the believers. In this regard, freedom of religious expression should be taken more seriously than mere freedom of choice.[26] This perspective was upheld by the Supreme Court's decision in *Sherbert v. Verner* in 1963, which produced the "compelling interest test." The test required the state (1) to show a compelling interest for restricting certain religious practices by a general regulation and (2) to assure that there is no alternative means to reach this interest without restricting these religious practices.[27]

A famous educational case in which the Court upheld religious exemption was *Wisconsin v. Yoder* (1972). The Court decided that Amish parents had legitimate religious reasons to require that their children be exempt from school attendance beyond the eighth grade because their free exercise of religion outweighed the state's interests in compelling student attendance. The Court emphasized that such an exemption can only be acceptable for religious reasons: "A way of life,

---

[25] "Frequently Asked Questions," http://travel.state.gov/passport/guide/faq/faq_881 .html, accessed on June 1, 2006 (emphasis added).

[26] According to Michael McConnell, by the Free Exercise Clause, the framers aimed to provide "a special, protected status to religious conscience not because religious judgments are better, truer, or more likely to be moral than nonreligious judgments, but because the obligations entailed by religion transcend the individual and are outside the individual's control." McConnell 1990, 1497. For a philosophical defense of this view, see Sandel 1999, esp. 84–93.

[27] *Sherbert v. Verner*, 374 U.S. 398 (1963). In *Sherbert*, the Court decided that an individual had the right to refuse to work on his or her Sabbath without relinquishing his or her unemployment benefits because the state had no compelling reason for denying that right. See also Reid 2002, 79–82; Flowers 2005, 32–3.

however virtuous and admirable, may not be interposed as a barrier to a reasonable state regulation of education if it is based on purely secular considerations; to have the protection of the Religion Clauses, the claims must be rooted in religious belief."[28]

The second argument rejects religious exemption unless it is specifically provided by state law. The Supreme Court had embraced this approach in some cases and established it in *Oregon v. Smith* (1990). The court approved the Oregon state policy of firing two Native Americans for using peyote (a mild hallucinogenic) although they used it in a religious ceremony. Justice Antonin Scalia delivered the Court decision: "To permit [religious exemption] would be to make the professed doctrines of religious belief superior to the law of the land, and in effect to permit every citizen to become a law unto himself."[29] Critics have claimed that the Court decisions against religious exemption have generally targeted religious minorities, such as Native Americans and Mormons.[30] In the polygamy case *Reynolds v. U.S.* (1878), the Court decided against the Mormons (see Chapter 3).[31] In *Lyng v. Northwest Indian CPA* (1988), the Court decided that the government had the right to construct a road that would cut through lands that were perceived as sacred by some Native American tribes.[32]

Oregon v. Smith created a substantial political reaction. In 1993, the House unanimously, and the Senate overwhelmingly (97–3), voted and President William Clinton promptly signed into law the Religious Freedom Restoration Act (RFRA) to overturn *Oregon v. Smith* and to restore the compelling interest test. The RFRA restricted state authority in regulating religious freedom by requiring states to use the "least-restrictive means" against religious practices.[33] Based on the

---

[28] *Wisconsin v. Yoder*, 406 U.S. 205 (1972).

[29] *Oregon v. Smith*, 494 U.S. 872 (1990).

[30] In the words of Stephen Carter, "Religions that most need protection seem to receive it least. Contemporary America is not likely to enact legislation aimed at curbing the mainstream Protestant, Roman Catholic, or Jewish faiths. But Native Americans, having once been hounded from their lands, are now hounded from their religions, with the complicity of a Supreme Court untroubled when sacred lands are taken for road building or when Native Americans under a bona fide religious compulsion to use peyote in their rituals are punished under state antidrug regulations." Carter 1993, 9. See also Jacobsohn 2003, 268–83; Boyle and Sheen 1997, 162; Michaelien 1987; McConnell 1992, 741–2; Witte 2004, 163.

[31] *Reynolds v. U.S.*, 98 U.S. 145 (1878). See Weisbrod 2002, 46–64.

[32] *Lyng v. Northwest Indian CPA*, 485 U.S. 439 (1988).

[33] Religious Freedom Restoration Act, 42 U.S.C. 2000bb. See also Witte and Green 1996, 536–47.

RFRA, in 1995, President Clinton issued the Memorandum on Religion in Schools, which stressed student freedom in displaying religious symbols: "When wearing particular attire, such as yarmulkes and headscarves, during the school day is part of students' religious practice ... schools generally may not prohibit the wearing of such items."[34]

Nevertheless, in 1997, in *City of Boerne v. Flores*, the Supreme Court held the application of RFRA as an unconstitutional restriction over states' authority.[35] As a reaction to the Court's decision, twenty states have incorporated the RFRA into their state law.[36] The decision also weakened the legal ground of Clinton's memorandum. In response, he issued a guideline on religious freedom in places that he had direct oversight on – federal workplaces: "An employee must be permitted to wear religious garb, such as a crucifix, a yarmulke, or a head scarf or hijab, if wearing such attire during the work day is part of the employee's religious practice or expression, so long as the wearing of such garb does not unduly interfere with the functioning of the workplace."[37]

In sum, students in American public schools can be exempt from generally applicable school dress codes with the excuse of their religious beliefs. Schools cannot single out religious attire in general or attire of a particular religion (e.g., the Muslim headscarf) for prohibition or regulation in the United States.[38]

Private Religious Education and State Funding of Religious Schools

Several groups have had their own private religious schools in the United States.[39] During 1999 to 2000, there were about twenty-seven thousand private schools with 5.3 million students, which constituted 24 percent of all schools and 10 percent of students in the United States.

[34] "President Clinton's Memorandum on Religion in Schools," *New York Times*, July 13, 1995.
[35] *City of Boerne v. Flores*, 521 U.S. 507 (1997). The court did not totally strike the RFRA down. In 2006, in *Gonzales v. O. Centro Espirita* (546 U.S. 418), it applied the RFRA to the federal government. See also Gedicks 2005, 1191–2.
[36] Davis 2004, 232.
[37] "Guidelines on Religious Exercise and Religious Expression in the Federal Workplace," August 14, 1997, http://clinton2.nara.gov/WH/New/html/19970819-3275.html.
[38] Davis 2004, 232–3.
[39] In 1925, in *Pierce v. Society of Sisters* (268 U.S. 510), the Supreme Court unanimously upheld education in private schools.

About 30 percent of all private schools were affiliated with the Roman Catholic Church and 50 percent with other religious groups. Half of all students in private schools were attending Catholic schools.[40] The number of Protestant schools substantially increased in the 1950s and 1960s. As a response to both the desegregation (of black and white students) and the ban on organized prayer and Bible reading in public schools, many white Protestant families, especially in the South, began to send their children to private Protestant schools.[41]

Religious groups also own institutions of higher education. By the mid-1990s, there were 1,300 accredited private colleges and universities in the United States, more than one thousand of which had religious affiliations (e.g., 240 of them were Catholic). Despite the secularization trend, half of these institutions still have a "strong religious orientation."[42] Private colleges and universities with religious affiliations are allowed to receive governmental funding regarding two criteria established by the Supreme Court. First, public money should be spent on secular elements and activities of these institutions. Second, they should avoid being pervasively sectarian by having institutional autonomy from religious hierarchies, maintaining academic freedom, and teaching courses with academic standards. Moreover, they should not have religious indoctrination as their primary purpose and discriminate against faculty or students with regard to religious affiliations.[43]

Private religious elementary and secondary schools, however, do not receive direct public (federal and state) funding except some indirect supplies (e.g., books). Yet a recent initiative, the voucher system, has provided an alternative to the financial separation. According to this system, the state reimburses the tuition expenses of the parents who send their children to private (either secular or religious) schools. As I will discuss later, the voucher system has been a marginal program implemented in only a few states.

[40] National Center of Education Statistics 2002, 3. The number of Jewish schools was 604 in 1990. Sarna and Dalin 1997, 246.
[41] Flowers 2005, 118. In 1954, in *Brown v. Board of Education* (347 U.S. 483), the Supreme Court outlawed the segregation of children in public schools based on race.
[42] Monsma 1996, 9. See also Fowler et al. 2004, 32.
[43] Monsma and Soper 1997, 36–9.

Religious Instruction and Prayer

Religious instruction has been prohibited in American public schools since the Supreme Court's decision in *McCollum v. Board of Education* in 1948. Later, in the early 1960s, the Court banned prayer and Bible reading in public schools with regard to the Establishment Clause. The particular prayer tried in the Court was: "Almighty God, we acknowledge our dependence upon Thee, and we beg Thy blessing upon us, our parents, our teachers and our Country."[44] Since that time, the Court has declared unconstitutional several related issues, such as a state law on "a moment of silence" and student-led prayer in football games. The U.S. Department of Education, under both the Clinton and George W. Bush administrations, issued guidelines to clarify the prayer issue regarding court decisions. The guidelines stressed that students in public schools were allowed to pray and read religious texts, individually or jointly, as an extracurricular activity, as long as these activities were not endorsed by teachers or administrators. They even noted that students could preach to each other without coercion.[45]

General Policy Trend toward Religion

The U.S. policies toward religion have had certain inconsistencies. The Supreme Court has made several polarized decisions on state-religion relations. On June 27, 2005, for example, the Court made two opposite decisions. In *McCreary County v. ACLU*, it decided that three Kentucky counties violated the Establishment Clause by displaying the Ten Commandments in courthouses and public schools.[46] In *Van Orden v. Perry*, however, the Court held that a Ten Commandments monument on the grounds of the Texas state capitol does not violate the Establishment Clause due to its historical and secular aspects.[47] One may argue that the Court decided regarding

---

[44] *Engel v. Vitale*, 370 U.S. 421 (1962).

[45] "Religious Expression in Public Schools, August 1995," http://www.ed.gov/Speeches/08–1995/religion.html, accessed on June 2, 2008; "Guidance on Constitutionally Protected Prayer in Public Elementary and Secondary Schools," February 7, 2003, http://www.ed.gov/policy/gen/guid/religionandschools/prayer_guidance.html. See also Dilulio 2007, 64–5.

[46] *McCreary County v. ACLU*, 545 U.S. (2005).

[47] *Van Orden v. Perry*, 545 U.S. (2005).

the different context of each case so therefore it is still consistent. However, both decisions were made by 5–4, which shows that their rationale was convincing for only one swing-vote justice (Stephen G. Breyer), whereas the other eight justices do not see any difference between the two cases and were therefore divided.[48]

U.S. policies toward religion in schools also indicate a paradox. On the one hand, American public schools are open to public religiosity regarding a pledge referring to God and student freedom to display religious symbols. On the other hand, court decisions have disallowed any religious instruction and organized prayer in schools. The main reason for these policy inconsistencies has been the ideological struggles between groups with dissimilar interpretations of secularism – conservatives and liberals.

CONSERVATIVES, LIBERALS, AND TWO TYPES OF SECULARISM

For the last two decades, several books on "culture wars" have examined "the struggle to define America" through "battles over ... education, law, and politics."[49] The two sides of this conflict are generally defined as the conservatives and liberals. This sociopolitical division is related to but not simply based on denominational differences in American society reflected in the following ratios: evangelical Protestants (26%),[50] mainline Protestants (18%), black Protestants (7%), Catholics (24%), people with no religion (16%), Mormons (2%), Jews (2%), Muslims

---

[48] Another example of inconsistency is the crèche debate. In 1983, in *Lynch v. Donnelly*, the Supreme Court decided by 5–4 that a city administration could display a nativity scene as part of a Christmas celebration because the crèche was a historical tradition with secular purposes. In *Allegheny v. ACLU* of 1989, the Court decided by 5–4 that the display of a crèche by a public authority was unconstitutional because it had religious purposes. (In the same decision, it approved a menorah display because it lacked an exclusively religious message and coexisted with secular symbols.) Again, these two different decisions were determined by the swing vote of Justice O'Connor, while other members did not see the two decisions as consistent and remained divided as 4 versus 4. *Lynch v. Donnelly*, 463 U.S. 783 (1983); *Allegheny v. ACLU*, 492 U.S. 573 (1989).

[49] Hunter 1991. See also Wuthnow 1990; Fiorina 2005; Schlesinger 1998; Huntington 2005.

[50] For diverse evangelical groups (e.g., fundamentalists and Pentecostals), see Zoba 2005, 62–80; Wills 2005, 30–3.

(1%), and others (4%).[51] Instead, it is mainly a division between conservative and liberal interpreters of religion.[52] The two groups with clear political preferences are the evangelicals, who are mostly conservatives, and the growing number of people with no religion, who overwhelmingly support liberalism.[53] The liberals are the so-called progressives, who seek more individual freedom and multiculturalism. The conservatives support the preservation of life, morality, and family values. This is why liberals defend the right to abortion, gay marriage, and euthanasia, while conservatives generally oppose them. The majority of conservatives vote for the Republican Party, whereas many liberals support Democratic candidates.[54] In presidential and House elections in the 2000s, 60 percent of those who said they frequently attended worship services voted for the Republican Party, while only 40 percent of them voted for the Democrats.[55]

The major issue of disagreement between these two groups is secularism. The conservatives support state accommodation of religion, while liberals tend to defend a wall of separation between the state and religious institutions. With regard to the specific issue of secularism and religion, scholars generally use the terms *accommodationist* and *separationist* to define conservative and liberal approaches.[56] I want to provide a more sensitive typology by adding two more categories. The extremists on the conservative side are the Christian Right, who want to establish a cultural dominance of Christianity in the United States.[57] On the liberal side, the extremists are the strict separationists, who aim to exclude religion from the public sphere.[58] Figure 4 and Table 9 locate these four groups regarding their ideologies and policy preferences. The Christian Right and strict separationists have had a marginal impact on

---

[51] The Pew Forum on Religion and Public Life, "U.S. Religous Landscape Survey," March 30, 2008, http://religions.pewforum.org/reports. See also Kohut et al. 2000, 18; Kosmin, Mayer, and Keysar 2001, 12–13; Bukhari 2003, 7.

[52] Wald 1996, 176–9; Wuthnow 1990, esp. 24; Kohut et al. 2000, 34–72; Green and Silk 2003; Layman 2001; Fowler et al. 2004, 292–3.

[53] The number of people with no religion increased from 8% in 1990 to 14% in 2001. Jacoby 2004, 6–7.

[54] Kohut et al. 2000, 73–98. For the relationship between religion and voting behavior in American politics, see Leege and Kellstedt 1993.

[55] Green and Silk 2003. See also Reichley 2002, 186.

[56] Wald 1996; Jelen 1998; Jelen and Wilcox 1995; Kobylka 1995.

[57] Fraser 1999, 239–40; Kramnick and Moore 2005, 153–67; Ravitch 1999, 19–43.

[58] Feldman 2005, 111–34.

TABLE 9. *Groups' Goals and Policy Preferences in the United States*

		Christian Right	Accommo- dationists	Separation- ists	Strict Separationists
GOALS	Exclusion of religion from the public sphere	NO	NO	NO	YES
	Cultural dominance of Christianity	YES	NO	NO	NO
POLICY PRE- FEREN- CES	Organized prayer in public schools	YES	YES	NO	NO
	State funding of religious schools	YES	YES	NO	NO

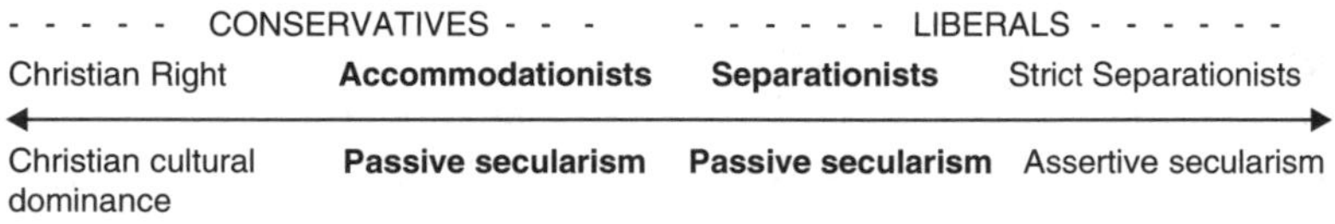

- - - - - CONSERVATIVES - - -   - - - - - - LIBERALS - - - - - -

Christian Right	**Accommodationists**	**Separationists**	Strict Separationists

◄──►

Christian cultural dominance	**Passive secularism**	**Passive secularism**	Assertive secularism

FIGURE 4. Continuum of Ideological Groups in the United States

current U.S. policies toward religion. Contemporary policies have been largely shaped by the accommodationists and separationists.[59] Despite their opposite policy preferences, these two mainstream groups share the goal of protecting passive secularism. They oppose a cultural establishment of Christianity and an assertive secularist exclusion of religion from the public sphere. That is why I define them as defenders of two different interpretations of passive secularism.

For the sake of generalization, I neglect diverse views within these groups. For example, the state funding of religious schools has been a

---

[59] Carl Esbeck calls these four groups (the Christian Right, accommodationists, separationists, and strict separationists) restorationists, nonpreferentialists, pluralistic separationists, and strict separationists, respectively. Esbeck 1986.

controversial issue with the conservatives, though currently they largely support it. According to John Jeffries and James Ryan, the "historic Protestant hostility to school aid sprang, at least in part, from antipathy toward Roman Catholics." Since the 1960s, the evangelicals have regarded the secularists as the main enemy and conservative Catholics as an ally. Therefore, their "emotional energy for opposing school aid evaporated."[60] Although "some fundamentalists continued to oppose any form of governmental assistance on the ground that it would lead to governmental control ... since the 1980s, the religious right increasingly had supported government aid for religious schools."[61]

Their opposite views on school prayer is a reflection of the conservatives and liberals' disagreement on the "true meaning" of the First Amendment, regarding both the Establishment and Free Exercise clauses. Liberals take organized prayer in public schools as an establishment of religion and a form of governmental discrimination against the followers of dissenting religions and nonbelievers.[62] For conservatives, in contrast, its ban means the establishment of secularism as an antireligious doctrine and violation of religious freedom of those who want the prayer.[63]

The conflicting policy preferences of these two groups also linked their opposite notions of neutrality.[64] For conservatives, neutrality generally means state impartiality to monotheistic religions. Conservative Supreme Court Justice Scalia, joined by Chief Justice Rehnquist and Justice Clarence Thomas, argued that the public honoring of God and the Ten Commandments is constitutional, because "[t]he three most popular religions in the United States, Christianity, Judaism, and Islam – which combined account for 97.7% of all believers – are monotheistic. All of them, moreover

---

[60] Jeffries and Ryan 2001, 349.
[61] Ibid., 345. See also McConnell 1999, 850–1.
[62] Ravitch 1999.
[63] See Monsma 1995, esp. 17–57. A debate on this issue took place between the Pontotoc County public school in Mississippi and the ACLU, which sued the school's prayer on behalf of a parent in 1995–6. See the video documentary, Grunberg and Crane 1999.
[64] The concept of neutrality is crucial in the debates on the meaning of secularism in the United States. Several Supreme Court decisions interpret the First Amendment through a requirement for state neutrality. The majority, concurring, and dissenting opinions in *Abington v. Schempp* (374 U.S. 203 [1963]) refer twenty-five times to *neutrality* and six times to the word *neutral*. For discussions on neutrality, see Monsma 1995; Feldman 2002b, 691n79.

(Islam included), believe that the Ten Commandments were given by God to Moses, and are divine prescriptions for a virtuous life." He also added that "it is entirely clear from our Nation's historical practices that the Establishment Clause permits this disregard of polytheists and believers in unconcerned deities, just as it permits the disregard of devout atheists."[65] For liberals, however, the state should also be neutral toward nonmonotheists. Liberal Justice John Paul Stevens, joined by Justice Ruth Bader Ginsburg, criticized Scalia's conception of neutrality as an "evil of discriminating" against polytheists and atheists, which is forbidden by the Establishment Clause.[66]

Conservatives

The conservatives argue that religion has positively contributed to American public life, and the framers' primary intent was to protect religion from governmental intervention, more than the reverse.[67] In their view, the federal government's power has expanded, particularly since World War II, at the expense of the private, mainly religious, institutions, especially on the issues of education and welfare services.[68] Due to this expansion, they argue, state-religion separationism has marginalized religion and created a "naked public square."[69] In the words of Stephen Monsma, "in the age of administrative state ... [i]f neutrality is defined purely in terms of no state recognition or support for religion, it, in fact, is not neutral but rather promoting a secular cultural ethos."[70] Although the accommodationists and the Christian Right share these views and certain policy preferences, they disagree on the primary nature of state-religion relations. The conservative Supreme Court justices, for example, have generally been accommodationists who have supported the dominance of passive secularism instead of a Christian cultural dominance.

---

[65] Justice Scalia's dissenting opinion, *McCreary County v. ACLU*, 545 U.S. (2005) (I removed the citations).

[66] Justice Stevens's dissenting opinion, *Van Orden v. Perry*, 545 U.S. (2005).

[67] Segers 1998.

[68] Durham 1996, 21, 24; Wood 1998, 3; Wood 1993, 1–4; Robbins 1987, 73.

[69] Neuhaus 1986. Carter argues that American law and politics have trivialized religion in the public sphere because "religion is treated ... as a hobby." Carter 1993, 51.

[70] Monsma 1995, 191; also 5, 40, 54. See also Monsma and Soper 1997, 6, 33, 222.

The Christian Right has gained salience by the increasing number of evangelicals, at the expense of the mainline Protestants, and their growing organizational capacity.[71] They were primarily organized in the late 1970s and the 1980s, under the leadership of Jerry Falwell and his Moral Majority.[72] Although in 1950 there were only eighteen major religious lobbies in Washington, D.C., this number increased to eighty by 1985.[73] In 1989, when the Moral Majority dissolved, Pat Robertson, another prominent televangelist, founded the Christian Coalition.[74] The Christian Coalition currently claims to have more than two million members.[75] In 1990, Robertson founded the American Center for Law and Justice (ACLJ). The ACLJ has focused on issues involving religious rights, judicial nominations, and protection of references to God in the national motto and the pledge. In addition to the ACLJ, other conservative associations, including Rutherford Institute, Christian Legal Society, National Association of Evangelicals, United States Catholic Conference, and National Jewish Commission on Law and Public Affairs, have defended conservative causes, particularly by litigating First Amendment issues.[76] Robertson is the founder of several other institutions such as Regent University (1977) and the Christian Broadcasting Network (1961).[77] Currently, there are 1,600 radio stations and 250 TV channels affiliated with the Christian Right.[78]

The most influential conservative TV channel, which has both accommodationist and Christian Right tendencies, is Fox News, which was founded in 1996. In December 2005, Fox News launched a campaign claiming that the liberals, especially the American Civil Liberties Union (ACLU), perpetrated a "War on Christmas." According to Fox News, the liberals removed references to Christmas in holiday displays and tried to replace "Merry Christmas" with "Happy Holidays."[79] As a result, the House of Representatives voted (401–22) on a resolution

---

[71] Huntington 2005, 341–3.
[72] Wald 1996, 223–7; Jelen 2000, 86–94; Casanova 1994, 147–66.
[73] Hertzke 1988, 5.
[74] Reichley 2002, 176–7.
[75] See the Web site of the Christian Coalition, http://www.cc.org/about.cfm.
[76] Kobylka 1995, 112–19.
[77] Wills 1990, 165–91.
[78] Martin 2002, 335.
[79] See T. Jeremy Gunn, "A Fictional 'War on Christmas,'" *USA Today*, December 18, 2005.

that "recognizes the importance of the symbols and traditions of Christmas."[80]

It is a mistake to define all conservatives as a bloc by confusing the moderate accommodationists with the Christian Right. A similar misperception is to identify liberals as a monolithic entity hostile to public religions.[81] The separationists, who try to erect a wall of a separation between the state and religion, differ from the strict separationists, who want to exclude religion from the public sphere and, therefore, are *assertive secularist* in my terminology.

Liberals

The assertive secularists go beyond the separationists by seeking not only a church-state separation but also a separation of religion and public life. One of the main assertive secularist associations is the American Atheists (AA). The most influential liberal association, the ACLU, also includes both separationist and assertive secularist individuals. Currently, it has half a million members and supporters, and annually handles about six thousand court cases about civil liberties. The conservatives have generally criticized the ACLU for "becoming increasingly obsessed with a one-sided view of ... the Establishment Clause" while ignoring the Free Exercise Clause and for devoting "its energies to preventing or stopping any public display or expression of religion."[82] The ACLU, in response, notes that it has defended religious rights of believers as well. In May 2005, for example, the ACLU sued a "Wisconsin prison on behalf of a Muslim woman who was forced to remove her headscarf in front of male guards and prisoners."[83] In November 2005, it filed a case about a Muslim woman who "was denied the option of using the Quran when she was being sworn in as a witness in a court proceeding."[84] Moreover, recently, the ACLU founded a new "Program on Freedom of Religion and Belief."

---

[80] H. Res. 579.

[81] Gedicks 1995, esp. 117–23.

[82] Garry 2005, 129.

[83] "ACLU's Defense of Religious Liberty," March 2, 2005, http://www.aclu.org/religion/tencomm/16254res20050302.html.

[84] The judge upheld the use of the Qur'an and other religious texts in court proceedings. "Judge Says Multiple Religious Texts Must Be Allowed for Swearing-In Proceedings,"

Another leading separationist organization is the Americans United for the Separation of Church and State (AU). The AU currently has more than seventy-five thousand members. A major Jewish association, the Anti-Defamation League (ADL), has also been a defender of separationism. The ADL generally presents itself as friendly toward religion in the public sphere. For example, unlike the ACLU and the AU, it defended the phrase "under God" in the pledge because that did not endorse any religion and was a part of the American culture.[85] I conducted interviews with the ACLU's and the ADL's directors in charge of state-religion issues. Both emphasized that they were for religious freedom and critical of assertive secularist policies in France, such as the ban on Muslim headscarves.[86]

Other influential liberal organizations include the People for the American Way (PFAW) and the American Jewish Congress (AJC).[87] PFAW, with its three hundred thousand members, focuses on challenging the activities of the Christian Coalition.[88] The AJC lawyer Leo Pfeffer played a major role in several separationist Supreme Court decisions through his *amicus curiae* briefs and publications. From the 1940s to the 1980s, Pfeffer "has probably argued more church-state cases before the United States Supreme Court than anyone else in American history."[89]

One of the main reference points for the liberals is the Supreme Court's *Everson v. Board of Education* decision in 1947, which defines the Establishment Clause as the following:

Neither a state nor the Federal Government can set up a church. Neither can pass laws which aid one religion, aid all religions, or prefer one religion over another.... No tax in any amount, large or small, can be levied to support any religious activities or institutions, whatever they may be called, or whatever

May 24, 2007, http://www.aclu.org/religion/govtfunding/29872prs20070524.html.
[85] "ADL Says Appeals Court Ruling on 'One Nation under God' Was Wrong," June 27, 2002, http://www.adl.org/presrele/rel%5Fchstsep%5F90/4120%5F90.asp.
[86] The author's personal interviews with T. Jeremy Gunn, Professor of Law and the Director of the ACLU's Program on Freedom of Religion and Belief, Washington, D.C., September 6, 2005, and Michael Lieberman, Director of the ADL's Civil Rights Policy Planning Center, Washington, D.C., September 6, 2005. I could not conduct an interview with the conservative ACLJ because it did not give me an appointment.
[87] Kobylka 1995, 112–19.
[88] Fraser 1999, 192–3.
[89] Wood 1985, x.

form they may adopt to teach or practice religion. Neither a state nor the Federal Government can, openly or secretly, participate in the affairs of any religious organizations or groups and vice versa. In the words of Jefferson, the clause against establishment of religion by law was intended to erect "a wall of separation between Church and State."[90]

Another basis for them is the Court's *Lemon v. Kurtzman* decision in 1971, which specifies three criteria to determine the constitutionality of legislation: "First, the statute must have a secular legislative purpose; second, its principal or primary effect must be one that neither advances nor inhibits religion; finally, the statute must not foster 'an excessive government entanglement with religion.'"[91] For the conservatives, the *Lemon* test is deeply problematic and should be overruled.[92] The ideological disagreements between the conservatives and liberals are not simple rhetoric but have had significant policy implications.

POLICY CONTROVERSIES BETWEEN THE CONSERVATIVES AND LIBERALS

The conservatives supported three recent Republican presidents – Reagan, George H. W. Bush, and George W. Bush. During the 2000 presidential campaign, George W. Bush said that Christ was his favorite philosopher-thinker.[93] In that campaign, even the Democratic candidates used religious language. Al Gore mentioned that when faced with important problems, he asked himself what Jesus would do. The Democratic candidate for vice-president, Joe Lieberman, was also eager to declare publicly his personal Jewish religious devotion.[94] Following his election, President Bush showed strong support for the conservative agenda. He pushed the Faith-based Initiative, which maintained federal grants to religious institutions for social services. This initiative was based on the Charitable Choice first enacted by

[90] *Everson v. Board of Education*, 330 U.S. 1 (1947). For critiques of *Everson*, see Dreisbach 2002; Jeffries and Ryan 2001, 369–70.
[91] *Lemon v. Kurtzman*, 403 U.S. 602 (1971).
[92] Carter 1993, 113.
[93] Mansfield 2004, xv.
[94] William Pfaff, "Take Religion out of the Politics," *International Herald Tribune*, January 7, 2000.

the Clinton administration and later extensively applied by Bush.[95] Charitable Choice required the federal government to provide equal opportunity to secular and religious organizations in the distribution of social welfare benefits.[96] In 2005, Bush declared that the federal government had directed about $1.2 billion to religious groups.[97] As another conservative policy, Bush called for a constitutional amendment against same-sex marriage.[98] Moreover, he supported the teaching of Intelligent Design in public schools.[99] According to Intelligent Design, the origin and development of life are based on a purposeful plan, rather than coincidental and chaotic natural selection. It seems to be a revised version of creationism and a new challenge to evolutionism.[100]

Bush's policies received support from conservatives and substantial criticisms from liberals. Liberal associations have opposed restrictions on gay marriage and the teaching of Intelligent Design in public schools. They have particularly criticized the Faith-based Initiative for allowing the mixture of public money and religious institutions. This mixture, for them, would mean governmental support behind proselytizing and religious discrimination in the recruitment of employees, regulation of religious organizations, and discouragement of volunteer contributions.[101]

In the controversies over secularism, the Supreme Court has played the leading role, being the highest court of appeal in the United States and having a monopoly on the interpretation of the Constitution

---

[95] State funding of religious social services existed before the George W. Bush administration. In the 1990s, the revenue of about 65% of Catholic Charities, 75% of the Jewish Board of Family and Children's Service, and 55% of Lutheran Social Ministries came from governmental funding. Monsma 1996, 1. See also Santorum 1997.

[96] Dilulio 2007, 82–115.

[97] James Lakely, "President Outlines Role of His Faith," *Washington Times*, January 12, 2005. See also Monsma 2002b, 6. For a conservative critique of Bush's Faith-based Initiative, see Kuo 2006.

[98] "Bush to Back Gay Marriage Ban Amendment," June 2, 2006, http://www.cbsnews .com/stories/2006/06/02/ap/politics/mainD8HVQLM00.shtml.

[99] "Bush Remarks on 'Intelligent Design' Theory Fuel Debate," *Washington Post*, August 3, 2005.

[100] Greenawalt 2004, 90–125; Jacoby 2004, 124–48; Wood 1986, 356–60.

[101] "The Bush 'Faith-Based' Initiative," February 20, 2001, http://www.au.org/site/ News2?page=NewsArticle&id=6088&abbr=pr&security=1002&news_iv_ ctrl=1376; "The Faith-Based Initiative and 'Charitable Choice,'" http://www.adl .org/religious_freedom/resource_kit/faith_based_initiative.asp, accessed on June 13, 2008.

TABLE 10. *Ideology and Supreme Court Nominations since Reagan*

President/Party	Justice	Ideology	Ideology Score[1]
Ronald Reagan/R	O'Connor	Moderate	0.415
Ronald Reagan/R	Scalia	Conservative	0.000
Ronald Reagan/R	Kennedy	Moderate	0.365
George H. W. Bush/R	Souter	Moderate	0.325
George H. W. Bush/R	Thomas	Conservative	0.160
George W. Bush/R	Roberts	Conservative	0.120
George W. Bush/R	Alito	Conservative	0.100
William Clinton/D	Ginsburg	Liberal	0.680
William Clinton/D	Breyer	Liberal	0.475

[1] The Ideology Score ranges from 0 (most conservative) to 1 (most liberal).
Sources: Segal n.d.; Epstein and Segal 2005, 110; Segal and Cover 1989.

in general and the First Amendment in particular. Despite all their efforts, the conservatives failed to amend the Constitution to overturn the Supreme Court decisions on school prayer, abortion, and some other controversial issues.[102] For that reason, they have focused on influencing the Supreme Court.[103] Following the Reagan administration, Republican presidents have largely nominated conservative justices, while the Democratic president, Clinton, preferred liberal nominees. Table 10 matches presidents and their nominees, in terms of their ideological affiliations. Conservative or liberal ideology also matters in the Senate voting regarding Supreme Court nominees.[104] Although justices' initial ideologies are important in their subsequent decisions,[105] ideological shifts are also possible after their appointment. Justice David Souter, for example, leant toward liberalism, which was different from his earlier position at the nomination process.

[102] Fraser 1999, 177–221.
[103] Robertson initiated a campaign, "Operation Supreme Court Freedom," in his TV program, "Club 700," in the summer of 2005, to pray to God for more vacancies on the Court. He seemed to be sure that any vacancy would be filled by President Bush's nomination of a conservative justice. Pat Robertson, "Operation Supreme Court Freedom," August 15, 2005, http://www.cbn.com/special/supremecourt/prayerpledge.asp.
[104] Epstein and Segal 2005, 108–13.
[105] Ibid., 125.

In addition to nominations, conservatives and liberals have tried to influence the Supreme Court through *amicus curiae* briefs. As a result, the Court's decisions on state-religion issues have reflected the opposing ideological views of the justices, as well as those who have lobbied to influence the decisions.[106] The conservatives seem to have been relatively more successful on this issue following the Reagan administration. As Kenneth Wald and Joseph Kobylka have evaluated, from 1943 to 1980, the Court had a separationist tendency by making thirteen separationist decisions (59%), eight accommodationist decisions (36%), and one mixed decision on significant state-religion cases. From 1981 to 2002, however, the numbers are almost reversed: fifteen separationist decisions (35%), twenty-six accommodationist decisions (60%), and two mixed decisions.[107] The Court's decisions on three controversial issues in schools have been particularly important regarding the conservative versus liberal split: school prayer, freedom of religious speech, and school vouchers.

School Prayer

Following the Supreme Court's prohibition of school prayer in 1962, certain states initiated moments of silence and prayer. Nevertheless, the Court struck down these legislations as well. In *Wallace v. Jaffree* in 1985, the Court examined the constitutionality of an Alabama law that required that public classrooms daily begin with a moment of "silent meditation or prayer" conducted by the teachers. A six-justice majority held the law unconstitutional with regard to the *Lemon* test, because the statute did not have a secular purpose and aimed to endorse religion. Chief Justice Warner E. Burger wrote a dissenting opinion: "To suggest that a moment-of-silence statute that includes the word 'prayer' unconstitutionally endorses religion, while one that simply provides for a moment of silence does not, manifests not neutrality but hostility toward religion."[108]

---

[106] On the First Amendment cases, Supreme Court justices' ideological positions (conservative or liberal) play important roles. This argument fits to the attitudinal approach in the literature. See Segal and Spaeth 2002; Segal and Cover 1989; Epstein and Knight 1998; Clayton and Gillman 1999.

[107] Wald 2003, 85–7; Kobylka 1995, 96, 102–3. For the Court's diverse views on the Establishment Clause, see Witte 2004, 185–232.

[108] *Wallace v. Jaffree*, 472 U.S. 38 (1985).

After the ban on teacher-led prayers in their classrooms, several public schools kept prayers in their ceremonies. Nevertheless, the Court also impeded that practice in *Lee v. Weisman* (1992). A middle school principal, Mr. Lee, invited a rabbi to offer nonsectarian prayers at the graduation ceremony. The prayers were the following:

INVOCATION: God of the Free, Hope of the Brave:
> For the legacy of America where diversity is celebrated and the rights of minorities are protected, we thank You. May these young men and women grow up to enrich it. For the liberty of America, we thank You. May these new graduates grow up to guard it. For the political process of America in which all its citizens may participate, for its court system where all may seek justice, we thank You. May those we honor this morning always turn to it in trust. For the destiny of America, we thank You. May the graduates of Nathan Bishop Middle School so live that they might help to share it. May our aspirations for our country and for these young people, who are our hope for the future, be richly fulfilled. AMEN.

BENEDICTION: O God, we are grateful to You for having endowed us with
> the capacity for learning which we have celebrated on this joyous commencement. Happy families give thanks for seeing their children achieve an important milestone. Send Your blessings upon the teachers and administrators who helped prepare them. The graduates now need strength and guidance for the future; help them to understand that we are not complete with academic knowledge alone. We must each strive to fulfill what You require of us all: to do justly, to love mercy, to walk humbly. We give thanks to You, Lord, for keeping us alive, sustaining us, and allowing us to reach this special, happy occasion. AMEN.[109]

Weisman, the Jewish father of a student attending the ceremony, sued the school administration and was supported by the ACLU in the court process. The District Court and the Court of Appeals decided that the prayer was a violation of the First Amendment. The George H. W. Bush administration asked the Supreme Court to overturn the decision and abolish the *Lemon* test.[110] The Court, however, decided that the inclusion of clergy to offer prayers at public school ceremonies "places subtle and indirect public and peer pressure on attending students" and violated the Establishment Clause. In his dissenting opinion,

---

[109] *Lee v. Weisman*, 505 U.S. 577 (1992).
[110] "Brief for the United States as *Amicus Curiae* Supporting Petitioners," *Lee v. Weisman*, 1990.

joined by three other justices, Scalia criticized the decision as contrary to the "American tradition of nonsectarian prayer to God at public celebrations." He also criticized the Court for inventing a "boundlessly manipulable test of psychological coercion."[111]

As the last remaining option, some public schools tried student-led prayers in ceremonies. The Court did not allow that either by its decision in *Santa Fe v. Doe* (2000). In a Santa Fe public high school, a student was delivering a Christian prayer as a public address before each home football game. One Mormon and one Catholic family sued to prevent this practice. Meanwhile, the school district issued a new policy that allowed student-led nonsectarian prayer at home games. The District Court modified the policy by allowing the prayer, but the Court of Appeals decided that the football prayer was unconstitutional. The school district appealed to the Supreme Court. The Court held in a 6–3 opinion that student-led, student-initiated prayer at football games of public schools violated the Establishment Clause because it took place on public school property and was authorized by the school administration. Chief Justice Rehnquist, in his dissenting opinion, joined by Justices Scalia and Thomas, wrote that "even more disturbing than its holding is the tone of the court's opinion; it bristles with hostility to all things religious in public life."[112] The ACLU applauded the decision as a "victory" and "triumph for religious liberty."[113]

In sum, the school prayer issue has been a failure for the conservatives. They could not reverse the Supreme Court's decisions on this issue by amending the Constitution. Moreover, the ban on prayer has been extended from the classroom to other public school spaces and activities. Even the conservative scholar and later federal judge Michael McConnell admits that it is impossible to reestablish school prayer: "In order to be broadly acceptable, a prayer would have to be so general and abstract that it would be largely meaningless.... Moreover, no matter how abstract and how general the prayer may be ... it will remain unacceptable to some children in

---

[111] *Lee v. Weisman*, 505 U.S. 577 (1992). See also Kobylka 1995, 122–3; Eastman 2000.

[112] *Santa Fe v. Doe*, 530 U.S. 290 (2000).

[113] "ACLU Hails 'Total Victory' for Religious Liberty in High Court's Rejection of School Stadium Prayers," June 19, 2000, http://www.aclu.org/scotus/1999/16294prs20000619.html.

this world of diverse beliefs."[114] This failure led the conservatives to focus on the freedom of religious speech.

Freedom of Religious Speech

Although the conservatives failed to bring prayer back into public schools, they succeeded in creating new spaces for religiosity in public schools through the principles of freedom of speech and equal access. In the early 1980s, the Supreme Court reversed some lower-level court decisions on the restrictions regarding student-led religious activities at universities. In *Widmar v. Vincent* (1981), the Court decided by 8–1 that the University of Missouri violated freedom of religious speech and equal access by banning a student group from using university rooms for prayers and Bible studies.[115]

The conservatives wanted to assure the free practice of religious clubs in public schools, beyond universities. Therefore, they lobbied for the bill of the Equal Access Act (EAA). Congress passed the bill (88–11 in the Senate and 337–77 in the House), and Reagan signed it into law in 1984. The EAA stresses:

It shall be unlawful for any public secondary school which receives Federal financial assistance and which has a limited open forum to deny equal access or a fair opportunity to, or discriminate against, any students who wish to conduct a meeting within that limited open forum on the basis of the religious, political, philosophical, or other content of the speech at such meetings.[116]

The Act also requires that the student meetings be voluntary with no interference to the orderly conduct of educational activities. The meetings should exist without sponsorship or participation of the school or government employees and nonschool persons. The constitutionality of the EAA was examined in *BOE of Westside Community Schools v. Mergens* (1990). The Court ruled by 8–1 that the EAA was constitutional and that students had the right to form a Christian club, like other nonreligious clubs, in their public schools.[117]

---

[114] McConnell 1998, 34.
[115] *Widmar v. Vincent*, 454 U.S. 263 (1981).
[116] Equal Access Act, 20 U.S.C. 4071–4.
[117] *BOE of Westside Community Schools v. Mergens*, 496 U.S. 226 (1990).

Another case on freedom of religious speech is *Lamb's Chapel v. Center Moriches* in 1993. The Court unanimously rejected a New York school district's decision to refuse a religious group's use of school property after hours to show films on social issues from a religious perspective, although it allowed nonreligious groups to do so.[118] The ACLJ defines the decision as a "victory" and a "turning point for Christians obtaining access to the marketplace of ideas."[119] In 1995, in *Rosenberger v. Rector*, the Court decided by 5–4 that a public university that pays printing costs for student publications should not exclude religious publications.[120] A more recent case on this issue was *Good News v. Milford Central* (2001). The AU defined the case as "the latest attempt to use schools to proselytize young children."[121] The Court, though, ruled by 6–3 that, regarding First Amendment free speech rights, a public school could not forbid a religious club for children from meeting at school facilities after hours simply because of its religious nature.[122] The ACLU criticized the ruling as a decision that "is likely to blur the line between public school and Sunday school" and as a permission for "after-school Evangelism."[123]

In short, the Court allowed voluntary religious collective activities in public school facilities out of class hours with regard to freedom of speech and equal opportunity. For some critics, the Court "equates religious speech with other forms of protected secular speech and thereby undermines religion's special constitutional status."[124] Many conservatives, however, are happy to have spaces for student-initiated religious meetings in public schools. The growing number of

---

[118] *Lamb's Chapel v. Center Moriches*, 508 U.S. 384 (1993).
[119] "Lamb's Chapel and the Use of Public Facilities," http://www.aclj.org/Issues/ Resources/Document.aspx?ID=639, accessed on June 9, 2006.
[120] *Rosenberger v. Rector*, 515 U.S. 819 (1995).
[121] "N.Y. Dispute Tests whether Religious Groups Can Evangelize Children on Campus after School Hours," February 22, 2001, http://www.au.org/site/News2?page=News Article&id=6086&abbr=pr&security=1002&news_iv_ctrl=1376.
[122] *Good News v. Milford Central*, 533 US 98 (2001).
[123] "In Setback for Religious Liberty, High Court Ruling Permits After-School Evangelism," June 11, 2001, http://www.aclu.org/scotus/2000/16325prs20010611 .html.
[124] Davis 1998, 136.

Christian clubs in American public schools, which has reached about ten thousand,[125] indicates the importance of these court decisions.

School Vouchers

School vouchers imply a certain amount of public funding (generally $2,500 to $5,000) provided to parents for the educational expenses of their children attending schools different from assigned public schools. The parents can use this funding to pay the tuition of either religious or secular private schools. One of school vouchers' intended results is the increasing competition between private and public schools. Another is to support low-income pupils to pursue education in private schools.[126] The conservatives have particularly supported this system because it allows an indirect public funding of religious schools.[127]

The liberals, however, have opposed it for the same reason. They have claimed that vouchers, by mixing public money and religious schools, violate church-state separation and lead to a religiously discriminatory and segregated school system. According to the ADL, "80 percent of vouchers would be used in schools whose central mission is religious training."[128] The liberals have also stressed that the vouchers would weaken public schools and alienate poor families who could not afford the tuition of private schools by limited vouchers. The National Education Association (NEA), the largest labor union in the United States with 2.7 million members, has shared these concerns and opposes school vouchers.[129]

Liberals expected that the Supreme Court would prohibit the voucher systems. Nevertheless, in *Mitchell v. Helms* (2000), the Court allowed by a 6–3 decision the use of federal funds to supply computer hardware, software, and library materials to religiously affiliated schools because the aid was made in a nondiscriminatory manner

---

[125] "ACLU Hails 'Total Victory' for Religious Liberty in High Court's Rejection of School Stadium Prayers," June 19, 2000, http://www.aclu.org/scotus/1999/16294prs20000619.html.

[126] Amanda Paulson, "Milwaukee's Lessons on School Vouchers," *Christian Science Monitor*, May 23, 2006.

[127] McConnell 1999.

[128] "School Vouchers: The Wrong Choice for Public Education," http://www.adl.org/religious_freedom/resource_kit/school_vouchers.asp, accessed on June 6, 2006.

[129] "Vouchers," http://www.nea.org/vouchers/index.html, accessed on June 6, 2006.

to both secular and religious schools.[130] The most crucial Court case for the voucher system was *Zelman v. Simmons-Harris* in 2002. The Court upheld in a 5–4 decision the constitutionality of Ohio's school voucher program that provided financial assistance to parents for expenses at private or out-of-district public schools. The Court did not define the program as unconstitutional despite the fact that during the 1999 to 2000 term of the program in the Cleveland area, "82 percent of schools participating in the voucher program were religious and that 96 percent of participating students enrolled in religious schools."[131] President Bush called the decision a "landmark ruling" while Attorney General John Ashcroft defined it as "historic" and "a great victory." Barry Lynn, the head of the AU, depicted it as "probably the worst church-state case in the last 50 years" because it "really brings a wrecking ball to a part of the wall separating church and state."[132]

Although the Supreme Court upheld its federal constitutionality, the voucher system has had several state-level impediments. Thirty-seven states have Blaine Amendments in their constitutions that prohibit state funding of religious schools, while many others have constitutional restrictions on public funding of private schools. For that reason, several state supreme courts have struck down bills on vouchers. The vouchers have also lacked popular support. About twenty voucher program proposals voted by referendum ballots have been rejected. The voucher proposals have not been successful in the legislative process either. About another twenty bills on school vouchers were voted down in state legislatures.[133] As a result, only Ohio (Cleveland) and Wisconsin (Milwaukee) now have citywide systems that allow the use of vouchers for religious private schools.[134] Florida

---

[130] *Mitchell v. Helms*, 530 U.S. 793 (2000). See also Monsma 2002a.

[131] *Zelman v. Simmons-Harris*, 536 U.S. 639 (2002).

[132] Quoted by Terry Friden, "Supreme Court Affirms School Voucher Program," June 27, 2002, http://www.cnn.com/2002/LAW/06/27/scotus.school.vouchers/.

[133] "School Vouchers: The Wrong Choice for Public Education," http://www.adl.org/religious_freedom/resource_kit/school_vouchers.asp, accessed on June 6, 2006.

[134] Maine and Vermont have vouchers systems that can be used only for nonreligious schools. Some states have tax credit programs, instead of vouchers, to support parents' tuition expenses. Kavan Peterson, "School Vouchers Slow to Spread," May 5, 2005, http://www.stateline.org/live/ViewPage.action?siteNodeId=136&languageId=1&contentId=29789.

had the only statewide program, which was struck down by the state
supreme court in 2004.[135] The court did not refer to the public funding
of parochial schools as a problem. Instead, it referred to the shrink-
ing public funds for public schools and the development of private
schools as an alternative that was not subject to the requirements of
the state.[136]

The federal government established a voucher program in
Washington, D.C.[137] In addition, it implemented the largest voucher
plan in 2006 in order to help the victims of Hurricane Katrina. The
NEA president called the project a part of "the worst assault on public
education in American history."[138]

The conservatives have achieved extremely limited success in their
attempts to maintain school vouchers, which seems to be between their
failure on school prayer and significant success on freedom of religious
speech. Their main accomplishment lies in the lack of a federal prohibition of school vouchers by the Supreme Court. Yet they have several
obstacles, including state constitutions and public opposition. For that
reason, school voucher systems have remained very marginal in the
United States.

CONCLUSION

State policies toward religion in the United States have been more
inclusionary than those in France and Turkey, mainly because passive
secularism has been the dominant ideology in the former. However,
the American state has pursued certain inconsistent and changing policies toward religion due to the struggles between conservatives and
liberals based on their opposite views on state-religion relations. The
conservatives generally prefer organized prayer in public schools and

---

[135] Utah initiated a statewide voucher system that was rejected by a referendum.
"Vouchers Killed," *Deseret News*, November 7, 2007.

[136] Governor Jeb Bush, a supporter of the program, criticized the court's decision. Lois
Romano, "Fla. Voucher System Struck Down," *Washington Post*, January 6, 2006.

[137] Among the schools that participate in the Washington, D.C., voucher program, 51%
are Catholic, 21% are non-Catholic religious, and 28% are nonsectarian schools.
Meghan Clyne, "School Vouchers Taking Hold in Washington," *New York Sun*,
November 14, 2005.

[138] Quoted by Meghan Clyne, "Bush to Sign 'Monumental' School Voucher Law," *New
York Sun*, December 30, 2005.

state funding of religious schools, while the liberals seek a wall of separation between the state and religion regarding these issues. The conservatives and liberals are not ideologically monolithic. They both include mainstream and extreme perspectives. Although the mainstreams of these two groups, accommodationists and separationists, agree on the basic framework of passive secularism, the extremists, Christian Right and assertive secularists, tend toward either the dominance of Christian culture or assertive secularism, respectively.

The struggle between the conservatives and liberals has been primarily ideological. Institutional or economic differences do not constitute the boundary between them or their basis of self-identification. The split between conservatives and liberals exists between different presidents, members of Congress, Supreme Court justices, and civic associations, regardless of their common institutional affiliations or shared socioeconomic status. Religious interpretations (conservative or liberal) and religious affiliations are directly related to individuals' identification with particular political ideologies. In this regard, the evangelicals are most likely to be conservative, while nonbelievers are largely liberal. Religious demography is, therefore, an important aspect of this ideological debate. The rising religious diversity in the United States has constituted an important basis for the liberals, whereas the conservatives still find strong popular support in American society, which is more religious than many other Western societies.[139]

Since the 1980 presidential election, the conservatives have been successful with the election of conservative presidents – Reagan, Bush (41st), and Bush (43rd) – and the appointments of several conservative justices to the Supreme Court. In terms of specific policies, however, the only area of success for them has been the cases defended through the freedom of religious speech in public schools. They have experienced extremely limited success on school vouchers and a clear failure on school prayer.

One may argue that restrictive American policies toward minorities contradict my argument about the dominance of passive secularism. I analyze the historical debates about the conditions of Catholics, Jews, and Mormons in Chapter 3. I show how these debates were part of the

---

[139] See Table 14. See also Putnam 2001, 65–8.

transformation of passive secularism in the United States. The main current controversy about this issue is the trouble facing Muslims in the aftermath of the terrorist attacks on September 11, 2001. About one hundred thousand Muslims have experienced security measures, including being investigated, interrogated, or arrested, mainly as a result of racial and religious profiling.[140] Muslim foundations and charitable organizations have also been targeted by police investigations.[141] Yet the mistreatment of Muslims occurred not because of, but despite, passive secularism in the United States. The major reason for that is the rising Islamophobia among policy makers and certain social actors, especially some tele-evangelicals such as Falwell, Robertson, and John Hagee.[142]

Due to dominant passive secularism, Muslims still enjoy religious freedom in the United States in terms of wearing religious dress, constructing mosques, opening Islamic schools, and founding organizations.[143] Three million to six million Muslims[144] who live in the United States have more than 375 private Islamic schools[145] and 1,209 mosques.[146] A Muslim scholar argues that the United States, apart from the Hajj, "is the only place in the world in which every ethnic Muslim group in the *ummah* and every Muslim school of thought currently in the world are found."[147] Moreover, American politicians have publicly recognized Islam. Presidents Clinton and Bush annually sent a message to celebrate the Muslim holiday of breaking the fast in addition to organizing an official *iftaar* dinner during the month of Ramadan in the White House.[148] Since 2001, the U.S. Postal Service has issued

---

[140] Cainkar 2008, 53.

[141] Cesari 2006b, 38–40; Cesari 2006a, 41–2; Saeed 2003, 41–4.

[142] Brand 2007; Cole 2007. Certain media outlets, such as CNN Headline News with its daily host Glenn Beck, have also contributed to Islamophobia. For a definition of *Islamophobia*, see Chapter 4.

[143] Cesari 2006b, 83.

[144] Bukhari 2003, 7.

[145] Muhammad 2003, 100.

[146] Bagby, Perl, and Froehle 2001, 2–3.

[147] Bakar 2003, 151.

[148] "Presidential Message: Eid Al-Fitr," November 4, 2005, http://www.whitehouse .gov/news/releases/2005/11/20051104–2.html; "President Hosts Iftaar Dinner," October 17, 2005, http://www.whitehouse.gov/news/releases/2005/10/20051017–5 .html. A point that makes *iftaar* dinners at the White House more interesting is that the Turkish President Necdet Sezer (2000–2007) cancelled the *iftaar* tradition at

a stamp to commemorate Islamic holidays.[149] The first Muslim representative, Keith Ellison, was elected to the U.S. Congress in 2006. In his ceremonial swearing-in, Ellison used a copy of the Qur'an originally owned by Thomas Jefferson and loaned by the Library of Congress.[150]

In the United States, passive secularism is deeply consolidated. The main ideological struggles focus on its different interpretations. That makes the United States different from France and Turkey, where ideological conflicts take place between assertive and passive secularism. This chapter, therefore, leaves two important questions to be answered by Chapter 3: why did passive secularism initially become dominant in the United States? How did the two struggling interpretations of assertive secularism emerge?

the Presidential Residence because that would contradict his assertive secularist ideology.

[149] "U.S. Postage Stamp Celebrating Muslim Holiday to be Issued by United States Postal Service," August 1, 2001, http://www.usps.com/news/2001/philatelic/sro1_054.htm.

[150] A second Muslim congressperson, Andre Carson, was elected in 2008.

3

Religious Diversity and the Evolution of Passive Secularism (1776–1981)

An inquiry about the current dominance of passive secularism in the United States requires an historical analysis. The lack of an *ancien régime* based on monarchy and hegemonic religion shaped the formation of passive secularism during the American founding period. America was a new country that had religious diversity. These initial conditions nurtured the emergence and dominance of passive secularism. In contrast, in France and Turkey, when the secular republic was founded, it had a perceived threat from the *ancien régime* based on old monarchy and the hegemony of Catholicism or Islam.

The alliance between the British monarchy and the Anglican Church in colonial America did not mean an *ancien régime* for three main reasons. First, the Anglican Church was established only in Virginia, South Carolina, North Carolina, Georgia, Maryland, and some counties of New York. Congregational churches were established in New England (including Massachusetts, Connecticut, and New Hampshire), and there was no establishment in Rhode Island, Pennsylvania, Delaware, and, arguably, New Jersey.[1] Second, even in the limited number of colonies "the Anglican establishment was during most times nominal and the church's control over religious concernments largely ineffective."[2] Last but not least, in the aftermath of the American Revolution, the

[1] Esbeck 2004, 1415, 1457–97; Hutson 2008, 1–94; McConnell 1990, 1421–30; Bailyn 1967, 247–8.
[2] Esbeck 2004, 1414.

British monarchy was largely regarded as a foreign power, instead of a local monarchy to be reestablished. Related to that, the Anglican Church in the United States did not have the popular support the Catholic Church and Islamic institutions had in France and Turkey. Therefore, following independence, it quickly became marginalized and permanently lost its status due to "its connection to the Crown and the loyalist sympathies of most of its clergy."[3] As a result, religious groups in America accepted the lack of an established church at the federal level and disestablishments at the state level "without nostalgia for an *ancien régime*."[4]

The analysis of American history is important to understand the emergence and transformations of passive secularism. Nevertheless, there is no single objective account of the American history of secularism. Both the conservatives (who want close state-religion relations) and liberals (who seek a wall of separation between the state and religion) have their own history writing.

According to the conservatives, the framers did not intend to establish a wall of separation. They point to the Declaration of Independence's references to God and Congress's tradition of having publicly funded chaplains for prayer before its sessions. For them, George Washington (1732–1799) was a good example because he referred to God and religion in his swearing-in, his declaration of a Thanksgiving Day, and his Farewell Address. The conservatives, therefore, disagree with the Supreme Court's separationist reading of the framers' original intent in the First Amendment in *Everson v. Board of Education*.[5]

They argue four main points, although not all conservatives make each of them. First, the framers' intent was to limit federal authority about establishing or prohibiting a religion, while leaving states with their own choice of establishing a church.[6] Second, the Court has misused Thomas Jefferson's (1743–1826) metaphor of a wall of

---

[3] McConnell 1990, 1436.
[4] Bellah 2005, 50.
[5] Hutson 1998, 75–81; Justice Scalia's dissenting opinion, joined by Justice Rehnquist and Justice Thomas, *McCreary County v. ACLU*, 545 U.S. (2005). According to Phillip Hamburger, "[o]nly in the twentieth century, after the amendment process had been abandoned, did an interpretive approach prevail, and, by this means, separation became part of American constitutional law." Hamburger 2004, 285.
[6] Munoz 2006, 634; Esbeck 2004, 1576; Jeffries and Ryan 2001, 292.

separation to interpret the First Amendment, because Jefferson did not support a strict separationism[7]; he was in France at the time the amendment was passed and ratified, and he used the metaphor fourteen years later.[8] Third, a separationist reading of James Madison (1751–1836) in *Everson* is also problematic because there is a proreligious perspective in his *Memorial and Remonstrance*.[9] Finally, the Court's separationist interpretation of the First Amendment was heavily influenced by the Blaine Amendments of the 1880s, which were anti-Catholic and nativist.[10] This conservative argument traces the "genealogy" of secularism in the United States through the unintended consequences of anti-Catholic policies, as opposed to the deliberately planned and founded secular institutions.

The liberals argue that the "American political society in the early republic adopted a decidedly secular tone."[11] They note that the framers did not include God in the Constitution due to the goal of founding a secular state.[12] Similarly, for them, of "the eleven states that ratified the First Amendment, nine … [defended] that any government financial assistance to religion constituted an establishment of religion and violated its free exercise."[13] The liberals' favorite historical figure is Jefferson, who used the metaphor of the wall of separation and refused to issue Thanksgiving proclamations to avoid violating the First Amendment.[14] Not only liberals, but also conservatives, depict

---

[7] Dreisbach 2002.

[8] McConnell 1990; Chief Justice Rehnquist's dissenting opinion, *Wallace v. Jaffree*, 472 U.S. 38 (1985). Jefferson was also criticized by his political opponents for being influenced by France and French thought. Kramer 1994.

[9] Hutson 1998, 70–4; McConnell 1990, esp. 1446; Carter 1993, 116; Wills 1990, 373–80. For Charles Reid, Madison was primarily committed to the free exercise of religion "as the surest way of fulfilling our obligation to the Creator," which "refutes contemporary efforts to root religious freedom in secular concepts, whether neutral principles or liberal notions of self-fulfillment." Reid 2002, 99; also 66–70.

[10] Hamburger 2004, 14–17, 193; Monsma 1996, 140–1; Justice Thomas's plurality opinion, shared by Chief Justice Rehnquist and Justices Scalia and Anthony M. Kennedy, in *Mitchell v. Helms*, 530 U.S. 793 (2000). For a Web site devoted to a critique of the Blaine Amendments, see http://www.blaineamendments.org/.

[11] McGarvie 2004, 20.

[12] Kramnick and Moore 2005.

[13] Curry 1986, 220. See also Flowers 2005, 18.

[14] Jefferson used this metaphor in his letter to the Danbury Baptist Association in 1802: "Believing with you that religion is a matter which lies solely between man and his God; that he owes account to none other for his faith or his worship; that the

Jefferson, like Benjamin Franklin, George Washington, and John Adams, as a deist who did not believe in the Trinity.[15] Jefferson, therefore, predicted that Americans would one day all become Unitarians.[16] He had his own version of Gospel where he picked and chose verses he recognized as more rational than others.[17]

According to the liberals, an important historical document that showed America's secular founding is the Treaty of Peace and Friendship with the ruler of Tripoli – a semi-independent province of the Ottoman Empire. It was signed in 1796 and unanimously approved by the Senate a year later. Its most important part is Article 11:

> As the government of the United States of America is not in any sense founded on the Christian religion, – as it has in itself no character of enmity against the laws, religion, or tranquility of Musselmen [*sic*], – and, as the said States never entered into any war or act of hostility against any Mehomitan [*sic*] nation, it is declared by the parties that no pretext arising from religious opinions shall ever produce an interruption of the harmony existing between the two countries.[18]

Similar to the conservatives' argument about the unintended consequences of anti-Catholicism, the liberals define several public references to God as simple results of anticommunism, as opposed to a genuine part of American tradition.[19] The liberals regard the national motto "In God We Trust" and the phrase "under God" in the pledge as the mere legacy of the anticommunist McCarthy era that attempted to differentiate the United States from the atheist Soviet Union.

I give credit to both of these two seemingly opposite historical readings. The conservative and liberal history writings are not mutually exclusive; they just emphasize two different but valid aspects of

---

legislative powers of the government reach actions only, and not opinions, I contemplate with sovereign reverence that act of the whole American people which declared that their legislature should 'make no law respecting an establishment of religion or prohibiting the free exercise thereof,' thus building a wall of separation between church and State." For two Supreme Court decisions that referred to Jefferson's metaphor of the wall, see *Reynolds v. U.S.*, 98 U.S. 145 (1878) and *Everson v. Board of Education* 330 U.S. 1 (1947).

[15] Dreisbach 2002, 18–20; Mapp 2003, 19, 23, 65, 73; Gaustad 2004, 65, 77, 94.
[16] Kramnick and Moore 2005, 100–2.
[17] Hutson 1998, 83–4; Mapp 2003, 17.
[18] Quoted by Marr 2006, 59; Boston 1997; Martin 2002, 328.
[19] Kramnick and Moore 2005, 143.

American history. The framers' views on state-religion relations clearly reflect diversity. As Phillip Munoz elaborates, Washington defended a closer relationship between the state and religion, while Jefferson was against that. Madison may be located in the middle of the two.[20] These three historical figures are important for contemporary understanding of the First Amendment because they are the most frequently cited persons in the U.S. Supreme Court's decisions on both Establishment and Free Exercise Clauses.[21]

The history of secularism in America shows both continuity and change. Passive secularism, which allows the public visibility of religion, has remained a dominant ideology, although it has constantly been redefined due to the struggles between its conservative and liberal interpretations. As a result, the historical pendulum has kept swinging between religious "establishment" and "disestablishment" in the United States. In fact, this swinging does not result in identical back and forth. Instead, it has resulted in a trend toward more state neutrality in regard to religions. Each of the establishment experiences, such as the establishment of Protestant denominations in several states prior to 1833, the semiestablishment of nondenominational Protestantism in the nineteenth century, and the establishment of monotheism in the 1950s, was more inclusionary than the previous form.[22]

Throughout these transformations, the changes of religious demography played crucial roles because religious affiliations are significant carriers of specific religious and ideological views. From the importance of religious diversity in the founding period to the later impact of Catholic and Jewish immigration, and to the recent rise of nonbelievers, religious demographical changes have affected transformations of religious and ideological views, balance of power, and reinterpretations of secularism in America.

I will first analyze the constitutional era, wherein the framers decided not to create an established church at the national level. Next, I will examine the semiestablishment of Protestantism in the nineteenth century. The disestablishment of Protestantism in the early twentieth century will be the third period in my analysis. Then, I will explore the

---

[20] Munoz 2003b; Munoz 2003a; Munoz 2006, 636.
[21] Hall 2006, 568.
[22] Silk 1998, 3; Monsma and Soper 1997, 18–25; Casanova 1994, 135–57.

1950s, when a new monotheist semiestablishment emerged. The final section will discuss the disestablishment of monotheism, which took place in the 1960s and 1970s. This period also resulted in a reaction and a new swinging of the pendulum by mobilizing the conservatives, particularly following Reagan's presidency in 1981, which was examined in Chapter 2.

THE RATIONALISTS AND EVANGELICALS: NO FEDERAL ESTABLISHMENT

From Independence to the Second Great Awakening (1776–1816)

A major narrative about the foundation of America is the immigration of the Puritans, who escaped from Europe because of religious persecution. This narrative includes two major arguments: one is valid, and the other is not. The valid argument is that the early Puritan immigrants were religious people who faced political persecutions.[23] That led to the importance of religion and the religion-friendly mood in American public life. For the Puritans, religion was mainly a source of opposition, rather than a partner of the oppressive political authority. That was a major reason for the difference between the popular perceptions of Protestantism in America and Catholicism in France. Therefore, "[u]nlike the French Revolution, the American Revolution had not turned against the churches or their clergy, had not rejected the religious past that had guided the colonial settlements."[24]

The invalid part of the narrative is that because various Protestants had been persecuted in Europe, they promoted religious freedom and tolerance in America. This is a doubtful claim, because oppressions do not automatically make people promoters of freedom. Religious liberty and tolerance was not the established mode in the American colonies.[25] The immigrants' general aim was not "religious freedom for all," but it was "freedom to follow God as they understood Him."[26] Therefore, dissenting Protestant denominations (e.g., Quakers and

---

[23] Hutson 1998, 2–48.
[24] Gaustad 2004, 8–9.
[25] Gill 2007, 61–75; Fraser 1999, 9.
[26] Esbeck 2004, 1415.

Baptists), Catholics, Jews, Native Americans, and African slaves faced religious discrimination at various levels in several colonies and then in certain states after independence.[27]

As already mentioned, nine out of the thirteen colonies had established churches. Roger Williams's Rhode Island and William Penn's Pennsylvania were among the four colonies that lacked established churches and had more religious freedom.[28] The Anglican Church, due to its ties with British colonialism and the dissenting Protestant denominations, was disestablished during and immediately after independence in North Carolina (1776), New York (1777), Virginia (1776–1779), Maryland (1785), and South Carolina (1790).[29] In Georgia (1798), it was disestablished after the First Amendment. Later on, the remaining Puritan churches were disestablished in Vermont (1807), Connecticut (1818), New Hampshire (1819), Maine (1820), and Massachusetts (1832–1833).[30] This shows that religious freedom in America was not a simple legacy of the first immigrants. Moreover, church-state separation in America was not an automatic result of Protestant Christianity, as the civilizationalist scholars would argue (see Chapter 1). Instead, in the colonial and founding periods, there were sharply different Protestant views on church-state relations.[31] Church-state separation and religious freedom in America were the product of a long political process, which included several ideological and structural factors.

The critical juncture for the dominance of passive secularism in the United States began with independence in 1776. An important step forward in this period was the Constitution's prohibition of a religious test for public employees (Art. VI). Then, the ratification of the First Amendment in 1791 completed the critical period with two religious clauses: "Congress shall make no law respecting an establishment of religion, or prohibiting the free exercise thereof." This entire process was a result of an overlapping consensus, rather than a zero-sum game, between two important groups – the rationalists influenced by Enlightenment and the evangelicals affected by the Great

---

[27] Boyle and Sheen 1997, 154; McGarvie 2004, 25–6.
[28] Spurgin 1989; Kramnick and Moore 2005, 46–66.
[29] Esbeck 2004, 1458.
[30] Ibid., 1458. See also Witte 2004, 117–21.
[31] Casanova 1994, 138–9.

Awakening.[32] Their consensus was "overlapping" because they have different, if not opposite, reasons to agree on the absence of a federally established church, in addition to disestablishments at the state level. The tension between these two groups, which began in the founding period and have continued until the present, resulted in diverse reinterpretations of passive secularism and its changing policy implications in the United States.

A clear representative of the rationalists was Jefferson while that of the evangelicals was Isaac Backus. Although both defended disestablishment of churches in states, they had dissimilar rationales.[33] For Jefferson, disestablishment will lead to the freedom and triumph of the reason, whereas for Backus it will result in the flourishing of the revealed religion.[34] Similarly, Thomas Lindsay argues that the agreement between rationalist Madison and dissenting Protestants in Virginia came from "opposite poles" because Madison's "pious appeals" in *Memorial* were simply "rhetorical."[35] In short, the goal of the rationalists (to make the state independent of the churches) and that of the evangelicals (to liberate the churches from state intervention) completed each other.[36] This consensual origin led to the dominance of religion-friendly passive secularism in America.

The seventeenth-century British philosopher John Locke provided the rationalists and evangelicals with an ideational bridge through his "complex combination of religious and philosophical logic."[37] Locke's liberalism was friendly with religion and emphasized individualism and negative freedom. It differed from Rousseau's anticlerical republicanism that promoted social unity and positive freedom.[38] For Locke, religious excellence was based on inward experience, whereas

---

[32] McConnell 1990, 1438–43; Witte and Green 1996, 502–14; Witte 1991, 491–7; Witte 2004, 21–39; Fraser 1999, 18.

[33] My categorization based on the rationalists and evangelicals is a generalization, which neglects certain aspects of complex reality. McConnell mentions a third group, "Republicans," including George Washington, who attached importance to religion as a basis of a virtuous society. McConnell 1990, 1441–3.

[34] Owen 2007. See also Esbeck 2004, 1427–48; Wills 1990, 341–53; Munoz 2006, 606n116, 117.

[35] Lindsay 1991, 1321, 1333.

[36] Murrin 2007, 37; Monsma 1995, 83–113.

[37] Feldman 2002a, 350. See also Dienstang 1996; Zuckert 2004; McGraw 2003, pt. I.

[38] For negative and positive freedom, see Berlin 1997; Constant 1988 [1819]. For Rousseau's republicanism, see Chapter 5.

the rulers' power consisted only of outward force. Therefore, the use of state power could result in hypocrisy, rather than real faith. Individuals should be free to choose their personal ways of salvation. The rulers should not intervene in this personal journey.[39] The state authority should be limited to the temporal civic ends without having any power to coerce individual conscience or act in the sphere of religion.[40]

The main structural condition that affected the consensual relations between the rationalists and evangelicals was the absence of an *ancien régime* based on the alliance between monarchy and hegemonic religion.[41] America emerged as a new republic without the threat of the reestablishment of an old local monarchy, or the challenge to modernize old political institutions justified by religion. Therefore, the rationalists did not become anticlerical or antireligious. The Declaration of Independence had the signs of this religious-friendly rationalism with its deistic references to "God," "Creator," "Supreme Judge," and "Divine Providence." When Alexis de Tocqueville visited America in the early nineteenth century, he recognized that religion in the United States was not seen as part of political oppression: "In France I had seen the spirits of religion and freedom almost always marching in opposite directions. In America I found them intimately linked together in joint reign over the same land."[42]

Moreover, American society experienced a substantial diversity of Protestant denominations, none of which could have a nationwide majority. The religious groups regarded the lack of an established church at the national level as a guarantee of their religious freedom and, therefore, a second best choice. For that reason, they also supported disestablishment at several states. An example of the dissenting churches' activism was Virginia. Following the disestablishment of the Anglican Church, Patrick Henry proposed a bill to maintain state funding of all Christian churches. The rationalists allied with dissenting church leaders to oppose the bill as articulated in Madison's *Memorial*. The Virginia legislature turned down the bill and passed

---

[39] Locke 1983 [1689], 26–7, 36–7.
[40] Ibid.; Locke 1980 [1690].
[41] Hartz 1991 [1955], esp. 5–6.
[42] Tocqueville 2000 [1835], 295.

the "Virginia Statute of Religious Freedom" written by Jefferson in 1786.[43] The minority Catholics were also against establishment of particular churches as observed by Tocqueville about half a century later. He notes that Catholic priests "all thought that the main reason for the quiet sway of religion over their country was the complete separation of church and state. I have no hesitation in stating that throughout my stay in America I met nobody, lay or cleric, who did not agree about that."[44]

My emphasis on religious diversity and the "second best option" is apparently close to a rational-choice explanation. I do not deny agents' strategic behaviors, but argue that ideas and ideologies come first because they define the identity and preferences of the agents. Based on their ideas, actors evaluate their conditions, use their rationality, and decide strategies. Religious groups during the American founding period were first and foremost attaching importance to their interests defined by religious ideas and then developing strategies to defend those interests. I agree with rational-choice scholars such as Gill and Roger Finke about the importance of certain conditions in the founding era, such as increasing religious diversity, vast geographic size, and the need for immigrant labor, for the emergence of religious freedom and a secular state in America. Yet I disagree with them on the priority of the material interests over ideas.[45]

In sum, certain conditions in the critical founding period, especially the lack of an *ancien régime* based on monarchy and hegemonic religion, explained the emergence of passive secularism in the United States. Initial conditions and relations in American state building were different from those in the French and Turkish experiences. This historical origin still impacts current state-religion relations in the United States through its ideological path dependence. The foundation of passive secularism, however, did not mean the end of ideological struggles, negotiations, and compromises. Instead, tensions between the rationalists and evangelicals in the founding period have persisted even to this day as continuous threads despite their changing dimensions.

[43] McGarvie 2004, 15–16; Miller and Flowers 1996, 835–9.
[44] Tocqueville 2000 [1835], 295.
[45] Gill 2007, 60–113; Finke 1990.

Certain states had already disestablished churches before the First Amendment. The state disestablishment process completed following the absence of a federal establishment. This trend, however, was not linear. The pendulum began swinging in the other direction in early-nineteenth-century America as a result of Protestant activism.

THE PROTESTANTS AND CATHOLICS: THE PROTESTANT SEMIESTABLISHMENT

From the Second Great Awakening to the Scopes Trial (1816–1925)

The Second Great Awakening deeply influenced American society by leading the Protestant churches to find new members and resulting in the emergence of new denominations. The 1816 foundation of the American Biblical Society, which published and distributed copies of the Bible, was an important milestone of the Awakening. The evangelical mobilization against the Sunday mail service (perceived as violation of the Sabbath) in 1810–1830 revealed that Protestant religious revival had certain political implications.[46]

By the early nineteenth century, the evangelicals established a sociocultural hegemony of Protestantism in the United States. The Protestant influence "encompassed the entire public realm of education and religious instruction, and it extended to the mass media and to societies and movements for moral and social reform."[47] Christianity was taken as "a part of the common law."[48] Public schools were acculturating students with nondenominational Protestantism. The federal government was supporting the Protestant missionaries, particularly in their attempt to convert Native Americans and Southern slaves, as well as their activities abroad.[49] Secularism was perceived as state neutrality toward Protestant denominations, rather than neutrality toward all religions.[50] Monsma calls this period "the de facto establishment of Protestantism."[51] This semiestablishment, in the words of Christian

---

[46] Feldman 2005, 54–6; Kramnick and Moore 2005, 131–49.
[47] Casanova 1994, 137.
[48] Witte and Green 1996, 533.
[49] Fraser 1999, 43, 83–103.
[50] Demerath and Williams 1987.
[51] Monsma 1995, 113–26.

Smith, "ordered the dominant culture" and "governed key social institutions" in America.[52] According to Sydney Ahlstrom, the heyday of Protestant "quasi-establishment" was the period between 1815 and 1860.[53] Later it started to decline due to several challenges.

One challenge was the division among Protestants and the use of religion for bloody conflicts during the Civil War (1861–1865), which experienced "a vociferous battle of words debating the sinfulness or godliness of slavery; a retributive, bloody, fratricidal war in which both sides claimed God's favor, and a widespread belief that out of carnage would come the fulfillment of Christ's millennial promise."[54] President Abraham Lincoln's (1809–1865) second inaugural address, which is full of references to God, is an example of religious public discourses at the time.

A major challenge against the Protestant semiestablishment was the influx of Catholic immigrants. In 1789, the Catholics numbered only thirty-five thousand among four million Americans. The Catholic population reached 1.7 million by 1850 and three million by 1860. That led to the anti-Catholic, nativist movement.[55] The Protestants sought to maintain their dominance in the public schools, which taught the Protestant King James version of the Bible,[56] in addition to the Protestant version of the Ten Commandments that prohibited idolatry.[57] The public schools' curricula were "rife with material that Catholics and Jews found offensive."[58] For that reason, the Catholics opened their own private schools and tried to receive public financial support.[59] To prevent the state from funding Catholic schools, the Protestants eagerly referred to the principle of church-state separation.[60] In 1876,

---

[52] Smith 2003b, 25.

[53] Ahlstrom 1972, 556.

[54] Deverell 1987, 1.

[55] Ahlstrom 1972, 555–68.

[56] Hamburger 2004, 220. In 1844, a school board in Philadelphia responded positively to the "request by the local bishop that Catholic children not be required to read from King James Bible." That led to a Protestant riot, as a result of which fifty-eight people were killed and more than a hundred were wounded. Ravitch 1999, 5–6. For another "Bible conflict" in 1872 in New York, see Feldman 2005, 72.

[57] Lacorne 2007, 106–12.

[58] Sarna and Dalin 1997, 16.

[59] Smith 1967; Greenwalt 2004, 14–16. In 1892, about a third of Catholic students were attending private schools. Feldman 2005, 88.

[60] Hamilton 1995, 249.

James Blaine proposed a constitutional amendment to prohibit public funding of sectarian schools:

No State shall make any law respecting an establishment of religion, or prohibiting the free exercise thereof; and no money raised by taxation in any State for the support of public schools, or derived from any public fund therefor, nor any public lands devoted thereto, shall ever be under the control of any religious sect; nor shall any money so raised or lands so devoted be divided between religious sects or denominations.[61]

Although the House passed the amendment (180–7), it was rejected in the Senate (by 4 votes). Nevertheless, the Blaine Amendments were added into the constitutions of thirty-seven states.[62]

The use of a separationist discourse against religious minorities was not confined to the Blaine Amendments. The Supreme Court also did it in *Reynolds v. U.S.* (1878) to uphold the federal Moral Anti-Bigamy Act of 1862 that prohibited polygamy. The Court rejected the Mormon demand of religious exemption from the law by stressing that the government had the authority to regulate religious practices. It was the first decision in which the Court interpreted the Free Exercise Clause. The Court proposed a separationist argument referring to Jefferson's metaphor of the "wall of separation." It took a clearly negative stand against polygamy by comparing it to human sacrifices as religious worship and defining it as "odious," "an offence against society," and "almost exclusively a feature of the life of Asiatic and African people."[63]

In 1890, the Court made two other decisions, in which its language was much more clearly "Christian" and anti-Mormon.[64] In *Davis v. Beason*, the Court criticized polygamy for being a crime "by the laws of all civilized and Christian countries" and recognized as such "by the general consent of the Christian world."[65] In *Mormon Church v. United States*, the Court depicted polygamy as a "nefarious doctrine," "barbarous practice," and a "blot on our civilization." The Court added, "It is contrary to the spirit of Christianity, and of the civilization which Christianity has produced in the western world." It also targeted the

---

[61] Quoted by Hamburger 2004, 297–8; Witte 1991, 489n2.
[62] Fraser 1999, 106–13; Sandel 1999, 76.
[63] *Reynolds v. U.S.*, 98 U.S. 145 (1878).
[64] Reid 2002, 70–2.
[65] *Davis v. Beason*, 133 U.S. 333 (1890).

Mormon Church by defining it as an "organization of a community for the spread and practice of polygamy" and, therefore, "a return to barbarism."[66]

The Supreme Court's reference to Christianity was not confined to its anti-Mormon decisions. In *Vidal v. Girard's Executors* (1844), the Court referred to the Bible as "a divine revelation," which was supposed to be taught in schools. It asked, "Where can the purest principles of morality be learned so clearly or so perfectly as from the New Testament?"[67] Nearly a half-century later, in *Holy Trinity Church v. U.S.* (1892), the Court put more emphasis on Christianity. It defined the American people as "a religious nation" and noted that "[e]very constitution of every one of the 44 states contains language which, either directly or by clear implication, recognizes a profound reverence for religion, and an assumption that its influence in all human affairs is essential." The Court went even further:

[T]he custom of opening sessions of all deliberative bodies and most conventions with prayer; the prefatory words of all wills, "In the name of God, amen;" the laws respecting the observance of the Sabbath ... ; the churches and church organizations which abound in every city, town, and hamlet; the multitude of charitable organizations existing everywhere under Christian auspices; the gigantic missionary associations, with general support, and aiming to establish Christian missions in every quarter of the globe. These and many other matters which might be noticed, add a volume of unofficial declarations to the mass of organic utterances that this is a Christian nation.[68]

The *Holy Trinity Church* decision, however, was an articulation of a declining view. In the words of Robert Handy, "between 1870 and 1920 especially the state courts were moving away from a perception of America as a Christian nation toward a secular-based perspective."[69] The evangelical forces were still fighting back. In the 1910s, eleven states made obligatory either or both Morning Prayer and Bible reading in public schools. That was something only one state – Massachusetts – had been enforcing before. In response, courts in five other states banned Bible reading in public schools. As

---

[66] *Mormon Church v. United States*, 136 U.S. 1 (1890).
[67] *Vidal v. Girard's Executors*, 43 U.S. 127 (1844).
[68] *Holy Trinity Church v. U.S.*, 143 U.S. 457 (1892).
[69] Handy 1991, 160.

a result, "the America of 1920" was different from "what it had been in 1880" because "the informal hegemony that the Protestant movement had long held over American religious and cultural life by its numerical pluralities and the power of its organizational networks was weakened."[70]

In 1910, the Catholic population reached sixteen million out of ninety-two million Americans.[71] They were no longer the only demographic challenge to the Protestant dominance because the Jewish immigrants also became influential.[72] The ADL was founded in 1913 to defend the rights and interests of the Jews. Beyond the change of religious demography, the spread of European secularist social sciences among the American elite also contributed to the weakening of Protestant semiestablishment.[73] Casanova rightly linked "the secularization of American higher education" to "the loss of Protestant cultural hegemony."[74] He calls this period "second disestablishment," after the First Amendment.[75] Scholars agree that the disestablishment of Protestantism was a long process. According to Handy, it took from 1880 to 1920, and for John Wilson and Donald Drakeman, it was the period between 1860 and 1920.[76]

THE SEPARATIONISTS AND EVANGELICALS: AFTER THE DISESTABLISHMENT OF PROTESTANTISM

From the Scopes Trial to Anticommunism (1925–1950)

Some scholars explain the disestablishment of Protestantism through modernization theory, arguing that American public life, especially education, "was secularized not as the result of direct attacks by militant secularists. Instead, as with modern civilization, generally, secular values and ways of thinking gradually (and for the most part

---

[70] Ibid., 189.
[71] Casanova 1994, 168; Macedo 2000, 60.
[72] Sarna and Dalin 1997, esp. 13; Handy 1991, 69–70.
[73] Smith 2003a.
[74] Casanova 1994, 137.
[75] Ibid., 137–45. See also Monsma 1995, 126–9.
[76] Handy 1991; Wilson and Drakeman 2003, 30.

unobtrusively) acquired power in the hearts and minds of people."[77] Christian Smith et al. rightly refute this explanation in their comprehensive *The Secular Revolution*.[78] They attach importance to human agency and ideological struggles in the disestablishment of Protestantism. In the words of Smith, "historical secularization of the institutions of American public life was not a natural, inevitable, and abstract by-product of modernization; rather it was the outcome of a struggle between contending groups with conflicting interests seeking to control social knowledge and institutions."[79]

One of these contending groups was the evangelicals, who tried to preserve the sociocultural dominance of Protestantism. At the opposite side, there existed a complex coalition of three major groups. The first one was the religious minorities such as Catholics and Jews. The second group comprised those who held secularism as a personal ideology, including social scientists, who embraced the secularization theory, and natural scientists, who embraced Darwinian evolution.[80] They were organized by associations like Freemasons and Freethinkers.[81] These scholars and scientific disciplines had "their new epistemologies and critical methods of interpretation," which "presented explanations of nature, society, and human culture that were often in conflict with established Protestant worldviews."[82] The third group was the new professionals, such as teachers, journalists, writers, artists, and businesspeople, who regarded Protestant principles and prohibitions, including Victorian moralism and censorship, as a barrier to their professionalism and their social mobility.[83]

These three (religious, ideological, and professional) groups attacked the Protestant semiestablishment. They secularized American higher education by founding new secular universities,[84] spreading European secularist scientific approaches,[85] and promoting a positivist

---

[77] Nord 1994, 96.
[78] Smith 2003a.
[79] Smith 2003b, vii.
[80] Smith 2003c, 36–47, 53–60; Wuthnow 1990, 26–7.
[81] Hamburger 2004, 360–75, 391–9, 451.
[82] Casanova 1994, 137–8.
[83] Smith 2003c, 36–7, 48–53; Kemeny 2003; Sikkink 2003, 326–8; Flory 2003.
[84] Smith 2003c, 74–8.
[85] Smith 2003d.

epistemology.[86] They also secularized public elementary and second-ary education by taking over the National Education Association[87] and upholding John Dewey's "progressive," secular, and humanist per-spective on education.[88] Moreover, they influenced the Supreme Court through maintaining new separationist legal perspectives, by lobbying for the appointment of liberal justices, and by writing *amicus curiae* briefs.[89] The final and fatal blow to the Protestant establishment came from the mainline Protestants, who eventually cooperated with these three groups and broke from the evangelicals.[90] The mainline Protestants later founded the Protestants United for Separation of Church in 1947 to institutionalize their support of separationism.[91]

The two events that sealed the end of the Protestant semiestab-lishment were the Scopes Trial in 1925 and the end of Prohibition in 1933.[92] In *Tennessee vs. John Scopes*, also known as the "Monkey Trial," John Scopes was charged with teaching the theory of evolution in violation of Tennessee state law, which prohibited teaching "any theory that denies the story of divine creation of man as taught in the Bible." The ACLU, which had been founded five years earlier to defend civil rights, was legally supporting Scopes, particularly with the hope of having a court decision on the unconstitutionality of state laws against evolutionism. The trial went beyond the guilt or inno-cence of Scopes, and even the constitutionality of Tennessee's law. It became a media show between Clarence Darrow, a proevolution agnostic, and William Jennings Bryan, an antievolution Christian. It turned into one of the most famous courtroom debates in American history. The separationist media paid special attention to the trial in order to ridicule the alleged failure of Bryan and his fundamentalist Christian perspective.[93]

---

[86] Garroutte 2003.
[87] Beyerlein 2003.
[88] Glenn 2002, 310–14; Thomas, Peck, and Haan 2003.
[89] Sikkink 2003; Macedo 2000, 139–45.
[90] Casanova 1994, 138.
[91] Later, this association changed its name to Americans United for Separation of Church and State.
[92] Dionne 2002, xiii; Reichley 2002, 169.
[93] Larson 2006; Kemeny 2003, 231; Feldman 2005, 135–49; Jacoby 2004, 245–51. Following the Scopes Trial, however, evolutionism did not become dominant in school curricula. It gained such a status in the late 1950s, as a result of the fear of Soviet

Prohibition was different from the Scopes Trial because it did not simply reflect a controversy around secularism and evangelical Protestantism, yet its end still meant a failure for evangelicals who had been its major defenders.[94] Throughout the nineteenth century, the temperance movement defended abstinence and gradually succeeded in limiting the alcohol consumption by social control and legal prohibitions in certain states. At the end of the century, organized groups supported by Protestant churches, such as the Woman's Christian Temperance Union and the Anti-Saloon League, launched a campaign against alcohol.[95] The Eighteenth Amendment to the Constitution, which was ratified in 1919, established the nationwide prohibition of the manufacture, sale, and transportation of alcohol. In the words of Joseph Gusfield, "Prohibition had become a symbol of cultural domination or loss. If the Prohibitionists won, it was also a victory of the rural, Protestant American over the secular, urban, and non-Protestant immigrant."[96] Yet the former's victory did not take long. In 1933, the Twenty-first Amendment abolished federal Prohibition and left the issue to the states and local administrations. The failure of Prohibition damaged the prestige of Protestant social activism, in terms of defending morality through legal restrictions.[97]

After more than a decade, a landmark court decision redefined secularism in the United States. *Everson v. Board of Education* in 1947 became the first case in which the Supreme Court applied the Establishment Clause to the states regarding the Fourteenth Amendment. Although the Court upheld state funding of bus transportation for parochial schools, the majority opinion written by Justice Hugo Black interpreted the Establishment Clause in a separationist way:

Neither a state nor the Federal Government can set up a church. Neither can pass laws which aid one religion, aid all religions, or prefer one religion over

---

technological advance, especially the launch of *Sputnik*. Wills 1990, 97–114, 127–31; Fraser 1999, 125 6.

[94] Casanova 1994, 144.

[95] Fowler et al. 2004, 19–21.

[96] Gusfield 1986, 110.

[97] Prohibition laws in certain states existed until 1966. Since then, there have been only some "dry" counties that have banned alcohol. Jan Palmowski, "Prohibition," *Oxford Reference Online*, http://www.oxfordreference.com/views/ENTRY.html?subview=Main&entry=t46.e1904, accessed on June 27, 2006.

another.... No tax in any amount, large or small, can be levied to support any religious activities or institutions, whatever they may be called, or whatever form they may adopt to teach or practice religion. Neither a state nor the Federal Government can, openly or secretly, participate in the affairs of any religious organizations or groups and vice versa. In the words of Jefferson, the clause against establishment of religion by law was intended to erect "a wall of separation between Church and State."[98]

The four dissenting justices' opinion written by Justice Robert H. Jackson also noted: "Separation means separation, not something less. Jefferson's metaphor in describing the relation between Church and State speaks of a 'wall of separation,' not of a fine line easily overstepped."[99]

After *Everson,* the Court continued to disallow the public funding of religious schools, any other types of state support for religious education, and any close connection between public schools and religious institutions. A year later, in *McCollum v. Board of Education,* the Court stressed that the First Amendment prohibits not only establishment of a particular religion but also the state's close relations with religion in general, even in a nondenominational manner. Regarding the complaint of an atheist parent, the Court decided that the use of public school classrooms during regular hours for voluntary religious instruction by a religious association (which included Protestants, Catholics, and Jews) and the close cooperation between the school authorities and this association violated the Establishment Clause. Justice Black stressed that "the First Amendment had erected a 'wall of separation' between Church and State which must be kept high and impregnable." He also added, "To hold that a state cannot ... utilize its public school system to aid any or all religious faiths ... does not ... manifest a governmental hostility to religion or religious teachings." Justice Felix Frankfurter, in his concurring opinion, joined by three other justices, defined the public school "as a symbol of our secular unity."[100]

The Court's emphasis on a wall of separation occurred at a time period when the state's role in society was expanding. That is why

---

[98] *Everson v. Board of Education* 330 U.S. 1 (1947). I repeated this quotation in Chapters 2 and 3 because it is an influential precedent.

[99] *Everson v. Board of Education* 330 U.S. 1 (1947).

[100] *McCollum v. Board of Education* 333 U.S. 203 (1948). For a critique of this decision, see Reid 2002, 85–7.

increasing legal separationism damaged not only the political but also the social influence of Protestantism. If separationism had been emphasized earlier, it would have been less harmful for the Protestant social dominance because, as Robert Wuthnow stresses, "prior to World War II, religion provided much of the nation's higher education, sponsored many of the nation's leading hospitals, and carried the lion's share of services for the elderly, handicapped and homeless."[101]

The Supreme Court played an important role in the consolidation of separationism in the American legal system as the dominant interpretation of passive secularism. The dominance of separationism ignited a religiously conservative countermovement in the 1950s.

THE ACCOMMODATIONISTS AND SEPARATIONISTS: THE ESTABLISHMENT OF MONOTHEISM

The Anticommunist Decade (the 1950s)

In the 1950s, one domestic and one international factor led the pendulum to swing into a new establishment. Domestically, the rising separationism created a reaction among the religious conservatives. Evangelicals, as well as conservative Catholics and Jews, became irritated by the Supreme Court's separationist decisions and mobilized toward a monotheist alliance. Internationally, the United States was waging the cold war against the "godless" communists. Anticommunism was an obsession during the so-called McCarthy era (1950–1954). Therefore, in the 1950s, it was important for American leaders to show to their nation and others how they possessed a distinct respect for God.

The Congress and President Dwight Eisenhower (1890–1969) played important roles in the formation of a monotheist establishment in the 1950s. In 1952, Congress passed legislation to declare that each year there would be a National Day of Prayer, which was signed into law by President Harry S Truman (1884–1972). Later, three more important legislations were signed by Eisenhower. In 1954, Congress added the phrase "under God" to the Pledge of Allegiance, which had existed

---

[101] Wuthnow 1990, 17.

since 1892 without a reference to God.[102] In 1955, Congress passed
the law that made it mandatory for all coinage and paper currency to
display the motto "In God We Trust."[103] Since 1864, this motto had
been used in a limited way, being impressed only on certain coins.
Another law was enacted in 1956 to declare "In God We Trust" the
national motto of the United States, replacing the old one, "E Pluribus
Unum" (Out of Many, One), which had been used since the founding
period.[104] Eisenhower's famous statement effectively summarizes the
official mood of this period: "Our government makes no sense unless
it is founded on a deeply held religious belief – and I don't care what
it is."[105] Beyond these official discourses, the monotheistic tone became
also dominant in public institutions, including the armed forces and
hospitals.[106]

Even the Supreme Court followed the zeitgeist of the 1950s and
took a more accommodating stand toward state-religion entanglements. An important case of the era was *Zorach v. Clauson* (1952).
Despite the dissention of three separationists – Justices Black, Jackson,
and Frankfurter – the Court upheld a "released time" program through
which public schools allowed students to miss classroom activities in
order to take religious instruction in religious institutions, because
no public facilities or sources were used, and students were attending
based on parental request.[107]

Justice William O. Douglas wrote the majority opinion with an
accommodationist perspective: "We are a religious people whose
institutions presuppose a Supreme Being." For him, the state should
be concerned about religion in respecting people's spiritual needs:
"When the state encourages religious instruction or cooperates with
religious authorities by adjusting the schedule of public events to
sectarian needs, it follows the best of our traditions. For it then
respects the religious nature of our people and accommodates the
public service to their spiritual needs." He differed from earlier
separationist precedents: "The First Amendment ... does not say

---

[102] 36 U.S.C. 172.
[103] 36 U.S.C. 186.
[104] 31 U.S.C. 5112(d)(1).
[105] Quoted by Demerath and Williams 1987, 78. See also Meacham 2007, 176–9.
[106] Kelley 1963.
[107] *Zorach v. Clauson*, 343 U.S. 306 (1952).

that in every and all respects there shall be a separation of Church and State. Rather, it studiously defines the manner, the specific ways, in which there shall be no concert or union or dependency one on the other." He added that a complete lack of entanglement might turn into a mutual hostility between state and religions: "Otherwise the state and religion would be aliens to each other – hostile, suspicious, and even unfriendly." An impenetrable wall of separation between state and religions was something practically impossible because, in such a condition, "[c]hurches could not be required to pay even property taxes. Municipalities would not be permitted to render police or fire protection to religious groups." A separationist reading would put the Constitution and American traditions in contradictory positions: "Prayers in our legislative halls; the appeals to the Almighty in the messages of the Chief Executive; the proclamations making Thanksgiving Day a holiday; 'so help me God' in our courtroom oaths – these and all other references to the Almighty that run through our laws, our public rituals, our ceremonies would be flouting the First Amendment." Moreover, it was not possible to satisfy each and every demand of separationism: "A fastidious atheist or agnostic could even object to the supplication with which the court opens each session: 'God save the United States and this Honorable Court.'" Finally, an impenetrable wall that requires state's "callous indifference" toward religion would be a favor to "those who believe in no religion over those who do believe."[108] This decision has become an important precedent for subsequent conservative justices with accommodationist perspective.[109]

During the 1950s, accommodationism emerged as the dominant perspective that reinterpreted passive secularism as state neutrality toward three monotheistic religions (Protestantism, Catholicism, and Judaism). It replaced separationism, which defended a wall of separation between state and religions. So the two main ideological camps in the debates on state policies toward religion in America became clearer. After its heyday in the 1950s, accommodationism faced a strong challenge from the separationists.

---

[108] Ibid.
[109] Leon Wieseltier, "The Mark of Zorach: Rehnquist's and Scalia's Commandments," *The New Republic*, June 29, 2005.

THE SEPARATIONISTS AND ACCOMMODATIONISTS:
DISESTABLISHMENT OF MONOTHEISM
AND ITS AFTERMATH

From the Prohibition of School Prayer to the Reagan Administration (1962–1981)

The separationists challenged the monotheist establishment in the 1960s. The increasing number of nonmonotheists (atheists, people without religion, and polytheists) in America contributed to this challenge.[110] The Supreme Court played a leading role in the disestablishment of monotheism. In 1962, in *Engel v. Vitale,* the Court decided that it was unconstitutional for public schools to officially compose particular school prayers and to require their recitation. The Court rejected the accommodationist position by stressing that denominational impartiality cannot make prayer in public schools constitutional. Justice Black delivered the Court's opinion: "Neither the fact that the prayer may be denominationally neutral nor the fact that its observance on the part of the students is voluntary can serve to free it from the limitations of the Establishment Clause, as it might from the Free Exercise Clause."[111] Another critical decision was *Abington v. Schempp* of 1963, in which the Court ruled against the voluntary recitation of Bible verses and the Lord's Prayer in public schools. Justice Tom C. Clark's majority opinion stressed that "the State may not establish a 'religion of secularism' in the sense of affirmatively opposing or showing hostility to religion."[112] But this statement was not convincing for Justice Potter Stewart, the only dissenter to *Engel* and *Abington.* He argued that the decisions violated the principle of neutrality by establishing "a religion of secularism" and confining religious exercises to private life.[113] Even more than two decades later, it was still unclear to what extent these two Court decisions changed

---

[110] Hammond 1987, 100–1.

[111] *Engel v. Vitale,* 370 U.S. 421 (1962).

[112] *Abington v. Schempp,* 374 U.S. 203 (1963). The Court combined this case with *Murray v. Curlett,* where the appellant was Madalyn Murray, who later founded the American Atheists.

[113] *Abington v. Schempp,* 374 U.S. 203 (1963). Justice Stewart gave the example of chaplains in the armed forces. Their funding "might be said to violate the Establishment Clause. Yet a lonely soldier stationed at some faraway outpost could

daily practices in America, because "conservatively estimated, more than 25 percent of the nation's schools still begin their day with prayers or Bible reading and possibly end them with released time religious instruction in the school buildings."[114]

Both the *Engel* and *Abington* decisions took place during the presidency of John F. Kennedy, who "in both his personal style and his political philosophy, was arguably the most secularist American president since Jefferson."[115] Kennedy particularly emphasized church-state separation to respond to the criticisms that as a Catholic, he would mix these two.[116] Beyond Kennedy, the Court's decisions were supported by separationist civic associations, such as the ACLU, and religious groups, such as liberal Protestants and Jews. The elite support of the decisions "was demonstrated when Leo Pfeffer, Counsel for the American Jewish Congress, rounded up 110 law school deans and professors of law and political science to sign a letter to the Senate Judiciary Committee supporting *Engel* and opposing school-prayer amendments."[117]

Despite this elite support, there was a mass resistance against the Supreme Court's decisions on school prayer. According to the public surveys from 1963 to 1994, the average ratio of opponents to the decisions was about 60 percent, while that of supporters remained only 35 percent.[118] The conservative Protestants and Catholics were the main groups that opposed the prohibition of prayer. "Beginning with the school-prayer decisions, conservative evangelicals came to see secularists as their real enemies. Catholics joined evangelicals in opposition to the increasing secularization of American public life, seeking the reintroduction of prayer in schools, aid to religious education, and an end to abortion."[119] They initiated several constitutional school prayer amendment proposals to overturn Court decisions, all of which became unsuccessful.[120]

---

surely complain that a government which did not provide him the opportunity for pastoral guidance was affirmatively prohibiting the free exercise of his religion."
[114] Demerath and Williams 1987, 86. See also Fisher 2005, 470–2.
[115] Jacoby 2004, 319. See also Kramnick and Moore 2005, 179–80.
[116] Balmer 2008, 6–46.
[117] Jeffries and Ryan 2001, 322.
[118] Kernell and Jacobson 1999, 145.
[119] Jeffries and Ryan 2001, 349.
[120] West 1991, 361–3; Wood 1986, 362.

The Supreme Court, however, continued its separationist decisions. In *Epperson v. Arkansas* in 1968, the Court decided that a state could not ban the teaching of evolutionism.[121] A decision that firmly consolidated separationism was *Lemon v. Kurtzman* (1971), in which the Court required a law having a secular legislative purpose, not advancing or inhibiting religion, and not fostering excessive state-religion entanglement.[122] The *Lemon* test became a core reference point for separationists to strike down any law and policy that might seem to have a religious intention.

During the 1960s the separationists succeeded in disestablishing monotheism through legal activism. Although they could not eliminate monotheistic official mottos and discourses, the separationists imposed certain policies onto public schools. The accommodationists, however, did not give up. There has been an action-reaction relation between these two groups for decades: each side has motivated the other to mobilization.[123] The accommodationists developed a strategy to support the Republican Party. They have been successful in this goal, which has also allowed them to influence Supreme Court nominees since the presidency of Reagan in 1981. Thus they have balanced the power of the separationists in the state-religion controversies as examined in Chapter 2.

CONCLUSION

The historical origin of secularism in the United States was very different from that of France and Turkey. When the American framers founded a new republic, there was no *ancien régime* based on the alliance between monarchy and hegemonic religion. Instead, America was a new country with diverse Protestant denominations. That

---

[121] *Epperson v. Arkansas*, 393 U.S. 97 (1968). Another example of separationist Court decisions on public schools is *Stone v. Graham* (449 U.S. 39) in 1980, which declared unconstitutional the posting of the Ten Commandments in classrooms. There were also a few cases in this period in which the Court tended to accommodationism. An example is *Board of Education v. Allen* (392 U.S. 236) in 1968, wherein the Court decided that a state might provide textbooks free of charge to all children, including those attending parochial schools, because these schools have both secular and religious aspects.
[122] *Lemon v. Kurtzman*, 403 U.S. 602 (1971).
[123] Kohut et al. 2000, 123.

shaped the formation and dominance of passive secularism, which tolerates public religiosity, unlike assertive secularism in France and Turkey.

The two main groups, the rationalists and evangelicals, who reached a consensus in the American founding era left the legacy of the tension between proseparation and proestablishment forces. The pendulum has been swinging between establishment and disestablishment as a result of the struggles and balance of power between these two competing groups. The absence of federal establishment and disestablishment in states was followed by the semiestablishment of Protestantism. The separationist movement in the early twentieth century disestablished Protestantism. Then the evangelicals allied with conservative Catholics and Jews to establish monotheism with accommodationist state policies. The separationists disestablished monotheism in the 1960s. These transformations meant changing the meaning of passive secularism in the United States. During the Protestant semiestablishment, passive secularism implied state neutrality toward all Protestant denominations. During the 1950s, it implied neutrality toward all monotheist religions. The debate on the meaning of passive secularism still continues, as elaborated in Chapter 2.

Throughout these debates and transformations, ideological views have played an important role. Ideology trumped economic and institutional affiliations because the defenders of opposing views could be found in the same economic classes and institutions. Although individuals form their preferences regarding their sincerely held ideologies, they can also pursue certain instrumental behaviors to reach these preferences. The Protestants' use of a separationist discourse for nativist, anti-Catholic purposes in the Blaine Amendments is an example of such a strategic behavior. This does not undermine the importance of sincerely held religious and ideological views, because the strategy of the Protestants was based on their preferences constructed by anti-Catholic ideas.

The chapter also emphasizes the role of human agency throughout the ideological struggles to reinterpret passive secularism and to shape state policies toward religion. Although certain structural factors, such as migration and the cold war, affected these changes, it was still up to human agents to adopt particular ideologies, get organized around them, and struggle to transform conceptions and policies. Even though migration caused the change of religious demography in America, it was still individuals who used religious affiliations as the carriers of religious and political views. Similarly, the cold war influenced state-religion relations in the United States when certain individuals took an ideational stand against communism and conducted policies to combat it.

PART II

FRANCE

4

Assertive Secularism and the Multiculturalist Challenge (1989–2008)

In October 1989, the principal of a public high school in Creil (near Paris) expelled three Muslim female students because of their headscarves. The issue gained national importance because it could become a precedent for other schools. The Minister of Education, Lionel Jospin, declared that he supported a solution based on dialogue between school administrators and parents.[1] Certain leftist and feminist intellectuals accused him of pursuing an appeasement policy and called for a general ban on wearing headscarves in schools.[2] To shift the burden away from himself, Jospin applied to the Conseil d'Etat (Council of State). The Council issued an opinion,[3] which emphasized that wearing a headscarf was not incompatible with *laïcité* (secularism).[4]

The supporters of a general ban on headscarves did not give up, and the debate on the issue continued passionately for years. A survey

---

[1] Remond 1995, 15.
[2] Elisabeth Badinter, Régis Debray, Alain Finkielkraut, Elisabeth de Fontenay, and Catherine Kintzler, "Profs, ne capitulons pas!" *Le Nouvel observateur*, November 2–8, 1989.
[3] The French Council of State, November 27, 1989; no. 346,893.
[4] Some French scholars have translated the term *laïcité* as *secularity*. Instead, I prefer the term *secularism*, which is most commonly used in the literature on state-religion relations in English (by American and Indian scholars). The term *secularism* is generally translated as *laïcité* into the French language while analyzing secularism in the United States. Zoller 2005. Similarly, in Senegal, where the French language is still in use, the constitution defines the republic as *laïque* despite the fact that the dominant state ideology in Senegal is passive, not assertive, secularism that accommodates public visibility of religions (especially Islam and Catholicism). Villalon 2006.

of six major French[5] and British[6] newspapers between 1989 and 1999 shows that the number of articles on the headscarf issue in French newspapers reached 1,174, whereas the British newspapers carried only eighteen articles.[7] The debate also raged in the courtrooms. The Council of State, the final appeals court on state-citizen cases in France, made case-by-case decisions on headscarves. Between 1992 and 1999, the Council overturned forty-one of the expulsion cases while upholding only eight of them.[8] To overrule the Council of State, the supporters of a ban pressed for a new law on secularism. A bill was accepted in the French Assembly and the Senate and signed into law by President Jacques Chirac in March 2004. The first article of the new law says, "In public primary, secondary, and high schools, the wearing of signs or dress with which the students manifest ostentatiously a religious affiliation is prohibited."[9]

Given the fact that there were fewer than 1,500 Muslim female students wearing headscarves, it is puzzling why this issue so deeply occupied French politics. To take the growing Muslim population under control is not a convincing explanation. Muslims in France are marginal in terms of political power. Among the 331 members of the Senate, there are only two members of Muslim origin, and, among 577 members of the Assembly, there is no Muslim deputy.[10] Even if Muslims were politically influential, policies toward religious symbols would not help control them because Muslims in France are not religious people. Their ratio of weekly mosque participation (5 percent)[11]

---

[5] *Le Figaro, Le Monde, Libération, L'Humanité, La Croix,* and *Le Monde de l'Education.*
[6] *The Times, Independent, Guardian, Morning Star, Church Times,* and *The Times Education Supp.*
[7] Liederman 2000, 371–2. For articles on headscarves in one of these newspapers, see *Libération* 2004.
[8] Haut conseil à l'intégration 2001, 66.
[9] The Law 2004–228 of 15 March 2004. As Jeremy Gunn emphasizes, the new law "applies about as equally to all religions as the law that prohibits all people from sleeping under bridges applies to the homeless and the wealthy." Gunn 2005a, 92n48.
[10] Klausen 2005, 22. Following his election in May 2007, President Nicolas Sarkozy appointed Rachida Dati, a Muslim woman of North African origin, as the minister of justice. "In Clubby France, A Muslim Woman as Justice Minister," *Christian Science Monitor* July 3, 2007.
[11] "L'islam nationalisé?" *Libération,* December 8, 2004, 4–5.

or being observant Muslims (10–12 percent)[12] is as low as the average weekly church participation in France (10 percent).[13] As already discussed in Chapter 1, a rational-choice perspective based on opportunity costs does not explain this puzzle because the headscarf ban did not contribute to the economy and created ruling costs. It also risked France's relations with some Muslim countries.[14]

An alternative approach rightly points to the impact of anti-immigrants and Islamophobics on French state policies toward Muslims. This approach, however, has two problems. First, as explained in Chapter 2, anti-immigrants and Islamophobics also exist in the United States. Beyond the investigations of thousands of Muslims, Islamophobia did not result in restrictive state policies toward Muslims in the United States, especially when it comes to students' religious symbols. Similarly, anti-immigrationism and Islamophobia are present in many other Western European countries,[15] such as Britain, the Netherlands, and Germany.[16] Yet none of these countries has attempted to ban students from wearing headscarves.[17] As I explained elsewhere, France is an exception in Western Europe by its restrictive policies toward Muslims.[18] In mainland France, Muslims have faced municipal

---

[12] Debré 2004, 67; Laurence and Vaisse 2006, 76; Klausen 2005, 140.

[13] The Survey of *CSA/La Vie/Le Monde*, "Les français et leur croyances," March 21, 2003, 41, 91, http://a1692.g.akamai.net/f/1692/2042/1h/medias.lemonde.fr/medias/pdf_obj/sondage030416.pdf.

[14] "Laïcité: La décision de M. Chirac suscite des critiques à l'étranger," *Le Monde*, December 22, 2003.

[15] The European Monitoring Centre on Racism and Xenophobia (EUMC), an EU institution, issued several reports on Islamophobia. It notes that Muslims in the EU countries "experience various levels of discrimination and marginalisation in employment, education and housing, and are also the victims of negative stereotyping by majority populations and the media. In addition, they are vulnerable to manifestations of prejudice and hatred in the form of anything from verbal threats through to physical attacks on people and property." EUMC 2006, 19. It refers to the Runnymede Trust, a United Kingdom–based nongovernmental organization, to define Islamophobia as: "1. Islam is seen as a monolithic bloc, static and unresponsive to change. 2. Islam is seen as separate and 'other'. It does not have values in common with other cultures, is not affected by them and does not influence them. 3. Islam is seen as inferior to the West. It is seen as barbaric, irrational, primitive, and sexist. 4. Islam is seen as violent, aggressive, threatening, supportive of terrorism, and engaged in a clash of civilizations." EUMC 2006, 61.

[16] Dekker and Noll 2007; Fetzer and Soper 2003, 247, 255; Cesari 2002, 10; Cesari 2006b, 3–4, 29–42; Pfaff and Gill 2006, 812–13.

[17] Willaime 2005a, 16.

[18] Kuru 2008.

and bureaucratic limitations to build mosques, there is no instruction on Islam (or other religions) in public schools, and there exist only three recently opened, very small Islamic schools.[19]

Second, France is also more restrictive toward religion in general (including Catholicism) in comparison to the United States and other Western European countries,[20] which cannot be explained by anti-immigrationism and Islamophobia. The ban on students' religious symbols in France also covers "large" Christian crosses, Jewish kippas, and Sikh turbans. At this point, the French policy differs from the German counterpart. Eight out of sixteen German states embraced laws banning teachers, not students, from wearing Muslim headscarves by defining it against "Christian" or "Western" values, without prohibiting other religious symbols.[21]

I argue that the headscarf ban and other exclusionary French policies toward Muslims are a reflection of the French state's restrictive attitude toward religion in general. French state policies toward religion have been shaped by the ideological struggles between the defenders of *laïcité de combat* (combative secularism) and *laïcité plurielle* (pluralistic secularism). Combative secularism aims to exclude religion from the public sphere whereas passive secularism allows the public visibility of religion. These two French concepts are similar to my terms of *assertive secularism* and *passive secularism*. I will use *assertive* and *passive*, instead of *combative* and *pluralistic*, while defining particular notions of secularism, to maintain conceptual consistency throughout the book. Assertive secularism has been dominant in France, like Turkey and unlike the United States, and it has led to exceptionally restrictive policies toward religion. The resistance of the

---

[19] These three schools exist in Aubervilliers – a suburb of Paris – (opened in 2001 and had eighty students in 2005), Lille (opened in 2003 with fifteen students), and Marseille (opened in 2005 with only one class). In 2008, the one in Lille became the first Islamic school qualified for state subsidies. There is also a private Islamic school funded by the French state in Réunion, the French overseas region in the Indian Ocean. "Les premières écoles privées en quête de financement," *Le Monde*, March 15, 2005. See also Debré 2004, 134; "Muslim Lycée Opens in Secular France, Raising Eyebrows," *New York Times* September 9, 2003; "French Muslims Find Haven in Catholic Schools," *New York Times*, September 30, 2008.

[20] France is the only country in Western Europe where there is no religious instruction in public schools.

[21] McGoldrick 2006, 115–17; Klausen 2005, 171.

passive secularists has also been significant in France. Concerning the headscarf issue, the ban took more than fifteen years to come into being because of this opposition. Moreover, on several policies, the assertive secularists have made certain compromises from their ideal educational system due to the passive secularist opposition.

My perspective does not deny the role of anti-immigrationism and Islamophobia. Instead, I take them seriously as intervening variables to explain French state policies toward Muslims. Although there are many Islamophobic and anti-immigrant rightist groups in other Western European countries, they lack assertive secularism as a dominant ideology. Therefore, these groups do not have a useful ideological discourse and an ideological ground for building coalitions with leftists to pursue restrictive policies toward Muslims. In France, however, assertive secularist ideology has led to a coalition of two old enemies – secularist leftists and anti-immigrant conservative rightists.

This chapter begins with an analysis of six policies toward religion in schools, which are crucial to understanding the debates on secularism in France. These policies are also examined in the chapters on the United States and Turkey as the main dependent variable. Then, I will analyze the ideological struggles between assertive and passive secularists. Finally, I will trace the impact of these ideological struggles on French state policies toward the Muslim minority.

THE FRENCH STATE'S POLICIES TOWARD RELIGION IN SCHOOLS

Among the following policies, the ban on student religious symbols and the lack of a pledge referring to God both indicate the difference of French policies from those in the United States and their similarity to those in Turkey. However, the legality of private religious education and substantial state funding of religious private schools show that French policies are more accommodating toward religion than the Turkish ones.

Students' Religious Symbols

The new law on secularism in France was first applied in the 2004–2005 education year. Some Muslim students wore bandanas to get around the ban. Yet the minister of education made a distinction between an

TABLE 11. *Muslim Female Students Wearing Headscarves in 2004–2005*

Muslim students who were expelled from their schools	47
Muslim students who wore discreet headscarves	12
Muslim students who agreed to remove their headscarves	533
Muslim students who studied at home	26
Muslim students who transferred to private Catholic schools	3
Muslim students who went to another country for education	67
Muslim students who left education (under 16 years old; estimation for Paris region)	25
Muslim students who left education (older than 16 years; estimation in general)	100
TOTAL	813

Source: Xavier Ternisien, "Des organisations musulmans évoquent 806 'victimes,'" *Le Monde*, March 14, 2005.

"ordinary bandana" and a bandana that switched to a *foulard islamique*. According to the minister, the latter is worn for a full day, worn every day of the week, and covers the hair entirely. It is, therefore, forbidden in public schools.[22] According to the report of the French Ministry of Education, the cases of wearing headscarves declined from 1,465 in 2003–2004 to 626 in 2004–2005.[23] In addition to these 626 Muslim students, the law was imposed on two Christian students wearing big crosses and eleven Sikh students wearing turbans. As a result of the disciplinary process, forty-seven Muslim and three Sikh students were expelled from their schools.[24] Table 11 summarizes the Muslim students' responses to the new law reported by the Committee of March 15 and Freedom, which was founded by several Muslim associations. The report's data is slightly different from that of the Ministry of Education, because the latter only counted students who tried to attend French public schools after the law.

[22] "Trois autres lycéennes exclues pour non-respect de la loi sur la laïcité à Mulhouse et dans l'Orne," *Le Monde*, October 21, 2004.
[23] The number of students wearing headscarves was 1,123 in 1994 and 1,256 in 2003. Debré 2004, 50.
[24] Ministère de l'éducation nationale de l'enseignement supérieur et de la recherche, "Application de la loi du 15 mars 2004 sur le port des signes religieux ostensibles dans les établissements d'enseignement publics," July 2, 2005, http://lesrapports.ladocumentationfrancaise.fr/BRP/064000177/0000.pdf. See also Laetitia Van Eeckhout, "L'exclusion de trois élèves sikhs devant le tribunal d'administratif," *Le Monde*, April 13, 2005.

Religious Instruction, Prayer, and the Pledge

By the laws on the secularization of education in the 1880s, Catholic dominance in French public schools was replaced with a secular outlook. Since that time, religious instruction has been abandoned, organized prayer has been disallowed, and a student pledge that refers to God has not existed in French public schools.

Private Religious Education and State Funding of Religious Schools

The religious communities have run private schools in France since the mid-nineteenth century. After having lost its impact on the public schools in the 1880s, the Catholic Church has focused on its private schools. According to recent data, almost 20 percent of all students in France attend private schools, about 95 percent of which are Catholic schools. State funding of these schools had been a serious issue of debate in the second half of the twentieth century. Currently in France, the state pays about 80 percent of the budgets (including the teachers' salaries) of the Catholic schools that sign an agreement to follow the national curriculum and to be open to students of all faiths.[25]

General Policy Trend toward Religion

The French policy toward religion has dual aspects. On the one hand, the French state, unlike the United States, has excluded religious symbols and discourses from the public sphere. There has been no prayer, reference to God, or oaths putting hands on the Bible in the French public institutions. Moreover, the French state is less sensitive with regard to freedom and autonomy of religious associations than the United States is. For example, France declared 173 sects as potentially dangerous, including Jehovah's Witnesses and the Church of Scientology. In 1998, France assigned a governmental institution – the Inter-ministerial Mission to Assert Sects – to monitor these groups.[26]

---

[25] Baubérot 2004c, 150; Coq 2004, 101; Klausen 2005, 144.

[26] "In the 'sect issue,' France may be said to practice cultural protectionism to preserve its domestic policy, just as it fights to protect its position in areas such as the film industry." Fautre, Garay, and Nidegger 2004, 617–8; also 595–602. See also Robert 2003, 652–5.

On the other hand, the popularity of private Catholic schools and their public funding reveals that French state policies toward religion are not completely exclusionary. The French state has been more sensitive to the religious demands of its citizens than Turkey. In France, students have had the opportunity to attend churches or other institutions for religious education on school-free Wednesdays, while in Turkey, the state has barely allowed any religious education, except religious instruction in public and private schools, which teaches a state-drafted version of Islam. In France, majority Catholics have particularly been accommodated in public schools: "While fish is generally served on Fridays in public school cafeterias [for Catholics who abstain from meat], little provision has been made for students who eat only halal meat."[27] Since the 1905 Law, which separated the Catholic Church and the state, the French public schools have had Catholic *aumôniers* (chaplains) for responding to student demands for religious counseling. "Although Protestants, Jews, and Muslims typically do not take advantage of this opportunity that the law provides, one estimate suggests that Catholic chaplains operate in approximately half of French public secondary schools."[28] There have also been chaplains in French prisons, hospitals, and barracks.[29] In 2004, there were 513 Catholic, 267 Protestant, 69 Muslim, 64 Jewish, and 3 Orthodox chaplains in French hospitals.[30] Until recently, there existed only Catholic (254), Protestant (71), and Jewish (49) chaplains in the military.[31] Yet in 2005, there began to be Muslim military chaplains.[32] In Turkey, however, there are no Muslim or non-Muslim chaplain in schools, the military, or many other public institutions. Furthermore, in terms of the rights to association and private religious education, France provides much more freedom to religious groups than Turkey does (see Chapter 6).

Chapter 1 explained the difference between these two countries, where assertive secularism is similarly dominant, through democracy

---

[27] Fernando 2006, 206.
[28] Gunn 2005a, 90. In 2000, more than 60% of French schools (2,594 out of 3,800) had chaplains. Massignon 2000, 363n2.
[29] Brechon 1995, 63.
[30] Conseil d'Etat 2004, 315n262.
[31] Durand-Prinborgne 2004, 96. See also Boniface 2001.
[32] "Création d'une aumônerie musulmane dans l'armée française," http://eurel.u-strasbg.fr/FR/index.php?RuBintialeSS=Débats%20actuels&intrubrique=Mars%202005&pais=5&rubrique=390&nompais=France, accessed on December 23, 2005.

in France and authoritarianism in Turkey. Assertive secularism in Turkey was established under a single-party rule and has been mainly protected since then by authoritarian military and judiciary. In France, however, it was established by a multiparty democracy and has had significant popular support. Under French democracy, the conservative Catholics have had more opportunities to challenge the assertive secularists in the public policy-making process. Because French state policies have been the result of the struggles between these forces, they have included several "exceptions." These exceptions can be summarized in three major issues.

First, in the region of Alsace-Moselle[33] the secularization laws have not been applied. The legal framework of the region is still based on the Concordat of 1801 and the Organic Laws of 1802–1808 (for these laws, see Chapter 5). The main reason for this exception is that this region was a part of Germany in 1871–1919, a period when legal secularization occurred. There have been four recognized religions in the region – Catholicism, Lutheranism, Calvinism, and Judaism. The French state has paid the salaries of these religions' clergy. Moreover, the French president has appointed Catholic bishops based on proposals from the pope. In public schools, it is not rare to see crucifixes on the walls, and there has been obligatory religious instruction taught by the clergies of the four religions. Moreover, the public University of Strasbourg in the region has had theology departments for these religions.[34]

Second, the French state has not imposed the secularization laws on six overseas colonies, where it has had various nonseparationist state-religion regimes.[35] In French Guyana, for example, Catholicism is the only recognized religion, and the Catholic clergy is paid by the French state. In Mayotte, personal law is based on Islamic law and the French government's representative has appointed the Grand

---

[33] Sometimes scholars use the term *Alsace-Lorraine*, instead of *Alsace-Moselle*, because the legal exceptions exist in both of the two departments of the Alsace region (Bas-Rhin and Haut-Rhin) and only one (Moselle) out of four departments of the Lorraine region.

[34] Conseil d'Etat 2004, 266–9; Bauberot 1994b; Willaime 2000; Gunn 2005a, 90; Wieviorka 1995, 63. There has been no Islamic instruction in schools or a Department of Islamic Theology in Alsace-Moselle. Massignon 2000, 360.

[35] Conseil d'Etat 2004, 265–72.

Kadi, who has been the supreme Muslim authority for religious and judicial issues.[36]

The third exception is that since the Law of 1905, the French state and local governments have owned and funded the maintenance of the grand majority of forty-five thousand Catholic churches,[37] in addition to half of the Protestant churches and a tenth of the synagogues.[38] The central and local governments have allowed Catholics, Protestants, and Jews to use these buildings.[39] These and other policies can be better understood by a detailed analysis of the struggles between the assertive and passive secularists.

ASSERTIVE AND PASSIVE SECULARISTS

In France, leftist parties generally defend the confinement of religion to private life, whereas rightist parties largely support the public visibility of religion. Nevertheless, French political parties, unlike their American and Turkish counterparts, have not fully represented the opposing sides in the debates on secularism, mainly because of their internal splits on this issue. Multiculturalist leftists and multiculturalist rightists, for example, have recently embraced passive, rather than assertive, secularism. Additionally, due to the foundation and demise of several republics, French politics has not had long-standing political parties, such as the Democratic and Republican parties in the United States, or Republican People's Party in Turkey. Last but not least, French political culture appreciates the rousseauian general will, while political parties by definition defend particular wills and interests. Since the 1789 Revolution's attack on the aristocrats, there has been a French ideal to remove the intermediaries (including parties) between the individual and the Republic.[40] For these reasons, I will focus on certain individuals and civic associations, instead of parties, as the supporters of passive and assertive secularism in France.

---

[36] Jean Baubérot, "Le mythe de l'exception," *Le Monde des Religions*, no. 8 (November–December), 2004, 20–3; Boyer 2005a, 37.

[37] Conseil d'Etat 2004, 318.

[38] Willaime 2005b, 74; Bertrand 2006, 296, 299.

[39] Burdy and Marcou 1995, 10; Baubérot 1994a, 63.

[40] The author's personal interview with Valentine Zuber, Professor of Sociology, EPHE, Sorbonne University; Paris, November 26, 2004. See also Bosworth 1962, 3–6.

One of the most influential civic associations on state-religion relations in France has been the Ligue de l'enseignement (League of Education).[41] The league was "the ancient bastion of the traditional notion of secularism" in France. In 1986, however, it declared that secularism needed a transformation by calling for a *nouvelle* (new), *ouverte* (open), and *plurielle* (pluralistic) secularism.[42] Since the league has been a pillar of the secular French education system, its call has been taken seriously by certain supporters and critics. That created a new debate between the defenders of dominant assertive secularism and those of alternative passive secularism.[43] The debate has focused on the issue of multiculturalism, which has challenged assertive secularist state policies in France through the rise of (Muslim and other) new religious identities, as well as the recognition of alternative state-religion regimes in other European Union (EU) members.[44]

Scholars who are sympathetic to assertive secularism generally refuse to discuss alternative types of secularism, because they believe that their own notion is the only true understanding of secularism. For that reason, the majority of comparative analyses on assertive and passive secularism in French literature have a critical stand for the former and sympathy for the latter. According to Jean-Paul Burdy and Jean Marcou, assertive secularism in France is "republican, monist, and anxious about the individual citizen's expression of his or her religious or communitarian affiliation in the public space," while passive secularism is "more democratic, flexible, and open to differences."[45] In the words of Guy Haarscher, assertive secularism is more "doctrinaire," "rigid," and "separatist" than passive secularism, which is more "open," "flexible," and "neutral."[46] An extreme version of assertive secularism in France, Pierre Brechon argues, can even claim to be an

---

[41] Martin 2005.
[42] Dereymez 1995, 253. See also Palau 2001; Bergounioux 1995, 18.
[43] Scksig, Kessel, and Roirant 1999; Zuber 2004; Ducomte 2001, 34, 41; Baubérot 1999, 130–6; Carens and Williams 1999.
[44] Baudouin and Portier 2001, 22–7; Willaime 2004a, 328–38; Wieviorka 1996; Zuber 2004, 33–4; Cesari 2001; Fernando 2006, 65–7; Safran 2003a; Bleich 1998; Gunn 2004, 462; Laurence and Vaisse 2006, 55.
[45] Burdy and Marcou 1995, 13–14.
[46] Haarscher 2004, 101.

alternative to religions and substitutes them with its "set of thoughts and rituals," as well as its dogmatic take on "reason and progress."[47]

Assertive Secularists

A major supporter of assertive secularism in France has been the *franc-maçons* (Freemasons). The Grand Orient and other divisions of the French Freemasons currently have about 110,000 members.[48] The *libre-penseurs* (Freethinkers) is a more philosophical (generally atheistic) organization than the Freemasons. These two associations have had overlapping members and a shared support of assertive secularism. Both have been critical of the league's suggestion of alternative passive secularism.[49] In 1991, several Freemasons and other assertive secularists founded the Comité Laïcité République (Committee on Secularism and the Republic, or CLR).[50] Patrick Kessel, the president of the CLR and a former grand master of the Grand Orient, notes that in certain cases they "would not engage in a dialogue," and they "would combat for" secularism.[51] He criticizes the league's notion of passive secularism for leading to social disunity and communitarianism. Like many other assertive secularists, Kessel contests any new versions of secularism because "the concept of secularism is full, dense, and rich enough that it is not necessary to associate it with adjectives."[52]

In addition to these associations, two intellectuals have been influential promoters of assertive secularism. One is Regis Debray – the socialist thinker, activist, and one of CLR's founders. The other figure is Henri Pena-Ruiz, a philosopher of secularism. For both, secularism requires a neutral public sphere free from all religious symbols and discourses. They assert that *laïcité* is a uniquely French concept and opposite of the American system of church-state relations. They obviously favor the former and criticize the latter. Debray claims that in France "the state is free from the influences of churches," whereas in the United States "the

---

[47] Brechon 1995, 65.
[48] "Les francs-maçons dans la rue pour la laïcité," *La Croix*, December 8, 2005.
[49] Baubérot 2005, 360; Dereymez 1995, 253; Xavier Ternisien, "Les associations laïques commémorent la loi de 1905 en ordre dispersé," *Le Monde*, December 11, 2005.
[50] See the Web site of the CLR at http://www.laicite-republique.org/.
[51] Seksig, Kessel, and Roirant 1999, 74.
[52] Ibid., 65–6.

churches are free from the influences of the state."[53] Pena-Ruiz argues
that the United States is not a secular state; therefore, the president is
sworn in by putting a hand on the Bible.[54] They seem to ignore various
types of secularism, take both countries monolithically, and neglect the
conservative Catholic influence over French politics and separationist
aspects of secularism in the United States.

These two thinkers disagree on the main reason for the distinction
between secularism in France and the United States. For Debray, the
reason is the two distinct, historically dominant religions in the two
countries. In France, the dominant Catholic Church supposed itself
as the eternal proprietor of truth and the good. Therefore, it impeded
freedom of thought, which made the French political elite anticlerical.
In the United States, dominant Protestant creed recognized the right to
disagree and became compatible with liberty and democracy. As a result,
in America, a state-church conflict was not experienced.[55] Debray's
argument is based on the civilizational approach that I criticized in
Chapter 1. This approach compares Catholicism and Protestantism
as monolithic entities, while disregarding liberal Catholic and illiberal Protestant voices. Pena-Ruiz, in contrast, attaches importance to
structural factors and the ways in which religious beliefs have been
interpreted, an approach with which I agree. He points out that

the French Protestants were favorable to the secularization laws and the separation adopted between 1880 and 1905; while the Protestants of Northern
Europe have stayed hostile to any separation, which would deprive them of
the advantages of the Lutheran state churches. As for Catholics, they are secularist in the North of Europe [where they are minority] and anti-secularist in
the South [where they are majority].[56]

In general, assertive secularists aim to confine religion to the individual's conscience or to the home. For them, secularism has always
had enemies – the Catholic clergy and the *intégristes*[57] in the past, and

[53] Debray 1992, 23.
[54] Pena-Ruiz 1999, 61.
[55] Debray 1992, 23.
[56] Pena-Ruiz 2003, 46.
[57] The assertive secularists have used the term *intégriste* to accuse someone (generally a
Catholic) of being an antisecular extremist. For them an *intégriste* believes that only
a religiously designed society can guarantee the integrity of the religious belief. Poulat
2004, 159.

the conservative Muslims at present – and it should be defended in a combative manner. They claim a monopoly over the true meaning of secularism by rejecting the possibility of its diverse interpretations. Pena-Ruiz, therefore, refuses to define secularism with adjectives: "Those who have covered words and want to call into question the strict separation of the state and religions define a 'modern,' 'open,' or 'pluralistic' secularism. In fact, such a project is not a simple redefinition, but a true destruction of secularism, which is neither closed nor open; neither hard nor soft." For him, the adversaries of secularism generally use it with adjectives.[58]

Passive Secularists

Since the end of World War II, Catholic institutions have embraced secularism as church-state separation and religious freedom, rather than secularism as an antireligious ideology and state fetishism.[59] Major associations of the second biggest religion in France, Islam, have embraced a similar view. In November 2004, I participated in a nationwide conference on secularism in France.[60] Fouad Alaoui, the secretary general of the Union des Organisations Islamiques de France (Union of Islamic Organizations of France, or UOIF) was invited to elaborate on the Muslim views on secularism. He stressed that they wanted a secularism that accepted the public visibility of religion in general and Islam in particular.[61] Alaoui is not an exception; Muslim associations have generally used a discourse of passive secularism to criticize assertive secularist policies of the French state.[62]

The League of Education, a union of educators with two million members, is an active supporter of passive secularism.[63] Because of its secular character and historical efficacy, the league has had more legitimacy than Catholic and Muslim associations to challenge assertive

[58] Pena-Ruiz 1999, 62–3. See also Pena-Ruiz 2003, 127.
[59] Portier 2005, 131–3; Poulat 2003, 150; Ognier 1994, 272–5; Bedouelle and Costa 1998, 12–13.
[60] "Les entretiens d'Auxerre: De la séparation des églises et de l'Etat à l'avenir de la laïcité," November 10–13, 2004, Auxerre.
[61] Alaoui 2005, 171–2.
[62] Fetzer and Soper 2005, 69.
[63] See the Web site of the league at http://www.laligue.org/laligue/rubriques/ligue/index .htm.

secularism. It has called for a rethinking of secularism in France based on new conditions of multiculturalism. Jean-Marc Roirant, the secretary general of the league, noted that "secularism has been fortunately embraced to protect the nation's cultural diversity, not to erase it."[64]

Among the intellectuals, the most influential supporters of passive secularism have been two professors at Sorbonne University and, simultaneously, in the Groupe Sociétés, Religions, Laïcités (Group of Societies, Religions, and Secularisms). The first is Jean Baubérot, historian of French secularism. Baubérot has promoted his arguments about multiple secularisms with a series of publications in the 1990s and 2000s.[65] He claims that secularism in France should be reconsidered in a way that would open it to changes and diverse interpretations. It should no longer be seen as a zero-sum game between the anticlerical secularists and antisecular Catholics. Rather, secularism should be regarded as a shared value based on mutual compromises. For Baubérot, new conditions require new pacts on secularism.[66] Unlike Debray and Pena-Ruiz, he regards secularism as a dynamic process in constant interaction with sociopolitical conditions. Baubérot stresses that there is no absolute or perfect secularism that needs to be fought for. Instead, secularism is an ongoing process of negotiation.[67] He has been critical of the depiction of secularism in France as exceptional and monolithic: "The problem is no longer, then, to defend, in a more or less contracted way, a pseudo 'French exception,' but to combine secularisms (yes, with an 's,' when we talk about secularism not as a principle, but as an empirical reality) and rights of being human."[68] He calls other French intellectuals to take a more humble position: "regarding secularism, France can give some, but it can also receive much [from other countries]."[69] Again, unlike Debray and Pena-Ruiz, he takes the American model seriously.[70] Baubérot emphasizes that some founders of French secularism in 1905, such as Jean Jaurès,

---

[64] Seksig, Kessel, and Roirant 1999, 65.
[65] Baubérot 1990; Baubérot 1994c; Baubérot 2004a; Baubérot 2004b; Baubérot 2004d.
[66] For Ruiz's critique of Baubérot's concept of "pact," see Pena-Ruiz 2003, 320.
[67] Baubérot 2003, 9.
[68] Ibid., 28.
[69] Jean Baubérot, "Le mythe de l'exception," *Le Monde des Religions*, no. 8 (November–December), 2004, 21.
[70] The author's personal interview with Jean Baubérot, EPHE, Sorbonne University; Auxerre, November 11, 2004.

referred to secularism in the United States to defend their plan of church-state separation.[71]

The second professor is Jean-Paul Willaime, a sociologist of religion and secularism. According to Willaime, France needs a "*laïcisation de la laïcité*" (secularization of secularism).[72] What he means is that the traditional notion of secularism in France has too many dogmatic aspects; it has almost become a worldly religion. France, therefore, needs "*une laïcité plus laïque*" (a more secular secularism), which would be less dogmatic and more open to "a certain return of religions to the public sphere."[73] The main pillar of Willaime's understanding of the secular state is neutrality. If the French state becomes less obsessive with its (assertive) secularist ideology, then it will become more neutral. "The more the secular state abandons its dominance over civil society, the more it will tend to recognize the contributions of religious groups to the public life. By doing that it becomes more secular."[74] For Willaime, the rise of multiculturalism is a major challenge to the dominant understanding of secularism in France.[75] Through a postmodern perspective, he brings not only secularism but also other meta-narratives in France, such as science and politics, into a critical discussion: "The secularization of secularism is also a critique of the mystifications of science and politics, a demythologization of all the secular forms of absolutization."[76]

The passive secularists, in short, criticize the exclusionary character of dominant assertive secularism. Several passive secularist associations and individuals have struggled to reshape French state policies toward religion.

POLICY CONTROVERSIES BETWEEN THE ASSERTIVE AND PASSIVE SECULARISTS

The debate between the assertive and passive secularists has had important policy implications. The assertive secularists, such as the

---

[71] Baubérot 2004a, 4, 87.
[72] Willaime 2005b, 68; Willaime 2004c, 375. The author's personal interview with Jean-Paul Willaime, EPHE, Sorbonne University; Auxerre, November 11, 2004.
[73] Willaime 2005c, 351n24.
[74] Ibid., 350.
[75] Willaime 2004c, 377.
[76] Willaime 2000, 393. See also Willaime 2004b.

Freemasons and Freethinkers, have had a common policy agenda. They have, for example, favored the abolishment of the exceptional status of Alsace-Moselle and called for the implementation of the secularization laws in this region.[77] The defenders of passive secularism, however, have not seen a problem with this exceptional status. Baubérot emphasizes that French state policies are not homogeneous and points to Alsace-Moselle as an example of flexibility for secular state policies in France.[78]

Education has been the main fault line between the assertive and passive secularists. The passive secularists have recently challenged the lack of religious instruction in public schools. They have argued that French youth have become increasingly ignorant about religion. Since 1982, the league has supported the reintroduction of religious instruction in public schools. In 1989, it submitted a report on "religious illiteracy" and a proposal for the reintroduction of religious instruction to the Ministry of Education.[79] According to the league, without learning the basics of religion, "the comprehension of the entire French history and civilization would be problematic." The league's initiative was a challenge to "combative [read assertive] secularism [according to which] religion should not be mentioned in school; religion is a private affair – individual and familial – which should not invade the public space of the school."[80] The Federation of French Protestants, which has brought together Reform and Lutheran congregations, has also supported the league's position. The federation and the league signed a common declaration in 1989 that stressed the necessity of a pluralistic debate on secularism, an education of religious culture in public schools, and a revision of the secularization laws to positively take account of the new religions' (e.g., Islam's) conditions in France.[81]

Certain assertive secularists have taken a balanced position on the league's proposal rather than simply rejecting it. Debray, for example,

---

[77] "Les francs-maçons dans la rue pour la laïcité," *La Croix*, December 8, 2005. For the Freemasons' and Freethinkers' views on secularism, see their Web sites at http://www.godf.org/structures_observ.html; http://librepenseefrance.ouvaton.org/index.htm.

[78] Jean Baubérot, "Le mythe de l'exception," *Le Monde des Religions*, no. 8 (November–December), 2004, 20–3.

[79] MacNeill 2000, 346.

[80] Brechon 1995, 66.

[81] "Vers un nouveau pacte laïque: Eléments de réflexion," April 1989, http://www.protestants.org/docpro/doc/0905.htm, accessed on March 24, 2007.

submitted a report on the education of religion to the minister of education in 2002. Although he admitted that French students needed to acquire basic information on religion to better understand secular courses that referred to religious concepts, Debray emphasized that the new courses should only describe religions from a philosophical and scientific perspective.[82] Therefore, he opposed a reintroduction of religious instruction as generally understood in other European countries.

These discussions on secularism in France have been marginal in comparison to the debates on policies toward the Muslim minority, in general, and headscarves, in particular. According to Gilles Kepel, the headscarf issue has created one of the biggest political debates in France since the Dreyfus affair.[83]

The French State and the Muslim Minority

The French colonial empire ruled several Muslim territories from the mid-nineteenth to the mid-twentieth centuries. Algeria had a special importance among these territories. The French state kept Islam under control in Algeria, from the appointments of imams and muftis, to the organization of the pilgrimage to Mecca. Even after the separation law of 1905 this control continued.[84] The Muslim population in the French mainland has grown since the end of the colonial period. The French state's first official recognition of Islam appeared in the aftermath of World War I. To commemorate the Muslim soldiers who fought in the French military during the war, the state led the construction of the Paris Mosque between 1922 and 1926.[85] Other than the Paris Mosque, there was practically no public evidence of Islam in French urban spaces until the 1970s. As Jocelyne Cesari stresses, "The collective dimension of Islam was confined to the intimate space of the residences, the hearths, the provided places at hotels, or the backs

---

[82] Debray 2002, 23.
[83] Kepel 1994, 11.
[84] Conseil d'Etat 2004, 265.
[85] The French state allocated half a million francs for the construction of the Paris Mosque. Azria 2003, 45. It also collaborated with the king of Morocco for the construction. Since 1957, Algeria has played a major role in sponsoring the mosque. Caeiro 2006, 73.

of the shops."[86] With their rising population, however, Muslims built mosques whose number has kept increasing: 5 in 1965, 68 in 1975, 274 in 1980, 922 in 1985, 1,020 in 1990,[87] 1,500 in 1999,[88] and 1,685 in 2004.[89] The Muslim population has recently reached between four million and five million, which constitutes 7 to 8 percent of the French population.[90] Only half of this Muslim population has French citizenship.[91]

Muslims in France have diverse affiliations with Islam. For some, it is first and foremost a divine religion, while for others it is primarily a cultural affiliation.[92] As Olivier Roy stresses, they exist along a wide spectrum, from Islamists to *"athées musulmans"* (atheist Muslims). Therefore, it is necessary to disconnect Islam as a religion and the problems of *banlieues* in France, such as the riots in November 2005, which have had several socioeconomic bases.[93] As an example, the unemployment rate among the Algerians under thirty with high school diplomas is 32 percent whereas the national average with similar qualifications is only 15 percent.[94]

Muslims do not constitute an intellectual bloc either. Soheib Bencheikh has developed an assimilationist perspective by embracing assertive secularism and not criticizing state policies.[95] That is why he was nominated by the Paris Mosque as the Mufti of Marseilles with unofficial support from the French state. The nomination did not give him any practical authority because he has lacked recognition from the local Muslim community.[96] The president of the Paris Mosque, Dalil Boubakeur, is also a close ally of the French state, but he has

---

[86] Cesari 1995, 180–1.

[87] Gastaut 2004, 92.

[88] Fetzer and Soper 2005, 87.

[89] Twenty of the mosques in France are for more than one thousand persons, fifty-four of them are for five hundred to one thousand persons, and the rest are smaller. "L'islam nationalisé?" *Libération*, December 8, 2004, 4–5.

[90] Khosrokhavar 2004, 43. The ethnic origins of Muslims in France are as follows: Algerians (1,550,000), Moroccans (1,000,000), Tunisians (350,000), Arabs from the Middle East (100,000), Turks (315,000), sub-Saharan Africans (250,000), converts (40,000), applicants for asylum and illegal immigrants (350,000), Asians (100,000), and others (100,000). Haut conseil à l'intégration 2001, 37–8.

[91] Laurence and Vaisse 2006, 196.

[92] Khosrokhavar 1997; Frégosi 2008.

[93] Roy 1999, 77. See also Keaton 2006.

[94] Laurence 2005, 40. See also Giry 2006.

[95] Bencheikh 1998; Bencheikh 1999.

[96] Caeiro 2006, 75.

represented a relatively balanced view.[97] More "Islamic" figures such as Tariq Ramadan have been popular among the young generation with Islamic tendencies. Although Ramadan's home country is Switzerland and he now teaches at Oxford, he has been influential in France because of being francophone. Ramadan has supported integration of Muslims into Europe as equal citizens rather than as a minority.[98] A recent *APSR* article defines him as the "most prominent contemporary advocate of the notion that Muslims can fully and without contradiction embrace their citizenship in European countries."[99] Nevertheless, because he is the grandson of Hasan al-Banna (the founder of the Muslim Brotherhood in Egypt), certain French magazines have accused Ramadan of being a fundamentalist.[100]

Among the French politicians, Nicolas Sarkozy is the one most involved with issues about Muslims. He had been the leader of the central-rightist Union pour un mouvement populaire (Union for a Popular Movement, or UMP) before he was elected as the President of France. In his *La République, les religions, l'espérance* (*The Republic, Religions, and Hope*), published in 2004, Sarkozy notes that the French state should have closer relations with its Muslim population.[101] He even proposes public funding of mosques, by revising the Law of 1905, which forbids the state's financial support of religious institutions.[102] Sarkozy's concern about Muslims comes from his desire to control them, rather than from sympathy. He frequently stresses that he wants to create an "*islam de France*" (French Islam), rather than an "*islam en France*" (Islam in France),[103] by assimilating Islam within the French culture.[104]

Sarkozy played the final leading role in the foundation of the Conseil français du culte musulman (French Council of the Muslim Faith, or

---

[97] Ibid., 75; Laurence and Vaisse 2006, 102–3.
[98] Ramadan 2005, 62–77; Ramadan 2003b, 31; Ramadan 2003a, 100–1.
[99] March 2007, 244.
[100] *L'Express*, October 18, 2004. In 2004, Ramadan received a tenured professorship at Notre Dame University, but the U.S. Department of State revoked his visa.
[101] Sarkozy 2004. See also Etienne de Montety, "Le livre-choc de Nicolas Sarkozy," *Le Figaro Magazine*, October 23, 2004; Sarkozy's interview with Denis Jeambar, *L'Express*, November 11, 2004.
[102] Sarkozy 2004, 121–32.
[103] Ibid., 100. See also Azria 2003, 31.
[104] Caeiro 2006, 71; Kaltenbach and Tribalat 2002, 180–3.

CFCM) in December 2002, when he was the ministre de l'intérieur et des cultes (minister of interior and "religious" affairs). The CFCM comprised several Muslim associations, such as the Paris Mosque, UOIF, the Federation National of Muslims of France (FNMF), and the Turkish Islamic Union for Religious Affairs (DİTİB). The FNMF was linked to Morocco and the DİTİB was the European division of Turkey's Diyanet.[105] The UOIF was criticized by the French media for being an Islamist organization. Nevertheless, Sarkozy favored its active role to expand the representational capacity of the CFCM, which only brought together associations that controlled 60 percent of mosques.[106] The French state has recognized the CFCM as a primary coordinator of several issues, such as the construction of mosques and Muslim cemeteries, the ritual of sacrificing animals in the Grand Holiday, validation of halal meat, the appointment of Muslim chaplains to hospitals and prisons, and the training of imams.[107]

Sarkozy's successor as minister of interior, Dominique Villepin, similarly from the UMP, also engaged with Muslims. In December 2004, Villepin stressed that 75 percent of the 1,200 imams in France were not citizens, and 33 percent of them did not speak French.[108] He noted that the imams needed to be trained in French public schools to install the secular aspect of their education. Moreover, Villepin lamented that some of the imams were funded by foreign countries, such as Saudi Arabia.[109] For that reason, he initiated a foundation of Muslims to fund the mosques in France in March 2005.[110]

Within the French state structure, the Council of State seems to be the most tolerant institution toward Muslims. In February 2004, the council issued a public report on secularism. It depicted the existence

[105] Recently, the FNMF gave birth to Rassemblement des musulmans de France (RMF) and the DİTİB named its French branch as Comité de coordination des musulmans turcs de France (CCMTF). "Il ne fait pas bon être indépendant dans l'islam de France," *Le Monde*, June 10, 2008.

[106] Caeiro 2006, 73; "L'islam nationalisé?" *Libération*, December 8, 2004, 4–5.

[107] Laurence and Vaisse 2006, 153; Zeghal 2005, 98.

[108] Forty percent of imams in France ethnically or as citizens are Moroccans, 25% are Algerians, and 13% are Turkish. Caeiro 2006, 75.

[109] "L'islam nationalisé?" *Libération*, December 8, 2004, 4–5.

[110] "La fondation pour les œuvres de l'islam de France," http://www.interieur.gouv .fr/rubriques/c/c2_le_ministere/c21_actualite/2005_03_21_CFCM/fondation.pdf, accessed on December 25, 2005.

of programs on religions (Catholicism, Protestantism, and Islam) on public TV and radio channels as a perceived step forward toward an "open-minded" secularism in France.[111] According to the report, non-Catholics, especially Muslims, lacked necessary conditions, such as sufficient number of mosques and chaplains (in barracks, prisons, and hospitals). It stressed that the majority of mosques are still simple prayer rooms made of "abandoned factories, houses, basements, and garages."[112] By this emphasis, the council implicitly suggested a limited legal reform that would allow state support to disadvantaged religions. Even such a limited reform was unacceptable for the assertive secularists, who wanted to leave the Law of 1905 unchanged. During the law's centennial anniversary, the Freemasons and the Freethinkers were in the streets of Paris to protect the law against its so-called enemies. They emphasized that the Law of 1905 should be "neither revised, nor purified, nor adapted."[113] The disputes on mosques and imams were relatively low-key in comparison to the real ground-shaking discussion on headscarves.

The Headscarf Ban

When the headscarf issue appeared in October 1989, Lionel Jospin from the Partie socialiste (Socialist Party, or PS) was the minister of education. In his speeches to the media and the National Assembly, Jospin stressed that school directors should establish a dialogue with students and their parents, rather than excluding them. The assertive secularists, including about fifty deputies from Jospin's own party, strongly criticized him.[114] They were disappointed because they expected a general ban on headscarves. For the assertive secularists, religious symbols should have no place in secular public schools. They also had two specific discourses to defend such a ban. One was republican: the school should be an emancipating and unifying republican institution, whereas headscarves supported communitarianism and ghettoization. The other was feminist: the headscarf was a symbol of patriarchal

---

[111] Conseil d'Etat 2004, 348.
[112] Ibid., 318–19.
[113] "Les francs-maçons dans la rue pour la laïcité," *La Croix*, December 8, 2005.
[114] Dereymez 1995, 251; Gastaut 2004, 95.

oppression and female inequality vis-à-vis men.[115] Two leading feminists argued that feminism required them to defend a strict (read assertive) secularism, which "supposes a neutral public space free of all religious beliefs." They defended "the prohibition of the headscarf in the places of education and common life (schools, factories, companies, bureaucracy)," and if necessary "on the street."[116]

The best example of the assertive secularist perspective was the open letter to Jospin written by Debray and four other intellectuals in October 1989. The letter was the antiheadscarf manifesto that set the tone of the following debates on the issue. According to the letter, Jospin was a defender of "the right to be different" and "new" (read passive) secularism: "The partisans of 'new secularism,' among whom you place yourselves, preach an indistinct tolerance." The authors defined their position as the opposite:

Neutrality is not passivity, nor freedom simple tolerance. Secularism has always been an issue of power struggle. Should we abandon – what you call – "combative secularism" for the sake of good feelings at this time when religions again have an appetite for combat? Secularism, as a principle, is and will remain a battle, like public education, the Republic, and freedom itself. Their survival imposes on all of us discipline, sacrifices, and a little courage. Nobody anywhere defends citizenship by lowering their arms with benevolence.[117]

For the authors, a major problem of Jospin and other defenders of passive secularism is their notion of education: "They want a school open to communitarian, religious, and economic pressures; a school where each professor is held to yield with the social environment; a school where each student is constantly returned to his or her parents, recalled to his or her condition, and bound by his or her 'roots': it is a school of social predestination." To the authors, "the secular and republican school" is and should remain "a place of emancipation." It is a place of "discipline" where "students are pleased to forget their community of origin." The French Republic should not be "a mosaic

---

[115] See Bowen 2006, 208–41.

[116] Anne Zelensky and Anne Vigerie, "Laïcardes, puisque féministes," *Le Monde*, May 30, 2003.

[117] Elisabeth Badinter, Régis Debray, Alain Finkielkraut, Elisabeth de Fontenay, and Catherine Kintzler, "Profs, ne capitulons pas!" *Le Nouvel observateur*, November 2–8, 1989.

of ghettos" and "the destruction of the school would precipitate that of the Republic." The school should address all equally, and, therefore must not permit students to display distinctive signs that mark religious affiliations. The headscarf is particularly unacceptable because it is "the symbol of the female submission." By authorizing this symbol de facto, Jospin gave "full power to the fathers and brothers, i.e., the hardest patriarchates of the planet." The letter criticizes Jospin for wrongly tolerating the Muslim "*intégristes* who are by definition the enemies of tolerance." The schoolteachers should not repeat this mistake and should not make compromises where the headscarf is concerned.[118]

Five other intellectuals – three social scientists, a women's rights activist, and the president of an antiracist organization (SOS-Racisme) – replied to this letter with another letter entitled "Pour une laïcité ouverte" (For an Open-minded Secularism). They defend a passive secularist perspective while criticizing Debray and others for proposing the exclusion of students from schools merely because of their headscarves. They stress the importance of respecting cultural diversity and warn that a general ban on headscarves would empower both the Muslim fundamentalists and the French extreme nationalists (e.g., Le Pen).[119]

Overwhelmed by the critiques, Jospin appealed to the Council of State to make a decision on the subject matter. In November 1989, the council issued an opinion that attached importance to religious freedom and emphasized that the wearing of religious symbols, such as headscarves, in schools was not inherently incompatible with the principle of secularism: "[I]n schools, the students' wearing of signs by which they intend to manifest their affiliations with a religion is not by itself incompatible with the principle of secularism as long as it constitutes the exercise of the freedom of expression and manifestation of religious beliefs...." The council also stressed that religious symbols should not disturb the functioning of educational activities by being used as "an act of pressure, provocation, proselytism, or propaganda."[120]

[118] Ibid.
[119] Joelle Brunnerie-Kauffmann, Harlem Désir, René Dumont, Gilles Perrault, and Alain Touraine, "Pour une laïcité ouverte," *Politis*, no. 79, November 9–15, 1989. See also Bowen 2006, 85.
[120] The French Council of State, 27 November 1989; no. 346,893.

Based on the council's opinion, Jospin issued a circular that gave the school directors the authority to regulate the issue through dialogue with parents and students.[121] From 1989 until the promulgation of the new law in 2004, the council regulated the wearing of headscarves in schools. During this period, many students were tolerated by the school administrators or returned to their schools by local courts. Among the forty-nine cases that reached the council between 1992 and 1999, only eight cases of expulsion were upheld.[122] In these few cases, students wearing headscarves and their parents staged street protests against the school administrations and therefore were perceived as harming the public order.[123]

In addition to individuals such as Debray, certain assertive secularist associations, including the Freemasons, Freethinkers, and CLR, defended a general ban on headscarves in public schools. According to Kessel, a leading Freemason and the president of the CLR, the headscarf affair has reemphasized that "secularism is an ongoing combat."[124] The passive secularists who opposed the ban were not confined to Jospin and the Council of State. The League of Education resisted a general ban and defended the council's position of examining the issue case by case.[125] Roirant, the secretary general of the league, declared their position by stressing that they "would like [it] better if the headscarves are not worn," but it is entirely up to the Muslim students "to decide it through their own consciences."[126] The league defended that it would be much better for a Muslim student wearing a headscarf to attend the school than to stay at home.[127] Other opponents of the ban have included the chief rabbi of France and,[128] unsurprisingly, major Muslim associations, the CFCM, UOIF, and FNFM.[129] They declared wearing headscarves as a religious prescription that one should be free to do in schools. Some assimilationist

---

[121] The Circular of Jospin, December 12, 1989. Debré 2004, 93; Gastaut 2004, 97.
[122] Haut conseil à l'intégration 2001, 66.
[123] Debré 2004, 92.
[124] Seksig, Kessel, and Roirant 1999, 74.
[125] Ibid., 70.
[126] Ibid., 75.
[127] Antoine de Baecque and Jacqueline Lalouette, "La laïcité est un mythe national français," *Libération*, October 15, 2005.
[128] Bowen 2006, 84; Frégosi 2008, 392–3.
[129] Caeiro 2006, 80; Killian 2003.

Muslims, such as Bencheikh, however, founded the Conseil français des musulmans laïques (French Council of Secular Muslims), which supported the ban on headscarves.[130]

Beyond being a typical debate between the assertive and passive secularists, the headscarf case has had a unique place in French politics. Until the headscarf debate, the rightist politicians had criticized assertive secularism and disagreed with the leftists on this issue (see Chapter 5). The headscarf debate, however, created an unprecedented coalition between the Right and the Left.[131] This coalition became visible in the French press. Although independent newspapers, such as *Le Monde*, had a relatively neutral position toward the headscarf, its "negative representation ... was almost prevalent in the articles published by *L'Humanité* and *Le Figaro*, ... respectively left and right of the center."[132] In other words, due to their anti-immigrationism and Islamophobia, the rightists supported the assertive secularist leftist proposal to ban the headscarf.[133]

A clear representative of this strategic alliance was François Bayrou, the minister of education from 1993 to 1997. Bayrou was from the Union pour la démocratie française (Union for French Democracy, or UDF), a center-right party inspired by Christian (Catholic) Democracy. In 1994, he initiated a project to increase public funding of private, mostly Catholic, schools. As a result of street protests by the assertive secularists against it, the project was cancelled.[134] Despite their substantial disagreement on public funding to Catholic schools, Bayrou and the assertive secularists agreed on banning headscarves in schools. In September 1994, Bayrou issued a circular to the directors of schools that declared the headscarf inherently ostentatious and therefore prohibited.[135] In July 1995, however, the Council of State cancelled Bayrou's circular by deciding that a general and permanent ban on headscarves was illegal.[136]

---

[130] Caeiro 2006, 78.
[131] Baubérot 2005, 360; Fetzer and Soper 2005, 73–85; Moruzzi 1994, 664.
[132] Liederman 2000, 375.
[133] According to Baubérot, current Islamophobia in France has certain similarities with French anti-Semitism in the first half of the twentieth century. Baubérot 2004d, 189.
[134] Beattie 2000.
[135] The Circular of Bayrou, September 20, 1994. See Durand-Prinborgne 2004, 105.
[136] Costa 1995, 80; Burdy and Marcou 1995, 27.

The French Catholic Church opposed a ban on headscarves.[137] That indicates that the ban was a result of the struggle between two opposite coalitions. The proban coalition included certain pro-Catholic rightist politicians allied with assertive secularists, while the antiban coalition involved the Catholic Church and other passive secularist Catholic forces. Islamophobia in France has not been promoted by the Catholic hierarchy, but it has been driven by certain historical memories – from the Battle of Tours against the Arabs in 732[138] to the colonization of Algeria in 1830–1962[139] – and contemporary sentiments against immigrants.[140] Joan Scott's *The Politics of the Veil* is a recent insightful analysis of the colonial legacy's negative impact on the contemporary French imaginary of Islam, in general, and headscarves, in particular.[141] As a result of the Left-Right coalition, the supporters of the ban, according to a report of the National Assembly, reached 72 percent of the French population in 2003. More specifically, 71 percent of sympathizers of the Left and 79 percent of the Right supported the ban.[142]

A ban did not take place during the premiership of Jospin between 1997 and 2002. In the first round of the 2002 presidential elections, Jean-Marie Le Pen, the leader of the far-right, anti-immigrant, and Islamophobic Front National (National Front, or FN) shook French politics. Le Pen received 17 percent of votes, while center-rightist President Chirac won only 20 percent and leftist Prime Minister Jospin won 16 percent. After his reelection, President Chirac took a clear, negative position against headscarves.[143] He appointed a commission

[137] Debré 2004, 181; Chadwick 2000b 192–3.
[138] Alain Ruscio, "Des Sarrasins aux Beurs, une vieille méfiance," *Le Monde diplomatique*, February 2004, 10.
[139] "Frantz Fanon and others have made it very clear that women's wearing the veil was an intense focus of symbolic struggle during the Algerian Revolution." Moruzzi 1994, 663. See also Shepard 2006, esp. 186–8; Burgat 2003, 22–3.
[140] In a 1999 survey in France, 66% of the respondents defined themselves as "racist" and 51% of them thought that "there were 'too many Arabs' in France." Cirtautas 2000, 97.
[141] Scott 2007, esp. 41–5.
[142] Debré 2004, 179. According to the Survey of CSA, the supporters of the ban constituted 69% of the population. "La majorité des Français favorables à une loi," *Le Monde* December 17, 2003.
[143] McGoldrick 2006, 83.

comprising twenty intellectuals and headed by a former minister, Bernard Stasi, to evaluate the issue.[144]

Members of the Stasi Commission were overwhelmingly selected from the assertive secularists, such as Debray and Pena-Ruiz. Baubérot was the only member who explicitly supported passive secularism. Alain Touraine could be regarded as another passive secularist member because of his multiculturalist views[145] and his coauthored letter for an open-minded secularism in 1989.[146] Nevertheless, during and after the Stasi Commission meetings, Touraine embraced an assertive secularist position.[147] As a member later mentioned, "there was no one with sensitivity about Islam" in the commission. "Réne Rémond had that for Catholicism and Patrick Weil for Judaism; Muhammed Arkoun has no real ties with the Muslim community."[148] As a result, Baubérot remained the only member of the Stasi Commission who did not vote for the proposal of a new law to ban students' religious symbols in public schools.[149] The commission submitted its final report and recommendations to Chirac in December 2003.[150]

To evaluate the same issue, the president of the National Assembly, Jean-Louis Debré, also appointed a commission under his leadership. In December 2003, the commission submitted a report favoring the perspectives of the assertive secularists, while ignoring those of the passive secularists. The report defined the wearing of headscarves as the simple result of family and social pressure.[151] It neglected the voices of Muslims while referring to Hanifa Chérifi as if she were an expert on Islam.[152] Chérifi, also a member of the Stasi Commission, had been the

---

[144] The commission included nine academics, three other members of national education, three politicians, two members of the Council of State, two members of civil associations, and a businessperson. Zuber 2004, 36.

[145] Touraine 1997.

[146] Joelle Brunnerie-Kauffmann, Harlem Désir, René Dumont, Gilles Perrault, and Alain Touraine, "Pour une laïcité ouverte," *Politis*, no. 79, November 9–15, 1989.

[147] Renaut and Touraine 2005.

[148] Quoted by Bowen 2006, 116. In its public hearings, the commission listened to only one student wearing a headscarf. Bowen 2006, 118, 246.

[149] Jean Baubérot, "Laïcité: le grand écart," *Le Monde*, January 4, 2004; Baubérot 2004f, 234.

[150] Stasi 2003. For a critique of the Stasi report, see Gunn 2004.

[151] Debré 2004, 8.

[152] The report does not refer to proheadscarf views, even those of non-Muslims. In October 2003, the French and international media extensively covered the story

French government's chief mediator with the students wearing head-scarves and their parents since 1994, and had no authority to speak on behalf of Muslims or Islam, other than having an Algerian origin and name. The report quoted her argument that there was no religious symbol in Islam; therefore, the headscarf was a mere symbol of fundamentalism and proselytizing. She was also quoted as stating that the headscarf was incompatible with individual freedom.[153] Consequently, the Debré Commission also proposed a new law to ban students' religious symbols in public schools.

Many scholars have disagreed with the Stasi and Debré reports' monolithic depiction of headscarves as simple signs of patriarchic pressure or Islamic fundamentalism.[154] Willaime notes that although some girls wear the headscarf because of parental or fundamentalist pressure, others "wear it as an affirmation of liberty and to demonstrate their personal autonomy."[155] French sociologists Françoise Gaspard and Farhad Khosrokhavar stress that in many cases, wearing headscarves shows "a desire for integration *without* assimilation, a desire on these women's part to be simultaneously French *and* Muslim."[156] American law professor Jeremy Gunn points out multiple meanings of wearing headscarves, in addition to familial and social pressure: "such as a matter of faith and belief, a feeling of cultural identity with Islam, a showing of solidarity with a sister who was harassed for wearing it, to annoy the French, to protest a father who is not a good Muslim, or as a statement of teenage rebellion."[157] American anthropologist John Bowen adds that for some women, wearing headscarves means "to be part of *breaking* with immigrant culture, a way of distinguishing between an Islam learned in France ... and the insufficiently Islamic

---

of Laurent Levy, a French Jewish lawyer, an avowed atheist, and the father of two Muslim teenagers, Lila and Alma. Levy waged a media and legal battle against the authorities of the public high school in the northern Paris suburb Aubervilliers, which expelled his daughters due to their headscarves. Neither the Debré report nor the Stasi paid attention to Levy's claims. Laurent Lévy, "Mauvaise fois," *Le Monde*, 17 October 2003. "Jewish Dad Backs Headscarf Daughters," BBC News Online, October 1, 2003, http://news.bbc.co.uk/1/hi/world/europe/3149588.stm.

[153] Debré 2004, 74–81, 157.
[154] Nordmann 2004; see also Roy 2007, 87.
[155] Willaime 2004c, 380.
[156] Gaspard and Khosrokhavar 2003, 65 (emphasis in original); Gaspard and Khosrokhavar 1995, 47.
[157] Gunn 2005a, 98.

traditions of the 'old country' ... , [and] a mark of discovery and self-identification as an individual."[158] Last but not least, Scott, American historian of France and an expert of gender studies, emphasizes that "many of the girls who donned headscarves defined their action as a personal choice, one made in the face of parental disapproval and as part of an individual search for the spiritual values."[159]

The French executive and legislature eagerly embraced the Stasi and Debré proposal of a new law to prohibit religious symbols. They ignored, however, the Stasi Commission's several other propositions, including to make one Jewish and one Islamic holiday official in France, where six of eleven official holidays had Christian origins.[160] President Chirac made a public speech to denounce the headscarf as a sign of social disunity and communitarianism.[161] Sarkozy had an inconsistent attitude during the debates on headscarves. Initially, he opposed a general ban. Later, having realized the rising popular support for the ban, he changed his position. Sarkozy even went to Egypt in December 2003 to meet with the sheikh of al-Azhar, Tantawi, and received a "fatwa" from him about France's right to ban headscarves.[162]

In early 2004, the French Parliament approved the legislative bill to prohibit student displays of religious symbols in public schools. Both the Chamber of Deputies (494 for, 36 against, and 31 abstentions) and the Senate (276 for and 20 against) passed the bill by a large majority. The ruling center-right UMP and the center-left PS massively voted for

---

[158] Bowen 2004a, 46–7 (emphasis in original). Bowen is also critical of the French ban on head-covered photos in identity cards: "[I]f a woman habitually wears a headscarf, would not a scarf-clad identity photo be the better form of identification? Yes, if the point were to establish her individual identity. No, if the point were (as I believe it is) to ensure that the public identity of individuals be undifferentiated, that they present themselves in public life as French and only as French." Bowen 2004b, 33.

[159] Scott 2007, 126.

[160] These holidays are the followings: Noël (Christmas Day), Pâques (Easter), Ascension catholique (Ascension Day), Pentecôte (Whit Sunday), Assomption (Assumption of the Blessed Virgin Mary), and Toussaint (All Saints' Day). "Official Public Holidays for 2005," accessed at the Web site of the French Embassy in the United States, http://www.ambafrance-us.org/atoz/holidays.asp, on May 2, 2006.

[161] "M. Chirac prône le 'sursaut républicain' et interdit le voile à l'école," *Le Monde*, December 18, 2003; "French President Urges Ban on Headscarves in Schools: Chirac Confronts Spread of Islam," *Washington Post*, December 18, 2003.

[162] "M. Sarkozy obtient l'appui de la plus haute autorité sunnite sur le voile islamique," *Le Monde*, December 12, 2003; Hervé Gattegno, "En Egypte, M. Sarkozy fait 'le service après-vente' d'une loi qui ne le convainc pas," *Le Monde*, January 1, 2004.

the bill, while smaller parties, such as center-right UDF and the Parti communiste français (French Communist Party, or PCF), split their votes.[163] On March 15, 2004, Chirac signed the bill into law.

The debate on headscarves between the assertive and passive secularists went on for a decade and a half. It was the coalition of the assertive secularists (generally leftists) and anti-immigrants/Islamophobics (generally rightists) that succeeded in imposing a ban on students' religious symbols. Following the ban, the coalition between the assertive secularist Left and conservative Right seemed to end. Sarkozy, who was elected as the president of France in May 2007, signaled the collapse of the coalition. He explicitly criticized assertive secularism during his first visit to the Vatican as president in December 2007.[164] In the same speech, he attached importance to France's Catholic roots, using a conservative rightist discourse.[165] A month later, Sarkozy visited Saudi Arabia, where he stressed the importance of religion for civilization and human life.[166] That created a huge reaction in France organized by several associations, particularly Freemasons and Freethinkers.[167] The debate provoked by Sarkozy shows that the tension between the assertive secularist leftists and conservative rightists in France may always intensify, though it has been postponed because both sides preferred to take care of the "headscarf question" first.

CONCLUSION

The French state, unlike the United States, has pursued exclusionary policies toward religion, particularly in schools. Its policies toward Muslims, including the one regarding headscarves, is a reflection of this general policy tendency. These restrictive policies are the result of the struggles between dominant assertive secularists and challenging passive secularists. Although the passive secularists failed to prevent the ban on headscarves, they had succeeded in resisting it for fifteen

---

[163] Klausen 2005, 176.
[164] "La République a besoin de croyants, dit Sarkozy," *Le Monde*, December 21, 2007.
[165] "L'intérêt de la République, c'est qu'il y ait beaucoup d'hommes qui espèrent," *Le Monde*, December 21, 2007.
[166] "Sarkozy ramène l'Eglise dans l'Etat," *Libération*, January 16, 2008.
[167] Marie-France Etchegoin, "Francs-maçons en colère," *Le Nouvel Observateur*, February 14, 2008, no. 2258.

years. State policies toward religion in France have been less restrictive than those in Turkey, despite the fact that assertive secularism has been dominant in both countries. The major reason for this distinction is the democratic regime in France, which has allowed the critics to oppose assertive secularist policies, and the semiauthoritarian regime in Turkey, which has limited resistance against assertive secularism.

Assertive secularism in France has been part of a larger French republican project, which has aimed to create a homogeneous national identity and a secular public sphere. Several processes, from globalization to the EU integration, as well as recently growing religions, especially Islam, have challenged this project and promoted multiculturalism. The assertive secularists have responded to these challenges with exclusionary policies, including those on Islam and 173 "dangerous cults." Certain old friends of the assertive secularists, such as the League of Education, have opposed those policies and embraced passive secularism. Some old enemies, such as certain rightists, however, have allied with the assertive secularists due to their worries about the immigrants and Islam. This alliance finally resulted in popular and political support for the ban on wearing headscarves in public schools. Yet there are still tensions between assertive secularist leftists and conservative Catholic rightists. For example, the assertive secularists criticized the official funeral of former president François Mitterrand in the Notre Dame Cathedral in January 1996 and the official order to lower flags in France to half-staff due to the death of Pope John Paul II in April 2005.[168] The recent debates on Sarkozy's criticisms of assertive secularism and appreciation of religion are another example of this ongoing tension.

Paradoxically, Islamophobia led many rightists to embrace certain discourses and policies of assertive secularism that they had strongly opposed. That seems similar to the American Protestants' use of separationist principles and policies, such as the Blaine Amendments, against the rising Catholic minority, as explained in Chapter 3. Nevertheless, the French Right's strategic coalition with the assertive secularists on the headscarf issue does not undermine the role of ideology in the public policy-making process. In contrast, it shows that ideology, at least as a constraining factor, plays an important role in shaping

---

[168] Chadwick 2000a, 4; Jeanneney 2004; Laurence and Vaisse 2006, 141.

actors' preferences and strategies. First, despite its instrumental use of the assertive secularist ideology, the French Right's reaction against headscarves is still ideological because it is based on certain negative views on immigrants and Islam, rather than some material interests. Second, there have been Islamophobic and anti-immigrant groups in other Western European countries too. However, Islamophobics and anti-immigrants in these countries have had neither a useful ideological discourse nor an ideologically driven ally (comparable to assertive secularism/secularists in France). That is why they have been unable to impose radically restrictive policies toward Muslims, such as a ban on students' wearing headscarves, in other Western European countries. Finally, the main opponents of the ban on the headscarf in France were multiculturalist individuals and groups. These individuals and institutions were mostly non-Muslim actors, who had no institutional or personal interest in defending the freedom to wear headscarves. They defended this freedom because of their adoption of passive secularist ideology, instead of material interests.

If French state polices have been shaped by the dominance of assertive secularism, then we need to ask why and how assertive secularism became dominant in France. Chapter 5 answers this question through an historical analysis.

5

The War of Two Frances and the Rise of Assertive Secularism (1789–1989)

Throughout medieval times, the Catholic Church was a dominant sociopolitical power in Western and Central Europe. France had special status in this situation as the *fille aînée de l'Eglise* (elder daughter of the Church).[1] Then, assertive secularism became the dominant ideology in such a Catholic country. The proponents and opponents of assertive secularism have different perspectives to explain this puzzle as Emile Poulat notes: "Our secularism has one history and two memories."[2] Beyond this ideological division there are two main approaches to the history of secularism in France. Baubérot attaches importance to continuity in his analysis. For him, the secularization of the French state was a gradual process. He defines the postrevolutionary period (1789–1806) as the first threshold of political secularization and the early Third Republic's secularization reforms (1881–1905) as the second threshold.[3] Pena-Ruiz criticizes Baubérot's process-oriented argument and stresses that there were several moments of back and forth, rather than continuity in the French history of secularism. Pena-Ruiz emphasizes the emergence of the secular state in 1795 and the return

---

[1] "During long centuries, the situation [in France] was relatively simple: the subjects were adopting the religion of the sovereign, the 'Most Christian King.'" Messner 2003, 77. Yet there was still a tension between *gallicanisme*, i.e., supporting the autonomy of the state and national church from the Vatican, and *ultramontanisme*, i.e., strict submission to the pope, in France. Troper 2000, 1273.

[2] Poulat 2003, 18.

[3] Baubérot 2004a, 8; Baubérot 1999.

to close church-state relations by the Concordat of 1801. According to his perspective, secularization reforms (1881–1905) meant a rupture from the Catholic past, rather than a result of an ongoing process.[4]

These two actually are not mutually exclusive perspectives. While examining the ideological dominance of assertive secularism, I use the change-based approach and take the early Third Republic (1875–1905) as the critical juncture. Catholicism was influential in the French polity before the Third Republic, while assertive secularism became dominant afterward. The continuity-based approach is also important for two points. First, the revolutionary period (1789–1801) constituted the ideological predecessor of the secular state building in the early Third Republic. Second, the establishment of assertive secularism did not mean the end of a two-century-long debate on state-religion relations in France. The struggle between the anticlerical assertive secularists and conservative Catholics has continued.

As explained in Chapters 1 and 3, the dominance of either assertive or passive secularism in a country is shaped by certain conditions and relations in the secular state-building period. The conditions in the French founding period were different from those in the United States and were relatively similar to those in Turkey. This historical comparison explains ideological comparisons among these three states. The existence of an *ancien régime* based on the cooperation between the monarchy and hegemonic Catholicism led to the emergence of assertive secularism in France and its dominance in the early Third Republic. The fact that the monarchy and Catholic establishment were supporting each other played an important role in the popularity of anticlericalism among the political opponents, particularly the republican elite.[5] Especially because several regime changes occurred back and forth between French monarchies and republics, the republicans faced a peril of the reestablishment of the monarchy and Catholicism, at least until the mid-twentieth century. That was an important reason that the assertive secularists were concerned about Catholicism's public influence and hence opposed its public visibility. Additionally, because Catholicism was the hegemonic religion in

---

[4] Pena-Ruiz 2003, 320–1.
[5] Tocqueville 1988 [1858], esp. 47; Weill 2004 [1929], 25, 33; Ricoeur 1998, 127–32; Englund 1992, 349–59; Skocpol and Kestnbaum 1990, 26.

France, the conservative Catholics did not see church-state separation as beneficial to them, and so they opposed it. Besides the lack of religious diversity, the organizational structure of the Catholic Church also played an important role in this issue. The church had a hierarchical structure that supported a monolithic voice against church-state separation.

In this regard, from the eighteenth to the mid-twentieth centuries, secular and Catholic thought in France were opposed to each other and had almost no common ground. French *Lumières* was different from "the Enlightenment as it appeared in Britain or America ... where religion, whether as dogma or as institution, was not the paramount enemy."[6] Since that time, the French progressive elite have preserved the idea that modernity and religion are incompatible and, therefore, the latter should be excluded from the public sphere.[7] In France, unlike America, republicanism and disestablishment emerged as almost entirely anticlerical views, without having any religious justification. Jean-Jacques Rousseau, the father of the republican idea of the general will,[8] for example, was strongly critical of Catholicism, arguing that it "is so apparently bad that it is a waste of time to enjoy demonstrating its badness."[9] He even proposed creating a "civil religion" because he regarded the Catholic Church as the enemy of the republican project. Voltaire was another critic of the Catholic Church. From 1814 to 1824, 1,598,000 copies of Voltaire's books were printed, while Rousseau's books reached 480,500 copies.[10] Beyond their influence over the elite, Rousseau and Voltaire's writings helped the emergence of an "anticlerical popular culture."[11] This ideological polarization led to the two-century-long conflict between secular republicans and conservative Catholics, which ultimately resulted in the dominance of assertive secularism in France.

---

[6] Himmelfarb 2003, 18. See also Baubérot and Mathieu 2002, 46–53; Gaillard 2004, 104; Zylberberg 1995, 38; Sewell 1985.

[7] See Baubérot 2004e, 441.

[8] In the words of Rousseau, "There is often a great difference between the will of all and the general will; the general will studies only the common interest while the will of all studies private interest, and is indeed no more than the sum of individual desires." Rousseau n.d. [1762], 72.

[9] Rousseau 2001 [1762], 174.

[10] Weill 2004 [1929], 55.

[11] Baubérot and Mathieu 2002, 157.

I will first analyze the early periods of this conflict – the Revolutionary period, 1789–1801, and the reestablishment of Catholicism, 1801–1870. Then, I will examine the dominance of assertive secularism in the early Third Republic. Finally, I will survey the moderation of assertive secularist policies in the aftermath of World War II.

THE REPUBLICANS AND MONARCHISTS: THE ROOTS OF ASSERTIVE SECULARISM

From the Revolution to the Concordat (1789–1801)

"In the France of the ancien régime, [the Catholic Church] sanctified the king, and the king defended the ancestral faith of the country as well as the worldly privileges of its ministers."[12] The French Revolution of 1789 abolished the monarchy and ended the Catholic Church's close engagement with the state.[13] It could not establish a stable alternative, and France therefore faced the chaos of state-religion relations for more than a decade.

In July 1790, the National Assembly passed the Civil Constitution of the Clergy, which sought to establish a national church independent of the pope. It required that church members elect bishops and priests, who would be paid by the state and take an oath of loyalty to the state and nation. That forced the priests to choose to be loyal to either the state or the pope.[14] Although few bishops and about half of the clergy took the oath, others refused to submit their loyalty to the state. Many of them fled France; the rest "were tracked down and imprisoned, or met in secret."[15] During this period, the state expropriated the lands of the church and guillotined about three thousand priests.[16] According to Tocqueville, the anti-Catholic mood of the revolution was based on the church's connection to the *ancien régime*: "It was far less as a religious faith than as a political institution that Christianity provoked

---

[12] Merrick 1990, 2. See also Furet 1992, esp. 3–40.
[13] For a classical analysis of the Revolution, see Burke 1987 [1790].
[14] Bedouelle and Costa 1998, 23; Haarscher 2004, 11; Le Tourneau 2000, 70; Laot 1998, 40.
[15] Gunn 2004, 435–6.
[16] Baubérot 2004a, 14; Emile Poulat, "Séparation de l'Eglise et de l'Etat en France: De la Révolution à 1905," *Le Monde des Religions*, no. 8, November–December 2004, 14.

these violent attacks. The Church was hated ... not because there was no room for the Church in the new world that was in the making, but because it occupied the most powerful, most privileged position in the old order that was now to be swept away."[17]

The French Constitution of 1791 declared religious liberty.[18] A year later, the assembly passed the law that made divorce legal.[19] Nevertheless, many revolutionary leaders kept regarding Catholicism and other organized religions as a threat to their republican revolution. Therefore, they banned religious ceremonies and manifestations in the public sphere.[20] Moreover, some revolutionaries constructed the Cult of Reason as an atheistic religion. Robespierre initiated a deistic religion, the Cult of the Supreme Being.[21] The revolutionaries were obviously affected by Rousseau's idea of civic religion, as well as his notion of the general will. Rousseau's influence can be traced in the Declaration of the Rights of Man and of the Citizen of 1789 (especially Art. 1 and 6). To show their respect, the postrevolution rulers moved Rousseau's remains across from the tomb of Voltaire in the Panthéon, the burial places of French national heroes.

In 1795, the first secular French state was declared. According to the new constitution, the state shall not recognize or subsidize any religions.[22] The enmity between the French Republic and Catholicism went beyond the French borders. French troops captured the pope in 1798, brought him to Southern France, and kept him there until his death.[23] The extreme anticlericalism of the French state largely continued until the Concordat of 1801.

The period from the revolution to the concordat experienced the polarization between the anticlericals and conservative Catholics. This period was also crucial for the development of the French secular legal system. The secular republic of 1795 was the historical predecessor of

---

[17] Tocqueville 1983 [1858], 6–7. Tocqueville also notes that the anticlerical revolutionaries "were convinced that in order to overthrow the institutions of the existing social order they must begin by destroying of the Church, on which these were modeled and from which, indeed, they derived." Ibid., 151.

[18] Durand-Prinborgne 2004, 24.

[19] Laot 1998, 44.

[20] Le Tourneau 2000, 75; Gunn 2004, 438.

[21] Fehér 1990.

[22] Zuber 2005, 109–10; Durand-Prinborgne 2004, 24.

[23] Warner 2000, 3.

the secular Third Republic. The Law of 1905, for example, referred to the Constitution of 1795.[24] Moreover, the French Constitutions of 1946 and 1958 (the current one) explicitly refer to the Declaration of the Rights of Man and of the Citizen as a valid legal document for contemporary France.

THE MONARCHISTS AND REPUBLICANS: THE REESTABLISHMENT OF CATHOLICISM

From the Concordat to the Third Republic (1801–1870)

On July 15, 1801, Napoleon Bonaparte (1769–1821) signed the concordat with Pope Pius VII (1740–1823). According to the concordat, which legally lasted until 1905, the French state recognized Catholicism as the religion of the majority of the French people. The concordat also institutionalized the French state's authority over the clergy. The state would pay clergy salaries and nominate the bishops. Moreover, the clergy would take an oath of allegiance to the state. In addition, the church gave up all claims to its confiscated lands. The concordat led to a *modus vivendi* between the anticlericals and conservative Catholics.[25] Despite the pope's protest, the French state also issued the Organic Laws in order to regulate its relations with Protestants in 1802 and with Jews in 1808.[26]

In 1814, following the defeat of Napoleon and the restoration of the Bourbon monarchy, the French state revised the concordat. It reestablished Catholicism as the state religion, while still emphasizing freedom of religion.[27] That implied the swing of the pendulum from disestablishment toward establishment. A legal result of this change was the prohibition of divorce again in 1816.[28] The status of the Catholic Church kept changing regarding the dynamic balance of power in France. In 1830, a new act between the state and church redefined Catholicism as the only "religion of the majority of the French people."[29]

[24] Durand-Prinborgne 2004, 24.
[25] Debré 2004, 15.
[26] Bedouelle and Costa 1998, 25; Durand-Prinborgne 2004, 25.
[27] Poulat 1987, 191; Durand-Prinborgne 2004, 25.
[28] Laot 1998, 39.
[29] Poulat 1987, 191.

In the aftermath of the 1848 Revolution, the Catholic Church secured its control over education. The Falloux Law of March 15, 1850, removed the restrictions on private education, "which had existed since the creation of the University by Napoleon" in 1806.[30] It allowed religious groups, especially the church, to open private parochial schools.[31] The church was keen to preserve its privileges, particularly its influence over the public school system. In 1864, Pope Pius IX (1792–1878) declared a list of eighty wrong and condemned opinions – the *Syllabus of Errors*. The list included the notion that the church and the state should be separate and the idea that everybody should have freedom of choice among religions with respect to his or her reason.[32]

During this period, the anticlericals tied themselves to republicanism whereas the conservative Catholics defended monarchy. Because republicanism was not the dominant regime in France at the time – except the short-lived Second Republic (1848–1852) – Catholicism preserved its privileged position in French sociopolitical life. Anticlerical republicanism, therefore, remained an opposition ideology. Yet the church's alliance with the monarchy, which was a political asset in the early and mid-nineteenth century, turned into a political liability with the foundation of the Third Republic.

THE SECULARISTS AND CONSERVATIVES: THE DOMINANCE OF ASSERTIVE SECULARISM

From the Third Republic to the Vichy Regime (1870–1940)

France's defeat by Prussia in the 1870–1871 War marked the end of the Second French Empire. The Third Republic, therefore, was declared in 1870. The adoption of the Constitutional Laws in 1875 particularly meant the beginning of a critical period of three decades, which would consolidate assertive secularism. During this period, the republicans used the term *laïcité* as the core of their anticlerical agenda, which aimed to exclude Catholicism, in particular, and religion, in

---

[30] Anderson 1970, 51.
[31] Debré 2004, 16.
[32] Laot 1998, 68.

general, from the public sphere.[33] This period implied a new phase in the ongoing "war of two Frances."[34] One France was the inheritor of the 1789 Revolution's values. It was republican, anticlerical, and secularist. It was represented by leftist (Republican, Socialist, Radical) parties, some civic associations (Freemasons, Freethinkers, League of Education),[35] and religious minorities (Protestants[36] and Jews).[37] The other France was tied to the *ancien régime*. It was monarchist and clerical, in the sense of supporting restoration of monarchy and preservation of the Catholic establishment. It included the Catholic Church, conservative media, and conservative politicians.[38]

In the mid-1870s, French society was overwhelmingly Catholic: "35,387,703 of the 36,000,000 people in France were listed in the official census as Catholics. The rest declared themselves Protestants (something under 600,000), Jews (50,000), or freethinkers (80,000)."[39] The number of the Catholic clergy was more than fifty-five thousand.[40] The conservative Catholics had number but not political organization. In 1879, for example, they succeeded in collecting 1,775,000 signatures for a petition against certain secularization laws. Yet they failed to stop those laws.[41] The Catholics were also trying to use the print media. In 1882, several conservative newspapers called for a popular resistance, even rebellion, against secularist policies.[42] In 1896, the total sale of conservative Catholic press was about half a million, including the national weekly *Le Pèlerin* (110,000), the national newspaper *La Croix* (180,000), and *La Croix*'s more than a hundred local weekly editions.[43] Nevertheless, the Catholic press "had a negligible political impact." It "could not swing public opinion

---

[33] Baubérot 2004d, 13–14.

[34] Poulat 1987.

[35] Larkin 1973, 42–6; Larkin 2002, 119–27; Franchi 1994, 216; Delasselle 2005, 123–4; Martin 2005.

[36] The Protestant minority, including both subsidized and nonsubsidized denominations, largely supported church-state separation in France assuming that they had a "stronger tradition of self-sufficiency than Catholicism." Larkin 1973, 111.

[37] Nord 1995.

[38] Wieviorka 1995, 85; Ducomte 2001, 3.

[39] Weber 1976, 339.

[40] Ibid.

[41] Kalyvas 1996, 124.

[42] Ozouf 1982, 80.

[43] Larkin 1973, 67.

away from the *laïques* at elections and it failed to curb anti-Catholic sentiment just before the separation."[44]

Similarly, the conservative Catholics were not effective in party politics or, therefore, in parliament. Their political inefficiency was mainly caused by the lack of unification. The lay Catholic organizations had internal conflicts.[45] The Catholic Church did not play the leading role to initiate or support Catholic civic associations and political parties. The Catholic Church was in a political apathy due to the perception that the Republic would not last long.[46] As Kalyvas emphasizes, the restoration of the monarchy "had looked certain until 1876, an extremely good bet until January 1879, and a serious possibility until roughly 1891."[47] Historically, France did not have good experiences of republicanism. The Third Republic "was a regime associated at best with the instability of the Second Republic and at worst with the Jacobinist terror of the First Republic." Theoretically, "the Republic was viewed as a regime … incompatible with large countries, fit only microstates," because the only republics in Europe at that time were Switzerland, Andorra, and San Marino.[48] For these reasons, the church focused on trying to replace the republic with a new monarchy, instead of supporting conservative politicians to compete with the secularists in the elections.

The negative results of this strategy were twofold. The first was the failure of conservative Catholic politicians, who experienced eleven electoral defeats until World War I.[49] The votes for conservatives declined from 3.4 million in 1889 to 1.3 million in 1893 and to 0.8 million in 1914.[50] Significant numbers of peasants were supporting the anticlerical republican politicians due to their "fear of a restoration of the Ancien Régime and its servitudes" (e.g., feudal dues such as tithes and forced labor).[51] The second result was a rising anticlericalism among the republicans. Due to its continuing alliance with

---

[44] Bosworth 1962, 30.
[45] Ibid., 26–8.
[46] Ibid., 28, 31.
[47] Kalyvas 1996, 141.
[48] Ibid., 139n27.
[49] Ibid., 144.
[50] Bosworth 1962, 27.
[51] Weber 1976, 250. See also Gould 1999, 59.

the monarchists, the church remained as a common enemy of the republicans.[52] In 1877, the republican leader Léon Gambetta formalized this enmity with his famous slogan: "*le cléricalisme, voilà l'ennemi!*" (the clericalism; here is the enemy!)[53]

The republican leaders had diverse party affiliations and personal beliefs. Some were atheists and completely against religion, while many others were agnostics, deists, Protestants, or nonobservant Catholics.[54] It was anticlericalism that kept them together like glue.[55] Additionally, several of them were influenced by the positivism of Auguste Comte.[56] By 1879, the republicans dominated both the Senate and the Chamber of Deputies. This allowed them to pass certain anticlerical laws. They primarily targeted the school system, attempting to shape the worldviews of future generations. The pope at the time, Leo XIII (1810–1903), was also attaching importance to education: "The school is the battlefield where it will be decided if the society will remain Christian or not."[57]

For the secularists, the competing public and Catholic schools were teaching two opposite value systems forming "*deux jeunesses*" (two youths) – as republican Prime Minister René Waldeck-Rousseau would call it later in 1900.[58] When they initiated the secularization policies, about a third of students in France were attending Catholic schools.[59] From a republican perspective,

[t]his meant that a large percentage of the future generation was not only cut off from contact with the principles of Republican virtue but was left to the mercy of "irrationalist" Christian concepts such as Revelation. Furthermore, since the Church was known to be largely monarchist in sympathy, it was suspected that these children would emerge as bigoted reactionaries, all straining to vote for the monarchists as soon as they were old enough. So the battle of Church and State under the Third Republic was largely one for intellectual control of the new generation. [60]

---

[52] Bergounioux 1995, 19.
[53] Quoted by Ozouf 1982, 50.
[54] Winock 2004, 45. E.g., Jules Ferry was a Protestant, and Emile Combes was a "spiritualist." Haarscher 2004, 74.
[55] Nicolet 1982, 249–77; Kalyvas 1996, 122.
[56] Winock 2004, 45.
[57] Quoted by Haarscher 2004, 25. See also Mayeur 2004.
[58] Quoted by Anderson 1970, 54.
[59] Ozouf 1982, 233–4.
[60] Larkin 1973, 23–4.

The League of Education, which had been founded by Freemason Jean Macé in 1866, provided the republican politicians with significant support to secularize the national school system.[61] In 1872, the league submitted a petition with 847,000 signatures to parliament to support reformation of elementary education as compulsory and free. The petition would eventually contain 1,267,267 signatures.[62]

It was republican Jules Ferry who promoted "free, obligatory, and secular" education through several new laws. From 1879 to 1885, Ferry undertook several cabinet positions, including premiership and ministry of public education. He appointed Ferdinand Buisson as the director of primary education, who would hold the position for seventeen years. Buisson had led an official expedition to the United States in 1876 to examine the primary school system. He was impressed by the free, partly obligatory, and nondenominational American public schools as documented by the 677-page report he edited.[63] Beyond his administrative position, Buisson played a crucial role in the secularization of the French school system as a philosopher of *laïcité*, drafter of important secularization laws, and the president of the League of Education.[64]

Ferry initiated several secularization reforms. In 1881, the public schools became free. In the following year, primary education became obligatory for boys and girls from ages six to thirteen. Moreover, religious instruction was replaced by courses on morality, which made the curricula fully secular in the primary schools. Ferry accommodated students' need for religious instruction by making Thursday (which would later be replaced by Wednesday) a school-free day, when students could attend religious courses in churches.[65] Reforms continued after Ferry. In 1886, the clergy members were no longer allowed to teach in public schools.[66] The law directly targeted fifteen thousand clerical teachers.[67] In addition to these educational reforms, the

---

[61] Brechon 1995, 66n9.
[62] Ozouf 1982, 229; Baubérot 1999, 107.
[63] Buisson 1878, esp. 1–20, 669–77.
[64] Buisson 2007 [1911]; Kahn 2005, 50–2.
[65] Cabanel 2005a, 243–7; Art. 2 of the law no. 11, 696; March 8, 1882.
[66] Debré 2004, 17; Durand-Prinborgne 2004, 26, 42; Baubérot 2004c, 149; Laot 1998, 43.
[67] Burdy 1995, 142.

TABLE 12. *Major Secularization Laws in France (1881–1889)*

The Law	The Reform
June 16, 1881	Primary education became free
March 28, 1882	Primary education became compulsory and secularized
July 27, 1884	Reestablishment of divorce
August 14, 1884	Abolishment of the prayer in parliamentary sessions
February 11, 1885	Secularization of hospitals
October 30, 1886	Secularization of public school personnel
July 15, 1889	Military service to the clergy became obligatory

Sources: Durand-Prinborgne 2004, 26, 42; Ducomte 2001, 27; Baubérot 2004c, 149.

secularists undertook certain policies to weaken religion's role in other public institutions. In 1884, for example, they abolished the recitation of a prayer at the beginning of parliamentary sessions.[68] The secularists imposed certain secularization reforms summarized in Table 12 and have succeeded in protecting them afterward.

The struggle between the secularist republicans and Catholic monarchists continued in the 1890s through public discussions such as the Dreyfus Affair. Alfred Dreyfus was a French military officer of Jewish origin. He was sentenced to imprisonment for life at Devil's Island for treason in 1894. Later, in 1898, it was discovered that much of the evidence against Dreyfus was forged and based on anti-Semitism. This discovery sharply divided the public between his supporters, largely republicans, and his opponents, mainly monarchists. Emile Zola, the republican novelist, published his famous open letter to the president – "J'Accuse." The new military court, however, covered up the forgery and sentenced Dreyfus with extenuating circumstances to ten years' imprisonment in 1899. Subsequently, the president pardoned him. Finally, it was revealed that the entire accusation was a conspiracy, and Dreyfus was exonerated in July 1906. The case resulted in the loss of credibility for the conservative forces, particularly for the Catholic Church and the army, and it empowered the public image of the republicans.[69]

---

[68] Durand-Prinborgne 2004, 26.
[69] Rebérioux 1975, 1–41; Larkin 1973, 70–9.

In addition to the Dreyfus Affair, their election victories embold-
ened the republicans for a second wave of secularization laws. They
passed the Law of Associations on July 1, 1901, which required all
religious associations to have state authorization. The law was particularly targeting Catholic orders such as the Jesuits.[70] In 1902, a
radical leftist, Emile Combes, became prime minister. Combes and
his cabinet members were Freemasons, as were a third of the deputies
and senators.[71] That was not an exceptional situation: "An estimated
40 percent of the republic's civilian ministers from 1877 to the out-
break of World War I were [masonic] lodge members."[72] According
to Maurice Larkin, Freemasonry was a symptom, not a cause, of
anticlericalism in France: "Masonic membership was generally a
means to an end: it was a form of solidarity which gave protection
and opportunities to men who shared a number of broad democratic
and secular assumptions. Its ideology was accepted because its basic
content corresponded with what most Radical freethinkers already
believed."[73]

Combes adamantly pursued anticlerical policies by strictly imple-
menting the Law of 1901 on associations. He initiated a new law on
July 7, 1904, that restricted all religious communities from provid-
ing education of any kind.[74] In his three-year term, Combes led the
closure of ten thousand Catholic schools and the expulsion of thirty
thousand members of Catholic orders, particularly Jesuits.[75] The
exclusion of the clergy from the school system resulted in their "mas-
sive exodus toward Belgium, the Catholic part of Switzerland, and
Italy."[76] France became a major source of Catholic missionary schools
worldwide because of the exiled clergy.[77] The secularist French rulers
generally tolerated, if not supported, Catholic missionaries abroad
because they were teaching the French language and spreading French

[70] Bosworth 1962, 88–90; Akan 2005, 124.
[71] Larkin 1973, 94–5.
[72] Nord 1995, 15.
[73] Larkin 1973, 94–5.
[74] In April 1904, the minister of justice withdrew crucifixes and religious emblems from
    the courtrooms.
[75] Cabanel and Durand 2005; Lalouette 2004, 66; Chanet 2004, 63 ; Baubérot 2004a,
    79–80.
[76] Burdy 1995, 143.
[77] Laurens 2004.

culture.[78] Even Gambetta had said that "anticlericalism was not an article of exportation."[79]

Ferry's and Combes's secularist policies had clear results in terms of the declining numbers of Catholic schools and teachers, as well as students in Catholic schools. In the 1876–1877 academic year, there were 51,657 secular (both public and private) and 19,890 religious (both public and private) schools. By 1906–1907, the number of secular schools increased to 78,444 while that of religious schools declined to 1,851. In the same period, the number of secular teachers increased from 65,811 to 153,078 whereas that of religious teachers declined from 46,684 to 7,387. Similarly, in that era, the number of students in secular schools increased from 3,027,560 to 5,357,812 and those in religious schools decreased from 1,841,527 to 227,213.[80]

A major political issue in 1904 was the parliamentary discussions about the proposals for a new law on church-state relations. The republicans had an internal disagreement about the content of the law. There were at least three different groups with distinct projects. The first group wanted an antireligious regime that would cause a socio-political de-Christianization. It included several Freethinker deputies, such as Maurice Allard. The second group was relatively less radical but clearly anticlerical. It wanted to dismantle the autonomy of the Catholic Church. It favored a system of concordat with a unilateral authority of the state over the church. Combes was the main supporter of this system. He wanted to keep Catholicism under state control because "the Church would be more dangerous separated than salaried."[81] That proposal was similar to what Turkey would adopt two decades later to keep Islam under state control.[82] The third group favored a law of church-state separation. It was less anticlerical than the two others. This group mainly comprised the leaders of the PS, such as Aristide Briand and Jean Jaurès.[83]

---

[78] Baubérot and Mathieu 2002, 274.
[79] Quoted by Poulat 1987, 142.
[80] Ozouf 1982, 233–4.
[81] Larkin 1973, 104. See also Cabanel 2005b.
[82] Baubérot 2000, 35–6.
[83] Cabanel 2004, 69–70; Kareh Tager, "100 ans de laïcité," *Le Monde des Religions*, no. 8, November–December 2004, 19.

In September 1904, Combes changed his position and declared his
support for church-state separation by giving his famous speech in
Auxerre.[84] In early 1905, however, he was forced to resign due to the
scandal of the *fiches* (cards). The conservative newspaper *Le Figaro*
revealed that the government was cooperating with the Freemasons
to record the religious and political views of the military officers
onto about twenty-five thousand cards. Their goal was to eliminate
observant Catholics from the ranks and to support the advance of the
republican secularist officers.[85] The scandal was a sign of an ongoing
discrimination against practicing Catholics in the French military and
civilian bureaucracy, which discouraged officers to attend masses.[86]

In late 1905, the plan of Briand and Jaurès prevailed, and the legislative bill was written in this direction. Despite the opposition of the
conservative Catholic parliamentarians, the bill was approved by a
majority in the Assembly (341 to 233) and the Senate (179 to 103).[87]
It was then promulgated by the president as law on December 9, 1905.
Several French scholars have defined the law as a policy of appeasement or even as a victory of liberalism and tolerance for two main
reasons.[88] First, the bill was written based on the moderate project of
Briand and Jaurès, instead of the radical alternatives. Second, the law
accommodates several aspect of religious life. For example, it attaches
importance to freedom of conscience and worship (Art. 1). It also
maintains chaplaincies to ensure the free exercise of worship in public
institutions, such as in schools, hospitals, and prisons (Art. 2).

Yet it is still an exaggeration to define the Law of 1905 as liberal
and tolerant.[89] The law directly targeted the Catholic Church at least
with respect to three major issues. First, it required all religious groups,
particularly the Catholics, to be registered by the state as *association*

---

[84] Merle 2005, 80–1; "Une fête locale, un discours nationale: 4 Septembre 1904,"
L'Yonne républicaine, November 9, 2004; Alain Gresh, "Apaiser la question religieuse
pour poser la question sociale: Aux origines des controverses sur la laïcité," *Le Monde
Diplomatique*, September 2003.

[85] Lalouette 2004, 67.

[86] Larkin 2002, esp. 71, 101.

[87] Larkin 1973, 144–5.

[88] Boyer 2004; Cabanel 2004, 70–1; Peiser 1995, 198; Baubérot 2004f, 235; Stasi
Commission, "Rapport au président de la République," December 11, 2003, 11,
http://lesrapports.ladocumentationfrancaise.fr/brp/034000725/0000.pdf.

[89] Gunn 2004, 465n201; Gunn 2004, 463–79.

cultuelles ("religious" associations), replacing their existing hierarchical organizations with a new bottom-up structure. With this requirement, the law was complementary to the Law of 1901, and both laws challenged the Catholic Church's "hierarchical structure by turning it into a congeries of locally organized and run parishes."[90] Second, the law banned the state funding of religion: "The Republic neither recognizes, nor salaries, nor subsidizes any religion" (Art. 2). That may sound like a simple church-state separation. Yet it was a unilateral abolishment of the concordat regime by removing the budget of the churches. As a result, forty-two thousand priests ceased to be paid.[91] That was, at least in the short run, a detrimental coup to the French Catholic Church. Last but not least, by the new law, churches and other types of religious buildings that were built by 1905 became public property (Art. 3–6, 12), except those built entirely by private funds from 1801 to 1905.[92] Religious communities would need state authorization to use their own buildings and the items inside them. Moreover, the state would record the inventory of all goods inside church buildings (Art. 3).[93] The implementation of this article created certain conflicts. When the state agents tried to enter the Catholic edifices to record the inventory, they frequently faced the protests of the clergy and local people. In several cases, the state used armed forces to enter the buildings. Physical resistance occurred in approximately five thousand out of sixty-three thousand parishes, where the recording took place.[94]

Moreover, the general tone of the law and several of its articles does not tolerate religions' public roles. The law prohibits religious symbols in public buildings with certain exceptions, such as the places of worship, cemeteries, and museums (Art. 28). It deliberately uses the words *culte* (61 times) and *cultuelles* (9 times), instead of *religion* (0 times) and *religieuse* (2 times). *Culte* means worship and rituals, and *cultuelle* implies something related to that. *Religion* and *religieuse*, however,

---

[90] Warner 2000, 66.
[91] Cabanel 2004, 70. See also Poulat 2000, 23. The state paid some pensions and transitional benefits to the clergy. Guerlac 1908, 275–6; Larkin 1973, 156–7.
[92] Larkin 1973, 152; Durand-Prinborgne 2004, 144.
[93] The Law of December 9, 1905, concerning the separation of the churches and the state, http://www.assemblee-nationale.fr/histoire/eglise-etat/sommaire.asp#loi, accessed on May 2, 2006.
[94] Winock 2004, 47, 49.

have broader meanings (similar to the meanings of the words *religion* and *religious* in English). With this emphasis, the law confines religions to the "sacred" (individual religiosity and collectivity for only worship and rituals), while discouraging their "profane" sociopolitical dimensions and impacts on the public sphere.[95] In the words of a current French top official in charge of *cultes*, "the word 'religion' (*religion*) has no place in French law." She adds, "*Le culte* involves three elements: the celebration of the *culte*, as in the mass; its buildings; and the teaching of its principles. That's all! Freedom of *culte* is limited to those three domains."[96]

The Catholic clergy and press, as well as Pope Pius X (1835–1914), were quick to condemn the law.[97] The new law particularly frustrated the church because it gave the state, including local administrations such as departments and communes, the ownership of all eighty-seven cathedrals, in addition to 40,197 parish churches and chapels of ease. The private individuals were given 688 churches and chapels. Only 2,318 such buildings were left to the religious associations.[98] Due to the Catholic reactions to the idea of renting the churches, parliament made a revision to allow them to use the churches free of charge in exchange for being partially responsible for the repair and maintenance of these buildings. Yet the law contained another major problem for Catholics. It gave the ownership of only 2,348 out of total 32,841 presbyteries, episcopal palaces, and seminaries to the religious associations. Almost all other such buildings were owned by the local authorities, who were eligible to rent or sell them to religious associations, or to use them in different ways.[99]

The legislative elections of 1906 were a major disappointment for conservative Catholics because the secularist republican parties increased their representation by sixty more seats in parliament, which largely meant that the Law of 1905 was endorsed by the voters.[100] Following the elections, the secularists made some legal changes to

[95] Portier 2002, 7n23; Cesari 1995, 171; Messner 2003, 4–5.
[96] Quoted by Bowen 2006, 17.
[97] Larkin 1973, 172.
[98] Ibid., 152–3.
[99] Ibid., 154–5.
[100] Winock 2004, 49; Guerlac 1908, 280.

accommodate the Catholic Church.[101] During World War I (1914–1918), they prioritized to unite the nation, rather than attack the conservative Catholics.[102] Nevertheless, they did not make a substantial compromise with the secularist agenda.[103] Throughout the rest of the Third Republic, assertive secularist policies largely persisted despite some electoral victories of pro-Catholic parties, such as the 1919 success of Bloc National.[104] In 1921, France resumed its diplomatic relations with the pope, which were broken off seventeen years prior.[105] Nevertheless, the Catholic Church preserved its general opposition to secularism throughout the Third Republic. The French Assembly of Cardinals and Bishops, for example, declared in March 1925 that "secularism in all spheres is fatal to the private and public good. Therefore the secularization laws are not laws."[106]

In sum, the early Third Republic (1875–1905) was the critical juncture in the history of secularism in France. It was the period when the dominance of Catholicism was replaced by assertive secularist ideology in the state structure, in particular, and in French public life, in general. Because education was the key domain of the ideological conflict in France, the secularists pursued aggressive policies against the clergy in the school system. The secularization of education became the main pillar of the ideological dominance of assertive secularism.

THE LEFTISTS AND RIGHTISTS: THE MODERATION OF ASSERTIVE SECULARIST POLICIES

From the Vichy Regime to the Muslim Question (1940–1989)

Conservative Catholics found an opportunity to challenge the secularists during the Vichy regime following the German invasion of

---

[101] Weil 2007, 21.
[102] Baubérot 2004d, 173.
[103] E.g., in March 1918, Cardinal Andrieu wrote a letter to Prime Minister Georges Clemenceau to stress that France was in a critical situation in several battlefields and a nationwide prayer was necessary. Clemenceau regarded the letter as an affront to secularism and did not even respond to it. Jeanneney 2004, 72–3. See also Bosworth 1962, 34.
[104] Warner 2000, 67.
[105] Debré 2004, 21.
[106] Quoted by Bedouelle and Costa 1998, 15. See also Papp 1998, 17.

1940. "Vichy, a self-declared 'Catholic' state, promised to eliminate Communism, Jews, Freemasons, and other rivals to Catholicism and authoritarianism, and restore Christian morals to public life."[107] Marshal Philippe Pétain, the Head of State of Vichy France, pursued certain pro-Catholic policies. For example, he maintained public funding to the Catholic schools and restored crucifixes in public schools and city halls. The Catholic newspapers, such as *La Croix*, welcomed these policies. The French Catholic Church condemned General Charles De Gaulle for his resistance to the Vichy regime.[108] The Vichy administration did not officially reestablish Catholicism and, in this regard, did not radically return to the pre-1905 concordat regime.

With the defeat of Germany in 1944, the Vichy regime collapsed. The Liberation government repealed the public funding of Catholic schools and removed the crucifixes from public buildings.[109] The French Catholic Church's support of the Vichy regime appeared to be a fatal mistake that damaged its credibility. The Liberation government, for example, asked for the "resignation of more than 30 of France's approximately 87 bishops for collaboration (the actual number dismissed was 7)."[110] Nevertheless, the reaction against the Church was moderated because many Catholics had been among the opponents of the Vichy regime. De Gaulle was also a practicing Catholic.[111] Following the collapse of the Vichy regime, the church tended to be less political and to focus on re-Christianizing the society. The church and its allies – conservative politicians – recognized that restoration of the monarchy or reestablishment of Catholicism was no longer possible.[112] In this regard, they ceased opposing republicanism and secularism.[113]

When secularism became a fundamental principle of the 1946 Constitution, the church and the conservatives, unlike their resistance to the Law of 1905, did not oppose it.[114] In November 1945, the French

[107] Warner 2000, 69. Se also Papp 1998, 145–75.
[108] Ognier 1994, 94, 254–65; Warner 2000, 69–70.
[109] Coq 2004, 101.
[110] Warner 2000, 128.
[111] Larkin 1973, 223.
[112] Warner 2000, 87.
[113] Gauchet 1998, 98.
[114] Article 1 of the 1946 Constitution says, "France is an indivisible, secular, democratic and social Republic." The current constitution (ratified in 1958) also includes the same article.

Episcopate made a declaration about the distinction between accept-able and unacceptable aspects of secularism. Secularism that meant "the sovereign autonomy of the state in its temporal domain" was acceptable for the Episcopate. It also favored secularism that implied religious liberty. However, secularism "as a philosophical doctrine with a materialist and atheist conception of the world" in addition to "a governmental system that imposes that conception to the private life of officers, to public schools, and the entire nation" was unacceptable. Secularism was also notorious "if it signifies the will of the state not to submit to any superior morality and only recognize its own inter-est as a basis of its actions." Such a state, according to the Episcopate, would be atheistic and dictatorial. An ideal state should take "God-given natural law" as its legal basis.[115]

The Episcopate's statement was a reflection of a broader transfor-mation among conservative Catholics in France. The main conserva-tive political party of the Fourth Republic, Mouvement Républicain Populaire (Popular Republican Movement), also became "the first political party of Catholic inspiration in France not to arouse the sworn hostility of *laïques*."[116] This trend was further consolidated by Vatican II's endorsement of religious liberty (1962–1965).[117] As a result, con-servative Catholics contributed to the development of secularism in general as a hegemonic principle in France. The old conflict between the secularist republicans and antisecular Catholic monarchists turned into a struggle between leftists, who defended assertive secularist pol-icies to exclude religion from the public sphere, and the rightists, who resisted these policies and asked for more public visibility of religion.

The main fault line between the leftists and rightists was the pub-lic funding of private, mainly Catholic, schools. The Catholic Church and rightist politicians supported state subsidies to these schools. In 1951, the rightists succeeded in sustaining state scholarships for students attending private schools.[118] Following the foundation of the Fifth Republic, they reached their main goal through the Debré Law of 1959, which maintained public financial support for private

---

[115] The entire declaration was quoted by Ognier 1994, 272–5. Certain parts were also quoted by Bedouelle and Costa 1998, 12–13.
[116] Bosworth 1962, 250.
[117] Talin 2001, 204.
[118] Healey 1968, 29.

schools. According to the law, which is still valid, the state funds private schools if they sign specific contracts. The two types of contracts include some obligations, such as to use authorized books and prepare students for official degrees. The contracts provide private schools with a certain amount of freedom in terms of assigning optional prayer and religious instruction.[119] The Guermeur Law of 1977 reinforced public financing of private schools.[120] These legal reforms meant "the swing of the pendulum back toward a greater tolerance of Catholic schools."[121]

In the early 1990s, of all students in France, 17 percent were attending private schools, and 33 percent attended these schools at least for some time during their education.[122] About 95 percent of the private schools were Catholic schools.[123] The state funding of these schools was debated from the mid-1980s to the mid-1990s. In 1984, Alain Savary, the minister of education in the PS government, initiated a project of unified education by cutting the funding of private schools. The leftists supported the project with the slogan "public money to public schools; private money to private schools."[124] For the opponents of the project, however, families who sent their children to private schools should not be penalized by paying both the tax and the tuition.[125] They included not only the pro-Catholic Right but also those who thought that the Catholic schools provided a high quality of education.[126] They staged street protests against the Savary project. The French Catholic Church also actively supported these demonstrations. The protest in Versailles in March 1984 included half a million people, while the larger one in Paris in June brought together about 1.5 million people. As a result of the relentless popular opposition, Prime Minister Pierre Mauroy resigned, and President François Mitterrand (1916–1996) declared the repeal of the Savary Bill.[127]

---

[119] The Debré Law of December 31, 1959, no. 59–1557, http://www.assemblee-nationale.fr/histoire/loidebre/sommaire.asp, accessed on May 2, 2006.
[120] Conseil d'Etat 2004, 334.
[121] Bosworth 1962, 282.
[122] Burdy and Marcou 1995, 10.
[123] Beattie 2000, 197.
[124] Pietri 1998, 78.
[125] Peiser 1995, 198, 206.
[126] Brechon 1995, 68; Francis 1992, 799.
[127] Dereymez 1995, 235; Coq 2004, 101–2; Baubérot 2004a, 113.

In 1993, Bayrou was the minister of education in the government of the rightist UDF. He initiated an opposite project aiming to enlarge the public funding of private schools. Bayrou's project also resulted in several street protests, organized this time by the leftists. In January 1994, about one million protesters filled the streets of Paris.[128] Later, the Constitutional Court declared the bill on the project to be unconstitutional, referring to the Preamble of the 1946 Constitution: "The provision of free, public and secular education at all levels is a duty of the State."[129] Thus the government abandoned the bill.[130]

After the failure of the Savary and Bayrou projects, the leftists and rightists recognized a *modus vivendi* based on a certain amount of public funding of private, mainly Catholic, schools, which signed contracts with the state. The rising public visibility of the Muslim minority also motivated the leftists and rightists to end their school battle.[131] Several leftists and rightists cooperated in the late 1990s and the early 2000s to ban Muslim headscarves, while temporarily disregarding points of disagreements between themselves as I explained in Chapter 4.

CONCLUSION

Assertive secularism became the dominant ideology in France as a result of a long-lasting conflict between the anticlerical secularists and conservative Catholics. These two forces regarded each other as enemies and perceived their struggle as a zero-sum game. They established either secular republics or Catholic monarchies through several back and forth regime changes from the French Revolution to the Fourth Republic. Throughout this conflict, the restoration of the *ancien régime* referring to the marriage of the monarchy and Catholic hegemony was a menace for the anticlerical republicans and an objective for the conservative Catholics. Although the conservatives gave up the idea of reestablishing the monarchy and Catholicism following World War II, they have still opposed the dominant assertive secularism in France.

---

[128] Brechon 1995, 68.
[129] The French Constitutional Court, January 13, 1994; no. 93–329 DC.
[130] Laot 1998, 134; Safran 2003b, 71.
[131] Mathy 2000, 109–10.

The struggle between the anticlericals and conservatives in France was primarily ideological. The state's economic gains, partly achieved by confiscating church properties during the early Third Republic, were very limited.[132] As Seymour Lipset and Stein Rokkan rightly emphasize, in France, as in many other European countries, church-state struggles primarily focused on ideational, rather than material, concerns: "It's true that the status of church properties and the financing of religious activities were the subjects of violent controversy, but the fundamental issue was one of morals, of the control of community norms." Therefore, "the fundamental issue between Church and State focused on the *control of education*."[133]

The French experience was sharply different from that of the United States, where secularism was a product of an overlapping consensus between secular and religious groups. This historical distinction explains opposite ideological developments and public policy orientations in the two cases. Parallel historical trajectories point to similar ideologies and policies in France and Turkey. Yet state policies in France have been relatively less exclusionary toward religion than those in Turkey. The main reason is that assertive secularism in France was established under a multiparty democracy and has had substantial popular support, while that in Turkey was brought about by single-party rule and has been preserved by the authoritarian military and judiciary against democratically elected politicians' demand for freedom to the public visibility of religion as elaborated in Chapters 6 and 7.

---

[132] It was only 200 million francs according to Baubérot 2004a, 81.
[133] Lipset and Rokkan 1967, 15 (emphasis in original). See also Gould 1999.

PART III

TURKEY

6

Assertive Secularism and the Islamic Challenge
(1997–2008)

On February 28, 1997, Turkey's National Security Council (MGK), consisting of President Süleyman Demirel, Prime Minister Necmettin Erbakan, three ministers, and six generals, had its monthly meeting. This particular summit resulted in a "soft" *coup d'état* against the premiership of Erbakan. The generals had already changed the security doctrine of the military by defining *irtica* (reactionism) as a primary national security threat similar to the Kurdish terrorist group Kurdistan Workers' Party (PKK). The generals succeeded in imposing this new doctrine on the civilian members of the MGK, in addition to forcing them to sign a program to fight *irtica*, which implicitly or explicitly included (1) the purge of bureaucrats suspected to be affiliated with Islamism and (2) the closure of the Qur'an courses and Imam-Hatip (Islamic) schools that taught students who did not finish the eighth grade.[1] The MGK's press declaration explains the rationale of the meeting by emphasizing that "secularism in Turkey is not only the assurance of political regime, but also ... a way of life."[2]

Following the MGK meeting, the generals continued to challenge the coalition government comprising Erbakan's Refah (Welfare) Party (RP) and Tansu Çiller's Doğru Yol (True Path) Party (DYP). The generals organized several briefings for the media and judiciary in

---

[1] See Appendix C.
[2] MGK, "Press Declaration," February 28, 1997, http://www.mgk.gov.tr/basinbildiri1997/28subat1997.htm.

order to explain the "reactionary threat to Turkey" and to emphasize
that they were willing and ready to use military force against such a
threat. The government resigned after a couple of months. The generals
were not alone in initiating the "February 28 process." They gained the
support of the Cumhuriyet Halk (Republican People's) Party (CHP),
Demokratik Sol (Democratic Left) Party (DSP), several members of the
judiciary, major media networks, and some civil society organizations.
During the February 28 process, about nine hundred military officers[3]
and several civil bureaucrats were expelled from their posts due to their
alleged Islamic ways of life; corporations run by conservative Muslims
were defined as "green capital" and discriminated against in governmental contracts and bids; wearing headscarves was strictly banned
in all educational institutions; and hundreds of Qur'an courses and
all secondary sections (grades 6–8) of the Imam-Hatip schools were
closed down.[4] The university admissions systems were changed to
make the admission of Imam-Hatip graduates almost impossible. New
restrictions were put over mosque construction, and existing mosques
were placed under stricter state control than before. Moreover, the
Constitutional Court dissolved the RP and banned Erbakan from politics for five years.[5] The young RP mayor of Istanbul, Recep Tayyip
Erdoğan, was the most likely candidate to succeed Erbakan. But he too
was sentenced to a ten-month imprisonment for reciting a poem,[6] which
resulted in his life-long ban from politics. The generals were confident
about the success and durability of their policies. In 1999, the Chief of
the Turkish General Staff, General Hüseyin Kıvrıkoğlu, declared that
the "February 28 process will continue a thousand years."[7]

[3] ASDER 2004; Arslan 2005a, 45–51.
[4] According to the MGK declaration on March 31, 2001, the number of Qur'an courses
closed down by the state reached 370, and the personnel of religious institutions
indicted was 12,071. "Kriz Aşılacak," *Milliyet*, March 31, 2001. See also Çetinkaya
2005.
[5] Kogacioglu 2004, 448–52.
[6] Erdoğan recited the following verses: "Minarets are our bayonets, domes are our hel-
mets, mosques are our barracks, believers are our soldiers" in one of his speeches.
In his defense, Erdoğan said that he recited the poem in a South East Anatolian city
to contribute to the (Turkish-Kurdish) solidarity. He also noted that the poem was
written by the founder of Turkish nationalism, Gökalp, and was published in a book
recommended by the ministry of education. Heper and Toktaş 2003, 169–73. Erdoğan
spent four months in prison.
[7] "İlk Kez Konuştu," *Sabah*, September 4, 1999.

Yet the February 28 process survived less than seven years. In 2001, Erdoğan and his followers founded the Adalet ve Kalkınma (AK) (Justice and Development) Party. In the national elections of November 3, 2002, the AK Party received 34.3 percent of the votes and became the ruling party with 363 of 550 seats in parliament. Three parties that ruled Turkey during the February 28 process, the DSP, Anavatan (Motherland) Party (ANAP), and Milliyetçi Hareket (Nationalist Action) Party (MHP), were left out of parliament by receiving only 1.2, 5.1, and 8.3 percent of the votes, respectively. The new parliament amended the constitution to make Erdoğan eligible again for public office. Erdoğan was elected to parliament and became the prime minister. In contrast to February 28 policies, the new parliament and cabinet included several politicians whose wives and daughters wore headscarves.[8] Moreover, parliament passed the seventh reform packet for adaptation to the EU norms, which included the reformation of the MGK, in August 2003. The packet changed the structure of the MGK, in terms of the appointment of a new civilian secretary general, removal of its influence within the state bureaucracy, and turning it into a completely advisory institution. This reform effectively ended the February 28 process, in terms of total military control over civilian politicians. Nevertheless, military involvement in politics has continued to a certain extent. In addition, certain policies imposed during the February 28 process are still effective, such as the ban on headscarves at universities and restrictions over Imam-Hatip schools and Qur'an courses.

Why has the Turkish state pursued policies toward religion, which have been much more exclusionary than those in the United States and even relatively more exclusionary than those in France? I argue that exclusionary policies in Turkey are products of dominant assertive secularist ideology and the semiauthoritarian role of the military and judiciary that limited the democratic opposition against these policies. The state-religion debate in Turkey occurs between two groups – the Kemalists and pro-Islamic conservatives. The Kemalists criticize the conservatives for not embracing secularism and for having a hidden

---

[8] Erdoğan is a graduate of the Imam-Hatip schools, and his wife wears a headscarf. His daughters and son could not pursue undergraduate and graduate education in Turkey and have attended American universities because his daughters have worn headscarves and his son was a graduate of the Imam-Hatip schools.

Islamist agenda. According to the conservatives, the Kemalists do not defend secularism; rather they defend an antireligious regime.[9] The debate between the Kemalists and conservatives is not simply a conflict between Islamism and antireligionism, but rather it is a discussion over the "true meaning and practice" of secularism. The Kemalists have defended assertive secularism, which aims to eliminate Islam, in particular, and religion, in general, from the public sphere, whereas the conservatives have tried to replace it with passive secularism, which allows the public visibility of religion.

I will first examine six state policies toward religion in schools already examined in chapters on the United States and France as the dependent variable. Then, I will examine the struggles between the assertive and passive secularists. Finally, I will trace the impact of these ideological conflicts on the public policy formation process, particularly on three controversial issues – headscarves, Imam-Hatip schools, and Qur'an courses.

THE TURKISH STATE'S POLICIES TOWARD RELIGION IN SCHOOLS

The Turkish state's policies toward religion, particularly in schools, have been exclusionary in comparison to the United States and even France as reflected in the following analysis.

Students' Religious Symbols

Following the February 28 process, wearing headscarves has been strictly banned in all public and private educational institutions, including K–12 schools and universities. This ban has covered all students, faculty, and staff members. This has been part of a general ban, which includes all civil servants and, in certain cases, is extended to citizens who want to visit public institutions, such as universities and military buildings.[10] I will elaborate on this issue later.

---

[9] The author's personal interviews with Turkish politicians and academics, Ankara and Istanbul, September 2004.

[10] Former President Necdet Sezer was disallowing women with headscarves to enter the Presidential Residence, including the wives of Erdoğan and other AK Party parliamentarians. When Erdoğan visited President Bush in January 2004, his wife, Emine Erdoğan,

Private Religious Education, Religious Instruction, and State Funding of Religious Schools

Since the closure of the *medreses* in 1924, private religious education of Islam has been prohibited in Turkey. Other religions have also had trouble in terms of religious education. The only theological school of the Greek Orthodox Church was closed down in 1972. Since that time the church's attempts to reopen the school have not been successful. Although this incident is linked to Greco-Turkish tensions, it is still a reflection of assertive secular state policies toward religion in Turkey.

The ban on private initiative to religious education and the societal demand for such an education led the state to pursue two policies: (1) it has provided obligatory religious instruction in public schools, and (2) it opened Qur'an courses, Imam-Hatip schools, and departments of theology. In its policies on religious instruction and public Islamic schools, the Turkish state does not seek to promote Islam. Instead, it aims at "[b]ureaucratizing religious functionaries and scholars so as to make them subservient to the state" and "controlling the legitimacy and representative capability of public religious discourses by defining a 'mainstream' Islam."[11]

Because private Islamic schools are not allowed in Turkey, Islamic movements have opened private secular schools, which have used the same curricula as secular public schools. These schools are still criticized by the assertive secularists because they are run by conservative Muslims. The state does not provide funding to these schools. In 2003, the AK Party government initiated a project to publicly fund the private school tuitions of ten thousand students from poor families. The project was blocked by the Council of State and then vetoed by President Ahmet Sezer, because they opposed the use of public money for private schools, some of which were run by Islamic movements. Due to financial problems and bureaucratic restrictions, the number of private schools has remained very limited; currently, only 1.9 percent of all students in Turkey attend private schools.[12]

---

was hosted at the White House. President Bush dropped in on Laura Bush's tea party to welcome Mrs. Erdoğan. That created a debate in Turkey on the opposite understandings and practices of secularism in the United States and Turkey.

[11] Pak 2004, 338.

[12] "Özel Okuldaki 50 bin Öğrenciye Devlet Desteği," *Zaman*, April 28, 2006.

Prayer and the Pledge

Organized prayer is not allowed in public or private schools in Turkey. Moreover, there are certain restrictions regarding students' private worship. A debate that occurred in May 2007 was a typical example of these restrictions. In a public school in Istanbul, a small group of female students were secretly recorded while praying (the Islamic worship *namaz*) in a discreet room outside of class hours. The assertive secularist media (including nine newspapers and five TV channels) covered the story as an illegal activity. The public prosecutor immediately started prosecution of the school principal and some teachers. The conservative media defended this voluntary prayer as part of the freedom of religious expression.[13]

In Turkey, students in all primary schools (grades 1–5) have to recite the following pledge every morning, which does not have any reference to God or religious values:

I am a Turk, I am trustworthy, I am hard working. My foremost principle: it is to defend my minors and to respect my elders, and to love my fatherland and my nation more than my self. My goal: it is to rise and to progress. O Atatürk the great! I swear that I will enduringly walk through the path you opened and to the target you showed. May my personal being be sacrificed to the being of the Turkish nation. How happy is the one who says: "I am a Turk."

The pledge is apparently a part of the state project of training students through secular nationalism.[14]

General Policy Trend toward Religion

The Turkish state's policies toward religion are inconsistent, if not contradictory.[15] On the one hand, the Turkish state pursues restrictive policies toward Islam. On the other hand, it provides Islamic instruction in public schools and operates public Islamic schools. Moreover, the state pays the salaries of the imams in mosques, who are all civil servants of the state's Directorate of Religious Affairs (Diyanet), though the construction and maintenance of mosques have been funded by

---

[13] "Namaz Düşmanlığına Tepki Yağdı," *Zaman*, June 1, 2007.
[14] For nationalist and statist philosophy of education in Turkey, see Çayır 2007.
[15] Selçuk 1999, esp. 48.

the people. As explained in Chapter 4, policy exceptions also exist in France toward the majority Catholicism, which is why some scholars define it as "catho-laïque."[16] These policies do not necessarily imply the Turkish state's positive attitude toward Islam for four reasons. First, as previously mentioned, the main rationale behind these institutions is not to support Islam, but rather it is to take Islam under state control.[17] The Diyanet, for example, controls all *vaaz*s (preaches before Friday prayer) and *hutbe*s (sermons during the Friday prayer) by even broadcasting the same *vaaz* in the mosques in an entire region through speakers, instead of having live imams, and asking the imams to choose their *hutbe*s from nationally standard books.[18] Second, through these institutions, the state wants to create an "individualized" version of Islam, which stays within one's own conscience or behind the walls of private homes and mosques, with almost no impact on the public sphere.[19] Third, the state confiscated the financial sources of the Islamic foundations in the founding period of the Republic and still controls these foundations. In exchange, at least, it has to pay imams' salaries. Last but not least, whenever Imam-Hatip schools, Qur'an courses, and even the Diyanet expand their impacts on society, the state intervenes to limit their capacity, despite the fact that these are also public institutions.

The Diyanet, therefore, remains a controversial institution. It plays an indispensable role in the assertive secularist agenda to keep Islam under control. That is why the Law of Political Parties forbade any political party program to propose the abolishment of the Diyanet.[20] Nevertheless, the assertive secularists also want to confine the Diyanet within certain limits, including restricting the number of imams. In 2003, the AK Party government wanted to hire fifteen thousand new imams because out of the 75,941 mosques in Turkey, 22,344 lacked imams.[21] The assertive secularists, however, resisted this new hiring through a

---

[16] Boyer 2005b, 46.
[17] Kara 2003, 92–106; Canatan 1997, 33–4; Keyder 2004, 69.
[18] Çakır and Bozan 2005, 34.
[19] Bozarslan 2004; Ulusoy 1999b.
[20] The 89th article of the Law of Political Parties; no. 2820.
[21] "İmam Ordusunun Gerekçesi İrtica," *Milliyet*, June 26, 2003. The number of staff in Diyanet reached 88,552 in 2004. Ali Bardakoglu, "Başyazı," *Diyanet*, March 2004, 1.

media campaign and succeeded in having it cancelled. They also aim to restrict the Diyanet's functions. An assertive secularist scholar lamented that although the Diyanet was formed as a tool to transmit secular ideology, it gradually evolved into an institution for proselytizing Islam.[22]

Alevis, an important popular basis of assertive secularism, are also critical of the Diyanet.[23] Because they do not have a homogeneous identification, it is difficult to assess the number of Alevis in Turkey. Three recent surveys have given the estimate of 10 percent for Alevis and 89 percent for Sunnis,[24] although several scholars have assessed the former as 15 to 20 percent. The Alevis generally criticize the Diyanet for favoring Sunni Islam.[25] Yet several Sunni intellectuals are also critical of the Diyanet for maintaining state authority over religion.[26]

In addition to the assertive secularist strategy to keep Islam under control, Turkish state policies are inconsistent because they are the product of the struggles between the dominant assertive secularists and challenging passive secularists.

ASSERTIVE AND PASSIVE SECULARISTS

During the cohabitation of Kemalist President Sezer and the conservative AK Party government from 2002 to 2007, the "true meaning" of secularism was frequently discussed. Sezer, as the main representative of assertive secularism, frequently stressed that secularism implied "separation of religious and this-worldly affairs," and, therefore, "religion should stay in its sacred place in individuals' conscience."[27] In his speech at the Military Academy, he even claimed that the state could intervene in "the individual faith and worship."[28] Prime Minister Erdoğan and the Speaker of Parliament, Bülent Arınç, defending passive secularism, have repeatedly emphasized that secularism is a guarantee of "freedom of religion and conscience."[29]

[22] Tanör 2001, 23–34.
[23] See Massicard 2005.
[24] Çarkoğlu and Toprak 2006, 38; Çarkoğlu and Toprak 2000, 139; "The Survey of *Milliyet* and Konda," *Milliyet*, March 21, 2007.
[25] Çakır and Bozan 2005, 270–82.
[26] Ali Bulaç, "Sistemin Hiyerarşisi ve 'Sünni Diyanet,'" *Zaman*, January 21, 2008.
[27] "Laiklik Özgürlük Demek," *Radikal*, February 6, 2004.
[28] "Gücün Yetmez Ahmet Bey," *Yeni Şafak*, April 14, 2006.
[29] "Laiklik'te anlaşamadılar," *Radikal*, February 6, 2006.

For assertive secularists, the twenty-fourth article of the constitution is the reference point: "No one shall be allowed to exploit ... religion ... for the purpose of maintaining personal or political interest or influence, or for even partially basing the social, economic, political, or legal fundamental order of the state on religious tenets."[30] Passive secularists, such as liberal law professor Mustafa Erdoğan, have criticized the article's statement of "exploiting religion" as too vague and that of "social and economic order of the state" as totalitarian.[31] Therefore, Erdoğan and Arınç have referred to the reason for the second article of the constitution, which notes that secularism "never means antireligionism" and "implies that each individual can be affiliated with any belief or denomination that he or she wants, can freely worship, and shall not be discriminated due to his or her religious belief."[32]

The assertive secularists, such as Sezer, have defined secularism as an official ideology and a way of life. For them, religious belief located in one's conscience should have no influence on this world.[33] The passive secularists, from Turgut Özal (1927–1993) to Erdoğan, have depicted secularism as a characteristic of the state, not of individuals, and have recognized that religion has implications beyond an individual's conscience.[34] Recently, Erdoğan declared that he could define himself as "a secular individual" in terms of "supporting the secular characteristic of the state," not in terms of believing in secularism as a sort of "religion."[35] In some countries, such as Belgium, secularism is considered "not as the basis of the state, but as one of the ideological components of society."[36] The Belgian state, therefore, funds the secularists among other religious groups.[37] Yet secularism in Belgium is one of several comprehensive doctrines, not the one officially recognized and imposed by the state on the people, as the assertive secularists envision doing in Turkey.

---

[30] Oktay Ekşi, "Erdoğan ve Laiklik ... ," *Hürriyet*, September 30, 2002.
[31] Mustafa Erdoğan, "Anayasa'nın 24. Maddesi ve Laiklik," *Zaman*, April 24, 2006.
[32] Arınç's interview with Mustafa Karaalioğlu, "Laiklik Tanımım Gerekçede Yazılı," *Yeni Şafak*, May 4, 2006. For Erdoğan, see "Anketlere Gore Barajı İki Parti Aşıyor; Üçüncüsü Sürpriz Olur," *Zaman*, May 5, 2006.
[33] "Laiklik Sosyal Barış İçin Şart," *Sabah*, February 6, 2005.
[34] Üstel 1995, 260; "Cami yerine Hastane Yapın," *Sabah*, June 14, 2004.
[35] "Erdoğan Soruları Yanıtladı," *Sabah*, May 15, 2007.
[36] Ducomte 2001, 41.
[37] Haarscher 2004, 51–3.

The debate on assertive and passive secularism has been the main pillar of the conflict between the Kemalists and conservatives.[38] The Kemalists have included the CHP, DSP, military generals, the majority of the high court members, the Association of Turkish Industrialists and Businessmen (TÜSİAD), and Doğan media group, including several newspapers (e.g, *Hürriyet* and *Milliyet*) and TV channels (e.g., Kanal D). The TÜSİAD and Doğan media group have supported a capitalist free market economy and, therefore, diverged from the Kemalist principle of economic statism. Nevertheless, they have defended the dominance of Kemalist assertive secularism, which aims to eliminate Islam from the public sphere. As Göle notes, Kemalism (*Kemalizm*) and Atatürkism (*Atatürkçülük*) are two different ideologies.[39] Kemalists are those who take Atatürk's six principles – secularism, nationalism, republicanism, statism, populism, and reformism – as unchangeable and nonnegotiable dogmas. The Atatürkists, however, reinterpret and update these principles in line with changing conditions as means to achieve the end – to reach the level of universal civilization.[40]

Kemalism is a sensitive issue in Turkey because there is a law (no. 5816) that criminalizes any criticisms of Atatürk as implemented in two recent well-known court decisions. Hakan Albayrak wrote an article in the newspaper *Milli Gazete* in 2000 arguing that Atatürk had been buried without Islamic ceremony. A few days later, he apologized for misinforming the readers and acknowledged the existence of such a ceremony. Yet he was sentenced to fifteen months of imprisonment for violating the Law on the Protection of Atatürk and served five months in prison.[41] The obvious paradox is that the secular courts took the claim about the lack of an Islamic ceremony as an insult. The second example is the case against Atilla Yayla, a professor of political science and the president of the Association for Liberal Thinking. In 2006, in a panel with fewer than forty listeners, he argued that "despite widespread official propaganda, the single-party era between 1925–1945, led mainly by Mustafa Kemal Atatürk, was not as progressive as it is claimed and was, in some respects, backward."

---

[38] Şükrü Hanioğlu, "İki Türkiye," *Zaman*, May 31, 2004. For a video documentary on secularism in Turkey, see Baristiran 2004.
[39] Göle 2000, 15–16. See also Turam 2006, 144–5.
[40] Atatürk n.d. [1927]; Genel Kurmay Başkanlığı 1983; Özyürek 2006; Aydın 2004.
[41] Ahmet Kekeç, "Hakan Albayrak Hapse Giriyor … ," *Yeni Şafak*, April 21, 2004.

He also added, "Europeans who see the ubiquitous representations of Ataturk here will ask: 'Why are the same man's pictures and statues everywhere?'"[42] The Kemalist media launched a campaign against Yayla defining him as a "traitor." In 2008, the court sentenced him to one year and three months in prison and postponed the sentence for a potential cancellation with the condition that he would not commit such a "crime" again in the next two years.[43] These two cases show the Kemalist domination and the ideological use of judiciary power in Turkey.

Despite the Kemalist dominance in the bureaucracy, the pro-Islamic conservatives have gained ground in civil society and the media. Conservative newspapers (e.g., *Zaman* and *Yeni Şafak*), TV channels (e.g., STV and Kanal 7), business associations (e.g., TUSKON and MÜSİAD), as well as conservative politicians, have tried to resist assertive secularist policies. Conservative politicians have largely taken places in conservative (the AK Party), nationalist (MHP), and center-right (DP[44] and ANAP) parties. The conservatives have preferred passive secularism, which allows public visibility of religion.

Major allies of the conservatives in the promotion of passive secularism in Turkey have been some liberal intellectuals – for example, Mustafa Erdoğan, Şahin Alpay, and Gülay Göktürk,[45] and associations, such as the Association for Liberal Thinking and the Turkish Economic and Social Studies Foundation (TESEV). The liberals have opposed the CHP and assertive secularists for their exclusionary stand toward religion. The liberals have also criticized the AK Party government for two reasons. First, the AK Party is not reformist enough. As reflected in the preservation of the Diyanet's status and obligatory religious instruction, the AK Party has largely conserved the status quo, rather than proposing a substantial reform for a real Islam-state separation. Second, although defending freedoms of Sunni Muslims, the AK Party has failed to present these freedoms in a broader perspective that encompasses all groups, such as Alevis, in Turkey.

---

[42] Atilla Yayla, "Freedom of Expression in Turkey," *International Herald Tribune*, December 6, 2006.

[43] "Atilla Yayla Gözetim Altında Tutulmayacak," *Zaman*, March 17, 2008.

[44] The True Path Party (DYP) changed its name to Democratic Party (DP) in 2007.

[45] Erdoğan 1997; Erdoğan 1998; Alpay 2003; Gülay Göktürk, "Zorunlu Din Dersi," *Bugün*, July 7, 2006.

Islamists have been critical of the AK Party for ignoring its Islamic roots and making Turkey be controlled by the EU. Islamism is a relatively marginal view in Turkey. According to recent survey data, supporters of an Islamic state based on Sharia law constitute only 9 percent of society.[46] Erbakan's Saadet Party (SP) represents moderate Islamist activism. This party does not defend an Islamic state, but it does not clearly support the secular state either. It opposes Turkey's membership in the EU. Certain media outlets (e.g., newspapers *Milli Gazete* and *Vakit*) can also be categorized as similar to the SP at this point. I would compare it with the Christian Right in the United States, in the sense that the SP defends at least a cultural hegemony of Islam in Turkey.

The difference between the conservatives and liberals resembles the distinction between accommodationists and separationists in the United States. The conservatives (e.g., the AK Party) are similar to the accommodationists in America (e.g., the Republican Party), in terms of legitimizing close state-religion relations, while the Turkish liberals, like the American separationists, seek a clear state-religion separation. The liberals, therefore, criticize the Diyanet's status. The conservatives, however, generally regard the Diyanet as necessary to avoid the anarchy that would happen if mosques were left to Islamic communities.[47] Arınç proposed that the Diyanet become an autonomous institution funded by private foundations rather than the state budget. His proposition, however, was either disregarded or rejected by the assertive secularists and the conservatives.[48] In general, there is popular support for the Diyanet. According to a public survey, 81.7 percent of the people support its existence.[49]

The following sections analyze assertive and passive secularists in Turkey. Several scholars have recognized the debate between these two groups by using different terminologies. Many of them have criticized the Turkish state's rigidly secular practices as *laikçilik* (secularist

---

[46] Çarkoğlu and Toprak 2006, 75.
[47] The author's personal interviews with AK Party politicians, September 2004, Ankara, Turkey.
[48] "Diyanet Kaldırılsın mı?" *Milliyet* May 6, 2006. See also Bekir Karlığa, "Diyanet İşleri Başkanlığının Dini Düşüncenin Gelişmesi ve Dini Hayatın Şekillenmesindeki Rolü," *Diyanet*, March 2004, 6–10.
[49] Çarkoğlu and Toprak 2000, 16.

extremism).[50] I prefer the term *assertive secularism* because it is less normative. Another alternative categorization calls the dominant ideology in Turkey *laicism*, different from *secularism* in the United States.[51] This categorization overemphasizes the difference between assertive and passive secularist regimes, ignoring their substantial commonalities – the lack of official religion and the absence of religious control over legislature and judiciary.

Assertive Secularists

Kemalist politicians, bureaucrats, businesspeople, and journalists have defended assertive secularism. They refer to the Turkish Constitutional Court for the definition of (assertive) secularism.[52] According to the court, secularism does not denote the separation of religion and the state, but it implies "separation of religion and worldly affairs." Secularism means separation of "social life, education, family, economy, law, manners, dress codes, etc. from religion."[53] For the court, secularism is beyond a political regime; it is "Turkey's philosophy of life." The court takes secularism as a comprehensive official doctrine, an overarching principle prior to all rights and freedoms, and a social engineering project to secularize society.[54] In this regard, the court's definition of *secularism* is mixed with *secularization*. Secularism is a constitutional regime that determines the political boundaries between state and religion. Secularization refers to social processes such as the decline of religion, in terms of belief, affiliation, and practice, and the individualization of religion, along with the erosion of its public role.[55] The court confuses these two different phenomena in its definition of secularism.

The Constitutional Court's understanding of secularism has two philosophical bases. First, the court adopts a modernist view, which

---

[50] Selçuk 1999; Vergin 2003.
[51] Davison 2003.
[52] Arslan 2005b.
[53] The Turkish Constitutional Court, January 16, 1997; no. 1998/1. For a critique of this decision, see Erdoğan 1999.
[54] Ibid.
[55] Casanova 1994, 19–39; Taylor 2007, 2–3. In the chapters on France, I used the term *secularization laws* when referring to French political reforms to secularize legal system and education. This was obviously different from the sociological secularization discussed here.

claims that an evolution has occurred from backward traditional societies to developed modern societies; one depends on religious dogmas and the other on science and reason.[56] Therefore, the court argues that secularism is beyond a political system: it is "the final phase of the institutional and ideational evolution of societies."[57] Second, the court has a civilizational view of Islam and Christianity. According to the court, Turkish secularism should be more rigid than secularism in Western countries with restrictions on religious freedoms because of the distinction between Islam and Christianity. It regards Islam as essentially a blueprint of society that encompasses life entirely. For controlling such a religion, a strict secularism, which confines religion to individual spirituality and does not allow it to play any social role, is necessary, though it may not be needed in Christian societies.[58]

The Constitutional Court has embraced and quoted Niyazi Berkes's work when defining secularism.[59] Berkes, a Kemalist scholar, has promoted a modernist and civilizational perspective in his *The Development of Secularism in Turkey*. He emphasizes the traditional versus modern dichotomy and celebrates the destruction of the former: "Without the breakdown of the traditional structure and attitudes, modern economic and technical aid may produce little change conducive to growth."[60] According to Berkes, "the bases of the [Islamic and Western] legal systems were different and irreconcilable, as they were the legal foundations of two different civilizations – medieval and modern."[61] There is a strong similarity between Berkes's book and Bernard Lewis's *The Emergence of the Modern Turkey* – another influential book with a modernist and civilizational perspective. Lewis agrees with Berkes while arguing that the Kemalist reforms meant that Turkey left Islamic civilization and became a part of Western civilization.[62]

To Berkes, state control over religion is inevitable in Turkey because a real separation of state and religion is not possible in a Muslim society

[56] For a former Constitutional Court judge's emphasis on the dichotomy between religious dogmatic and secular scientific education, see Aliefendioğlu 2001, 82–3.
[57] The Turkish Constitutional Court, March 7, 1989; no. 1989/12.
[58] Ibid.
[59] The Turkish Constitutional Court, January 16, 1997; no. 1998/1.
[60] Berkes 1998 [1964], 507.
[61] Ibid., 170.
[62] Lewis 1968, 234. For a critique of Lewis's modernist vision, see Zürcher n.d.

due to the political essence of Islam. In this regard, "Kemalist secularism implied political, legal, and educational restrictions upon religion."[63] For that reason, "to understand Kemalist secularism as a matter of separating church and state is ... erroneous and irrelevant." Berkes adds, "Kemalist secularism was nothing but a rejection of the ideology of Islamic polity,"[64] and, therefore, it "lacked a positive doctrine."[65] Berkes is worried that a real state-religion separation would energize the social role of Islam.[66] Therefore, conservative Muslisms, who are aware of the Kemalist control over Islam, may call for a real separation of state and religion "not on an Islamist principle but, strangely, on the grounds of the constitutional right to free exercise of religion."[67] So, he rightly predicted the transformation of pro-Islamic groups from opposing secularism to advocating passive secularism.

Another classical assertive secularist book is Çetin Özek's *Türkiyede Laiklik (Secularism in Turkey)*. Özek, like Berkes, embraces modernism and civilizationalism. He asserts that modernization and secularization of Western societies should be taken as a model for Turkey, because all religions undermine the "value of human beings," spread "fatalism," defend "a social system based on economic exploitation," and "opiate the oppressed and the poor by the idea of the hereafter."[68] Özek also argues that secularist state policies in Turkey are rightly "stricter and more interventionist" toward religion than those in Western countries, because a majority of Turks are Muslims. Islam, unlike Christianity, is not only a religion but also a political ideology; therefore, Muslims would always resist secularism. Such a resistance did not come from Christian fundamentalists in Western societies such as France because of the apolitical nature of Christianity.[69] Turkey should get rid of Islam to become a part of the universal civilization – the modern West.[70]

---

[63] Berkes 1998 [1964], 480–1. See also Berkes 1955.
[64] Berkes 1998 [1964], 499.
[65] Ibid., 502.
[66] Berkes resembles Karl Marx, who lamented in "On the Jewish Question" that the separation of church and state in the United States empowers public religiosity. Marx 1994, 6–7.
[67] Berkes 1998 [1964], 499–500.
[68] Özek 1962, 152, 527.
[69] Ibid., 74–5, 112, 116, 522. Özek defines Islamic law as "centuries-old desert law." Ibid., 143, 153.
[70] Ibid., 520.

The Constitutional Court, Berkes, and Özek have a shared understanding of secularism, modernity, and Islam. Even the scholars of modernization theory and civilizationalism discussed in Chapter 1 would find this understanding based on their theories extremely simplistic and reductionist. Modernization did not result in "linear progress" in the "West" or elsewhere. Neither Islam nor Christianity is monolithic as reflected in their complex local interpretations and their followers' diverse interactions with states. This book particularly points to the political activism of the Catholics in France and the evangelicals in the United States. Moreover, the assertive secularists would not have been able to impose avowedly "rigid" policies toward Islam, if Muslims in Turkey had been so threatening and reactionary to secularism.

In short, the assertive secularists regard Islam as an inherently political religion and an impediment to the modernization of Turkish society. Sociopolitically, they have tried to exclude Islam from the public sphere. Theologically, they have aimed to create a new interpretation of Islam, which is confined to individual conscience and does not intervene in personal ways of life, from drinking alcohol to wearing a bikini.

Passive Secularists

The central rightist parties were the main advocates of passive secularism in Turkey from the 1950s to the 1990s (see Chapter 7). The pro-Islamic conservatives experienced a transformation in the late 1990s as a result of their adaptation to the globalization process and the state oppression they faced during the February 28 process.[71] The conservatives started to support Turkey's membership in the EU and to offer passive secularism as an alternative to dominant assertive secularism. Ali Bulaç, the influential Islamist writer, declared that state-based "political" Islamism was dead. He called for a new individual-based "civil" Islamism, which did not contradict secularism as a political regime.[72]

The Gülen movement initiated by Fethullah Gülen, who has been in a semivoluntary exile in the United States since 1999, played a leading role in this transformation. Gülen has generally avoided polarized debates. "When the headscarf ban prevented most of the covered

[71] Kuru 2005a; Kösebalaban 2005; Dağı 2004; Çınar and Duran 2007.
[72] Bulaç's interview, *Aksiyon* November 7–13, 1998. See also Bulaç 2001, 11–65.

girls from going to school, the Gülen movement was first to insist on girls' schooling at the cost of compromising their headscarf."[73] The movement has coordinated more than five hundred schools in around one hundred different countries, in addition to eight universities. These schools have secular curricula and teach English and Turkish, in addition to the local languages. The movement is also affiliated with several media outlets worldwide, including internationally broadcasting STV and the newspaper *Zaman*, which is printed in about ten different countries. It is also linked to a business association, TUSKON, representing twelve thousand businesspeople.[74] In the late 1990s, the Gülen movement founded the Journalists and Writers' Foundation (JWF), which began to organize the Abant workshops to head off sociopolitical polarization and to search for a new social contract in Turkey. Each annual Abant workshop has included about fifty Turkish intellectuals from sharply different ideological backgrounds. The first workshop in 1998 was devoted to Islam and secularism. Its press declaration emphasized that God's ontological sovereignty is compatible with the political sovereignty of the people. The second meeting also examined the relationships among state, society, and religion.[75] Later, these workshops gained an international dimension. In 2004, the seventh meeting, "Islam, Democracy, and Secularism: The Turkish Experience," took place in Baltimore, Maryland, at the Johns Hopkins University. In the same year, the eighth meeting was organized in the European Parliament, in Brussels, to discuss Turkey's membership in the EU.[76] The events organized by the JWF have become a public forum where the Gülen movement has elaborated its new discourse of promoting intercultural dialogue and supporting Turkey's membership in the EU, democratization, and passive secularism.[77]

---

[73] Turam 2006, 115.

[74] Kuru 2003; Agai 2003; Kalyoncu 2008; Gürbüz 2007. See also Sabrina Tavernise, "Turkish Schools Offer Pakistan a Gentler Vision of Islam," *New York Times*, May 4, 2008; "Fethullah Gülen'in Eğitim İmparatorluğu," *Yeni Aktüel*, no.13, October 11–17, 2005.

[75] Gazeteciler ve Yazarlar Vakfı 1998, 1999.

[76] The author's personal observations in the seventh and eighth Abant meetings, Baltimore, MD, April 19–20, 2004 and Brussels, December 3–4, 2004.

[77] For Gülen's views on the EU, see Kösebalaban 2003. For his perspective on democracy, see Gülen 2001.

The late 1990s was also an era of transformation for Erbakan's Milli Görüş movement. Following the closure of their party as part of the February 28 process, the RP parliamentarians founded the Fazilet (Virtue) Party (FP).[78] In 2000, three leaders of the Milli Görüş's youth – Erdoğan, Arınç, and Abdullah Gül – emphasized their prosecular views by criticizing the idea of an Islamic state.[79] Despite the FP's pro-EU and democratic discourse,[80] the Constitutional Court dissolved it in 2001, arguing that the party defended the freedom to wear headscarves and was therefore antisecular. That deepened the rift between the elders of the Milli Görüş led by Erbakan and the young generation led by Erdoğan. The former founded the SP, whereas the latter established the AK Party.[81] The SP made a return to the anti-EU discourse whereas the AK Party took a step further to defend Turkey's membership in the EU, as well as to support passive secularism. In the elections of November 3, 2002, the SP was marginalized with 2.5 percent of the national votes while the AK Party became the leading party with 34.3 percent of the votes.

The AK Party rejected any affiliation with Islamism[82] and identified its normative framework as "conservative democracy."[83] The party's official publication, *Conservative Democracy*, defines this new ideology by stressing common sense, prudence, and gradual change, unlike its two alternatives – socialism and liberalism – which may promote ideological rationalism and radical changes. *Conservative Democracy*, therefore, rejects rationalist utopias, Jacobinism, and social engineering. At this point, its sources of inspiration include Michael Oakeshott and Edmund Burke.[84] Erdoğan emphasized that the AK Party's understanding of conservatism did not mean the conservation of established institutions and relations but implied the protection of important

[78] White 2003.
[79] Erdoğan's and Arınç's interviews, *Zaman*, February 6, 2000; Gül's interview, *Hürriyet*, February 8, 2000.
[80] Öniş 2001.
[81] Mecham 2004; Tepe 2005.
[82] "Erdoğan: Millî Görüş' ün Değil Demokrat Parti'nin Devamıyız," *Zaman*, May 17, 2003.
[83] Yavuz 2006. The author's personal interviews with AK Party politicians, Ankara, September 2004.
[84] Akdoğan 2003. Yalçın Akdoğan largely used Bekir Berat Özipek's PhD diss. on conservatism while writing *Conservative Democracy*. See also Akdoğan 2006.

values and principles while pursuing progress. He stressed that using religion as a political instrument was harmful to social peace, political diversity, and religion.[85]

The AK Party defines secularism as a principle that "implies that the state remains neutral toward all religions and thoughts" and "maintains peace among diverse beliefs, schools of thoughts, and perspectives."[86] Its party program depicts secularism as "an assurance of the freedom of religion and conscience" and rejects "the interpretation and distortion of secularism as enmity against religion." The program adds, "It is also unacceptable to make use of religion for political, economic, and other interests or to put pressure on people who think and live differently by using religion."[87] According to the AK Party, secularism needs to be empowered by democracy to maintain religious freedom and social harmony: "A particular understanding of secularism as a monopolistic, totalitarian, and Jacobin ideology or way of life, would result in conflict, rather than social peace."[88] Arınç is a leading AK Party politician who challenges assertive secularism. For him, secularism "is an unchangeable principle of the Turkish Constitution and will stay as such forever. On the other hand, it should be adapted to new conditions and the characteristics of the Turkish society."[89] According to Arınç, "rigid secularist policies in Turkey have turned social life into a prison," and therefore, "the reinterpretation of secularism is required to reach social peace."[90] The new interpretation of secularism, he stresses, should be based on individual freedoms.[91]

Because the AK Party is a conservative party, its attitude toward non-Muslim citizens is important to evaluate to what extent it embraces passive secularism and seeks state neutrality toward all religions. Non-Muslim communities, which constitute only one hundred thousand out of Turkey's population of seventy-two million, have

---

[85] Erdoğan 2004.

[86] AK Parti n.d., 13–14. See also Erdoğan 2004, 7–17.

[87] AK Parti 2002.

[88] Akdoğan 2003, 105.

[89] Arınç's speech in the Turkish Parliament: "Demokrasi Manifestosu," *Zaman*, April 24, 2006.

[90] "Arınç: Laiklik, Hayatı Cezaevine Çevirmemeli," *Zaman*, April 26, 2006.

[91] The author's personal observation at the Diyanet's Third Symposium, Ankara, September 20, 2004; see also "Zirvede Laiklik Atışması," *Radikal*, September 21, 2004.

faced official restrictions since the founding of the republic.[92] In 2003, the European Commission criticized Turkish state policies, such as the "absence of legal personality, education and training of ecclesiastic personnel as well as full enjoyment of property rights of religious communities."[93] The AK Party initiated certain reforms to alleviate conditions of non-Muslim minorities and to adjust Turkey to the EU standards on this issue. "Members of Turkey's non-Muslim communities are unanimous in declaring that, since the ruling ... AK Party came to power in November 2002, relations with the government have improved considerably."[94] In 2003, the AK Party group led the parliament to change the legal framework concerning religious places, replacing the word *mosque* with "place of worship." This allowed all religions to open temples in Turkey.[95] In 2004, the AK Party government cancelled the state surveillance of non-Muslims by abolishing the Subcommittee for Minorities, which had been monitoring non-Muslim citizens for forty-two years.[96] Moreover, Erdoğan has made several visits to Jewish synagogues and Christian churches in Turkey, a gesture that has been appreciated by these communities. That is why the Armenian Orthodox Patriarch Mesrob II announced that Armenians would vote for the AK Party in the 2007 elections.[97]

Nevertheless, non-Muslim communities still face several bureaucratic hurdles in Turkey.[98] Because the assertive secularists have focused on the exclusion of religion from the public sphere, they have not taken non-Muslim communities' problems seriously. Moreover, they have been worried about non-Muslims' rights of association because if the Christians and Jews were free to have legal entities, found new associations, and open new temples, then independent Muslim communities in Turkey would want these freedoms too.[99] For example, in 2006, Sezer vetoed a parliamentary bill that recognized the legal status

[92] Öktem 2002, 375; Oran 2007.
[93] Quoted by WRR 2004, 30.
[94] Jenkins 2004, 54.
[95] The law passed in Parliament on July 15, 2003.
[96] Şükrü Küçükşahin, "Sessiz Azınlık Devrimi," *Hürriyet*, February 23, 2004.
[97] "Ermeni Cemaati Seçimlerde Ak Parti'yi Destekleyecek," *Yeni Şafak*, June 4, 2007.
[98] Jenkins 2004, 59. See also the papers presented at TESEV Conference, "Cemaatler ve Cemaatlerin Hukuki Sorunları," May 15, 2004, http://www.tesev.org.tr/etkinlik/azinlik_dilleri.php.
[99] See İsmet Berkan, "AB ve Din Özgürlüğü Eksikliği," *Radikal*, May 26, 2004.

and full property rights of non-Muslim foundations. He argued that the bill would wrongly allow the expansion of the economic activities and social status of these religious foundations.[100] The AK Party passed the law again in February 2008. This time President Gül signed it into law. Yet the CHP and MHP applied to the Constitutional Court to declare it unconstitutional.[101] In sum, the passive secularist AK Party initiated reforms to solve certain problems of Christians and Jews, despite the opposition of the assertive secularists in Turkey.

POLICY CONTROVERSIES BETWEEN THE ASSERTIVE AND PASSIVE SECULARISTS

The assertive and passive secularists have mainly disagreed on policies toward religion in schools because they both attach importance to shaping the worldview of the younger generation. A particularly controversial issue is the obligatory religious instruction (mainly on Islam) through the course "Religious Culture and the Knowledge of Ethics," which was put into the Turkish Constitution (Art. 24) by the Kemalist military administration following the September 12, 1980, *coup d'état*. For several Kemalists, religious instruction is a means to have a state monopoly over the education of Islam. According to numerous conservatives, this course partially satisfies societal demand regarding education on Islam. The AK Party, therefore, wants to preserve it.[102] However, neither Kemalists nor conservatives have a monolithic attitude on this issue. Some conservatives argue that the content of this course is quite different from their own understanding of "true Islam." A book written on this critique is *Bu Din Benim Dinim Değil (This Religion Is Not My Religion)*.[103] Due to their dissatisfaction with the religious instruction in public schools, which takes only a few hours a week, many conservative families have sent their children to Imam-Hatip schools. Certain Kemalists criticize religious instruction in schools for being contradictory to their understanding of secular education. Additionally, several Alevis claim that the content of the

---

[100] "Sezer Vakıflar Yasası'nı Lozan'a Aykırı Buldu," *Zaman*, November 30, 2006.
[101] Şahin Alpay, "Laiklik, AKP ve CHP," *Zaman*, March 13, 2008.
[102] "AB'ye Cevap: Din Konusu Bizim Bileceğimiz İştir," *Yeni Şafak*, February 16, 2005.
[103] Dilipak 1995.

course is dominated by a Sunni perspective.[104] Recently the European
Court of Human Rights accepted the application of an Alevi father
decided that the obligatory religious education in Turkish schools was
a violation of the European Convention of Human Rights. This decision may eventually lead Turkey to allow parents who want their kids
to be waived from this course to do so.[105]

Another controversial issue was the state funding of private schools.
Although private Islamic schools are not allowed in Turkey, there are
some secular private schools run by conservative Muslims. Many
of these private schools are affiliated with the Gülen movement. In
2003, the AK Party government initiated a policy of funding private
school tuition for ten thousand students from poor families. Minister
of Education Hüseyin Çelik issued a circular about that. The assertive
secularists organized a media campaign arguing that the project was
promoting the schools run by conservative Muslims, especially the
Gülen movement. They claimed that 89 out of 415 private schools in
the project belonged to Islamic movements, and these schools would
receive 2,218 out of 10,000 students.[106] The Council of State cancelled
Çelik's circular. Then, the AK Party group in parliament passed a legislative bill that framed the project. President Sezer, though, vetoed the
bill because it would allocate public funds to certain private schools,
which educate students in a way that "contradicted the principle of
secularism."[107] Because of the assertive secularist resistance, the AK
Party did not repass the bill and cancelled the project.

The conservative and center-rightist parties, including the AK
Party, MHP, DP, and ANAP, have won about 70 percent of the votes
in elections during the last three decades.[108] Yet they have had limited

---

[104] Çakır and Bozan 2005, 283–5.

[105] "AİHM: Din Dersi Zorunlu Olamaz," *Radikal*, October 10, 2007.

[106] "En Özel Okullar," *Sabah*, July 26, 2003.

[107] Sezer's veto of the bill no. 4967, August 13, 2003, http://www.cankaya.gov.tr/tr_
html/ACIKLAMALAR/13.08.2003–2376.html.

[108] In the national legislative elections of July 22, 2007, the conservative and center-rightist
parties received 68% of the votes (AKP [47%], MHP [14%], DP [5%], and SP [2%]),
whereas the assertive secularist CHP-DSP alliance received only 21%. The Kurdish
nationalist Democratic Society Party, which ran through independent candidates,
received about 5%. This party's deputies are largely assertive secularists, while its
constituency is heavily conservative. "DTP Tabanla Uyumlu Değil," *Milliyet*, July 30,
2007.

impact on state policies toward religion due to assertive secularist dominance in the military and judiciary. The presidency has played the key role for the preservation of the assertive secularist domination in these state institutions, because the president approves the appointment of high-ranking generals and top civil bureaucrats, as well as appointing high court judges and presidents of universities. Except for Celal Bayar (1950–1960) and Özal (1989–1993), presidents of Turkey have always been assertive secularists. The main reason why parliament repeatedly elected assertive secularist presidents was the military interventions that forced deputies not to vote for conservative or liberal candidates.

Turkey experienced stressful events that started a year before the presidential election scheduled for 2007. In February 2006, the Council of State decided that it was inappropriate for a school principal to wear a headscarf even on the street. The passive secularists condemned the decision as a violation of religious freedom. Two months later, an assassin shot the judges who made this decision and killed one of them. The Kemalists accused the AK Party government regarding the event because Erdoğan had criticized these judges. Yet the police uncovered that the murderer was linked to a "deep-state" terrorist organization, Ergenekon, run by ultranationalist retired military officers, who set up conservatives with the assassination.[109]

In April 2007, the Kemalists brought together about one million protesters in several major cities to prevent the AK Party from electing the new president. The AK Party, however, nominated Gül, the vice prime minister and minister for foreign affairs, for the presidency. The assertive secularists opposed Gül, whose wife wore a headscarf. Gül needed to receive two thirds of the votes (367/550) in the first two rounds. In the third round, however, more than half (276/550) would be enough. On April 27, Gül received 357 votes out of 361 deputies present in the first round. Gül was planning to be elected in the third round, similar to presidents elected before him. Nevertheless, the CHP applied to the Constitutional Court, arguing the quorum

---

[109] In 2008, the police arrested several alleged members of the Ergenekon, including retired military generals. The public prosecutor charged them with the assassinations of judges, intellectuals, and Christians, particularly by using grenades of the Turkish military to create an atmosphere of anarchy and to make conditions ready for a *coup d'état*. "Devlet, Derin Devlete Karşı," *Sabah*, January 23, 2008.

of 367 deputies was required and asked for the cancellation of the first round. At midnight, the military issued a statement on its Web site threatening direct intervention, which was later referred to as an "e-coup." The CHP supported the military's statement,[110] while the AK Party government declared that the military was under its authority. Gül did not withdraw his candidacy. The Constitutional Court upheld the CHP's claim about the quorum of 367 and cancelled the first round. The two passive secularists among the eleven members of the court voted against the decision.

Ergun Özbudun, one of Turkey's top professors of constitutional law, criticized the court's decision as a political maneuver that clearly contradicted the text and original intent of the constitution, as well as the precedents of the presidential elections.[111] The so-called 367 decision was not an exceptionally politicized and ideological decision of the Turkish Constitutional Court. As Ceren Belge points out, since its foundation following the 1960 military coup, the court has prioritized defending the Kemalist dominance in the state establishment against the democratically elected politicians, instead of defending civil liberties.[112]

As a response, the AK Party called for early parliamentary elections. Moreover, the AK Party, with the support of the ANAP, passed a constitutional amendment to elect the president by people's direct vote. President Sezer and the CHP opposed the amendment, because it was more likely that a majority of the people would vote for a conservative candidate. Sezer vetoed the amendment. When parliament passed it again, Sezer took the amendment to the referendum because he did not have the second veto authority. Sezer and the CHP applied to the Constitutional Court to get the amendment and referendum cancelled. Yet the court rejected their applications by a 6–5 vote. In the parliamentary elections that took place in July 2007, the AK Party increased its votes to 47 percent, vis-à-vis fourteen contesting parties, in addition to independents. A month later, parliament reinitiated the presidential election, despite the CHP's boycott, and elected Gül. In October 2007, the constitutional amendment that

[110] "Öymen: Genelkurmay'ın Bildirisi Bizimle Uyuşuyor," *Zaman*, April 22, 2007.
[111] "Cumhurbaşkanlığı Krizinin Götürdükleri," *Zaman*, May 14, 2007.
[112] Belge 2006, 671.

turned the future presidential elections into popular elections was voted by 69 percent.[113]

In December 2007, the MHP initiated a constitutional amendment to lift the headscarf ban at universities.[114] The AK Party agreed with the MHP. Many professors supported this initiative; 3,549 of them signed a petition online to end all discrimination and to make all dress free at universities.[115] The assertive secularist media together with the CHP and DSP ran a campaign against the amendment. The public prosecutor of the High Court of Appeals, Abdurrahman Yalçınkaya, threatened the AK Party and the MHP with a closure case.[116] Assertive secularist professors also opposed the amendment. Professor Celal Şengör, who was elected to the Council for Higher Education (YÖK) by the Inter-Universities Committee, distributed a letter to the committee members to condemn the amendment as being against modern civilization. He argued that religions were mere superstitions already withered away by science and had no place at universities. He also warned parliament that if headscarves became free the professors would close universities.[117]

Despite the opposition, parliament overwhelmingly (411 to 103) voted the following two amendments, and President Gül signed them into law: (to Art. 10; the additional part is emphasized) "State organs and administrative authorities shall act in compliance with the principle of equality before the law in all their proceedings *and in benefiting from all public services*" and (to Art. 42) "No one can be deprived of his or her right to higher education for reasons not openly mentioned by laws. The limits of the use of this right will be determined by law." The amendments do not refer to religion at all. They focus on (1) equality for students while receiving education as a public service in order to keep the ban on headscarves for the faculty and staff and (2) the freedom of higher (college and graduate) education in order to continue the ban on schools. The president of the YÖK, Yusuf Ziya Özcan, who

[113] Taşpınar 2007.

[114] "Bahçeli: Başörtüsü Yasağına Rızamız Yok, Kaldırılmalı," *Zaman*, December 14, 2007.

[115] The text and signatures are at http://universitedeozgurluk.blogspot.com/, accessed on February 13, 2008.

[116] "MHP'den Formül Savcı'dan Uyarı," *Sabah*, January 18, 2008.

[117] İsmet Berkan, "Vahim Bir Mektup," *Radikal*, January 31, 2008.

had been recently appointed by Gül, issued a circular to declare the freedom of all dresses including headscarves at universities.

A majority of university presidents, however, kept imposing the ban and the Council of State cancelled the circular. The CHP and DSP applied to the Constitutional Court. The court struck down the amendments referring to secularism and defining its "ideational frameworks" as "Renaissance, Reformation, and Enlightenment." It claimed that if some students wore headscarves at universities, that would be a pressure to those who did not wear them. It also noted that the courts should be active in banning headscarves because parliament was unable to "limit religious freedoms" given the fact that it was "a political institution" elected by the people and the "majority of the people in [Turkey were] ... affiliated with a particular religion [Islam]." The two passive secularist judges, again, voted against the decision. Haşim Kılıç, president of the court, stressed the following points in his dissenting opinion: (1) The court violated article 148 of the constitution that prevented it from evaluating the contents of constitutional amendments, removed parliament's authority to amend the constitution, and diminished the balance of power between judiciary and legislature. (2) The court's violation of parliament's authority is also a disregard of the people's sovereignty. (3) There is no other modern country that bans religious symbols at universities. (4) "Universities are not barracks" and cannot discipline students regarding "a uniform model."[118]

Motivated by the headscarves debate, Prosecutor Yalçınkaya opened a closure case against the AK Party in the Constitutional Court and asked for a five-year ban from politics for Erdoğan, Arınç, and sixty-eight other AK Party politicians, in addition to Gül (although the president cannot be charged with anything except for treason according to the constitution). The case contributed a new term to the Turkish political lexicon: *judiciary coup d'état*. Because of several external and internal factors, such as EU pressure, fragile economic conditions, the arrest of two top retired generals as part of the Ergenekon case by the accusation of planning a coup against the AK Party government, and the fact that the AK Party did not have an alternative in parliament for founding a new government, this attempt remained abortive. In July

---

[118] The Turkish Constitutional Court, June 5, 2008; no. 2008/116.

2008, the court did not close down the AK Party but defined it as a basis of antisecular activities and cut half of its annual public funding (about 20 million dollars).[119]

The prosecutor's indictment was a simple collection of AK Party politicians' speeches about religious freedom and their failed attempts to alleviate the conditions of university students wearing headscarves, Imam-Hatip school graduates, and the Qur'an courses.[120] These three are the most controversial issues between the assertive and passive secularists. In a public survey, 42 percent of the interviewees claim oppression of religious people in Turkey.[121] These interviewees mentioned issues "related to education policies such as the headscarf ban, closure of Koran [sic] courses and Imam-Hatip schools. These examples cover a total of 77 per cent of all examples given by those who claim that religious people are being oppressed in Turkey."[122] Given the prominence of these three issues, a separate look at each is warranted.

The Headscarf Ban

Women wearing headscarves cannot get any level of education, become elected politicians, or enter several public buildings, such as university campuses, even as visitors in Turkey. Because the ban is an arbitrarily imposed de facto policy, its limitations are unknown. In some cases, it is extended to result in the expulsion of women wearing headscarves from university dormitories and even courthouses.[123] This is problematic given the fact that about 63 percent of women wear some kind of headscarf in Turkey.[124] According to the European Stability Initiative, despite the rhetoric of the emancipation of women, Turkey still has the embarrassing rank of 105 in the Global Gender Gap Index 2006, and

---

[119] The Turkish Constitutional Court, July 30, 2008; no. 2008/2.
[120] The indictment also included the AK Party's previously mentioned abortive initiative of funding needy students' tuitions in private schools.
[121] Çarkoğlu and Toprak 2000, 69–70.
[122] Çarkoğlu 2004, 129. Among these interviewees, 65% mentioned the headscarf ban, 7% noticed the closure of the Qur'an courses, and 6% recognized the closure of the Imam-Hatip Schools as the main examples of oppression against religious people. Çarkoğlu and Toprak 2000, 69; Çarkoğlu 2004, 130.
[123] "Rektör, Şehitliği Ziyarete Gelen Aileleri Gece Yarısı Pansiyondan Kovdu," *Zaman*, May 11, 2008; "Türban Tartışması Hukukçuları Böldü," *Sabah*, November 8, 2003.
[124] Çarkoğlu and Toprak 2006, 58.

one of the reasons for that is the exclusion of women with headscarves from public life.[125]

After the foundation of the republic, assertive secularist policies developed a dichotomy between educated, urban, and "modern" women, on the one hand, and uneducated, rural, and "traditional" women, on the other. The main symbolic line between these two is having the head uncovered or covered. In the late 1980s, the daughters of the second group began to attend universities with their headscarves.[126] That sociological transformation was seen as a threat by the assertive secularists, and they decided to use state power to eliminate it.

Following the *coup d'état* in 1980, the military rulers founded the YÖK to control universities. The YÖK decided to expel students with headscarves in 1982 based on the order of the military government. The Council of State confirmed the YÖK's policy of expulsion in several cases. In 1984, the council unanimously decided that

some of our daughters who are not sufficiently educated wear headscarves under the influence of their social environments, customs, and traditions – without giving any special thought to it. Yet it is known that some of our daughters and women who are educated enough to resist their social environments and customs wear headscarves just to oppose the principles of the secular Republic, showing that they adopt the ideal of a religious state. For those people, the headscarf is no longer an innocent habit, but a symbol of a world view that opposes women's liberty and the fundamental principles of our Republic....Therefore, the decision to expel the plaintiff from the university does not contradict the laws. She is so against the principles of the secular state that she resists removing her headscarf even when she comes to university for higher education.[127]

The leading conservative/center-right party, the ANAP, initiated two legislative bills to lift the ban on headscarves at universities. During the first initiative, the leader of the ANAP was Özal, who was also the prime minister (1983–1989). In 1988, parliament, led by the ANAP majority, passed a bill that provided freedom to wear any dress at universities.[128] Kemalist President Kenan Evren vetoed

---

[125] European Stability Initiative 2007, 27, 31.
[126] Göle 1996.
[127] The Turkish Council of State, December 13, 1984; no. 1984/1574.
[128] The bill passed in parliament on November 16, 1988; no. 3503.

the bill, arguing that an absolute freedom of dress is against Atatürk's principles and reforms, secularism, modernism, and the principle of equality.[129] In response, parliament passed another bill in the same year, which made "modern dress and appearance" obligatory but allowed covering the neck and hair with a headscarf for religious belief.[130] Evren applied to the Constitutional Court, arguing the unconstitutionality of the legislation. The court struck down the law as unconstitutional due to the principle of secularism because the law took religious belief as a reason for legal exemption. According to the court, that particular legislation, which allowed wearing headscarves at universities, might provoke religious conflicts, threaten the unity of the state and nation, and destroy the public order. Moreover, the legislation "abolishes the constitutional boundaries of religious freedom by allowing religion to pass beyond the individual's spiritual life and to cause behaviors that influence social life." According to the court, "the dress issue is limited by the Turkish Revolution and Atatürk's Principles and it is not an issue of freedom of conscience....To attend classes with antimodern attire [i.e., headscarf] has no relevancy to freedom or autonomy."[131] The court quoted from the previously mentioned decision of the Council of State:

The dress code is not just an issue of physical appearance. Secularism is a transformation of mentality. It is a must for a modern healthy society. An individual is a unity composed of his or her inner and outer lives, sentiments and thoughts, and body and spirit. The dress code is a means to reflect the personal character. Regardless of whether it is religious or not, anti-modern dresses that contradict the Laws of Revolution cannot be seen as appropriate. Religious dresses, in particular, constitute a deeper incongruity since they contradict the principle of secularism.[132]

Only one member of the court, Mehmet Çınarlı, wrote a dissenting opinion. Çınarlı had four main arguments: (1) the banning of headscarves violates the individual freedoms protected by the constitution; (2) the constitution gives authority to parliament to limit freedoms for

[129] Evren's veto of the bill no. 3503, November 18, 1988; no. 1662–8088.
[130] The law passed in parliament on December 10, 1988; annex 16 added to law no. 2547.
[131] The Turkish Constitutional Court, March 7, 1989; no. 1989/12.
[132] Ibid.

the sake of the public order, and if parliament decides to enrich certain freedoms, the judiciary has no authority to restrict them; (3) Atatürk's speeches and the Laws of Revolution do not include anything against headscarves; and (4) the court's definition of the headscarf, as either a political symbol or backward tradition, does not reflect reality. According to the Diyanet's official declaration,[133] wearing headscarves is a religious duty, and many of the veiled students have tried to fulfill this duty.[134]

Following the court's decision, parliament passed another bill, which was similar to the first bill vetoed by Evren and lacked the issue of religious exemption: "As long as they do not violate existing laws, dress codes are free at universities."[135] Then President Özal signed it into law. The Social Democratic Populist Party, the major assertive secularist party at that time, applied to the Constitutional Court. The court this time did not declare the law unconstitutional, but interpreted it as disallowing headscarves at universities because they are against the principle of secularism.[136] Since then, the assertive secularists have argued that headscarves are prohibited by the court decisions. The passive secularists, however, claim that the law that made the headscarf free at universities remains valid, and that there is no other constitutional or other legal regulation about headscarves. For them, the ban on headscarves is an assertive secularist practice without any legal basis.

Because of this legal controversy, universities did not pursue a consistent policy toward headscarves until the 1997 coup. Even in the same university, some departments imposed the ban whereas others did not, based on the personal opinions of the deans and heads of departments. In 1992, Özal appointed Mehmet Sağlam, who was against the ban, to the YÖK. Under the presidency of Sağlam, few universities imposed the ban on headscarves. In 1995, however, President Demirel appointed Kemal Gürüz as the president of the YÖK. Gürüz strictly imposed the ban in all universities during the February 28 process. Following the

---

[133] The decision of the Diyanet's High Council for Religious Affairs, December 30, 1980; no. 77. The president of the Diyanet, Ali Bardakoğlu, repeated in January 2008 that covering the head is a religious duty for women.

[134] The Turkish Constitutional Court, March 7, 1989; no. 1989/12.

[135] The law passed in parliament on October 25, 1990; annex 17 added to the law no. 2547.

[136] The Turkish Constitutional Court, April 9, 1991; no. 1991/8.

1999 parliamentary elections, the ban was also extended to all elected politicians. At the time, Merve Kavakçı from the FP was elected to parliament as first deputy with a headscarf. Prime Minister Ecevit and DSP deputies did not allow her to take the oath in parliament by shouting adamantly "Out! Out!" Later, she lost her citizenship with the excuse that she became an American citizen without the permission of the Turkish government.[137]

In 2003, President Sezer appointed Erdoğan Teziç, another keen supporter of the ban, to the YÖK. Under Teziç's presidency, the ban was extended to wearing wigs (by students who wanted to hide their own hair) even in departments of theology.[138] According to Teziç, civil servants should not wear headscarves even on the street, for example, "while shopping in a bazaar."[139] In May 2004, the AK Party group in parliament passed a legislative bill that would remove Teziç and reorganize the YÖK.[140] Sezer vetoed the bill, and the AK Party did not pass it again due to the assertive secularist media campaign and the YÖK's street protests. Before the previously mentioned constitutional amendment in 2008, the AK Party did not take another initiative to lift the ban during its six-year ruling. Erdoğan had only some limited proposals on this issue. In 2004, for example, he proposed limiting the ban to public universities and making headscarves free at private universities.[141] Yet none of his proposals was taken seriously by the assertive secularists.

In addition to the courts and the YÖK, the main defenders of the headscarf ban have been the assertive secularist media and the CHP. In December 2007, *Milliyet* published a survey to alarm assertive secularists by the increasing number of those wearing headscarves. Although its presentation through headlines seemed politicized, the survey was informative. It noted that the percentage of women wearing headscarves in Turkey increased from 64 percent in 2003 to 69 percent in 2007. The main reason for wearing headscarves appeared to be one's religious beliefs (73%), while other reasons included customs and

---

[137] Göle 2005, 87–8; Kavakçı 2004.
[138] "SDÜ İlahiyatta Şimdi de Peruk Yasağı," *Zaman*, September 11, 2006; "Peruklu Diye Okula Kaydını Yaptırmadılar," *Zaman*, July 6, 2006.
[139] Teziç's interview to Nur Batur, *Hürriyet*, February 10, 2006.
[140] The bill passed in parliament on May 13, 2004; no. 5171.
[141] "Türbanda Ara Formül," *Radikal*, July 10, 2004; "Başbakandan Türban Formülü," *Sabah*, July 7, 2005.

traditions (14%), habit (4%), adaptation to the social environment
(3%), parental demands (3%), and spouse's demand (3%).[142] Only a
small percentage of women wearing headscarves regarded the headscarves as a symbol against the secular state (5–10%). Those who do
not wear headscarves have a higher percentage (34%) of seeing it as
antisecular. The supporters of the headscarf ban at universities constituted only 22 percent, whereas 78 percent opposed the ban.[143]

CHP President Deniz Baykal argues that the headscarf is "a
symbol of theocracy," and "if the headscarf becomes free, then in
5–10 years no woman will be able to walk on the street with her
head uncovered."[144] During the constitutional amendment debates in
2008, Baykal repeated the alleged differences between two types of
headscarves – the *türban* and the *başörtüsü*. According to Baykal and
other assertive secularists, wearing a *türban* is not an Islamic act; it
is a recently emerged political symbol. Therefore, it should be prohibited at universities, if not in the entire public sphere. *Başörtüsü*,
however, is a centuries-old tradition of the Turkish woman.[145] For
passive secularists, such as Taha Akyol and Nazlı Ilıcak, this is not
a convincing argument for three main reasons.[146] First, it is hard to
differentiate between the *türban* and the *başörtüsü* except by the fact
that the latter is tied under the chin. The term *türban* was introduced
by the YÖK's first president, İhsan Doğramacı, as a modern alternative
to the traditional *başörtüsü*. But later, the assertive secularists gave a pe-
jorative connotation to the term as a symbol of Islamism. Second, both
the *türban* and the *başörtüsü* are prohibited at universities, schools,
and many other public institutions. Finally, the traditional dress of the
Turkish woman historically includes certain types of veiling, such as
the *çarşaf* (chador), which were much more incompatible with modern
fashions than the *türban*. The assertive secularists, who were critical of

[142] According to *Zaman*'s survey, 75% of women declared to wear headscarves for their
    religious beliefs, 11% of them for the demands of parents and husbands, and 6% of
    them for tradition and habit. *Zaman*, February 9, 2008.
[143] "The Survey of *Milliyet* and Konda," *Milliyet*, December 3–4, 2007.
[144] "Başörtüsüne Özgürlük İsteyen CHP'liler Baykal'ı Kızdırdı," *Zaman*, December
    5, 2003; Baykal's interview with Murat Yetkin, "20 Yıl Sonra Kızının Başı Zorla
    Kapatılsın İster misin?" *Radikal*, April 18, 2006.
[145] "Baykal: Türban Yabancı Üniforma," *Milliyet*, January 30, 2008.
[146] Taha Akyol, "Türban ve Başörtüsü," *Milliyet*, January 30, 2008; Nazlı Ilıcak,
    "'Babaannelerin' ve 'Torunların' Başörtüsü," *Sabah*, November 10, 2007.

the traditional dress of Turkish women for decades, began praising them to be able to criticize a relatively more recent and "modern" dress (*türban*).

During the headscarf debates in the late 1990s and early 2000s, the assertive secularists mainly used the "legal/political" argument that "religious symbols should not be allowed in the public sphere." Yet in the recent debate, Baykal and others started to use a "theological" argument that "wearing a headscarf is not a requirement of Islam, but a sign of Islamism." For the majority of the French assertive secularists, the former argument is convincing while the latter is absurd because they are not interested in defining what is Islamic and what is not. In Turkey, the popular support for the headscarf ban has been very limited (22%),[147] in comparison to that in France (72%).[148] The reasons for the distinction between public opinions in these two countries are threefold. First, in France, the Islamic headscarf is a symbol of an immigrant religious minority, while in Turkey, Islam has been the religion of the overwhelming majority of society. Second, the ban in France is confined only to public schools, whereas the ban in Turkey encompasses all educational institutions. Finally, the levels of religiosity are different in the two societies. The ratios of believing in God, being affiliated with a religion, and attending a mosque or church weekly are much lower in France (61%, 55%, and 10%) than they are in Turkey (99%, 99%, and 69%).[149] The exclusion of religious symbols from public schools is relatively easier in less religious French society, in comparison to highly religious Turkish society.

The Imam-Hatip Schools

The Imam-Hatip schools are public schools run by the ministry of education. They teach the same curriculum as other secular public schools, along with additional courses, such as the reading of the Qur'an, the exegesis of the Qur'an, Islamic law, and the history of religions. From the 1980 coup to the 1997 coup, the number of these

---

[147] Çarkoğlu and Toprak 2006, 71; "The Survey of *Milliyet* and Konda," *Milliyet*, December 4, 2007. Similarly, the ban on headscarves for female civil servants is supported by only 25% of the people, whereas 75% are against it. Çarkoğlu and Toprak 2006, 71.

[148] Debré 2004, 179.

[149] See Table 14 in the conclusion.

schools increased from 374 to 612 due to societal demand and support of the conservative governments.[150] Beyond their number, the efficiency of these schools increased as their graduates became active in Turkish sociopolitical life. The assertive secularists have wanted to make these schools vocational schools confined to training imams and *hatip*s (Muslim preachers) as elaborated by the TÜSİAD's report in 1990.[151] The conservatives, however, tried to preserve these schools as regular schools whose graduates could attend any university.

The February 28 administration, a mixture of civilian government and military generals, pursued two policies in order to marginalize the Imam-Hatip schools. First, it implemented a policy that increased the compulsory (secular) education from five to eight years. By doing that, it closed down the sixth through eighth grades of the Imam-Hatip schools. Second, through a revision in the university entrance system, the administration made it almost impossible for the graduates of Imam-Hatip schools to enter universities, with the exception of departments of theology.[152] These students were also not allowed to enter police academies as they had already been disqualified for military academies. When the February 28 coup was staged during the 1996–1997 academic year, the Imam-Hatip schools were at their peak with 511,502 students, which constituted 10 percent of all secondary and high school students.[153] As a result of these two particular policies, the number of students at these schools decreased to 64,534 – an 87 percent drop – by the 2002–2003 academic year.[154]

AK Party politicians did not problematize the closure of Imam-Hatip secondary schools. They have focused on allowing Imam-Hatip high school graduates to enter universities again. In 2004, the AK Party group in parliament passed a bill to relatively improve the

[150] Ruşen Çakır, İrfan Bozan, and Balkan Talu, "İmam-Hatip Liseleri: Efsaneler ve Gerçekler," June 14, 2004, http://www.tesev.org.tr/etkinlik/134–144.pdf.
[151] Kaplan 2006, 36–72.
[152] As a result of these two policies, secondary sections of other vocational schools were also closed and their graduates lost the right to attend universities, except in departments directly related to their vocations.
[153] "Din Öğretimi Genel Müdürlüğüne Bağlı Okullar," accessed on the Web site of the Ministry of Education at http://www.meb.gov.tr/Stats/ist97/MYHTML30.htm, on February 25, 2005; Yavuz 2003, 127.
[154] "İmam-Hatip Liseleri," CNN Turk Online, May 28, 2004, http://www.cnnturk.com .tr/OZEL_DOSYALAR/haber_detay.asp?pid=392&haberid=9269.

opportunities for graduates of all vocational schools, including the Imam-Hatip schools, to enter universities. Conservative and center-right parties, such as the DYP, supported the bill.[155] The assertive secularists, however, organized a media campaign against it. President Sezer vetoed the bill by arguing that allowing Imam-Hatip graduates to enter universities would violate the principle of secularism, which implied "the separation of social life, education, family, economy, and law from the rules of religion."[156] The international media was interested in this discussion. The *New York Times* criticized Sezer's veto as "a setback to religious freedom and equal opportunity." The editorial added, "Turkey's 536 religious schools are coeducational and, with the exception of Koran [*sic*] study, teach the same curriculum as nonreligious schools. Their 64,500 students are as much Turkey's future as are the sons and daughters of the secular elite."[157] Following the assertive secularist reaction and Sezer's veto, the AK Party did not pass the bill again.

From 1997 to 2007, students who were once registered in the Imam-Hatip schools were not allowed to transfer to other schools. Moreover, the majority of Imam-Hatip graduates could not attend departments of theology because the YÖK cut about 90 percent of the students that these faculties admitted and allowed them to accept only a nationwide total of 950 students per year.[158] The YÖK also removed these departments' right to train teachers for religious instruction in schools. In 2005, the AK Party tried to alleviate the conditions of Imam-Hatip graduates. Minister Çelik issued a circular to allow Imam-Hatip students to take certain extra exams to get an additional degree from a regular school, which would allow them to enter universities. The Council of State cancelled the circular. The assertive secularist media supported the council's decision and asked the AK Party to give up on the Imam-Hatip struggle.[159]

[155] "DYP'den İmam-Hatip Desteği," *Sabah*, May 6, 2004.

[156] Sezer's veto of the law no. 5171, May 28, 2004, http://www.cankaya.gov.tr/tr_html/ACIKLAMALAR/28.05.2004-2729.html.

[157] "Mosque and State in Turkey," *New York Times*, June 6, 2004.

[158] "İmam-Hatip Liseleri," *Yeni Şafak*, July 2, 2005; Ahmet Taşgetiren, "İHL'ler ve Ötesi, *Yeni Şafak*, April 5, 2004.

[159] "Çıkmaz Yolda İnat," *Hürriyet*, February 9, 2006; Ertuğrul Özkök, "Noktayı Koyma Zamanı Geldi," *Hürriyet*, February 10, 2006.

Why did conservative parents not give up and still insist on sending their children to the Imam-Hatip schools despite all these restrictive policies? The major answer is that conservative parents want their children to receive both Islamic and secular education in these schools.[160] Imam-Hatip schools are particularly important for girls. Female students have attended these schools since 1976, and their ratio reached to 44 percent of total students in the 1997–1998 academic year.[161] In a recent survey, half of the female students noted that if they had not attended the Imam-Hatip schools, their conservative parents would not have sent them to school at all.[162] People not only have sent their children to these schools voluntarily, but they have also constructed the school buildings. According to the 1991 data, private associations funded 66 percent of the building of the Imam-Hatip schools, whereas 19 percent of them were funded by state-private cooperation and only 10 percent were financed largely by the state. Moreover, in 2006, 85 percent of the population supported Imam-Hatip graduates' right to enroll in any university.[163] Despite this popular support of Imam-Hatip schools, the assertive secularists did not make any compromise from their policies against these schools.

The Qur'an Courses

The Turkish state has tried to control private Qur'an courses since the 1920s by either closing them or turning them into official courses under the auspices of the Diyanet and controlled by the ministry of education. Yet Islamic communities have opened illegal Qur'an courses, generally behind the façade of legal dormitories. In 1997, in the briefings to the media and high court judges, the generals presented the Qur'an courses and Imam-Hatip schools as reservoirs of votes for Islamists.[164] The February 28 administration substantially marginalized the Qur'an courses by introducing the policy of eight-year education. The Qur'an courses that had been teaching students who did not finish the eighth

---

[160] "İmam-Hatip Liseleri," *Yeni Şafak*, June 27–July 7, 2005.
[161] Özdalga 1999, 428.
[162] Ruşen Çakır, İrfan Bozan, and Balkan Talu, "İmam-Hatip Liseleri: Efsaneler ve Gerçekler," June 14, 2004, http://www.tesev.org.tr/etkinlik/134–144.pdf.
[163] Yavuz 2003, 127. Çarkoğlu and Toprak 2006, 55.
[164] "'Şeriat'a Dikkat' Kitapçığı," *Sabah*, April 26, 1997.

grade were closed down. Only summer courses were allowed to teach graduates of the fifth grade. So the teaching of the Qur'an to students under the age of twelve became completely prohibited even in summer. In their briefings, the military generals had exaggerated the number of students in the legal and illegal Qur'an course as 1,685,000.[165] According to the data from the Diyanet, the number of male students enrolled in the official Qur'an courses was 47,291 in 1996. Due to the February 28 policies, it decreased to 8,766 in 2000. The decrease among the females (from 111,155 to 76,340) was not so sharp.[166]

In December 2003, the AK Party attempted to improve the conditions of the Qur'an courses through a new regulation prepared by the Diyanet. The new regulation included some minor changes, such as the authorization to open evening classes, the reduction of the minimum student requirement from fifteen to ten, the removal of time limits (two months) in summer, and the permission to open dormitories.[167] These changes resulted in considerable opposition by the assertive secularists. They accused the AK Party of harboring a hidden Islamist agenda. President Sezer, who opposed the new regulation, met with Mehmet Aydın, minister of the state in charge of religious affairs, and successfully pressured him to cancel the regulation.

The conditions of the Qur'an courses became worse in February 2005 with a judgment by the Council of State. In a 16–7 vote, the council rescinded a specific regulation, which had increased the education time from three days to five days a week in summer Qur'an courses. Moreover, the council applied to the Constitutional Court to declare unconstitutional the law that permitted teaching the Qur'an in summer to students who had finished fifth grade. According to the council, it is the duty of the state to educate citizens loyal to secularism, and, therefore, it should not allow antisecular education. Secular education should be solid and continuous. Religious education, even in summer, will negatively affect a student's secular training before finishing the eighth grade.[168]

Debates on the Qur'an courses flared up again in May 2005. Mainly because the official courses could not teach the Qur'an to children

[165] "İşte Brifing," *Sabah*, June 12, 1997.
[166] Çakır and Bozan 2005, 87.
[167] "Kuran Kursları Okullara Giriyor," *Radikal*, December 5, 2003.
[168] "Danıştay," *Radikal*, February 10, 2005; Nazlı Ilıcak, "Laiklik Dinsizlik mi?" *Dünden Bugüne Tercüman*, February 10, 2005.

younger than fifteen (or in summer, twelve) years old, several unofficial courses were opened. These courses have been monitored and raided by the gendarmes. The assertive secularists wanted the new criminal code to include imprisonment from six months to two years for the staff of these courses. The AK Party group, however, passed the bill with a possible imprisonment from three months to one year, which may also be turned into the payment of a fine.[169] The assertive secularist media declared the bill as granting permission to undertake illegal Qur'an education. Sezer vetoed the bill. The AK Party group repassed the bill, overruling Sezer's veto.[170] Erdoğan defended the new law and the right to teach the Qur'an to children. He said that children should be as free to read the Qur'an as they are free to read "Teksas-Tommiks" (i.e., comic books).[171] All these statements and failed policies of the AK Party politicians regarding headscarves, Imam-Hatip schools, and Qur'an courses later constituted the prosecutor's indictment against the party.

CONCLUSION

The Turkish state's policies toward religion, particularly in schools, have been much more exclusionary than American polices. Policies in Turkey have been even more restrictive than those in France due to the combination of the assertive secularist ideology and the semi-authoritarian military and judiciary in Turkey. The Kemalists have defended the existing dominance of assertive secularism, which has led exclusionary policies toward not only Islam but also all other religions. The conservatives, however, have defended passive secularism as an alternative.

The struggle between the Kemalists and the conservatives obviously has certain aspects related to interests. Assertive and passive secularist ideologies may be used by certain individuals as means in their power politics and competition over economic interests. Yet ideologies still play a crucial role in the formation of interests. Even the arguments based on class struggle should not disregard that ideology is an

---

[169] The bill passed in parliament on May 27, 2005; no. 5357.
[170] The law passed in parliament on June 29, 2005; no. 5377.
[171] "Teksas Tommiks Okuyan Çocuk Kur'an da Öğrenebilir," *Zaman*, June 18, 2005.

important parameter to define classes in Turkey. Several members of the Kemalist elite, especially in the military and judiciary, came from low-income families or even villages. Similarly, the conservatives include many who can economically and socially be categorized as elite. In this regard, the division between the Kemalists and conservatives cannot be simply explained by socioeconomic or institutional boundaries, thus ignoring their ideological polarization.

Therefore, assertive and passive secularist ideologies are far from being epiphenomenal or simple reflections of institutions. Given the institutional structure of state-religion relations in Turkey, including the Diyanet, Imam-Hatip schools, and religious instruction in schools, one would think that Islam is favored by the Turkish state. However, because of the dominance of assertive secularist ideology, Islam is an excluded, not favored, religion in the Turkish public sphere. These institutions are mainly intended to construct a particular version of Islam, which is a simple affair of individual conscience without any public impact. These institutions are part of an assertive secularist project to create, in the words of Ahmet Yaşar Ocak, a "Kemalist Islam."[172]

The AK Party has tried to resist the assertive secularist policies, just as other conservative/center-right parties did in the past. Nevertheless, it has not been successful as seen by the persistence of assertive secularist policies toward the headscarf, Imam-Hatip schools, and Qur'an courses. The AK Party politicians were hoping that the EU membership process would lead to the moderation of these policies, in particular, and assertive secularism, in general. Some European institutions have played such a role. The Netherlands Scientific Council for Government Policy, for example, noted that "the issue of Islam in Turkey is not so much a problem of the influence of religion on the state as a problem of the influence of the state on religion. This is because government intervention in religion is stronger in Turkey than in EU member states."[173] Yet the majority of the EU institutions have generally focused only on the rights of the Alevis and non-Muslims, while simply ignoring violations

---

[172] Ocak 1997, 18.
[173] The council also stresses that "the constitutional restrictions on the democratic process aimed at protecting the secular state system [in Turkey] are incompatible with the principles of the EU. This observation applies equally to the role of the military as a guardian of this system." WRR 2004, 9.

of the majority Sunni population's religious freedoms.[174] Moreover, on June 29, 2004, in the *Leyla Şahin v. Turkey* case, the European Court of Human Rights decided that the Turkish state had the right to expel students wearing headscarves from their universities.[175] This decision substantially disappointed the Turkish conservatives.

In Turkey, there has been a tension between the ideological dominance of assertive secularism in state institutions and the highly religious nature of society.[176] That is why conservative parties, which have accommodated Turkish society's demands regarding religious education and public visibility of religion, have received the overwhelming majority of votes in elections. Thus, the Kemalist elite have been concerned about a truly democratic regime – a government by the people. As Göle stresses, there has been a conflict between the Kemalist understanding of secularism and democracy.[177] In the words of Hakan Yavuz, "Kemalism has been superficially Western in form while remaining rigidly authoritarian and dogmatic in substance. It continues to stress republicanism over democracy, homogeneity over difference, the military over the civilian, and the state over society."[178] The February 28 process is an example of the tension between the Kemalist elite's assertive secularist ideology and the highly religious Turkish society. This struggle will not end unless a shift from assertive to passive secularism occurs, or unless there is a decline of religiosity in Turkish society.[179]

---

[174] The U.S. Department of State's "Reports on International Religious Freedom" are more objective than several EU reports because the former mention all state oppressions, including those over not only non-Muslims and Alevi Muslims but also Sunni Muslims, such as the purge of "religiously observant" Muslim officers from the Turkish military and the ban on wearing headscarves by university students and civil servants. U.S. Department of State 2006.

[175] McGoldrick 2006, 140–72. For a critique of the *Şahin* decision, see Gunn 2005b; Arslan 2005a, 72–96.

[176] See Tables 14 and 15 in the conclusion.

[177] Göle 1997, 48; Göle 1995, 86.

[178] He continues, "[Kemalism's] quixotic quest to radically recast Turkish culture, history, and identity has ensured a permanent *kulturkampf* against society, guaranteeing, ironically, Turkey's failure to make the transition to a Western-style liberal democracy." Yavuz 2000, 34. For critiques of Kemalism, see also Yavuz and Esposito 2003; Kasaba 1997.

[179] For some scholars, even a decline of societal religiosity would not solve the deeper problem because Kemalism has trouble with any kinds of politics. Kemalism "restricts the legitimate sphere of politics, reduces politics to proper administration

If assertive secularism is so contradictory to the religious character of the majority of the Turkish society, then how did it initially become the dominant ideology in Turkey? Chapter 7 searches for an historical answer to this question.

to achieve the already (prepolitically) set goals/tasks, emphasizes unity over diversity in an absolutist manner and denies the integrative aspects of political activity.... [T]here is a clash between the Kemalist state and any political activity of society." Çınar 2004, 159.

7

Westernization and the Emergence of Assertive Secularism (1826–1997)

Assertive secularism became the dominant ideology in the founding of the Turkish Republic due to the impact of the Ottoman *ancien régime*. In the Ottoman Empire, Islamic law was dominant in legal and judicial systems. The *Şeyhülislam* – the head of the ulema (doctors of Islamic sciences) – held important political authority within the monarchical system. The ulema played significant roles in the center (Istanbul) and other parts of the empire. They were responsible for religious services, education, legal interpretation, judiciary, management of the foundations, and taxation.[1]

The Ottoman Empire was not a theocracy for two main reasons. First, Islamic law was not the only source of legislation. The sultans were making certain laws based on political needs.[2] The Turkish name of Suleiman the Magnificent (1494–1566), for example, was Kanuni (the lawmaker). Second, the Ottoman ulema were civil servants paid by the state and under the political control of the sultan.[3] Moreover, like the ulema in other Sunni countries, they were different from the Catholic clergy and Shia ulema in the sense that their differences from laypeople were functional instead of theological. The legitimacy of the Ottoman ulema largely came from the state's endorsement, their knowledge, and the people's acceptance, instead of from a specific religious hierarchy.

[1] Okumuş 1999, 152–71. See also Timur 1986.
[2] Karpat 2001, 156–7; Daver 1955, 27–30.
[3] Barkey 2008, 104–8.

The Ottoman sultans ruled the core of the Muslim territories and claimed to be the caliphs of the Muslims for centuries.[4] In the Ottoman *millet* system, the Turks were considered part of the Muslim *millet* (religious community) rather than a separate entity.[5] In the early twentieth century, however, the successor to the empire, the Republic of Turkey, was founded on the basis of a secular nationalism. It is puzzling that the Ottoman Empire, where Islamic institutions were fundamental, gave birth to Turkey, where assertive secularism has been dominant.

Scholars have debated whether the emergence of modern Turkey displays a rupture from or a continuation of the Ottoman Empire. Following the foundation of the Turkish Republic, the rupture argument was dominant. "The essential novelty of the Kemalist republic and its making a clean break with the Ottoman past was the theme, not only of Kemalist historiography itself, but of literally dozens of books published in the West."[6] Later on, scholars, including Niyazi Berkes, Erik Zürcher, and Şerif Mardin, have stressed the continuity between the empire and the republic.[7]

Both sides are right on certain aspects of this controversial issue. On the one hand, the Turkish Republic was an extension of the Ottoman Empire because it inherited the secular institutions of the empire, such as the schools, courts, and laws. On the other hand, the republic represented a radical change because it eliminated the Islamic institutions left from the empire. This synthesis of continuity and change describes not only institutions but also ideology and policy. Assertive secularism was embraced by several members of the Ottoman elite as an oppositional ideology in the late nineteenth century, when Islamism was dominant. Later, it became dominant by the foundation of the republic, whose framers were the former Ottoman elite. If one looks at the Ottoman institutions and ideologies as a static entity, then the empire

---

[4] Kayalı 1997, esp. 17.

[5] Karpat 1973, 31–40; Barkey 2008, 109–53; Küçükcan 2003, 480–4.

[6] Zürcher 2004b, 99. For examples of the rupture argument, see Ahmad 1993, esp. ix, 77; Daver 1955, 43. Aykut Kansu also emphasizes rupture rather than continuity. Yet he is still critical of the Kemalist historiography: for him the turning point is 1908, not 1923. Kansu 1997.

[7] Berkes 1998 [1964]; Zürcher 2004a; Mardin 1989; Mardin 1973; Mardin 1997d. Metin Heper also argues, "Continuity rather than change characterizes Turkish political culture. Ottoman political norms emerged and developed during the many centuries of the Empire. They persist today, affecting numerous aspects of contemporary Turkish politics." Heper 2000, 63. See also Bottoni 2007.

would seem different from the republic. However, if one regards the Ottoman experience as a continuously evolving process, the republic appears to be its result.

In chronological order, the reformist elites in the late Ottoman Empire were three major groups: the Tanzimat bureaucrats, the Young Ottomans, and the Young Turks. The first group held a pragmatic view of Westernization. They wanted to "save the empire" by imitating the European model through institutional reforms and European-style education. They did not have a consistent ideological position vis-à-vis secularism or Islamism. The Young Ottomans, however, leaned toward Islamism. They thought that modernizing reforms was compatible with the preservation of the Islamic identity of the empire. The Young Turks, though, ideologically differed from their predecessors. Several of them embraced European, especially French, secular social sciences and political ideologies. Yet a secular state was still an elite fantasy at that time. Mustafa Kemal Atatürk (1881–1938) and other framers of the Turkish Republic were the successors of the Young Turks. As Mardin puts it, "Young Ottoman theories were partly of Islamic origin. In the ideas of the Young Turks this substratum is weaker and it disappears completely in Atatürk."[8]

The late Ottoman and republican elite did not invent assertive secularism; they imported it from France, in addition to many other European ideologies, such as republicanism and nationalism. The Turkish word *laiklik* (secularism) comes from the French *laïcité*. Turkey embraced assertive secularism, like France and unlike the United States, mainly because of the reformist elites' reaction to the Ottoman *ancien régime* based on the alliance between the monarchy and hegemony of Islam. Due to its significant role in justifying the *ancien régime*, in the eyes of the republican elite, Islam was a barrier against modernization. Therefore, they decided to eliminate Islam from the republic's public sphere. Conservative Muslims were willing to protect their dominance by opposing a secular regime. That shaped the severe conflict between the secularists and Islamists, which eventually led to the dominance of assertive secularism in Turkey.

This chapter examines the Ottoman era in three periods, adapting from Berkes's periodization.[9] It also explores the republican era with

---

[8] Mardin 2000 [1962], 404.
[9] Berkes 1998 [1964].

regard to three periods. It divides the history of secularism in Turkey into these six periods for the sake of analytical clarity. That does not undermine the fact that the breaks between the periods were actually not so sharp, and reality was more complex than these parsimonious summaries.

THE BUREAUCRATS AND THE ULEMA: THE RISE OF THE BUREAUCRATIC STATE

From the Janissaries to Abdülhamid II (1826–1876)

From its foundation in 1299 to the Treaty of Karlofça in 1699, the Ottoman Empire was militarily influential in Eastern Europe. Then the balance of power changed in favor of other European countries. That was very disturbing to the Ottoman elite, who were accustomed to a position of superiority. The military, scientific, and economic challenges from Western Europe, as well as the domestic problems of governance, empowered the idea of reform mainly through the imitation of Western institutions.[10] Sultan Mahmud II (1785–1839) was dedicated to Westernization. When he was enthroned in 1808, the Janissaries, the elite infantry unit in the Ottoman army, was the main barrier against the reforms he was planning. The Janissaries was founded in the early fourteenth century, and its number was more than one hundred thousand in the early nineteenth century. Taking a lesson from the previous Sultan Selim III (1761–1808), who wanted to reform the military and was therefore assassinated by the Janissaries, Mahmud II did not directly challenge them for about two decades.

In 1826, the Janissaries revolted against Mahmud II's attempt to reform the military structure. The sultan received the support of the ulema, the people of Istanbul, and a number of divisions within the military. He ordered the bombardment of the Janissaries' barracks, execution of the remaining ones, and declared the abolishment of their institution. This was a turning point in the history of Ottoman Westernization that changed the domestic balance of power.[11] By the elimination of the Janissaries, "the ulema lost a main source of

[10] Findley 1980, 114–20.
[11] Zürcher 2004a, 39–40.

leverage over the court and the bureaucracy."[12] After that, Mahmud II founded new military divisions as well as the School of Medicine (1827) and the Military Academy (1834). With these new Western-type institutions, "the traditional links between the military and the religious institutions had been broken decisively."[13]

Mahmud II reformed the state structure by creating a centralized bureaucratic system based on specialization. His reforms were a challenge to the ulema and to the Islamic nature of the Ottoman state. Mahmud II also weakened the ulema by putting the administration of Islamic foundations in the hands of the governmental bureaucracy.[14] Some of his reforms, however, were formalistic. He ordered his photos to be put in public buildings and reformed the dress codes of the civil servants by requiring the wearing of pants and fez. Because of these reforms, he was criticized as "*gavur padişah*" (infidel sultan) by traditionalists.[15]

Mahmud II died in 1839, right before the announcement of the Tanzimat Edict. Following his death, the bureaucrats, such as Mustafa Reşid, Fuad, and Ali Paşas, continued the reforms and dominated Ottoman politics for about three decades until another influential sultan ascended to the throne.[16] The Tanzimat Edict addressed Muslim and non-Muslim citizens alike. It marked the end of the old *millet* system, which identified citizens regarding their religious communities. The new policy was Ottomanism, which aimed to create a politically unified "Ottoman nation."[17] The new penal code of 1843 maintained the equality of Muslims and non-Muslims in the empire. A year later, "the death penalty against apostasy from Islam" was abrogated.[18] The Islahat Edict in 1856 enforced this new premise. It provided equality to non-Muslim citizens of the empire by abolishing their *zımmi* (protected) secondary status. This new citizenship policy was intended to solve some domestic problems and to respond to the European powers' pressure concerning the non-Muslim minorities. It meant a substantial transformation of the legal and philosophical foundation of the empire.[19]

---

[12] Hanioğlu 2008, 59.
[13] Berkes 1998 [1964], 111.
[14] Okumuş 1999, 152–71. In 1836, Mahmud II founded the Directorate of the Foundations. Chambers 1964, 317–18; Sugar 1964, 156.
[15] Hanioğlu 2008, 4.
[16] Ibid., 60.
[17] Mardin 2000 [1962], 155–64.
[18] Zürcher 2004a, 61.
[19] Karpat 2001, 75–6.

The Tanzimat period was a continuation of Mahmud II's reforms, in terms of the marginalization of the ulema by the bureaucrats.[20] Several jobs, which had been undertaken by the ulema, were transferred to new bureaucratic positions, such as mayor and neighborhood/village headman.[21] In addition to the institutional division, there was an ideational disagreement between the Westernized bureaucrats and the Islamic ulema. "Through their secularizing reforms, the bureaucrats of the *Tanzimat* were alienated from both the doctors of Islamic law and the folk, whereas in the past a common idiom and code of conduct linked these elements."[22]

One of the two main fault lines between the bureaucrats and the ulema was the legal reforms. The foundation of secular, mixed, and commercial courts resulted in a demand for new legal codes. The bureaucrats sought to adopt French commercial and civil codes, while the ulema aimed to codify the Islamic law.[23] In one of his discussions with the ulema, Mustafa Reşid Paşa said that the Sharia had nothing to do with the legal reforms. The ulema accused him of apostasy, and he was temporarily removed from his position by the sultan. Yet he returned to the post and succeeded in the promulgation of the French commercial code in 1850.[24] As to the civil law, however, both the bureaucrats and the ulema made compromises and reached an agreement in 1867 to appoint Ahmed Cevdet Paşa (both a doctor of Islamic law and a bureaucrat) to preside over the Mecelle Committee, which would prepare the new civil code.[25] Although the project was never fully completed due to the rising rivalry between the bureaucrats and the ulema, the committee succeeded in preparing the code primarily based on the Hanafi School of Islamic law. The Mecelle was used as the civil code of the empire until its demise.[26]

The second controversial issue between the ulema and the bureaucrats was educational reforms. On the one hand, the ulema were concerned about new Western-type secular schools. On the other, they lacked a

[20] İnalcık 1964, 56–62.
[21] Okumuş 1999, 206–13, 323, 334–5.
[22] Mardin 1989, 9–10.
[23] Berkes 1998, 160–7.
[24] İnalcık 1964, 62; Lewis 1968, 110–14; Okumuş 1999, 324, 328–31.
[25] Mardin 1961, 274, 278; Ortaylı 1983; Onar 1955, 294.
[26] Mecelle was also used in several former Ottoman regions after their independence: Albania until 1928, Lebanon until 1932, Syria until 1949, and Iraq until 1953. Yavuz 1986, 96.

sufficient alternative educational project to propose. In the classical system, the Ottoman Empire "never accepted responsibility for the basic education of its citizens or subjects. Hence no formal system of public education then existed."[27] The schools of the classical period were Enderun Mektebi (for training top bureaucrats), *medrese* (for training the ulema), *sübyan mektebi* (local primary schools), or paid *lala* (private home teachers).[28] The Tanzimat rulers added new secular institutions of higher education, such as the Civil Service School, to the military schools founded by Mahmud II.

During the Tanzimat period, the European influence on the education system was visible at both the ideational and personal levels. "The military schools of the Tanzimat were from the beginning centers of modernization, which some observers even saw as centers of 'materialism.'"[29] In the Military Medical School, "[t]he majority of the teaching staff was composed of Europeans, converts, and non-Muslim natives."[30] At first, the Ottoman education system preserved its elitist view and emphasized "the role of the *lycée* and higher education at the expense of mass popular education."[31] It was much later that mass education was taken to be a duty of the state and that primary education became compulsory.[32] Galatasaray Sultanisi was founded in 1868 by the Ottoman state partly as a result of the French pressure.[33] It became the most prestigious public high school in Istanbul by instructing in French and training top bureaucrats. The first director of Galatasaray "was a Frenchman, succeeded by an Armenian; the third and fourth were Greek."[34] In 1877, the fifth director, Ali Suavi, was appointed as the first Muslim. In this multireligious school, only half of the students were Muslims.[35] The main resistance to the school came from the pope and some other non-Muslim leaders because Galatasaray took "the French *laïque* school" as the model.[36]

---

[27] Frey 1964, 211.
[28] Ibid.
[29] Mardin 1997c, 123.
[30] Berkes 1998 [1964], 177.
[31] Ward and Rustow 1964, 455.
[32] Frey 1964, 214–15.
[33] Fortna 2002, 102–3.
[34] Berkes 1998 [1964], 189.
[35] Mehmedoğlu 2001, 145–54.
[36] Berkes 1998 [1964], 189–90; also 406.

The periods of Mahmud II and the Tanzimat were very important for the Westernization reforms of the Ottoman institutions. These reforms resulted in the coexistence of secular and Islamic schools, courts, and laws. In these periods, the reforms were made through a pragmatic view toward the goals of Westernization.[37] The bureaucrats did not have an explicitly secular ideology. A new period began in 1876 with the enthroning of Abdülhamid II (1842–1918), who would reemphasize the Islamic character of the empire.

THE YOUNG OTTOMANS: RE-ISLAMIZATION

From Abdülhamid II to the Second Parliament (1876–1908)

In the 1860s and 1870s, the split between the bureaucrats and the ulema blurred. In 1865, several intellectuals founded Genç Osmanlılar Cemiyeti (Society of Young Ottomans) with the goal of creating a constitutional regime. Many Young Ottomans were not ulema, yet they were critical of the Westernist Tanzimat bureaucrats and generally had Islamist views.[38] The most influential of them was Namık Kemal, the promoter of the concepts of "fatherland" and "freedom" in the Empire. Kemal was both an Islamist and a reformist.[39] He played an important role in the declaration of a European-style Ottoman constitution. At the same time, he tried to keep the constitution conforming to Islamic principles.

In 1876, the Young Ottomans allied with the Westernist bureaucrats led by Mithad Paşa, to engineer two *coup d'états*. They eventually placed Abdülhamid II on the throne after he had promised to declare a constitution and open a parliament. Abdülhamid II fulfilled these two promises right after he was enthroned.[40] The Ottoman Parliament had two branches: the Assembly of Representatives

---

[37] Mardin 1989, 136; Mardin 2000 [1962], 118.
[38] İnalcık 1998 , 8–10; Kayalı 1997, 22–3.
[39] Kemal 1962 [1910]; Mardin 2000 [1962], 283–336.
[40] The opening of the Ottoman Parliament was appreciated by both Westernists and Islamists. Esat Efendi, a civil servant and journalist, published an essay on constitutionalism, *Hükümet-i Meşruta (Constitutional Government)*, in 1876. He noted that several features of parliamentary regime, such as the system of checks and balances, separation of powers, limitations over the sultan's power, and non-Muslims' representation in parliament, were compatible with and even required by the Sharia. Full text quoted by Tunaya 1978.

elected by the people and the Assembly of Notables appointed by the sultan. The former comprised 115 (69 Muslim and 46 non-Muslim) representatives, and the latter included 26 appointees.[41] Within a year, Abdülhamid II prorogued parliament and implemented an absolute rule. The Young Ottomans were either imprisoned or exiled.

Abdülhamid II reemphasized Islam as a source of Ottoman identity and foreign policy. Both the Young Ottomans' Islamic intellectual tendencies and Abdülhamid II's Islamist policies meant the swing of the pendulum from Westernism to Islamism. A primary reason for this transformation was that the Christian minorities in the Balkans (e.g., Greeks, Serbs, and Romanians) had already achieved independence. Moreover, the empire received a large number of Muslim refugees from the Balkans and Caucasus, who escaped from the newly independent states and Russia.[42] These transformations meant a much larger Muslim majority in the empire. It was then more reasonable to pursue an Islamist policy that brought together different Muslim groups, instead of the Tanzimat's Ottomanism.[43] Moreover, the Ottoman Empire was one of the few independent Muslim states in the world. Abdülhamid II used his title of caliph to defend the rights of Muslim minorities and sometimes used it as a political card to play against European colonial empires.

Abdülhamid II was a pious Muslim, but "not an Islamist reactionary." He "played the piano and spoke French…; was fond of theatre, opera and operettas … ; and wrote short plays in French."[44] Although Abdülhamid II attached importance to Islam in his identity politics and foreign policy, "many of his close personal associates were non-Muslims…. During his tenure a large number of Christians entered government service and occupied high positions over Muslim subordinates."[45] Abdülhamid II took a big step forward in the expansion of the school system. Under his rule, the number of public

---

[41] "İlk Parlamento," accessed at the Web site of the Turkish Parliament, http://www.tbmm.gov.tr/tarihce/kb2.htm, on March 16, 2006.

[42] McCarthy 2004; Zürcher 2000, 171.

[43] Karpat 1988; Karpat 1973, 106–7; Karpat 2001; Kayalı 1997, 31. See also Akçura 1976 [1904].

[44] Tezel 2005, 74.

[45] Karpat 2001, 155.

primary schools increased from 200 to more than 5,000, secondary schools increased from 250 to 620 (of which 74 were for girls), and high schools increased from 5 to 104.[46]

Abdülhamid II tried to impose Islamic ethics on students by putting courses about Islam into the curricula.[47] Nevertheless, he could not stop the spread of materialism and positivism in Ottoman schools and universities.[48] German philosopher Ludwig Büchner's *Force and Matter*, the most influential book of materialism at that time, became the favorite of Ottoman medical doctors.[49] The military schools were also dominated by Western ideologies and isolated from the society. They trained students through a "utopian mentality" in a way that they were "segregated from Ottoman everyday life."[50] This materialist education system also cultivated an anti-Islamic view among the young elite. Islam became the scapegoat that would be blamed for the socioeconomic backwardness of society. This perspective was something new in the late nineteenth century. Ziya Paşa, an Islamist and reformist Young Ottoman,[51] lamented this issue in his famous verses:

> Islam, they say, is a stumbling-block to the progress of the state,
> This story was not known before, and now it is the fashion.
> Forgetting our religious loyalty in all our affairs,
> Following Frankish ideas is now the fashion.[52]

The Abdülhamid era had two opposite trends. On the one hand, it was the period when the sultan and the Young Ottomans tried to reestablish the dominance of Islamism. On the other hand, it was the period when certain materialist views were imported from Europe and transmitted to the Ottoman youth, particularly through the educational system. Under these circumstances, the Young Turks arose as the new elite of the late nineteenth and early twentieth centuries.

---

[46] Tezel 2005, 76.
[47] Fortna 2000.
[48] Somel 2001, 4–5, 275; Bağcı 1997, esp. 219.
[49] Özervarlı 2007, 80; Berkes 1998 [1964], 181.
[50] Mardin 1997b, 204–5.
[51] Mardin 2000 [1962], 337–59.
[52] Translated and quoted by Lewis 1968, 139.

THE YOUNG TURKS: THE SEEDS
OF ASSERTIVE SECULARISM

From the Second Parliament to the Republic (1908–1923)

The Young Turks (*Jeunes Turcs*), unlike the Young Ottomans, criticized Islamic institutions for the persistence of traditionalism and opted for Westernization. They opposed the rule of Abdülhamid II. Many Young Turks were speaking French, as is reflected in their publications in French, readings of French thinkers, and institutionalization in Paris.[53] Several of the Young Turks became members of or were influenced by the French and Italian freemason lodges, both of which had negative attitudes toward religions' public impacts.[54] The Young Turks also founded their own secret societies. The most effective of them was İttihad ve Terakki Cemiyeti (Committee of Union and Progress, or CUP), founded in 1889.[55] The founders of the CUP were four students of the Military Medical School: two Kurds, one Albanian, and one Circassian.[56] At the outset, the CUP represented only an intellectual opposition to Abdülhamid II. Later, several young military officers joined the CUP and staged a series of revolts and *coup d'états*.[57]

In 1908, the Young Turks successfully forced Abdülhamid II to promulgate the constitution and reopen the Ottoman Parliament. In the new parliament, there were 288 deputies, including "147 Turks, 60 Arabs, 27 Albanians, 26 Greeks, 14 Armenians, 10 Slavs, and 4 Jews."[58] As the Young Turks gained political power, the pendulum swung back from Islamism to Westernism. The Young Turks' secularist views created a reaction among traditionalist soldiers and low-ranked officers, which led to the "31 March Incident" in 1909. The military officers affiliated with the CUP suppressed the insurgence and dethroned Abdülhamid II. In 1913, three leaders of the CUP, Enver, Talat, and Cemal Paşas, made a final coup and founded an oligarchy, which ruled the empire until its defeat in World War I (1914–1918).

[53] Hanioğlu 1990.
[54] Zarcone 2006, esp. 137–8.
[55] Hanioğlu 1985.
[56] Temo 1987 [1939]; Lewis 1968, 197.
[57] Hanioğlu 2000, 3–7, 314; Zürcher 2000, 151–7.
[58] Ahmad 1969, 28.

Westernization was a major goal for the CUP. For that reason, it founded several Western-style schools, in addition to reorganizing the Darülfünun (university in Istanbul). The CUP rule also pursued certain policies that weakened the political power of the ulema. In 1916, the *Şeyhülislam* was eliminated from the cabinet, the Sharia courts were transferred from his jurisdiction to that of the ministry of justice, and the administration of foundations, mosques, and *medrese*s was moved from his jurisdiction to that of the new ministry of religious affairs and foundations.[59]

In terms of ideology, the CUP was divided by the central statism and positivism of Ahmed Rıza (speaker of parliament) and the nationalism of Ziya Gökalp (ideologue), on the one hand, and liberalism and decentralized individualism of Prince Sabaheddin (political activist), on the other.[60] All three were influenced by French sociologists. In the words of Lewis, Auguste Comte's "positivist sociology inspired Ahmed Rıza to the first expositions of Union and Progress, and profoundly influenced the subsequent development of secularist radicalism in Turkey." Moreover, "it was in sociology, especially that of Emile Durkheim, that Ziya Gökalp found the conceptual framework within which he constructed the first elaborate theoretical formulation of Turkish nationalism." Finally, Prince Sabaheddin was "seeking a philosophy for his own rival school, found it in the teachings of Le Play and more especially of Demolins, whose ideas formed the basis of Sabaheddin's doctrines of individual initiative and decentralization."[61] According to Lewis, a "common feature of all these schools is their tendency to treat sociology as a kind of philosophy, even of religion, and as a source of quasi-revealed authority on moral, social, political, and even religious problems."[62] Other French thinkers who influenced the Young Turks with their positivistic views included Ernest Renan and Gustave Le Bon.[63]

During the CUP rule, Rıza's and Gökalp's views became dominant. Being marginalized in the CUP, Sabaheddin founded his own Teşebbüs-ü Şahsi ve Adem-i Merkeziyet Cemiyeti (League of Private Initiative and

[59] Berkes 1998, 416.
[60] Hanioğlu 2000, 82–129, 293–4.
[61] Lewis 1968, 231.
[62] Ibid.
[63] Hanioğlu 1985, 614–17; Zürcher 2005, 25.

Decentralization) as an opposition.[64] Central statism and positivism resulted in the popularity of radically secularist ideas among the late Ottoman elite. One may speculate that if Sabaheddin's liberalism based on decentralization and individualism had become dominant,[65] it might have led to the emergence of a passive secularist ideology like that of the United States or a liberal established-religion regime like that in England. Nevertheless, in the late Ottoman era, central statism, instead of liberalism, became dominant due to the sociopolitical conditions of the Empire. The Ottoman *ancien régime* depended on the sultanate and Islamic institutions. The Young Turks regarded both as a barrier against Westernization. Therefore, they embraced anticlerical and illiberal ideologies to challenge these two old institutions. Moreover, the positivist and elitist education alienated the Young Turks from the Muslim majority population. They claimed to have a civilizing mission that required pursuing top-down policies over the people, rather than liberal policies that respected individualism. Additionally, the empire had lost several territories and was still experiencing threats of many new secession demands. As Lewis emphasizes,

> The growing menace, from dissident nationalism and foreign imperialism, to the integrity of the Empire made decentralization seem a dangerous if not suicidal formula. The growing pre-eminence of the army in the revolutionary movement gave the direction of the latter to an institution and a profession that were inevitably imbued with a spirit of authoritarian centralism. Neither private initiative nor decentralization held much appeal for the Prussian-trained officers of the Turkish army.[66]

In addition to the military training,[67] the German influence was effective on civil education in the last decade of the empire.[68] Abdullah Cevdet, a founder of the CUP and the symbol of anti-Islam Westernism, was affected by German popular materialism. His journal *İctihad*, which was publishing Büchner's materialist writings, had a circulation of between three thousand and four thousand.[69] For Cevdet, a total

[64] Küçükömer 2002, 70–2.
[65] Sabahattin 2002 [1973].
[66] Lewis 1968, 204–5.
[67] Ortaylı 2006.
[68] Gencer 2003.
[69] Hanioğlu 2005, 29, 85.

Europeanization was necessary, and this required the abandonment of Islam by the Ottomans: "There is no second civilization; civilization means European civilization, and it must be imported with both its roses and its horns."[70] He also argued that "science is the religion of the élite, whereas religion is the science of masses."[71] According to Şükrü Hanioğlu, Cevdet did not want to be seen as anti-Islamic because that would limit his influence. Instead, he "maintained that Ottoman intellectuals should replace Islamic notions with 'scientific' ones, but always stitching them onto an Islamic 'jacket.'" Moreover, he criticized "those who openly promoted positivism and asked them to use *hadiths* instead of the motto of Comte to make their ideas more palatable to the Muslim masses."[72]

In the words of Erik Zürcher, a set of ideas including "anti-clericalism, scientism, biological materialism, authoritarianism, intellectual elitism, distrust of the masses, social Darwinism and nationalism ... soaked up in the France of the *fin de siècle* was then transmitted by Young Turk thinkers and publicists to the Kemalist activists." The Kemalists were, more than their predecessors, "in a position to fashion their state and society after their ideas."[73] The Kemalists also inherited certain "dreams" from the Young Turks. Kılıçzade Hakkı Bey, a prominent Westernist, published a blueprint of Westernist reform project in Cevdet's journal, *İctihad*, in 1913. The project was entitled "A Very Vigilant Sleep" and, to avoid prosecution, written as if it were a report of a dream. The plan included the closure of *medreses*, *tekkes* and *zaviyes* (Sufi lodges); the ban on the vows to the Muslim Saints; the replacement of the fez with a new national hat; the prohibition on unmarried women's veiling, especially during their education; the ban on wearing the turban and cloak for those other than the certified ulema; the reformation of the Turkish language and alphabet; and the reconstruction of the legal system.[74] It was hard to believe that these marginal ideas would be made official state policies by the Kemalists a decade later. According to Hanioğlu, the Kemalist ideology "may be traced back to the rise

---

[70] Translated and quoted by Lewis 1968, 236.
[71] Translated and quoted by Hanioğlu 1997, 135.
[72] Ibid., 136. See also Hanioğlu 2006, 57–63.
[73] Zürcher 2005, 26. See also Mardin 1997c, 121; Deringil 1993, 170–1.
[74] The complete translation of this article was published as an appendix in Hanioğlu 1997, 150–8.

of Ottoman materialism and [Westernism] … but its victory over the alternatives available at the time was surprising."[75] That is why I define the early Republican period (1923–1937) as a critical juncture, when institutions are in flux and powerful agents can make choices that will have long-lasting results.

THE KEMALISTS: THE DOMINANCE OF ASSERTIVE SECULARISM

From the Republic to Democratic Party (1923–1950)

After the defeat of the Ottoman Empire in World War I, the Turks waged the War of Independence (1919–1922) against Greece and several other invaders.[76] Because Istanbul was under Franco-British occupation, the Turkish Parliament was opened in Ankara. Parliament was a mixture of Westernists and Islamists. It included one hundred twenty-five civil bureaucrats, fifty-three military officers, and fifty-three ulema, in addition to those with other professions.[77] Parliament authorized Mustafa Kemal Paşa ("Atatürk" after 1934) to lead the war. Mustafa Kemal and other leaders used an Islamic discourse during the war to maintain social solidarity and mobilization[78] because "Islam constituted the medium of communication between the elite and the mass cultures."[79]

Following the victory, parliament abolished the Ottoman Sultanate in November 1922. Turkish politics was substantially reconstructed in 1923. In June, Mustafa Kemal's opposition in parliament – the Second Group (which included several Islamists) – was eliminated by the parliamentary elections. In July, Turkey signed the Lausanne Treaty with the victors of World War I. In September, Mustafa Kemal founded the Halk Partisi (People's Party), including all but one deputy in parliament.[80] In October, parliament declared the founding of the Turkish Republic. Mustafa Kemal was elected as the first president by the

---

[75] Hanioğlu 2008, 210.
[76] This war is also named the "Greco-Turkish War."
[77] Sugar 1964, 161.
[78] Zürcher 2000, 161–70.
[79] Kadıoğlu 1998, 11.
[80] T.B.M.M. 1924, 31, 33.

unanimous vote of deputies who were present in the voting (158 out of 287). The Halk Partisi, which became CHP in 1924, ruled the country for twenty-seven years as a single party, except for two short, abortive biparty experiences – Terakkiperver Cumhuriyet Fırkası (Progressive Republican Party)[81] from 1924 to 1925 and Serbest Cumhuriyet Fırkası (Free Republican Party) in 1930.

Mustafa Kemal and his followers pursued a Westernization program based on the ideological dominance of assertive secularism. The Constitution of 1924 had included the statement the "The religion of the Turkish Republic is Islam." The oaths of the president and the members of parliament had also been made in the name of Allah. In 1928, the reference to Islam as an established religion was removed from the constitution, and the oaths became based exclusively on personal honor.[82] Finally, in 1937, the principle of secularism was added to the constitution. Şükrü Kaya, the minister of the interior at the time, explained the government's support of this amendment in parliament with the following words: "We are determinists in our view on history and pragmatist materialists in our affairs.... We note that religion should stay in individuals' consciences and temples without intervening to material life and worldly affairs. We are not letting them intervene and we will not let them intervene."[83]

For the Kemalists, the reforms since the Tanzimat period did not fully succeed because of the coexistence of the secular and Islamic institutions, particularly schools, laws, and courts. The new republic should eliminate this duality.[84] "In the Kemalist regime the direction was reversed toward unification. The writings of the period abounded with criticisms of the dichotomies in life, ranging from law to musical taste and personal attire."[85] Ziya Gökalp, who influenced both the Young Turks and Kemalists, had lamented the diversity of schools as an anarchic situation during the Ottoman era and stressed the need for unification. According to him, there had been three types of schools in the late Ottoman Empire "the *medrese*, the foreign school,

---

[81] This party declared in its program that it was "respectful to religious thoughts and beliefs." Quoted by Yılmaz 2005b, 93. Rustow 1959, 547–9.

[82] T.B.M.M. 1928, 115–16.

[83] T.B.M.M. 1937, 60–1.

[84] Ward and Rustow 1964, 446–7.

[85] Berkes 1998 [1964], 468.

and the *mektep*, the Turkish imitation of the second. 'Talk to a Turk for ten minutes,' Gökalp said, 'and you can discover in which school his mentality has been molded.'"[86] By "foreign school" Gökalp meant hundreds of schools established by Christian missionaries (mainly from France and the United States) all over the Ottoman Empire.[87] Elsewhere, Gökalp emphasized the same point differently:

> In this country there are three layers of people differing from each other by civilization and education: the common people, the men educated in *medrese*s, the men educated in secular schools. The first still are not freed from the effects of Far Eastern civilization; the second are still living in Eastern civilization; it is only the third group which has had some benefits from Western civilization. That means that one portion of our nation is living in an ancient, another in a medieval, and a third in a modern age. How can the life of a nation be normal with such a threefold life? How can we be a real nation without unifying this threefold education?[88]

Sharing these concerns, parliament passed the Tevhid-i Tedrisat (Unification of the Education) Law on March 3, 1924, which would cause the closure of 479 *medrese*s and create a unified secular school system under the control of the ministry of education. The law also opened a department of theology at Darülfünun and required the ministry of education to organize Islamic education.[89] That led to the foundation of twenty-nine Imam-Hatip schools. Later, the Kemalists became more exclusionary toward Islamic education. They eliminated religious instruction from the school curricula in 1927 (except the villages) and removed Arabic and Persian courses in 1929.[90] They closed down all Imam-Hatip schools in 1930 and the department of theology at Darülfünun in 1933. From that time until 1949, there was no legal education of Islam in Turkey except for a few Qur'an courses.[91]

---

[86] Quoted by ibid., 409.

[87] Ortaylı 1983, 165–78; Gencer 2003, 81, 85, 186.

[88] Translated and quoted by Frey 1964, 209. This is similar to French republicans' lament of "two youths" educated by secular and Catholic schools in the early Third Republic (see Chapter 5).

[89] The Law on the Unification of Education, no. 430 in T.B.M.M. 1942 [1924], 242.

[90] Kaplan 1999, 159–60; Özdalga 1999, 418.

[91] The number of the Qur'an courses was nine (232 students) in 1932 and thirty-seven (938 students) in 1942. Frey 1964, 222–3. By 1948, the number increased to ninety-nine (5,751 students). Reed 1955, 122.

The Kemalist reforms also included the abolishment of political Islamic organizations. On March 3, 1924, parliament replaced the Ministry of Religious Affairs and Pious Foundations with the Directorate of Religious Affairs (the Diyanet) and the Directorate of Pious Foundations, both under the prime minister's office. The new law emphasized the distinction between sociopolitical life, and Islamic belief and worship; the former was under the authority of parliament and the latter would be managed by the Diyanet.[92] On the same day, parliament also abolished the caliphate and expelled the Ottoman family members from Turkey after a discussion.[93]

By his speech in parliament, Minister of Justice Seyit Bey convinced the opponents of the abolishment. Seyit Bey, also an expert on Islamic law, stressed that (1) Islam did not require a political institution such as the caliphate and allowed people to decide their own political institutions; (2) the caliphate had been based on the representation of the people, and the new and true representative of the Turkish people was parliament; (3) the Prophet Muhammad stated that the true caliphate would last only thirty years after him and then would be followed by the corrupt regime of sultanate; (4) many other Muslim nations did not recognize the Ottoman caliphs, particularly during World War I; and (5) the lack of a caliph would not create a problem for Islamic worship.[94] During this debate, even the speaker of parliament, Fethi Okyar, used an Islamic discourse and argued that the Turks were seen as "*seyfülislam*" (the sword of Islam) by all other Muslim nations even before the Ottoman sultans received the title of caliph in the sixteenth century.[95] The debate shows that the Islamic discourse was still effective, though it was in decline, in the early republican era.

The civil law was another arena wherein the Kemalists attacked the duality of "the secular" and "the Islamic." Throughout the late nineteenth and early twentieth centuries, there were several attempts, such as the aforementioned Mecelle project, to reconcile secular and Islamic civil laws. In the early republican era, parliamentarians debated alternative projects of a new civil code. Pro-Islamic conservatives, such as Seyit

[92] The law no. 429 in T.B.M.M. 1942 [1924], 241.
[93] The law no. 431 in ibid., 243.
[94] T.B.M.M. 1924, 40–61.
[95] Ibid., 64.

Bey, favored a civil law based on Islamic principles.[96] Seyit Bey and other conservatives were not alone in opposing the total Westernization of the legal system. The nationalists also wanted to draft a civil law that "came out of the Turkish spirit,"[97] and they did not want to "adopt or borrow the codes of Germany or Switzerland in a few months."[98] Seyit Bey was removed from office in November 1924.

The new minister of justice, Mahmut Esat (Bozkurt in 1934), was a keen supporter of adopting the European laws.[99] Mahmut Esat had a PhD in law from Switzerland, and, according to Mardin, had a personal influence on Mustafa Kemal in terms of embracing absolute Westernization.[100] Mahmut Esat once proposed a replacement of Islam with Christianity as the religion of Turks.[101] In 1926, Mahmut Esat led the adoption of the Swiss Civil Code, Italian Criminal Code, and German Commercial Code. The adoption of European laws was the point at which "Kemalism deviated from the Turkist view based on Gökalp's theory of the dichotomy of culture and civilization."[102] Although Gökalp, a founder of Turkish nationalism, wanted to make a distinction between Turkish culture and Western civilization, the Kemalist reforms did not pay attention to such a distinction.[103] Gökalp was seeking a synthetic approach by saying "I am from the Turkish nation, Islamic umma, and Western civilization."[104] "While Gökalp had taken an accommodationist stance arguing for the mutual compatibility of Islam, Turkish culture and contemporary civilization, Kemal [sic] had adopted a model that required the total privatization of religion and full secularization of social life."[105]

The Kemalists used nationalism as a complement to assertive secularism. They justified certain de-Islamization policies not only on the basis of Westernization, but also by eliminating the Arab and

---

[96] Ibid., 60–1.
[97] This is the statement of parliamentarian Şükrü Saraçoğlu. Ibid., 60.
[98] Berkes 1998 [1964], 468.
[99] Yılmaz 2002, 118–19.
[100] Mardin 1997b, 213.
[101] Çıtak 2004, 231, 240.
[102] Berkes 1998 [1964], 468.
[103] Gökalp 1976 [1918]; Timur 1986, 123–4. For a general discussion on culture and civilization, see Elias 2000, 3–44.
[104] Gökalp 2007 [1923], 210. See also Gökalp 1976 [1918].
[105] Kandiyoti 1991, 40.

Persian impacts and returning to the "pure" Turkish culture.[106] Yet they marginalized certain nationalists, particularly those who followed Gökalp's idea that Islam, Turkism, and Westernism were compatible. The closure of the main nationalist association, Türk Ocakları (Turkish Hearths), in 1931 was part of this marginalization.[107] The Kemalists also diverged from classical Turkish nationalist perspective, by attempting to create a new pre-Islamic origin for Turks in Anatolia by defining the Sumerians (2900 BC–1800 BC) and Hittites (1600 BC–1200 BC) as Turks.

The abolishment of the caliphate, the ministry of religious affairs and foundations, and Islamic laws meant the end of Islamism at the state level. The Kemalists also targeted Islamic social organizations. On November 30, 1925, they passed a law that shut down the *türbes* (tombs of Muslim Saints) and closed down all *tekkes* and *zaviyes*, where followers of tariqas had recited God's names, received Sufi training, and organized around a hierarchy. The law also banned religious titles of both Sunnis and Alevis, such as *şeyh, derviş, mürit, dede, seyit, çelebi, baba, emir, nakip,* and *halife.*[108] That made all religious positions illegal, except the imams in mosques who became the Diyanet's civil servants. While banning these centuries-old institutions, Mustafa Kemal no longer needed an Islamic discourse. Instead, he used a modernist discourse:

I flatly refuse to believe that today, in the luminous presence of science, knowledge, and civilization in all aspects, there exist, in the civilized community of Turkey, men so primitive as to seek their material and moral well-being from the guidance of one or another *şeyh*. Gentlemen, you and the whole nation must know, and know well, that the Republic of Turkey cannot be the land of *şeyhs*, dervishes, disciples, and lay brothers. The straightest, truest Way (tarikat) is the way of civilization.[109]

Table 13 lists important Kemalist reforms, half of which have been under constitutional protection since 1961. These reforms, as Nur Yalman notes, aimed "to set up a new culture, with new men ... uncontaminated by ... a past that was regarded as backward.... And since

---

[106] Göle 1996, 44–7.
[107] Cetinsaya 1999, 362–6.
[108] The law no. 677. Daver 1955, 160.
[109] Translated and quoted by Lewis 1968, 410–11.

TABLE 13. *Major Kemalist Reforms (1924–1935)*

Abolishment of the caliphate	1924
Unification of education (closure of the *medreses*)	1924
Closure of the *tekkes, zaviyes,* and *türbes*	1925
Enforcement of wearing the top hat	1925
Adoption of the Western calendar	1925
Adoption of the Swiss Civil Code	1926
Adoption of the Latin alphabet	1928
Adoption of European measurements	1931
Ban on the Arabic *ezan* (call to prayer)	1932
Ban on certain titles (e.g., Efendi, Bey, Paşa)	1934
Ban on certain religious dresses (e.g., cloak)[110]	1934
Adoption of Sunday as holiday	1935

Source: The Turkish Constitution of 1982, Art. 174.

Islam was at the heart of the *ancien régime*, it is Islam that receives the heaviest blow."[111]

The Islamists were against these reforms. Yet the Kemalist regime oppressed any political opposition, let alone an Islamist one. A failed armed opposition was the Şeyh Said Revolt of 1925, which mixed Islamism and Kurdish nationalism. In the same year, the Hat Law resulted in several protests because the hat "was considered a symbol of Christian Europe."[112] The violation of the law (i.e., not wearing the European top hat) was punished by a one-year imprisonment, and, furthermore, some protesters were executed.[113] Beyond the Hat Law, there was resistance against the reforms in general. "The Independence Tribunals played their part in suppressing this resistance. Under the Law on the Maintenance of Order nearly 7500 people were arrested and 660 executed."[114]

During this period, many Islamic scholars experienced state persecution. Mehmed Akif Ersoy, the poet of the National Anthem,

[110] The Kemalist reforms did not include an explicit dress code for women. Some implicit "measures were introduced, making it disadvantageous for any but the old to remain under cover.... The families of government employees were expected to attend public functions unveiled." Berkes 1998 [1964], 474.
[111] Yalman 1973, 154.
[112] Zürcher 2004a, 173.
[113] Chehabi 2004, 212–17; Daver 1955, 176–8.
[114] Zürcher 2004a, 173.

semivoluntarily went into exile in Egypt and died there. Bediüzzaman Said Nursi and Süleyman Hilmi Tunahan faced imprisonment and torture. They initiated underground social movements that eventually attracted millions of supporters. Nursi wrote *Risale-i Nur* (*Epistles of Light*) to show that Islamic faith and modern science are compatible.[115] He avoided politics in an ascetic manner: "I seek refuge in God from Satan and [party] politics."[116] He also added, "Ninety-nine percent of Islam is about ethics, worship, the hereafter, and virtue. Only one percent is about politics; leave that to the rulers."[117] Tunahan devoted his life to teaching the reading of the Qur'an in Arabic, which became difficult after the declaration of Latin script as the only legal alphabet. Along the same lines, Nakşibendi and Kadiri tariqas went underground and continued their spiritual teachings. When Turkey became a multiparty democracy in 1950, these Islamic groups gained relatively more public visibility.

In addition to eliminating it from the public sphere, the Kemalists tried to reform Islam in order to make it a matter of one's conscience. They wanted to create an Islam in their own image.[118] To reach this common goal, the Kemalists had diverse strategies. Some of them were expecting that Islam would gradually be reformed, particularly through the Diyanet and state control over Islamic education.[119] Others were not patient; they wanted to initiate the reform as quickly as possible. In June 1928, an official commission led by Fuad Köprülü wrote a report on reforming mosques. They proposed the Turkification of the *ezan* and prayers, as well as the putting of pews and musical instruments into mosques.[120] Turkification of the prayers was briefly tried and immediately cancelled. The only proposal that was really adopted was the Turkification of the *ezan*. It was first recited in 1932, and with the ban on the Arabic original in the following year, the Turkish *ezan* was enforced by the law and remained as such until 1950.[121] Falih Rıfkı Atay, a close friend and biographer of

---

[115] Kuru and Kuru 2008; Sarıtoprak 2008; Abu Rabi 2003; Mardin 1989.
[116] Nursi 1996b [1929–1934], 368.
[117] Nursi 1996a [1909], 1922.
[118] Aktay 1999; Arat 2004, 320; Zürcher and Linden 2004, 101.
[119] Arslan 1996, 66–70.
[120] For the English translation of this report, see Feroze 1976, 169–72.
[121] Daver 1955, 168–74.

Atatürk, summarizes this experience: "Kemalism is actually a great and substantial religious reform.... Kemalism repealed all Islamic obligations except acts of worship.... Atatürk also initiated the reforms of worship starting with the Turkification of *ezan* and prayer."[122] In this regard, it is very difficult to see the Kemalist understanding of secularism as the separation of Islam from the state.[123]

The Kemalists were aware of religion's important functions as an institution. Some leading Kemalists were affected by Durkheim,[124] who defined religion as a reflection of society, instead of being transcendental.[125] The Kemalists, therefore, wanted to use reformed Islam as an instrument to create a homogeneous nation. They excluded both non-Muslim religious (e.g., Orthodox Christian) and non-Turkish ethnic (e.g., Kurdish) affiliations from the official identity policy.[126] In the Lausanne Treaty, they defined Turkish citizenship according to Islam, by accepting Muslims (both Turks and Kurds) as regular citizens and non-Muslims as minorities. The Lausanne Treaty also included a population exchange with Greece. Turkey sent 1.2 million Orthodox Christians (including those who were speaking Turkish, the Karamanlı) to Greece in exchange for four hundred thousand Ottoman Muslims regardless of their ethnic origin.[127] Another paradoxical policy of the secular Turkish state was the wealth tax enforced between 1942 and 1944, which resulted in the extreme overtaxation of non-Muslims, who were, on average, allegedly wealthier than Muslims in Turkey.[128]

The CHP's authoritarian rule was not confined to its policy toward religions. Newspapers were taken under governmental control or closed down already in 1925. Two-thirds of professors and instructors were purged from Darülfünun in 1933, while it was in the process of becoming Istanbul University.[129] In 1935, the Turkish Women's Union "decided, at the request of the [CHP] leadership, to disband.... The Turkish Freemasons' lodges, whose members had often been prominent

[122] Atay 1980 [1968], 393–4.
[123] Çıtak-Aytürk 2005, 215.
[124] For Durkheim's impact on Mustafa Kemal and Gökalp, see Spencer 1958.
[125] Pals 1996, 88–123.
[126] Yıldız 2001. Currently Kurds constitute about 15% of the population in Turkey. "The Survey of *Milliyet* and Konda," *Milliyet*, March 21, 2007. See also Akyol 2006, 184.
[127] Zürcher and Linden 2004, 143.
[128] Neyzi 2002, 146; Kuyucu 2005, 371.
[129] Zürcher 2004a, 180–1.

in the Young Turk movement from the beginning of the century, were closed down in the same year, as was the union of journalists."[130]

Following Atatürk's death in 1938, İsmet İnönü (1884–1973) became the president. In the aftermath of World War II, Turkey chose to become a part of the "Free World" led by the United States. That encouraged İnönü to accept a new multiparty system.[131] The CHP remained in power by manipulating the first multiparty elections in 1946 with "open voting and secret counting." The CHP Congress in the following year experienced substantial debates on religious education. The participants agreed on the definition of (assertive) secularism as "isolation of religious ideas from the affairs of the state and this world" and that of religion as "an affair of conscience."[132] Yet some CHP parliamentarians criticized the lack of any institution to teach Islam for more than a decade, as well as the Diyanet's docile position without administrative autonomy, sufficient financial sources, and jurisdiction to train imams.[133] The critics stressed that (1) the Christians in Turkey had more rights than Muslims, in terms of religious education, (2) the villagers could not find enough imams for burial ceremonies, and (3) Western democracies (e.g., the United States) are more accommodating toward religion than Turkey.[134] Although these criticisms were rejected by the dominant group in the congress, they were still important to show that even the CHP members characterized its policies as too radical.[135]

The internal criticisms, in addition to the new Democratic Party (DP) opposition, led the CHP government to some policy changes, such as allowing people to go to the Hajj using foreign currency, which was under state monopoly. In 1949, the government opened eight ten-month Imam-Hatip courses.[136] In the same year, İnönü appointed Şemsettin Günaltay, a long-term CHP politician and a scholar of both physical sciences and Islam, as the prime minister. The Günaltay

---

[130] Ibid., 180.
[131] Kasaba 1993, 50–1.
[132] CHP 1948, 448.
[133] Ibid., 448–51, 457.
[134] Ibid., 450–1, 455, 457.
[135] In Ankara, "[n]ot a single mosque of any size was built during the 27-year" CHP rule. Ahmad 1993, 92.
[136] Tarhanlı 1993, 24.

government opened a department of theology at Ankara University and initiated optional religious instruction in the primary schools.[137] The CHP did not go beyond these lip services to Muslim demands due to its assertive secularist ideology. In the 1950 elections, the CHP received only 39 percent of the votes, whereas the DP became the leading party with 53 percent.

In sum, the period from the declaration of the republic to the constitutional amendment enshrining secularism as a principle (1923–1937) was the critical juncture for the dominance of assertive secularism in Turkey. This period made a clear distinction between the Ottoman era, when assertive secularism was a marginal ideology, and the republican era, when it became dominant. This critical period has had an influential ideological and institutional legacy.

THE LEFTISTS AND RIGHTISTS: THE MODERATION OF ASSERTIVE SECULARIST POLICIES

From Democratic Party to September 12 Coup (1950–1980)

In 1950, the DP won the parliamentary elections, and its leader Adnan Menderes became prime minister. Throughout the 1950s, the DP won all other elections, and Menderes remained prime minister for ten years. Economically, the DP was liberal, whereas the CHP was defending statism. The DP government tried to distance itself from assertive secularism and conducted certain policies to provide more religious freedom.[138] In 1950, the DP group in parliament led the lifting of the ban on Arabic *ezan*. When both Turkish and Arabic options became available, mosque personnel immediately returned to reciting the Arabic *ezan*.[139] Other proreligious policies of the DP included the reintroduction of optional religious instruction in all public schools, the opening of nineteen Imam-Hatip schools, and religious broadcasting on the public radio.[140] As a result, the Kemalists criticized the DP for encouraging *irtica*.

---

[137] Rahman 1982, 92–8; Paçacı and Aktay 1999; Frey 1964, 222–3.
[138] Kasaba 1993, 54.
[139] Daver 1955, 173.
[140] Kaplan 1999, 224.

On May 27, 1960, Kemalist military officers staged a *coup d'état*. They closed down the DP and executed Menderes and his two prominent cabinet members. They also purged 235 out of 260 generals and 5,000 other military officers, as well as 147 university professors.[141] Several of the junta leaders wanted to forcibly Turkify the *ezan* again.[142] Yet they lost the voting on this issue within the junta meeting by a slight margin. A year later, Turkey returned to the multiparty system. In the second half of the 1960s, the Adalet (Justice) Party (AP) and its leader Prime Minister Süleyman Demirel represented the legacy of Menderes, in terms of having overwhelming popular support in elections and conducting accommodating policies toward religion.[143] During Demirel's first premiership several Imam-Hatip schools were opened; their number reached seventy-one in 1969.[144]

Following the mid-1960s, political opponents in Turkey started to be defined as leftists (e.g., the CHP) and rightists (e.g., the AP). In 1970, political Islamists split from the AP and founded their own party under the leadership of Erbakan – Milli Nizam (National Order) Party (MNP). In terms of foreign policy, Erbakan was anti-Western and seeking close relations with Muslim countries. In terms of the economy, Erbakan, a professor of mechanical engineering, emphasized heavy industrialization. On March 12, 1971, the Kemalist officers staged a coup against Prime Minister Demirel. The coup had several ideological connotations, and a major one was to be against Islamism. Under the military influence, the Constitutional Court closed down the MNP. The government and parliament, controlled by the military, shut down the secondary sections (grades 6–8) of the Imam-Hatip schools, in addition to redesigning their remaining part (grades 9–11) as vocational schools with graduates who could not enter universities except through their departments of theology.

Bülent Ecevit, the secretary general of the CHP, opposed the 1971 coup. He became popular and replaced İnönü as the CHP president. Under his leadership, the CHP became the leading party in several elections in the 1970s. In 1972, Erbakan founded a new party,

---

[141] Zürcher 2004a, 243.
[142] Mardin 1982, 184.
[143] For the debates between the AP and CHP parliamentarians on the Diyanet and Qur'an courses, see T.B.M.M. 1965a, 590–5; T.B.M.M. 1965b, 352–3.
[144] Yavuz 2003, 123; Akşit 1991, 146.

Milli Selamet (National Salvation) Party (MSP). Erbakan took part in Ecevit's coalition government as vice–prime minister in 1974. He succeeded in opening the secondary sections of the Imam-Hatip schools and in allowing its graduates to enter all departments at universities.[145] In the second half of the 1970s, Erbakan continued his support to these schools as vice–prime minister in two coalition governments of Demirel.

From 1950 to 1980, state policies toward religion, particularly on education, became relatively more moderate, despite the persistent dominance of assertive secularism. The opening of new Imam-Hatip schools and Qur'an courses, as well as of several departments of theology, was a sign of this change. The main reason for this transformation was the influence of center-right and moderate Islamist parties. Center-right parties, such as the DP and AP, were defending passive secularism, which would allow public visibility of Islam. Therefore, they differed from the assertive secularist CHP. One of the ideologues of the DP and AP's passive secularism was Ali Fuad Başgil, the dean of the law school at Istanbul University and, later, a senator of the AP. In his *Din ve Laiklik* (*Religion and Secularism*), Başgil stresses that Muslims in Turkey should call for a true separation of the state and Islam to gain their religious freedom. In his words, Muslims should ask only one favor from the secular state (as Diogenes the Cynic asked from Alexander the Great): "Don't stand between me and the sun."[146] In 1980, a new period began that would witness the rising visibility of Islam in the Turkish public sphere.

THE KEMALISTS AND CONSERVATIVES: THE CHALLENGE TO ASSERTIVE SECULARISM

From September 12 Coup to February 28 Coup (1980–1997)

The declared aim of the military *coup d'état* on September 12, 1980, was to end the anarchism and terrorism arising in the late 1970s. The generals also pointed to Islamist activities, such as the MSP's Konya rally, as one of the motives for staging the coup. The military rule closed

---

[145] Yavuz 2003, 125; Toprak 1981, 96–121.
[146] Başgil 1977 [1954], 149.

down all political parties and oppressed all political groups.[147] The generals pursued inconsistent policies toward Islam. On the one hand, they wanted to use Islam as a bulwark against communism and, therefore, were relatively attracted to the idea of a Turkish-Islamic synthesis that combined Turkish nationalism with a Muslim identity.[148] They appointed Turgut Özal, a successful conservative bureaucrat, as vice–prime minister. The 1982 Constitution drafted by the military administration made religious instruction in schools obligatory. The generals also attached importance to building relations with Muslim countries, such as Pakistan. In 1982, Turkey was represented for the first time by its prime minister at the summit of the Organization of the Islamic Conference. On the other hand, Evren and the other generals who staged the coup were staunch Kemalists. They indoctrinated Kemalism particularly through education to fill the vacuum that occurred after the oppression of leftist and rightist ideologies. They imposed a ban on headscarves through the YÖK, the institution they founded to control universities.

In 1983, the military administration allowed only three parties to participate in elections. Although the generals supported another party, the center-rightist ANAP won the elections, and its leader Özal became the prime minister. In the 1990s, the terms *leftist* and *rightist* lost their central roles in Turkish politics for several reasons. The end of the cold war resulted in the decline of the Left-Right cleavage not only in Turkey but also worldwide. Turkey's dependence on the International Monetary Fund also contributed to the similarly liberal economic policies of all parties in government. Moreover, leftist CHP and DSP drifted toward Turkish nationalism and cut their ties with Kurdish leftists that had existed in the 1970s and 1980s. Last but not least, the rise of the Islamic movements empowered conservative politicians at

---

[147] As three Turkish nongovernmental organizations, 78'liler Vakfı, İnsan Hakları Derneği, and Türkiye İnsan Hakları Vakfı, reported, during the three years that followed the 1980 coup, about 650,000 people were arrested, 230,000 were indicted, 14,000 were expelled from citizenship, 517 were sentenced to capital punishment, 50 were executed, and 171 were killed by official torture. Moreover, 3,854 teachers, 120 professors, and 47 judges were fired. Four hundred journalists were sentenced to prison for a total of 3,315 years. Thirty-nine tons of newspapers and magazines were disposed of because of political censorship. Vahap Coşkun, "Evren'den Demokrasiye İkinci 'Darbe'!" *Zaman*, March 4, 2006.

[148] Cetinsaya 1999, 369–76; Yavuz 2003, 69–74.

the expense of the center-right, and this led to the emergence of the Kemalist versus conservative split.

Özal was more pro-Islamic than Menderes and Demirel in terms of his personal piety and his policies toward religion. In 1988, he became the first Turkish prime minister who went to the Hajj. During his premiership (1983–1989) and presidency (1989–1993), Özal challenged the Kemalists by promoting conservative politicians and bureaucrats, as well as by supporting the Imam-Hatip schools. He had a particular struggle with the Kemalists on the headscarf issue, as analyzed in Chapter 6. Özal also led the abolishment of three articles of the Turkish Penal Code that prohibited communism (Art. 141 and 142) and Islamism (Art. 163). Article 163 had been used to arrest and imprison thousands of members of Islamic movements and tariqas.

Özal also indirectly facilitated the rise of Islamic movements with his liberal policies, which weakened the state monopoly over economic and sociocultural life. He replaced import-substitution industrialization with an export-led liberal economy. Before Özal, there was a monopoly of the one-channel public TV, the public radio station, and public universities. He encouraged private media and education. In addition to Özal's liberal policies, the global rise of communication technologies challenged the Turkish state's sociocultural dominance and provided Islamic movements the opportunity to set up their own institutions.[149] Islamic movements have developed several media networks. Conservative newspapers reached hundreds of thousands in their circulations. The Gülen movement opened hundreds of schools in Turkey and abroad. Until the 1990s, the Kemalist project had succeeded in creating an elite as the guardian of assertive secularism. In the 1990s, however, a pro-Islamic alternative elite emerged with a different worldview and lifestyle from those of the Kemalists.[150] An example of this counterelite was the new pro-Islamic bourgeoisie, the so-called Anatolian Tigers.[151] The new elite demanded public visibility of Islam, which would have certain political implications.

---

[149] Kuru 2005a.
[150] Göle 1997; Göle 2000; Göle 2002. According to two surveys at Ankara University, the number of students who believe in the following Islamic creeds sharply increased from 1978 to 1996: believing in God (54% to 81%), the day of resurrection (64% to 77%), the Qur'an (47% to 77%), and heaven and hell (36% to 75%). Mutlu 1996, 355.
[151] Maigre 2005; Filiztekin and Tunalı 1999.

Contrary to Islam's increasing public influence, center-right parties – the ANAP and DYP – distanced themselves from conservatism. In 1991, two years after Özal left the ANAP to be president, Mesut Yılmaz became the leader of the ANAP. Similarly, when the leader of the DYP, Demirel, became president in 1993, Tansu Çiller replaced him. Yılmaz and Çiller were personally and politically much less conservative than Özal and Demirel. That helped the moderate Islamist Erbakan's RP appeal to the conservative voters. In 1994, the RP won the mayor's seats in Turkey's two biggest cities, Istanbul and Ankara. In the national parliamentary elections, the RP increased its votes from 7 percent in 1987 to 21 percent in 1995, which made it the leading party.[152] Erbakan became the prime minister in 1996 in the RP-DYP coalition. Although the RP had an Islamic rhetoric, Erbakan did not pursue a politically or economically Islamist policy in government. In terms of foreign policy, however, he opposed Turkey's membership in the EU[153] and led the foundation of an international organization among eight Muslim countries, the Developing Eight (D-8).[154] For the Kemalists, Erbakan's premiership was the last straw, and the military staged the soft *coup d'état* on February 28, 1997, as elaborated in Chapter 6.

CONCLUSION

The Ottoman *ancien régime* based on the alliance between the sultan and hegemonic Islamic institutions originated the assertive secularist ideological dominance in the Turkish Republic. The Westernist Turkish elite regarded Islam as a defender of traditionalism and a barrier against Westernization. Many Islamists, such as Mehmed Akif, were critical of the traditionalist interpretations of Islam and remained open to modernization policies.[155] Yet they wanted to modernize the country within an Islamic, not a Western, sociocultural and even political framework, by preserving the hegemonic position of Islam. That led to the conflict between the Westernist secularists and the Islamists as the origin of

---

[152] Gülalp 2001.
[153] Dağı 1998.
[154] The members of D-8 are Turkey, Iran, Egypt, Pakistan, Bangladesh, Indonesia, Malaysia, and Nigeria.
[155] Ocak 1999, 88–9; Bulaç 1992.

assertive secularism in Turkey. This historical process reflects substantial similarities with France, where the existence of the *ancien régime* resulted in the conflictual origin of assertive secularism, and differences with the United States, where the absence of an *ancien régime* led to the consensual basis of passive secularism.

The origin of secularism in Turkey, unlike that of the United States, was not based on state neutrality toward different religious communities, because, setting aside the Sunni-Alevi split, the overwhelming majority of the Turkish population have been Muslims. Moreover, unlike France, there was no inherent tension between the clergy, on the one hand, and laypeople and political authority, on the other. There was no clergy or pope in the Ottoman Empire; the ulema and Sufi leaders were in society and under the sultan.[156] In this regard, the main historical basis of assertive secularism in Turkey was the Young Turks' and then the Kemalists' perceived dichotomy between Westernization and Islam.[157]

In the early nineteenth century, the Ottoman rulers decided to reform their institutions by imitating Western models. The abolition of the Janissaries, the Tanzimat Edict, and the First and Second Parliaments were stations in the Ottoman long march toward Westernization. At first, it was a pragmatic policy, but then it turned into an ideological project. In the late nineteenth and early twentieth centuries, the Ottoman elite received a secular education in the public schools or the missionary schools in the empire. The more they embraced materialism and positivism, the more they adopted a European, instead of a Muslim, lifestyle and worldview. They began to blame Islam for the decline of the empire and the "backwardness" of the society. These views were formalized through assertive secularism, which was originally a marginal elite view largely imported from France.

The Turkish case indicates certain processes that are important for the establishment of an ideological dominance. At first, a set of ideas that frame the ideology should be transmitted to the youth through education. Then the new ideology requires an increasing number of followers. Finally, suitable structural conditions are necessary for the new ideology to replace the old one. Throughout this process, schools played a central role in the Turkish case: the "history of

---

[156] Arslan 1999, 141–7.
[157] Göle 1996, esp. 131–40.

'Westernization' or 'modernization' in Turkey is in large measure the history of secular education there – of a school system which turned out more and more 'modern' graduates until the balance was tipped in favor of European ways."[158] Atatürk and his cadre had already embraced assertive secularism in their youth among the Young Turks. They wanted to exclude Islam from the public sphere and to reform it as an individualized religion confined to the conscience.

The Kemalists succeeded in establishing assertive secularism during the founding of the republic, which was a critical juncture, when the old regime was declining and the new regime was unpredictable, and charismatic leaders like Atatürk had enormous leverage to change dominant ideology and institutions. During this critical period, both agency and structure were ready for change in Turkey. The Kemalist vanguards were dedicated to making assertive secularism dominant. The international conditions were available because European powers, such as Britain, supported a secular state in Turkey.[159] The domestic rivals, especially the sultan and ulema in Istanbul, were too weak vis-à-vis parliament in Ankara, which was the victor of the War of Independence. Atatürk, as the war hero and first president of the republic, controlled the military and eliminated opponents in parliament. That enabled the Kemalists to abolish Islamic institutions and pursue top-down reforms to Westernize society.

The Kemalists not only established assertive secularism as the dominant ideology, but they also secured its long-term prevalence by creating an exclusively secular educational system. Institutional socialization has also been important for its preservation. Public institutions, such as the military, the judiciary, and universities, have eliminated those who have not been loyal enough to assertive secularism. As a result, there is a strong ideological similarity between current Kemalists and their forerunners in the 1920s and the 1930s.

Chapter 6 quoted some critics of contemporary Kemalism. For many scholars, the main problem of Kemalism stems from its historical origin. According to Mardin, Kemalism could not fill the moral and philosophical vacuum that resulted from the exclusion of Islam

---

[158] Frey 1964, 209.
[159] For European encouragement to the secularization of the Turkish legal system during the Lausanne Conference, see Davison 1964, 91–3.

from the Turkish public sphere.[160] Kemalist modernization, he stresses, failed to understand not only its own local Islamic context, but also the Western model that it tried to imitate:

The Western, foreign source of republican reform – that is, imitation – impeded deeper cultural moorings for the new methodology, a foundation that, in the past, had been provided by Islam as ideation. The reform movement had no identifiable philosophical foundation. Its Jacobanism [*sic*], possibly its deepest root, was pragmatic and practical, that is fleshed out as a "project." The republic took over educational institutions and cultural practices (museums, painting and sculpture, secularism) from the West without realizing that these were just the tip of an iceberg of meanings, perceptions, and ontological positions.[161]

It is not possible to analyze the Kemalist reforms without taking assertive secularist ideology seriously. A simply interest-based approach would have a hard time explaining certain reforms, from the Hat Law to the ban on the Arabic *ezan*, which had little to do with material interests. Economically, these reforms did not contribute to development. Politically, they were very risky and costly because they resulted in a popular opposition. Ideology was the main impulse behind these reforms. In some cases, the Kemalists made certain compromises from their assertive secularist ideals given structural constraints. Following the 1980 coup, for example, Kemalist generals tried to use Islam to a certain extent against the communist threat. Yet even this *strategic* policy had an *ideological* (anticommunist) basis.

The golden era for the assertive secularists was the period from 1933 to 1949, when there was not a single legal school or university teaching Islam. The transition from single-party authoritarianism to democracy, which allowed the resistance of the center-right and conservatives, even moderate Islamists, meant the end of this period. Since then, the Kemalists have lamented the gap between their ideological utopia and the realities of state-religion relations in Turkey. As Chapter 6 pointed out, the CHP has never won the majority in parliament through a democratic election, mainly because of the incompatibility between its assertive secularist ideology and the people's religiosity. That has indicated the tension between assertive secularism

---

[160] Mardin 1991, esp. 127; Mardin 1994, 164–5.
[161] Mardin 1997a, 65.

and democracy in Turkey. Because the military has been the guardian of assertive secularism, this tension has been reflected in civil-military relations.[162] Ernest Gellner also notes the vicious cycle between the Kemalist generals and center-right/conservative politicians: "First, the army ... allows free elections to take place. A party wins that would betray the Kemalist tradition, so the army steps in.... Then, after a time, it hands the government back again, and so on."[163] These cyclical relations appeared in the coups and the returns of the center-right and conservatives in 1960 and 1965, 1980, and 1983, and, as explained in Chapter 6, in 1997 and 2002.[164]

[162] Cizre 1999, 63–5; Karabelias 1999, 139.

[163] Gellner 1997, 243.

[164] The main outlier of these cycles was leftist/Kemalist Ecevit, who opposed the 1971 coup. Ecevit made his CHP the leading party in 1973 and did not allow the return of Demirel. Ecevit did not oppose the 1997 coup, yet as vice–prime minister, he protected the Gülen movement against the generals. In the 1999 elections, Ecevit made his DSP the leading party and prevented the return of Erbakan.

Conclusion

This book examines two opposite policy tendencies toward religion. U.S. policies are generally tolerant toward religion in the public sphere, while the French and Turkish states largely try to confine it to the private domain. According to the American legal system, neither the federal government nor states can prohibit religious symbols in general, or symbols of a particular religion, by singling them out. In France and Turkey, however, the state has singled out students' religious attire to exclude them from public schools without having a general regulation due to a practical (e.g., health or security) purpose. If the headscarf had been a secular fashion, then it would not have been banned in France and Turkey.

I analyze this policy difference through ideological dominances and struggles in these three cases. In the United States, two major groups, the accommodationists and separationists, have had several disagreements on state-religion relations. Yet they both oppose state policies that would prohibit individuals' display of religious symbols in the public sphere. In this regard, these groups defend two different interpretations of passive secularism. In France, however, the combative secularists have succeeded in establishing the dominance of assertive secularism, which aims to exclude religion from the public sphere. The pluralistic secularists oppose this dominance and want to replace it with passive secularism, which tolerates public visibility of religion; but so far, they have not been successful. In Turkey, the Kemalists have defended dominant assertive secularism despite the challenge of the conservatives and liberals, who have promoted passive secularism.

IDEOLOGICAL DOMINANCE AND PUBLIC POLICIES

This book challenges the mainstream view in the social sciences, which tends to attach importance to strategic and instrumental behaviors, while disregarding actors' ideas. Therefore, it criticizes approaches that present public policies as results of class struggles or strategies to maximize utility. Instead, it stresses the importance of ideologies in the formation of individuals' preferences. The ideological struggles to take over key positions in the high courts or armed forces in the three cases show how political actors place relatively more importance on ideologies than on institutional affiliations. In the case of the Kemalists, for example, a conservative military officer is first and foremost a conservative affected by his or her ideology, rather than a simple military officer shaped by the institutional structure of the armed forces. Nevertheless, passive and assertive secularism, like other ideologies, can impact policies only if there are human actors who embrace these ideologies, form particular policy preferences based on them, and struggle to materialize these policy preferences.

The book also challenges statist analyses that overemphasize state rulers as policy makers isolated from society with a central understanding of the national interest. The critics of the statist perspective, such as Joel Migdal, have brought social forces into the analysis of state policy formation.[1] My analysis agrees with Migdal's state in society approach by revealing the fragmentation of state actors through ideological camps and by exploring state policies through a process-oriented perspective that avoids a monolithic and impenetrable view of the state. State actors may disagree with each other on the meaning of secularism and particular policies toward religion while being in agreement with their societal allies. Both secular and religious movements include several state and nonstate actors based on shared ideological views and policy agendas.[2]

---

[1] Migdal 2001; Migdal, Kohli, and Shue 1994.

[2] Mayer Zald rightly asks, "Does anyone believe that Ronald Reagan was part of the conservative movement before he ran for the presidency and not after?" Zald 2000, 10.

In a social scientific analysis, causes and effects are generally parts of broader chains of actions and reactions. In this regard, although the book uses ideological dominance as an explanatory variable in contemporary chapters, it also takes it as a dependent variable in the historical chapters. The establishment of a new ideological dominance generally requires a long historical process. First, ideologies emerge in the works of some native thinkers, or they are imported from other intellectually influential countries. They then find certain followers among the elite through publications and school education. Next these followers organize and mobilize to challenge the dominant ideology. Finally, these activists need available structural conditions (such as wars, economic crisis, or critical elections) to replace the old dominant ideology with a new one in both abstract institutions (the constitution, laws, and the market) and organizations (schools, courts, and barracks). On the one hand, ideological dominance is never absolute; it always exists alongside a resistance and a challenge to its authority.[3] On the other hand, a dominant ideology shapes even its own opponents. In the course of time, conservative Catholics in France and Islamists in Turkey gave up their resistance against the secular state and began defending a religion-friendly (passive) version of secularism rather than a religious establishment.

ANCIEN RÉGIME AND IDEOLOGICAL PATH DEPENDENCE

I argue that certain historical factors in the initial formation of secularism, particularly the presence or absence of an *ancien régime* based on the cooperation between monarchy and hegemonic religion, shaped the emergence and dominance of either passive or assertive secularism. In the United States, passive secularism emerged as a result of an overlapping consensus between the rationalists and evangelicals. The consensus was possible because the former was not antireligious and the latter was open to the idea of church-state separation. A severe conflict between the republican elite and the Catholic Church in France and between the Kemalists and Islamists in Turkey was the origin of assertive secularism's dominance in both countries. The conflict was foreseeable because the republicans and Kemalists were

[3] Scott 1985; Wedeen 1999.

against religion's public role, while the Catholic Church and Islamists were against state-religion separation. The ideological positions of these secular and religious groups were mainly shaped by sociopolitical conditions. The republicans and Kemalists perceived the revival of the *ancien régime* to be a major threat, whereas in America, a new immigrant country, there was no such threat. America had religious diversity, which encouraged several Protestant denominations to see church-state separation at least as the second-best choice. In France and Turkey, however, Catholics and Muslims already had hegemony, and therefore separation held little promise for them.

After the emergence and dominance of the two types of secular ideologies, certain ways of ideological struggle also follow comparable trajectories in these three cases. I will give four examples. First, in France and Turkey, the supporters of assertive secularism have tried to delegitimize their religious opponents for more than a century by portraying them as religious fanatics. The terms they have used are *intégriste* in France and *irticacı* (or *mürteci*) in Turkey.[4] In the United States, however, the term *fundamentalist* has never been used to define an illegal activity or a security threat. All versions of the Christian Right have been legitimate political actors in America. Second, the history of secularism is full of plots and contra-plots between the republicans and conservative Catholics in France, as well as between the Kemalists and pro-Islamic conservatives in Turkey. To take over the armed forces by eliminating the observant Catholic officers was important for the French republicans. For that reason, they were secretly recording these officers as seen in the *scandale des fiches* of 1904. The same method has been used by the Kemalists in Turkey for decades to purge the allegedly "Islamist" and avowedly observant Muslim officers. Especially in the last decade, several *fişleme skandalı* have been revealed and debated in the Turkish media. This kind of secret recording and purge is not a part of the history of secularism in the United States. Third, the secularization of laws in France and Turkey has specifically marginalized certain religious traditions. In both countries, religious marriage has been a crime if it is not preceded by a civil marriage. In the United States, however, it is not a crime; moreover, religious leaders are authorized to conduct both civil and

---

[4] *İrtica* is identified as a national security threat by Turkey's National Security Council.

religious marriages together. Finally, because the French state has been faced with an increasing Muslim population, it recently initiated the foundation of a centralized umbrella organization, the CFCM, to create an "Islam of France." This new organization led by the French state resembles Turkey's Diyanet, which institutionalizes state authority over Islam. Such an organization is unthinkable in the United States.

Despite their historical and ideological similarities, France and Turkey still have certain policy divergences. French policies toward religion are relatively more tolerant than those of Turkey. I explained this difference through diversity of their *ancien régime*s, which also impacted the rise of democracy in France and authoritarianism in Turkey. The founding period of assertive secularism in France (1875–1905) took place under a multiparty democracy, unlike the foundation of assertive secularism in Turkey by the single-party rule (1923–1937). Moreover, since that time, assertive secularism in France has had a democratic basis, while it has always been protected in Turkey by the authoritarian military and judiciary. In democratic France, street protests helped the assertive secularists and their critics in 1994 and 1984, respectively, in terms of affecting state policies toward Catholic private schools. In semiauthoritarian Turkey, however, the conservative Muslims failed to affect state policies with their street protests against the closure of the secondary part of the Imam-Hatip schools and the ban on headscarves in 1997 and 1998. The conservatives gained nothing but being arrested and in some cases imprisoned as a result of these protests.[5]

FUTURE PROSPECTS

Beyond this *ex post* analysis of past policies of the French and Turkish states, this book's analytical framework may also help predict the future of assertive secularism in these two countries. In the early Third French Republic, conservative Catholics planned to contain the republican influence in parliament by the monarchist control over the presidency and the army. They even supported plots of military coup against the republic to reestablish monarchy. Yet the assertive secularist

---

[5] "Sultanahmet'te Gövde Gösterisi," *Milliyet*, May 12, 1997; "Türbanda Gövde Gösterisi," *Milliyet*, October 12, 1998.

republicans eventually took control of all political and bureaucratic institutions through popular support and democratic elections. In the Turkish case, in contrast, it has been the assertive secularists who tried to limit the power of the elected parliament through the Kemalist dominance in the presidency, military, and judiciary. They also supported several military interventions, especially in 1960, 1997, and 2007. In this regard, one may predict the decline of assertive secularism in Turkey due to increasing democratization in the future.

Another future prospect for France and Turkey is the possibility of change from assertive to passive secularism as the dominant ideology. Such a transformation is possible despite this book's emphasis on historical path dependence. The historical legacy of the *ancien régime* does not last forever; the successor regime can become ancient in the course of time, which may lead to the emergence of a third regime. Moreover, besides the importance of historical path dependence, contemporary ideological struggles are still dynamic. As the previously mentioned metaphor of a swinging pendulum indicates, secular state policies have not followed a clearly linear trajectory. Instead, in all three countries, there are certain periods that differ from each other due to some "micro-critical junctures." In this regard, policy makers are not historically determined robots; instead, they are open to the learning process. Once an ideology emerges in a context, it can be transferred to other places through schools and publications. Political actors in a country can replace assertive secularism with passive secularism (or vice versa) as the dominant ideology. To materialize such a transformation, however, takes time and requires convenient structural conditions, as well as committed agency.

This change also is possible given the book's highlighting of religious diversity and hegemony, because France and Turkey no longer have hegemonic religions. In France, the Catholics, even nominally, constitute only about 50 percent of the society. Although the overwhelming majority of Turks are Muslims, Islam does not have hegemony over politics, the economy, or even society. Moreover, there are various identities (Sunni and Alevi), associations (the Diyanet, tariqas, and movements), and political views among Muslims in Turkey that make establishment of one single interpretation of Islam almost impossible. Additionally, as already seen in the cases of Ireland and Poland, passive secularism and religious majority (even hegemony) can coexist contingent on political position and relations of the majority religion.

Researchers can further examine the relationships between historical conditions, ideological struggles, and state policies in their analysis of other types of regime change (e.g., democracy and authoritarianism) or policy formation (e.g., ethnic and racial policies). They can analyze ideologies as (1) explanatory variables to explain how ideologies shape policies and (2) dependent variables to explore how ideologies emerge and become dominant. In particular, the book's analysis of the *ancien régime* has an implicit policy recommendation. It stresses that religious groups should not build alliances with authoritarian regimes, if they do not want to face the rise of anticlerical (or antireligious) movements and an assertive secularist (or antireligious) regime. Religions' political relations are more important than their so-called essences, as emphasized in the following section.

SECULARISM, ISLAM, AND CHRISTIANITY

This work primarily analyzes state interaction with Protestants (in the United States), Catholics (in the United States and France), and Muslims (in France and Turkey). The American case shows partially strategic decisions of the Protestant denominations about the absence of a federal establishment and disestablishments in states, in addition to their instrumental use of secularism to oppose public funding of Catholic schools in the late nineteenth century. The French case indicates the changing perspectives of the Catholic Church toward secularism, which transformed after World War II. Muslims in both Turkey and France have had diverse and dynamic political views, which reveal that they are not chained by so-called religious essentials. In short, several parts of the book emphasize that political interpretations of Christianity and Islam have played more important roles in state-religion debates than have the so-called essences of these religions as defined by civilizationalist scholars. Further research is needed for an exploration of this issue.

In this regard, the type of religion does not have a mono-causal impact on state-religion regimes. In general, interpretations of religions and religiosity of societies are more important factors needed to understand state-religion relations. In the three cases, the relationship between societal religiosity and type of secular ideology plays important roles regarding state-society synchronization. In the United States, a high level of societal religiosity coexists with passive secularism that tolerates such religiosity. In France, historically, there was a severe tension between the observant Catholic portion of society and the assertive secularist ideology. The tension was contained due to (1) the moderation of state policies in terms of accommodating Catholic demands, such as state funding of Catholic schools, and (2) secularization of the French society.[6] Today, the low religiosity of French society fits with the assertive secularist ideology of the state; both might be largely comfortable with the absence of religion in the public sphere.[7] Turkey is paradoxical by having the most religious society and the most extremist assertive secularist state policies among the three. Because Turkish society is highly religious, a combination of assertive secularist parties could not receive more than 30 percent of votes in the last three decades. Thus the assertive secularists largely support military and judiciary interventions against elected conservative politicians. This conflict reflects the tension between assertive secularism and democracy in Turkey. In Table 14 , I compare the levels of societal religiosity in my three cases[8] based on three criteria: percentages of those believing in God, affiliating with a particular religion, and

---

[6] See Roberts 2000. Weekly church participation in France decreased from 36% in 1958 to 21% in 1974. Brechon 1995. According to Eurobarometer, this ratio decreased from 23% in 1970 to 5% in 1998. World Value Survey notes the decline from 11% in 1981 to 8% in 2001 in France, whereas it points to the increase from 43% in 1981 to 46% in 2001 in the United States. Norris and Inglehart 2004, 72, 74. In Turkey, it is hard to trace such a longitudinal change because the reliable data started to be collected recently.

[7] State ideology does not have a mono-causal impact on religiosity. An assertive secularist ideology in France has coexisted with a declining religiosity, whereas there is no such decline in Turkey. Another relevant comparison would be between France and England. In both countries societal religiosity is similarly very low despite the fact that one has a secular state and the other has an established church.

[8] The populations of these countries are 72 million (Turkey), 304 million (the United States), and 64 million (France). The CIA's World Factbook, https://www.cia.gov/library/publications/the-world-factbook/index.html, accessed on May 5, 2008. The rough number of temples in Turkey are 78,000 mosques, 300 churches, and 36 synagogues; in the United States, 330,742 (311,750 Protestant and other non-Catholic, and 18,992 Catholic) churches and 1,209 mosques (no data available for synagogues); in France, 46,100 (45,000 Catholic and 1,100 Protestant) churches, 1,685 mosques, and 300 synagogues. "Türkiye'nin İbadethaneleri," *Sabah*, May 13, 2008; Lindner 2007; Bagby, Perl, and Froehle 2001, 2–3; Conseil d'Etat 2004, 318; Bertrand 2006.

TABLE 14. *Current Levels of Religiosity in Turkish, American, and French Societies*

	Belief in God (%)	Affiliation with a Religion (%)	Religious Participation Once a Week (%)
Turkey	99	99	69
United States	96	85	40
France	61	55	10

Source: For all three cases: World Values Surveys 1999 and 2001, http://www.worldvaluessurvey.org/, accessed on August 1, 2006. For the United States: Kosmin, Mayer, and Keysar 2001; Kohut et al. 2000, 18, 24. For France: The Survey of *CSA/ La Vie/Le Monde,* "Les français et leur croyances," March 21, 2003, 41, 91, http://a1692.g.akamai.net/f/1692/2042/1h/medias.lemonde.fr/medias/pdf_obj/sond-age030416.pdf; "Les Français et la prière," *Le Pèlerin Magazine,* April 13, 2001; Dominique Vidal, "La France des 'sans-religion,'" *Le Monde Diplomatique,* September 2001: 22–3. For Turkey: Çarkoğlu and Toprak 2000, 41, 45; "The Survey of *Milliyet* and Konda," *Milliyet,* March 21, 2007; "The Survey of *Milliyet* and A&G," *Milliyet,* May 31, 2003.

TABLE 15. *Societal Religiosity and Secular Ideology*

		Level of Societal Religiosity	
		High	Low
Type of Secularism	Passive	United States	Netherlands
	Assertive	Turkey	France

attending churches/mosques weekly.[9] Table 15 shows the relations between the level of religiosity and type of secular ideology.[10]

The synchronization or disharmony between religiosity and dominant ideology also has certain implications on the relationship between secularism, liberalism, and democracy. U.S. policies seem to be largely

[9] There is a debate about the validity of surveys to measure religiosity. Heclo 2007, 72. My analysis is not primarily interested in the exact religiosity, but it focuses on comparison of the three cases. If surveys provide exaggerated numbers in Turkey and the United States, then this will also be the case in France. If people in Turkey and the United States want to present themselves as being more religious than they actually are, then this still shows that it is important to be religious in these societies.
[10] Several commentators asked me about a possible fourth case in the table. There are many cases that combine passive secularist ideology and low religiosity. One example is the Netherlands, where public visibility of religion is tolerated, while people's religiosity (belief in God [58%], affiliation with religion [55%], and religious participation once a week [14%]) is very low. World Values Surveys 1999, http://www.worldvaluessurvey.org/, accessed on August 1, 2006.

liberal democratic because they respect individual rights and, generally, follow people's demand. French policies that violate individual freedoms, such as the ban on headscarves, are not liberal but can be still defined as democratic, because 72 percent of the population supported the ban.[11] Turkish policies, again such as the ban on headscarves, are neither liberal nor democratic because 78 percent of the population opposes it.[12] Future analyses can elaborate on these cases and others regarding the relationship between secularism, liberalism, and democracy.

More detailed studies are also needed on certain points that this book provides about Islam's relation to the secular state. It particularly analyzes Turkey in order to understand this complex relationship. In the early twentieth century, several founders of new Muslim states, including Reza Shah Pahlavi of Iran (1878–1944), Amanullah Shah of Afghanistan (1892–1960), and President Sukarno of Indonesia (1901–1970), were influenced by Atatürk's founding of a secular state.[13] There is also a contemporary debate about Turkey's role, from the Middle East to Central Asia, as a political model. According to some scholars, Kemalist (assertive) secularism can never be an appealing model for Muslim countries because it is "perceived as an oppressive and superficial attempt at imposing Western dress, life-style and symbols on Muslims."[14] Others take the cohabitation of the Kemalist elite and the AK Party government as a sign of the moderation of state-Islam relations, which can make Turkey a source of inspiration.[15] This book agrees with both perspectives by noting the problems of assertive secularism and the promises of passive secularism in a Muslim country.

Beyond the Turkish case, the book provides some insights into the question of compatibility between secularism and Islam. It stresses the diversity of state-religion regimes in forty-six Muslim countries

---

[11] Debré 2004, 179.
[12] Çarkoğlu and Toprak 2006, 71; "The Survey of *Milliyet* and Konda," *Milliyet*, December 4, 2007.
[13] Sukarno was "more influenced by Mustafa Kemal [Atatürk] than any other reformer" particularly on the issue of state-religion relations. Anshori 1994, 8, 110. For a comparative analysis of Atatürk and Reza Pahlavi, see Atabaki and Zürcher 2004.
[14] Ömer Taşpınar also adds, "That the headscarf, let alone the veil, is turned into a highly charged symbol, jeopardizing the future of secularism in Kemalist Turkey, proves to the Arab world that the Turkish model itself lacks domestic legitimacy." Taşpınar, 7. See also Uğur 2004, 340–2.
[15] Turam 2006; Fuller 2004, 51–2; Çavdar 2006.

(see Appendix C), which refutes the thesis that Islam and secularism are inherently incompatible. It also notes that such a question will be misleading unless the researcher is aware of passive and assertive types of secularism, as well as diverse interpretations of Islam. Secularism is perceived as an antireligious ideology in several Muslim societies. The main reason for that is the dominance of assertive secularism in countries such as Uzbekistan and Tunisia.[16] These Muslims may rethink secularism if they recognize alternative passive secularism, which is dominant in some other states with Muslim populations, such as Senegal and Indonesia.[17] This issue obviously requires further research.

In short, the practical or theoretical tensions between Muslim societies and assertive secularism are not based on the so-called exceptionalism or political essence of Islam. Assertive secularism is very likely to be incompatible with any religion that has public claims. The historical and current struggles between the conservative Muslims and assertive secularists in Turkey have not differed sharply from controversies between the conservative Catholics and assertive secularists in France. In general, state-religion controversies in countries affiliated with Islam, Christianity, or other religions have concentrated on very similar issues, such as state neutrality and religious freedom.

The changing meanings of the state neutrality toward all religions have been at the core of debates on secularism in America where religious diversity has kept deepening. Policies related to the Establishment Clause, therefore, have created the sharpest controversies. Policies that are exclusively linked to the Free Exercise Clause, such as those related to students' religious symbols, however, have been much less controversial. The debates on secularism in France and Turkey, however, have largely focused on the issue of religious freedom. Assertive secularism in these countries has had a social engineering project to exclude religion from the public sphere, which has led to violations of religious freedom. Although many may regard secularism as a solution for state-religion problems, secularism itself is still dealing with the paradoxes of state neutrality and religious freedom. Perhaps, these paradoxes and ongoing controversies are the dynamics of secularism.

---

[16] Webb 2007; al-Ghannouchi 2000; An-Na'im 1999; Keddie 1997, 25–30; Esposito 2000; Sayyid 2003, 77.
[17] Villalon 2006; An-Na'im 2008, 223–66.

Appendix A: State-Religion Regimes
Index of 197 Countries

COUNTRY	REGIME	OFFICIAL RELIGION
Afghanistan	Religious	Islam
Albania	Secular	
Algeria	Established	Islam
Andorra	Established	Catholic Church
Angola	Secular	
Antigua and Barbuda	Secular	
Argentina	Established	Catholic Church
Armenia	Established	Armenian Church
Australia	Secular	
Austria	Secular	
Azerbaijan	Secular	
Bahamas	Established	(Christianity constitutionally favored)
Bahrain	Religious	Islam
Bangladesh	Established	Islam
Barbados	Secular	
Belarus	Established	(Orthodox Church legally favored)
Belgium	Secular	
Belize	Secular	
Benin	Secular	

(*continued*)

(*continued*)

COUNTRY	REGIME	OFFICIAL RELIGION
Bhutan	Established	Buddhism
Bolivia	Established	Catholic Church
Bosnia and Herzegovina	Secular	
Botswana	Secular	
Brazil	Secular	
Brunei	Religious	Islam
Bulgaria	Established	(Orthodox Church constitutionally favored)
Burkina Faso	Secular	
Burma	Secular	
Burundi	Secular	
Cambodia	Established	Buddhism
Cameroon	Secular	
Canada	Secular	
Cape Verde	Secular	
Central African Republic	Secular	
Chad	Secular	
Chile	Secular	
China	Antireligious	
Colombia	Established	(Catholic Church – Concordat)
Comoros	Established	(Islam constitutionally favored)
Congo, Democratic Republic of the	Secular	
Congo, Republic of the	Secular	
Costa Rica	Established	Catholic Church
Côte d'Ivoire	Secular	
Croatia	Established	(Catholic Church – Concordat)
Cuba	Antireligious	
Cyprus, Greek	Established	(Orthodox Church constitutionally favored)
Cyprus, Turkish	Secular	
Czech Republic	Secular	
Denmark	Established	Lutheran Church
Djibouti	Established	(Islam legally favored)
Dominica	Secular	
Dominican Republic	Established	Catholic Church
Ecuador	Secular	

COUNTRY	REGIME	OFFICIAL RELIGION
Egypt	Established	Islam
El Salvador	Established	Catholic Church
Equatorial Guinea	Secular	
Eritrea	Secular	
Estonia	Secular	
Ethiopia	Secular	
Fiji	Secular	
Finland	Established	Lutheran and Orthodox Churches
France	Secular	
Gabon	Secular	
Gambia, The	Secular	
Georgia	Established	(Orthodox Church constitutionally favored)
Germany	Secular	
Ghana	Secular	
Greece	Established	Orthodox Church
Grenada	Secular	
Guatemala	Established	(Catholic Church constitutionally favored)
Guinea	Secular	
Guinea-Bissau	Secular	
Guyana	Secular	
Haiti	Established	(Catholic Church – Concordat)
Honduras	Established	(Catholic Church legally favored)
Hungary	Secular	
Iceland	Established	Lutheran Church
India	Secular	
Indonesia	Secular	
Iran	Religious	Islam
Iraq	Established	Islam
Ireland	Secular	
Israel	Established	Judaism
Italy	Established	(Catholic Church – Concordat)
Jamaica	Secular	

(*continued*)

(*continued*)

COUNTRY	REGIME	OFFICIAL RELIGION
Japan	Secular	
Jordan	Established	Islam
Kazakhstan	Secular	
Kenya	Secular	
Kiribati	Secular	
Korea, North	Antireligious	
Korea, South	Secular	
Kosovo	Secular	
Kuwait	Established	Islam
Kyrgyz Republic	Secular	
Laos	Antireligious	
Latvia	Secular	
Lebanon	Secular	
Lesotho	Secular	
Liberia	Secular	
Libya	Established	Islam
Liechtenstein	Established	Catholic Church
Lithuania	Secular	
Luxembourg	Secular	
Macedonia	Secular	
Madagascar	Secular	
Malawi	Secular	
Malaysia	Established	Islam
Maldives	Religious	Islam
Mali	Secular	
Malta	Established	Catholic Church
Marshall Islands	Secular	
Mauritania	Religious	Islam
Mauritius	Secular	
Mexico	Secular	
Micronesia, Federated States of	Secular	
Moldova	Established	(Orthodox Church legally favored)
Monaco	Established	Catholic Church
Mongolia	Secular	

COUNTRY	REGIME	OFFICIAL RELIGION
Montenegro	Secular	
Morocco	Established	Islam
Mozambique	Secular	
Namibia	Secular	
Nauru	Secular	
Nepal	Secular	
Netherlands	Secular	
New Zealand	Secular	
Nicaragua	Secular	
Niger	Secular	
Nigeria	Secular	
Norway	Established	Lutheran Church
Oman	Religious	Islam
Pakistan	Religious	Islam
Palau	Secular	
Palestine	Established	Islam
Panama	Established	(Catholic Church constitutionally favored)
Papua New Guinea	Secular	
Paraguay	Established	(Catholic Church constitutionally favored)
Peru	Established	(Catholic Church constitutionally favored)
Philippines	Secular	
Poland	Established	(Catholic Church – Concordat)
Portugal	Established	(Catholic Church – Concordat)
Qatar	Established	Islam
Romania	Secular	
Russia	Secular	
Rwanda	Secular	
Samoa	Established	(Christianity constitutionally favored)
San Marino	Secular	
São Tomé and Príncipe	Secular	
Saudi Arabia	Religious	Islam
Senegal	Secular	
Serbia	Secular	

(*continued*)

(*continued*)

COUNTRY	REGIME	OFFICIAL RELIGION
Seychelles	Secular	
Sierra Leone	Secular	
Singapore	Secular	
Slovak Republic	Secular	
Slovenia	Secular	
Solomon Islands	Secular	
Somalia	Established	Islam
South Africa	Secular	
Spain	Established	(Catholic Church – Concordat)
Sri Lanka	Established	Buddhism
St. Kitts and Nevis	Secular	
St. Lucia	Secular	
St. Vincent and the Grenadines	Secular	
Sudan	Religious	Islam
Suriname	Secular	
Swaziland	Secular	
Sweden	Secular	
Switzerland	Secular	
Syria	Secular	
Taiwan	Secular	
Tajikistan	Secular	
Tanzania	Secular	
Thailand	Established	Buddhism
Timor-Leste	Established	(Catholic Church constitutionally favored)
Togo	Secular	
Tonga	Secular	
Trinidad and Tobago	Secular	
Tunisia	Established	Islam
Turkey	Secular	
Turkmenistan	Secular	
Tuvalu	Secular	
Uganda	Secular	
Ukraine	Secular	
United Arab Emirates	Established	Islam

COUNTRY	REGIME	OFFICIAL RELIGION
United Kingdom	Established	Anglican and Presbyterian Churches
United States	Secular	
Uruguay	Secular	
Uzbekistan	Secular	
Vanuatu	Established	(Christianity constitutionally favored)
Vatican	Religious	Catholic Church
Venezuela	Established	(Catholic Church – Concordat)
Vietnam	Antireligious	
Yemen	Religious	Islam
Zambia	Established	Christianity
Zimbabwe	Secular	

NOTE

(1) As Table 1 in Chapter 1 summarizes, 197 countries in this dataset are divided into four categories: religious states (12), states with established religions (60), secular states (120), and antireligious states (5).

(2) While preparing this index, I mainly used the U.S. Department of State's "2007 Report on International Religious Freedom."[1] I read the report's detailed analysis of each country, in addition to referring to countries' constitutions. I categorize countries according to two criteria: (1) whether legislature and judiciary are controlled by religious institutions, and (2) whether there exists an official religion. I categorize those that fulfill (1) both criteria as "religious" states, (2) the second but not the first as states with "established" religions, (3) neither of the two as "secular" states, and (4) neither of the two, in addition to being hostile to all or many religions, as "antireligious" states.

Some countries are difficult to categorize because they do not explicitly have official religions, yet they still favor a particular religion through their constitutions, legal codes, or agreements with churches. To point out these cases, I put explanations within parentheses in the index to indicate their distinction from countries where there are clear official religions.

(3) I also match the results with Tad Stahnke and Robert Blitt's report on 44 Muslims countries,[2] Jonathan Fox's Religion and State dataset of 175 countries,[3] *World Christian Encyclopedia* edited by David Barrett et al.'s index of 227 countries,[4] and Robert Barro and Rachel McCleary's revisions on

[1] U.S. Department of State 2007.
[2] Stahnke and Blitt 2005a; Stahnke and Blitt 2005b.
[3] Fox 2008.
[4] Barrett, Kurian, and Johnson 2001.

the Barrett index.[5] I basically used the U.S. Department of State's list of 191 countries and separately evaluated four countries (Kosovo, Taiwan, Palestine, and Turkish Cyprus), which are examined as separate sections under Serbia, China, Israel, and Cyprus in the "2007 Report on International Religious Freedom." Kosovo recently became independent, and the other three are separately analyzed by Fox (except Palestine) and Barrett. I also added the United States and Vatican and increased the number in my index to 197.

(4) My results are very similar to those of Stahnke and Blitt except six cases as explained in Appendix C. Fox's index includes more (10) categories than mine (4); therefore it is normal that the two do not perfectly match. Yet almost all of their major disagreements (18 out of 20) are the countries that I classify as "state with established religions" with an explanation in parentheses.

My index's main disagreement appears to be with that of Barrett. In an earlier work, I used Barrett's index of 227 states and reached the result of twenty-two antireligious states (categorized by Barrett as A: atheistic), ninety-five secular states (categorized by Barrett as S: secular), and ten religious states and one hundred states with established religions (categorized by Barrett as R, RD, RA, RB, RG, RH, RI, RJ, RL, RM, RO, RR, RC, RT, or RX, meaning "religious" with specific types).[6] Having prepared my own index, I realize that Barrett's number of atheistic states is exaggerated. Out of his twenty-two, I found only five of them atheistic (antireligious), thirteen (mostly postcommunist countries) not atheistic, and the remaining four unknown (because they are not in my index). His number of religious states, 110, is also exaggerated. I found only sixty-seven of them are actually religious (states with established religions and religious states),[7] thirty-six of them are not, and seven of them to be examined (not in my index). Barro and McCleary fixed twenty-four of these thirty-six cases in their revision of Barrett's index. The main reason why they could not fix them all is that they categorize six secular post-Soviet republics as having official religions.

---

[5] Barro and McCleary 2005.

[6] Kuru 2007.

[7] The total number is seventy-two, because two states defined as atheistic and two states defined as secular by Barrett appeared to be states with established religions, and I added one country that is not on his list.

Appendix B: Human Development and Official Religion in 176 Countries

Country	HDI	O.R.	Country	HDI	O.R.
HIGH DEVELOPMENT			Philippines	0.771	0
Iceland	0.968	1	Tunisia	0.766	1
Norway	0.968	1	Fiji	0.762	0
Australia	0.962	0	St. Vincent and the Grenadines	0.761	0
Canada	0.961	0	Iran	0.759	1
Ireland	0.959	1	Paraguay	0.755	1
Sweden	0.956	0	Georgia	0.754	1
Switzerland	0.955	0	Guyana	0.75	0
Japan	0.953	0	Azerbaijan	0.746	0
Netherlands	0.953	0	Sri Lanka	0.743	1
Finland	0.952	1	Maldives	0.741	1
France	0.952	0	Cape Verde	0.736	0
United States	0.951	0	Jamaica	0.736	0
Denmark	0.949	1	El Salvador	0.735	1
Spain	0.949	1	Algeria	0.733	1
Austria	0.948	0	Vietnam	0.733	0
Belgium	0.946	0	Palestine	0.731	1
United Kingdom	0.946	1	Indonesia	0.728	0
Luxembourg	0.944	0	Syria	0.724	0

(continued)

(*continued*)

Country	HDI	O.R.	Country	HDI	O.R.
New Zealand	0.943	0	Turkmenistan	0.713	0
Italy	0.941	1	Nicaragua	0.71	0
Germany	0.935	0	Egypt	0.708	1
Israel	0.932	1	Moldova	0.708	1
Greece	0.926	1	Uzbekistan	0.702	0
Singapore	0.922	0	Honduras	0.7	1
Korea, South	0.921	0	Mongolia	0.7	0
Slovenia	0.917	0	Kyrgyzstan	0.696	0
Cyprus, Greek	0.903	1	Bolivia	0.695	1
Portugal	0.897	1	Guatemala	0.689	1
Brunei	0.894	1	Gabon	0.677	0
Barbados	0.892	0	South Africa	0.674	0
Czech Republic	0.891	0	Vanuatu	0.674	1
Kuwait	0.891	1	Tajikistan	0.673	0
Malta	0.878	1	Botswana	0.654	0
Qatar	0.875	1	São Tomé and Príncipe	0.654	0
Hungary	0.874	0	Namibia	0.65	0
Poland	0.87	1	Morocco	0.646	1
Argentina	0.869	1	Equatorial Guinea	0.642	0
United Arab Emirates	0.868	1	India	0.619	0
Chile	0.867	0	Solomon Islands	0.602	0
Bahrain	0.866	1	Laos	0.601	0
Slovakia	0.863	0	Cambodia	0.598	1
Lithuania	0.862	0	Myanmar	0.583	0
Estonia	0.86	0	Bhutan	0.579	1
Latvia	0.855	0	Comoros	0.561	1
Uruguay	0.852	0	Ghana	0.553	0
Croatia	0.85	1	Pakistan	0.551	1
Costa Rica	0.846	1	Mauritania	0.55	1
Bahamas	0.845	1	Lesotho	0.549	0
Seychelles	0.843	0	Congo, Rep. of	0.548	0
Cuba	0.838	0	Bangladesh	0.547	1
Mexico	0.829	0	Swaziland	0.547	0
Bulgaria	0.824	1	Nepal	0.534	0
St. Kitts and Nevis	0.821	0	Madagascar	0.533	0

Country	HDI	O.R.	Country	HDI	O.R.
Tonga	0.819	0	Cameroon	0.532	0
Libya	0.818	1	Papua New Guinea	0.53	0
Antigua and Barbuda	0.815	0	Haiti	0.529	1
Oman	0.814	1	Sudan	0.526	1
Trinidad and Tobago	0.814	0	Kenya	0.521	0
Romania	0.813	0	Djibouti	0.516	1
Panama	0.812	1	Timor-Leste	0.514	1
Saudi Arabia	0.812	1	Zimbabwe	0.513	0
Malaysia	0.811	1	Togo	0.512	0
Belarus	0.804	1	Yemen	0.508	1
Mauritius	0.804	0	Uganda	0.505	0
Bosnia and Herzegovina	0.803	0	Gambia	0.502	0
Russian Federation	0.802	0	**LOW DEVELOPMENT**		
Albania	0.801	0	Senegal	0.499	0
Macedonia	0.801	0	Eritrea	0.483	0
Brazil	0.8	0	Nigeria	0.47	0
MEDIUM DEVELOPMENT			Tanzania	0.467	0
Dominica	0.798	0	Guinea	0.456	0
St. Lucia	0.795	0	Rwanda	0.452	0
Kazakhstan	0.794	0	Angola	0.446	0
Venezuela	0.792	1	Benin	0.437	0
Colombia	0.791	1	Malawi	0.437	0
Ukraine	0.788	0	Zambia	0.434	1
Samoa	0.785	1	Côte d'Ivoire	0.432	0
Thailand	0.781	1	Burundi	0.413	0
Dominican Republic	0.779	1	Congo, Dem. Rep. of	0.411	0
Belize	0.778	0	Ethiopia	0.406	0
China	0.777	0	Chad	0.388	0
Grenada	0.777	0	Central African Republic	0.384	0
Armenia	0.775	1	Mozambique	0.384	0
Turkey	0.775	0	Mali	0.38	0
Suriname	0.774	0	Guinea-Bissau	0.374	0
Jordan	0.773	1	Niger	0.374	0

(*continued*)

(*continued*)

Country	HDI	O.R.	Country	HDI	O.R.
Peru	0.773	1	Burkina Faso	0.37	0
Ecuador	0.772	0	Sierra Leone	0.336	0
Lebanon	0.772	0			

NOTE

This table compares 176 countries' development scores, based on UNDP's "Human Development Index" (HDI) of 2007–2008, with their adoption (1) or lack (0) of an official religion (O.R.), based on my index in Appendix A.

I grouped countries according to UNDP's own categories of High Development (HDI score equal to or more than 0.800), Medium Development (HDI score more than 0.500), and Low Development (HDI score less than 0.500).[1]

[1] UNDP, "Human Development Reports," http://hdr.undp.org/en/statistics/, accessed on May 19, 2008.

Appendix C: State-Religion Regimes in Forty-Six Muslim Countries

Religious (Islamic) States (11)	States with an Established Religion (Islam) (15)	Secular States (20)	Antireligious States (0)
1. Afghanistan	1. Algeria	1. Azerbaijan	
2. Bahrain	2. Bangladesh	2. Burkina Faso	
3. Brunei	3. Comoros	3. Chad	
4. Iran	4. Djibouti	4. Guinea	
5. Maldives	5. Egypt	5. Kazakhstan	
6. Mauritania	6. Iraq	6. Kosovo	
7. Oman	7. Jordan	7. Kyrgyzstan	
8. Pakistan	8. Kuwait	8. Mali	
9. Saudi Arabia	9. Libya	9. Niger	
10. Sudan	10. Malaysia	10. Senegal	
11. Yemen	11. Morocco	11. Tajikistan	
	12. Qatar	12. Turkey	
	13. Somalia	13. Turkmenistan	
	14. Tunisia	14. Albania	
	15. United Arab Emirates	15. Gambia	
		16. Indonesia	
		17. Lebanon	
		18. Sierra Leone	
		19. Syria	
		20. Uzbekistan	

NOTE

This table explains the data summarized in Table 4 based on my index in Appendix A. In the third column, countries one through thirteen have constitutions that explicitly mention the word *secular* while defining the state or the republic. The rest (14–20) are also secular states regarding their lack of established religion and their secular legal systems, although the word *secular* does not exist in their constitutions. Except for a few cases, such as France and Russia, the majority of secular states worldwide do not use this word in their constitutions.

My data is very similar to the U.S. Commission on International Religious Freedom's report on forty-four Muslim countries edited by Stahnke and Blitt.[1] They noted ten constitutionally declared Islamic states and twelve countries with Islam declared as the state religion. The numbers in my table for these categories are, respectively, eleven and fifteen for two reasons. First, Stahnke and Blitt categorize Somalia and Sudan as states with "no constitutional declaration," because at the time of the report, Somalia had no recognized constitution and Sudan was in the process of drafting a new one. In my index, Sudan is a religious state, and Somalia is a state with an established religion. Second, Stahnke and Blitt classify Comoros and Djibouti as states with "no constitutional declaration." I put these two states under the categories of "Islam as established religion." According to the U.S. Department of State's "2007 Report on International Religious Freedom," although it is not explicitly established, Islam is either constitutionally or legally favored in these two cases.

Stahnke and Blitt have eleven constitutionally declared secular states. My number is thirteen because I added Kazakhstan, where the Muslim population recently became the majority, and Kosovo, a newly independent state. Finally, they have eleven countries with no constitutional declaration about Islam or secularism. I have seven (14–20 in the third column) because I put Somalia, Sudan, Comoros, and Djibouti under other categories.

I did not add Palestine (established) and Turkish Cyprus (secular) into the table because they are not internationally recognized as sovereign states. Nigeria (secular, 50%), Eritrea (secular, 50%), Ethiopia (secular, 45%), and Bosnia (secular, 40%) are not in the list because Muslims in these countries do not constitute more than half of the population, although Islam is the largest religion.[2]

---

[1] Stahnke and Blitt 2005a, esp. 7; Stahnke and Blitt 2005b, esp. 955.
[2] U.S. Department of State. 2007.

Appendix D: Turkey's National Security Council Decisions, February 28, 1997

(1) There shall be no compromise to the antiregime activities that target the Turkish Republic, which is a democratic, secular, social, and law-based state. The Revolution Laws defended by article 174 of the constitution should be implemented without a compromise. It is the government's duty to make its policies compatible with the Revolution Laws.

(2) The public attorneys should act against violation of the Revolution Laws. The tariqa lodges that violate the Revolution Laws should be closed down.

(3) It is observed that wearing *sarık* (turban) and cloak is encouraged. Those whose dresses contradict the Revolution Laws should not be honored.

(4) The abolishment of article 163 of the constitution created a legal vacuum, and that resulted in the strengthening of reactionary movements and antisecular attitudes. There should be new legal regulations to fill this vacuum.

(5) The education policies should again be compatible with the spirit of the Law on the Unification of Education.

(6) Obligatory education should increase to eight years.

(7) The Imam-Hatip schools were open to satisfy a societal need [of imams]. The Imam-Hatip schools that are beyond this need should be converted to vocational schools. Additionally, the reactionary groups' Qur'an courses should be closed down, and their schools should be regulated by the ministry of education.

(8) There is an ongoing fundamentalist infiltration into the state bureaucracy and municipalities. The government should stop this infiltration.

(9) All actions that aim to abuse religious issues (such as mosque construction) for political purposes should be ended.

(10) The pump rifles should be taken under control and, if it is necessary, the sales of the pump rifles should be banned.

(11) Iran's attempts that aim to destabilize the regime in Turkey should be closely watched. There should be policies to prevent Iran from intervening in Turkey's domestic affairs.

(12) The regulations, which maintain effective working of the judiciary, guarantee judicial independence, and protect it from the activities of the government, should immediately be created.

(13) Recently, there has been a big increase of provocations that target the members of the Turkish Armed Forces (TAF). These provocations have resulted in discontent in the TAF.

(14) The officers and petty officers expelled from the TAF because of their involvement to reactionary activities have been hired by the municipalities. That should be prevented.

(15) The speeches and behaviors of parties' mayors, regional chairmen, and town chairmen should be accountable by the Law on Political Parties.

(16) The tariqas' economic strengthening through their financial institutions and foundations should be carefully monitored.

(17) The messages transmitted by the TV channels and particularly the radio stations, which have antisecular attitudes, should be carefully monitored and these broadcastings should adapt to the constitution.

(18) The illegal money transfers of the Milli Görüş Foundation to some municipalities should be stopped.

Source: Milliyet, April, 27, 1997 (Because their official version has been kept secret, there exist various versions of these decisions.)

Bibliography

Interviews and Academic Conversations

Mehmet Aydın, Minister of the State in Charge of Religious Affairs; Washington, DC, April 19, 2004.

Mustafa Çalık, Editor of the journal *Türkiye Günlüğü*; Ankara, September 4, 2004.

Yalçın Akdoğan, Political advisor to Prime Minister Tayyip Erdoğan; Ankara, September 6, 2004.

Burhan Kuzu, President of the Constitutional Commission of the Turkish Parliament; Ankara, September 13, 2004.

Necmettin Cevheri, former Minister of the State in Charge of Religious Affairs; Ankara, September 13, 2004.

Mir Dengi Fırat, Vice-President of the AK Party; Ankara, September 14, 2004.

Mustafa Erdoğan, Professor of Law and founder of the Association for Liberal Thinking; Ankara, September 14, 2004.

Atilla Yayla, Professor of Political Science and President of the Association for Liberal Thinking; Ankara, September 14, 2004.

Ali Bardakoğlu, President of the Diyanet; Ankara, September 15, 2004.

Mehmet Görmez, Vice-President of the Diyanet; Ankara, September 15, 2004.

İhsan Dağı, Professor of International Relations, METU; Ankara, September 16, 2004.

Zana Çıtak, Assistant Professor of International Relations, METU; Ankara, September 17, 2004.

Haşim Kılıç, Vice–Chief Justice of the Turkish Constitutional Court; Ankara, September 20, 2004.

Binnaz Toprak, Professor of Political Science, Boğaziçi University; Istanbul September 21, 2004.

Ayşe Kadıoğlu, Professor of Political Science, Sabancı University; Istanbul, September 22, 2004.

Hamit Bozarslan, Professor of Sociology, EHESS; Paris, October 6, 2004.
Rüştü Naiboğlu, Retired Army General; Ankara, October 16, 2004.
Nilüfer Göle, Professor of Sociology, EHESS; Paris, October 21, 2004.
Semih Vaner, Professor of Political Science, AFEMOTI; Paris, October 25, 2004.
Nevzat Ceylan, Businessman; Paris, October 29, 2004.
Semra Meral, PhD Candidate, Political Science, Sorbonne University; Paris, October 30, 2004.
Rita Hermon-Belot, Professor of History, EHESS; Paris, November 5, 2004.
Emile Poulat, Professor of History, EHESS; Paris, November 10, 2004.
Jean Baubérot, Professor of History, EPHE, Sorbonne University; Auxerre, November 11, 2004.
Jean-Paul Willaime, Professor of Sociology, EPHE, Sorbonne University; Auxerre, November 11, 2004.
Fouad Alaoui, Secretary General of the Union of Islamic Organizations of France; Auxerre, November 12, 2004.
Valentine Zuber, Professor of Sociology, EPHE, Sorbonne University; Paris, November 26, 2004.
Ali Bulaç, Author and Columnist in *Zaman*; Brussels, December 3, 2004.
Rev. Sahag Mashalian, Armenian Patriarchate of Istanbul; Brussels, December 3, 2004.
Sabrina Pastorelli, PhD Candidate, Sociology, EPHE, Sorbonne University; Paris, December 8, 2004.
Frank S. Ravitch, Professor of Law, Michigan State University; Chicago, IL, April 9, 2005.
Philip Munoz, Assistant Professor of Political Science, Tufts University; Arlington, VA, May 21, 2005.
William Evans, Public Affairs Director of the LDS Church; by phone, August 30, 2005.
T. Jeremy Gunn, Professor of Law and the Director of the ACLU's Program on Freedom of Religion and Belief; Washington, DC, September 6, 2005.
Michael Lieberman, Director of the ADL's Civil Rights Policy Planning Center; Washington, DC, September 6, 2005.
Mark Button, Assistant Professor of Political Science, University of Utah; Salt Lake City, UT, September 12, 2005.
Rabbi Anson Laytner, Executive Director of the American Jewish Committee in Seattle; Seattle, WA, October 3, 2005.
Cole Durham, Professor of Law and the Director of the BYU International Center for Law and Religion Studies; Provo, UT, January 27, 2006.
Cynthia Moe-Lobeda, Assistant Professor of Theology, Seattle University; Seattle, WA, March 17, 2006.
Jocelyne Cesari, Professor of Islamic Studies, Harvard University; Madison, WI, March 25, 2006.
Michael S. Rassler, Executive Vice President, and Tina Friedman, Director of Community Relations, United Jewish Federation; San Diego, CA, March 16, 2007.

Court Decisions

The U.S. Supreme Court

Vidal v. Girard's Executors, 43 U.S. 127 (1844).
Reynolds v. U.S., 98 U.S. 145 (1878).
Davis v. Beason, 133 U.S. 333 (1890).
Mormon Church v. United States, 136 U.S. 1 (1890).
Holy Trinity Church v. U.S., 143 U.S. 457 (1892).
West Virginia v. Barnette, 319 U.S. 624 (1943).
Everson v. Board of Education, 330 U.S. 1 (1947).
McCollum v. Board of Education, 333 U.S. 203 (1948).
Zorach v. Clauson, 343 U.S. 306 (1952).
Brown v. Board of Education, 347 U.S. 483 (1954)
Engel v. Vitale, 370 U.S. 421 (1962).
Abington v. Schempp, 374 U.S. 203 (1963).
Sherbert v. Verner, 374 U.S. 398 (1963).
Board of Education v. Allen, 392 U.S. 236 (1968).
Epperson v. Arkansas, 393 U.S. 97 (1968).
Walz v. Tax Commission, 397 U.S. 664 (1970).
Welsh v. United States, 398 U.S. 333 (1970).
Lemon v. Kurtzman, 403 U.S. 602 (1971).
Wisconsin v. Yoder, 406 U.S. 205 (1972).
Stone v. Graham, 449 U.S. 39 (1980).
Widmar v. Vincent, 454 U.S. 263 (1981).
Lynch v. Donnelly, 463 U.S. 783 (1983).
Wallace v. Jaffree, 472 U.S. 38 (1985).
Goldman v. Weinberger, 475 U.S. 503 (1986).
Edwards v. Aguillard, 482 U.S. 578 (1987).
Allegheny v. ACLU, 492 U.S. 573 (1989).
Board of Education v. Mergens, 496 U.S. 226 (1990).
BOE of Westside Community Schools v. Mergens, 496 U.S. 226 (1990).
Oregon v. Smith, 494 U.S. 872 (1990).
Lee v. Weisman, 505 U.S. 577 (1992).
Lamb's Chapel v. Center Moriches, 508 U.S. 384 (1993).
Rosenberger v. Rector, 515 U.S. 819 (1995).
Agostini v. Felton of 1997, 521 U.S. 203 (1997).
City of Boerne v. Flores, 521 U.S. 507 (1997).
Mitchell v. Helms, 530 U.S. 793 (2000).
Santa Fe v. Doe, 530 U.S. 290 (2000).
Good News v. Milford, 533 U.S. 98 (2001).
Zelman v. Simmons-Harris, 536 U.S. 639 (2002).
Elk Grove Unified School District v. Newdow, 542 U.S. 1 (2004).
McCreary County v. ACLU, 545 U.S. (2005).
Van Orden v. Perry, 545 U.S. (2005).

The French Council of State

November 27, 1989; no. 346,893.

The French Constitutional Court

January 13, 1994; no. 93–329 DC.

The Turkish Council of State

December 13, 1984; no. 1984/1574.

The Turkish Constitutional Court

March 7, 1989; no. 1989/12
April 9, 1991; no. 1991/8.
January 16, 1997; no. 1998/1.
June 5, 2008; no. 2008/116.
July 30, 2008; no. 2008/2

Periodicals

In English

American Prospect
Christian Science Monitor
International Herald Tribune
New Republic
New York Sun
New York Times
USA Today
Washington Post
Washington Times

In French

La Croix
L'Express
Le Figaro magazine
Le Monde
Le Monde diplomatique
Le Nouvel observateur
Libération
Sciences humanes
L'Yonne républicaine

In Turkish

Aksiyon
Bugün
Diyanet
Hürriyet
Milliyet
Radikal
Sabah
Yeni Aktüel
Yeni Şafak
Zaman

Historical Documents and Publications

Akçura, Yusuf. 1976 [1904]. *Üç Tarz-ı Siyaset*. Ankara: Türk Tarih Kurumu.
Atatürk, M. Kemal. n.d. [1927]. *Nutuk I-III*. Istanbul: Türk Devrim Tarihi Enstitüsü.
Atay, Falih Rıfkı. 1980 [1961]. *Çankaya*. Istanbul: Bateş.
Buisson, Ferdinand, ed. 1878. *Rapport sur l'instruction primaire à l'exposition universelle de Philadelphie en 1876*. Paris: Imprimèrie nationale.
   2007 [1911]. *La Foi laïque: extraits de discours et d'écrits*. n.p.: Le Bord de L'Eau.
CHP. 1948. *Yedinci Kurultay Tutanağı*. Ankara: C.H.P.
Gökalp, Ziya. 1976 [1918]. *Türkleşmek, İslâmlaşmak, Muasırlaşmak*. Istanbul Devlet Kitapları.
   2007 [1923]. *Türkçülüğün Esasları* in *Kitaplar 1*. Istanbul: Yapı Kredi.
Kemal, Namık. 1962 [1910]. *Renan Müdafaanamesi: İslamiyet ve Maarif*, edited by M. Fuad Köprülü. Ankara: Milli Kültür.
Locke, John. 1980 [1690]. *Second Treatise of Government*. Indianapolis, IN: Hackett Publishing.
   1983 [1689]. *A Letter Concerning Toleration*. Indianapolis, IN: Hackett Publishing.
Nursi, Bediüzzaman Said. 1996a [1909]. *Divan-ı Harbi Örfi* in *Risale-i Nur Külliyatı*. Istanbul: Nesil.
   1996b [1929–1934]. *Mektubat* in *Risale-i Nur Külliyatı*. Istanbul: Nesil.
Rousseau, Jean-Jacques. 2001 [1762]. *Du contrat social*. Paris: GF Flammarion.
   n.d. [1762]. *The Social Contract*. Translated by Maurice Cranston. New York: Penguin.
Sabahattin, Prens. 2002 [1918]. *Türkiye Nasıl Kurtarılabilir?* Translated by İnan Keser. Istanbul: Liberte.
T.B.M.M. 1924. *T.B.M.M. Zabıt Ceridesi*, Vol. 7, Devre II, İçtima 1. Ankara: T.B.M.M. Matbaası.
   1928. *T.B.M.M. Zabıt Ceridesi*, Vol. 3, Devre III, İçtima 1. Ankara: T.B.M.M. Matbaası.

1937. *T.B.M.M. Kavanin Mecmuası*, Vol. *17*, *Devre V*, *İçtima* 2. Ankara: T.B.M.M. Matbaası.

1942 [1924]. *T.B.M.M. Kavanin Mecmuası*, Vol. *2*, *Devre II*, *İçtima 1*. Ankara: T.B.M.M. Matbaası.

1965a. *Millet Meclisi Tutanak Dergisi*, Vol. *39*, *Dönem I*, *Toplantı 4*. Ankara: T.B.M.M. Matbaası.

1965b. *Millet Meclisi Tutanak Dergisi*, Vol. *41*, *Dönem I*, *Toplantı 4*. Ankara: T.B.M.M. Matbaası.

Temo, İbrahim. 1987 [1939]. *İbrahim Temo'nun İttihad ve Terakki Anıları*. Istanbul: Arba.

Tocqueville, Alexis de. 2000 [1835]. *Democracy in America*. Translated by George Lawrence and edited by J.P. Mayer. New York: Perennial Classics.

Tunaya, Tarık Zafer. 1978. "Osmanlı Anayasacılık Hareketi ve 'Hükümet-i Meşruta.'" *Boğaziçi Üniversitesi Dergisi* 6: 227–37.

Books and Articles

Abu Rabi, Ibrahim, ed. 2003. *Islam at the Crossroads: On the Life and Thought of Bediüzzaman Said Nursi*. Albany: State University of New York Press.

Agai, Bekim. 2003. "The Gülen Movement's Islamic Ethic of Education." In *Turkish Islam and the Secular State: The Gülen Movement*, edited by M. Hakan Yavuz and John L. Esposito. Syracuse, NY: Syracuse University Press.

Ahlstrom, Sydney E. 1972. *A Religious History of the American People*. New Haven, CT: Yale University Press.

Ahmad, Feroz. 1969. *The Young Turks: The Committee of Union and Progress in Turkish Politics, 1908–1914*. New York: Oxford University Press.

1993. *The Making of Modern Turkey*. New York: Routledge.

Ahmad, Mumtaz. 1991. "Islamic Fundamentalism: The Jamaat-i-Islami and the Tablighi Jamaat." In *Fundamentalisms Observed*, edited by Martin E. Marty and R. Scott Appleby. Chicago: University of Chicago Press.

AK Parti. 2002. *Parti Programı*. n.p.: AK Parti.

n.d. *Siyasal Kimlik*. n.p.: AK Parti.

Akan, Murat. 2005. "The Politics of Secularization in Turkey and France: Beyond Orientalism and Occidentalism." PhD diss. Columbia University.

Akdoğan, Yalçın. 2003. *Muhafazakar Demokrasi*. Ankara: AK Parti.

2006. "The Meaning of Conservative Democratic Political Identity." In *Emergence of a New Turkey: Democracy and the AK Parti*, edited by M. Hakan Yavuz. Salt Lake City: University of Utah Press.

Akşit, Bahattin. 1991. "Islamic Education in Turkey: Medrese Reform in Late Ottoman Times and Imam-Hatip Schools in the Republic." In *Islam in Modern Turkey: Religion, Politics and Literature in a Secular State*, edited by Richard Tapper. New York: I. B. Tauris.

Aktay, Yasin. 1999. *Türk Dininin Sosyolojik İmkanı*. Istanbul: İletişim.

Akyol, Mustafa. 2006. *Kürt Sorununu Yeniden Düşünmek*. Istanbul: Doğan Kitap.

al-Ghannouchi, Rachid. 2000. "Secularism in the Arab Maghreb." In *Islam and Secularism in the Middle East*, edited by John L. Esposito and Azzam Tamimi. New York: New York University Press.

Al-Rasheed, Madawi. 2002. *A History of Saudi Arabia*. New York: Cambridge University Press.

Alaoui, Fouad. 2005. "Des conditions de l'intégration de l'islam dans le cadre républicain." In *Les Entretiens d'Auxerre: De la séparation des Églises et de l'État à l'avenir de la laïcité*, edited by Jean Baubérot and Michel Wieviorka. n.p.: L'aube.

Aliefendioğlu, Yılmaz 2001. "Laiklik ve Laik Devlet." In *Laiklik ve Demokrasi*, edited by İbrahim Ö. Kaboğlu. Istanbul: İmge.

Alpay, Şahin. 2003. "Türk Modeli Laikliğin 21. Yüzyılda Geleceği." In *Devlet ve Din İlişkileri-Farklı Modeller*, Konseptler ve Tecrübeler. Ankara: Konrad Adenauer Vakfı.

An-Na'im, Abdullahi Ahmed. 1999. "Political Islam in National Politics and International Relations." In *The Desecularization of the World: Resurgent Religion and World Politics*, edited by Peter L. Berger. Washington, DC: Ethics and Public Policy Center.

———. 2008. *Islam and the Secular State: Negotiating the Future of Shari'a*. Cambridge, MA: Harvard University Press.

Anderson, Benedict. 1998. *Imagined Communities: Reflections on the Origin and Spread of Nationalism*. London: Verso.

Anderson, John. 2007. "Putin and the Russian Orthodox Church: Asymmetric Symphonia." *Journal of International Affairs* 61 (1): 185–201.

Anderson, Robert. 1970. "The Conflict in Education: Catholic Secondary Schools (1850–70): A Reappraisal." In *Conflicts in French Society: Anticlericalism, Education and Morals in the Nineteenth Century*, edited by Theodore Zeldin. London: George Allen and Unwin.

Anshori, Ibnu. 1994. "Mustafa Kemal and Sukarno: A Comparison of Views Regarding Relations between State and Religion." MA thesis. McGill University.

Arat, Yeşim. 2004. "Boundaries of the Nation-State and the Lure of the Islamic Community in Turkey." In *Boundaries and Belonging: States and Societies in the Struggle to Shape Identities and Local Practices*, edited by Joel S. Migdal. New York: Cambridge University Press.

Arjomand, Said Amir. 1988. *The Turban for the Crown: The Islamic Revolution in Iran*. New York: Oxford University Press.

Arslan, Ahmet. 1996. "Türk Laikliği ve Geleceği Üzerine Bazı Düşünceler." *Liberal Düşünce* (1): 54–84.

———. 1999. *İslam, Demokrasi ve Türkiye*. Ankara: Vadi.

Arslan, Zühtü. 2005a. *Avrupa İnsan Hakları Sözleşmesinde Din Özgürlüğü*. Ankara: Liberal Düşünce Topluluğu.

———. 2005b. "Jüristokratik Demokrasi ve Laiklik: Türk Laikliğinin Siyasal İşlevi Üzerine." *Liberal Düşünce* (38–9): 45–54.

Asad, Talal. 2003. *Formations of the Secular: Christianity, Islam, Modernity*. Stanford, CA: Stanford University Press.

ASDER, Adaleti Savunanlar Derneği. 2004. *Ben Disiplinsiz Değilim*. Istanbul: ASDER.

Atabaki, Touraj and Erik Jan Zürcher, eds. 2004. *Men of Order: Authoritarian Modernization under Ataturk and Reza Shah*. New York: I. B. Tauris.

Aydın, Ertan. 2004. "Peculiarities of Turkish Revolutionary Ideology in the 1930s: The Ülkü Version of Kemalism, 1933–1936." *Middle Eastern Studies* 40 (5): 55–82.

Azria, Régine. 2003. *Le fait religieux en France*. Paris: La Documentation Française, no. 8033.

Bagby, Ihsan, Paul M. Perl, and Bryan T. Froehle. 2001. "The Mosque in America: A National Portrait." Washington, D.C., Council on American-Islamic Relations, April 26, http://www.cair.com/Portals/o/pdf/The_Mosque_in_America_A_National_Portrait.pdf.

Bağcı, Rıza. 1997. *Bizim Edebiyatımız: Nesiller, Şahsiyetler, Eserler*. İzmir: Kaynak.

Bailey, David C. 1974. *Viva Cristo Rey! The Cristero Rebellion and the Church-State Conflict in Mexico*. Austin: University of Texas Press.

Bailyn, Bernard. 1967. *The Ideological Origins of the American Revolution*. Cambridge, MA: Harvard University Press.

Bakar, Osman. 2003. "The Intellectual Impact of American Muslim Scholars on the Muslim World, with Special Reference to Southeast Asia." In *Muslims in the United States*, edited by Philippa Strum and Danielle Tarantolo. Washington, DC: Woodrow Wilson International Center for Scholars.

Balmer, Randall. 2008. *God in the White House: A History*. New York: Harper One.

Baristiran, Omer. 2004. *Secularism: The Turkish Experience. An Academic DVD*. Philadelphia: University of Pennsylvania Press.

Barkey, Karen. 2008. *Empire of Difference: The Ottomans in Comparative Perspective*. New York: Cambridge University Press.

Barrett, David B., George T. Kurian, and Todd M. Johnson. 2001. *World Christian Encyclopedia: A Comparative Survey of Churches and Religions in the Modern World*. New York: Oxford University Press.

Barro, Robert J. and Rachel M. Mccleary. 2005. "Which Countries Have State Religions?" *The Quarterly Journal of Economics* 104 (4): 1331–70.

Başgil, Ali Fuat. 1977 [1954]. *Din ve Laiklik*. Istanbul: Yağmur.

Bates, Robert H. 1981. *Markets and States in Tropical Africa*. Berkeley: University of California Press.

Baubérot, Jean. 1990. *Vers un nouveau pacte laïque?* Paris: Seuil.

1994a. "Republique laique." In *Religions et laïcité dans l'Europe des douze*, edited by Jean Baubérot. Paris: Syros.

1994b. "Annexe: l'Alsace-Lorraine, la difference au coeur du jacobinisme." In *Religions et laïcité dans l'Europe des douze*, edited by Jean Baubérot. Paris: Syros.

Baubérot, Jean, ed. 1994c. *Religions et laïcité dans l'Europe des douze*. Paris: Syros.

1999. "Two Thresholds of Laicization." In *Secularism and Its Critics*, edited by Rajeev Bhargava. Delhi, India: Oxford University Press.

2000. "D'une comparaison: Laïcité française, laïcité turque." In *Turquie, les mille visages: Politique, religion, femmes, immigration*, edited by Isabelle Rigoni. Paris: Editions Syllepse.

2003. "Secularism and French Religious Liberty: A Sociological and Historical View." *Brigham Young University Law Review* (2): 461–4.

2004a. *Histoire de la laïcité en France*. Paris: PUF, Que sais-je?

2004b. *La Laïcité à l'épreuve : Religions et libertés dans le monde*. n.p.: Universalis.

2004c. "Brève histoire de la laïcité en France." In *La Laïcité à l'épreuve : Religions et libertés dans le monde*, edited by Jean Baubérot. n.p.: Universalis.

2004d. *Laïcité 1905–2005, entre passion et raison*. Paris: Seuil.

2004e. "The Place of Religion in Public Life: The Lay Approach." In *Facilitating Freedom of Religion or Belief: A Deskbook*, edited by Tore Lindholm Jr., W. Cole Durham, and Bahia G. Tahzib-Lie. Leiden, The Netherlands: Martinus Nijhoff.

2004f. "La laïcité: le chêne et le roseau." In *La laïcité dévoilée: Quinze années de débat en quarante rebonds*. n.p.: *Libération* and éditions de l'Aube.

2005. "Conclusion." In *Les Entretiens d'Auxerre: De la séparation des Églises et de l'État à l'avenir de la laïcité*, edited by Jean Baubérot and Michel Wieviorka. n.p.: l'Aube.

Baubérot, Jean and Séverine Mathieu. 2002. *Religion, modernité et culture au Royaume-Uni et en France: 1800–1914*. Paris: Seuil.

Baudouin, Jean and Philippe Portier. 2001. "La laïcité française. Approche d'une métamorphose." In *La laïcité, une valeur d'aujourd'hui? Contestations et renégociations du modèle français*, edited by Jean Baudouin and Philippe Portier. Rennes, France: Presses Universitaires de Rennes.

Beattie, Nicholas. 2000. "Yeast in the Dough? Catholic Schooling in France, 1981–95." In *Catholicism, Politics, and Society in Twentieth-Century France*, edited by Kay Chadwick. Liverpool: Liverpool University Press.

Bedouelle, Guy and Jean-Paul Costa. 1998. *Les laïcités à la française*. Paris: Puf.

Belge, Ceren. 2006. "Friends of the Court: The Republican Alliance and Selective Activism on the Constitutional Court of Turkey." *Law and Society Review* 40 (3): 653–92.

Bellah, Robert. 2005. "Civil Religion in America." *Daedalus* 134 (4): 40–55.

Bencheikh, Soheib. 1998. *Marianne et le Prophète: L'Islam dans la France laïque*. Paris: Bernard Grasset.

1999. "Les Croyants les plus proches de la 'laïcité à la française' sont les musulmans." *Hommes and Migrations* (1218): 14–21.

Bennigsen, Alexandre and Chantal Lemercier-Quelquejay. 1981. *Step'de Ezan Sesleri: Sovyet Rejimi Altındaki İslâm'ın 400 Yılı*. Translated by Nezih Uzel. Ankara: Selçuk.

Berger, Peter L. 1999. "The De-secularization of the World: A Global Overview." In *The Desecularization of the World: Resurgent Religion and World Politics,* edited by Peter L. Berger. Washington, DC: Ethics and Public Policy Center.

Bergounioux, Alain. 1995. "La laïcité, valeur de la République." *Pouvoirs* (75): 17–26.

Berkes, Niyazi. 1955. "Historical Background of Turkish Secularism." In *Islam and the West,* edited by Richard N. Frye. The Hague: Mouton and Co.

1998 [1964]. *The Development of Secularism in Turkey.* New York: Routledge.

Berlin, Isaiah. 1997. "Two Concepts of Liberty." In *The Proper Study of Mankind: An Anthology of Essays,* edited by Henry Hardy and Roger Hausheer. London: Chatto and Windus.

Berman, Harold J. 1996. "Religious Rights in Russia at a Time of Tumultuous Transition: A Historical Theory." In *Religious Human Rights in Global Perspective: Legal Perspectives,* edited by Johan D. van der Vyver and John Witte Jr. The Hague: Martinus Nijhoff.

Bertrand, Jean René. 2006. "State and Church in France: Regulation and Negotiation." *GeoJournal* 67 (4): 295–306.

Beyerlein, Kraig. 2003. "Educational Elites and the Movement to Secularize Public Education: The Case of the National Education Association." In *The Secular Revolution: Power, Interests, and Conflict in the Secularization of American Public Life,* edited by Christian Smith. Berkeley: University of California Press.

Bhargava, Rajeev, ed. 1999. *Secularism and Its Critics.* Delhi, India: Oxford University Press.

2007. "The Distinctiveness of Indian Secularism." In *The Future of Secularism,* edited by T. N. Srinivasan. New York: Oxford University Press.

Billings, Dwight B. 1990. "Religion as Opposition: A Gramscian Analysis." *American Journal of Sociology* 96 (1): 1–31.

Blancarte, Roberto. 2005. "Un regard latino-américain sur la laïcité." In *Les Entretiens d'Auxerre: De la séparation des Églises et de l'État à l'avenir de la laïcité,* edited by Jean Baubérot and Michel Wieviorka. n.p.: L'aube.

Bleich, Erik. 1998. "From International Ideas to Domestic Policies: Educational Multiculturalism in England and France." *Comparative Politics* 31 (1): 81–100.

2002. "Integrating Ideas into Policy-Making Analysis: Frames and Race Policies in Britain and France." *Comparative Political Studies* 35 (9): 1054–76.

Boniface, Xavier. 2001. *L'aumônerie militaire française, 1914–1962.* Paris: Cerf.

Boston, Rob. 1997. "Joel Barlow and the Treaty with Tripoli: A Tangled Tale of Pirates, a Poet and the True Meaning of the First Amendment." *Church and State* 50 (6): 11–14.

Bosworth, William. 1962. *Catholicism and Crisis in Modern France: French Catholic Groups at the Threshold of the Fifth Republic.* Princeton, NJ: Princeton University Press.

Bottoni, Rossella. 2007. "The Origins of Secularism in Turkey." *Ecclesiastical Law Journal* 9: 175–86.

Bowen, John R. 2004a. "Does French Islam Have Borders? Dilemmas of Domestication in a Global Religious Field." *American Anthropologist* 106 (1): 43–55.

2004b. "Muslims and Citizens: France's Headscarf Controversy." *Boston Review* (February–March): 31–5.

2006. *Why the French Don't Like Headscarves: Islam, the State, and Public State*. Princeton, NJ: Princeton University Press.

Boyer, Alain. 2004. *1905 : La Séparation Églises-États*. Paris: Editions Cana.

2005a. "Comment l'Etat laïque connait-il les religions?" *Archives de sciences sociales des religions* (129): 37–49.

2005b. "La législation anticongréganiste 1901–1904." In *Le Grand Exil: Des Congrégations Religieuses Françaises 1901–1914*, edited by Patrick Cabanel and Jean-Dominique Durand. Paris: Cerf.

Boyle, Kevin and Juliet Sheen, eds. 1997. *Freedom of Religion and Belief: A World Report*. New York: Routledge.

Bozarslan, Hamit 2004. "Islam, laïcité et la question d'autorité dans l'Empire ottoman et en Turquie kémaliste." *Archives des sciences sociales des religions* (125): 99–113.

Brady, Henry E. and David Collier. 2004. *Rethinking Social Inquiry: Diverse Tools, Shared Standards*. Lanham, MD: Rowman and Littlefield.

Brand, Laurie A. 2007. "Middle East Studies and Academic Freedom: Challenges at Home and Abroad." *International Studies Perspectives* 8 (4): 384–95.

Brechon, Pierre. 1995. "Institution de la laïcité et déchristianisation de la société française." *Cahiers d'études sur la Méditerranée orientale et le monde turco-iranien* (19): 59–78.

Bruce, Steve. 2002. *God Is Dead: Secularization in the West*. Malden, MA: Blackwell.

Bukhari, Zahid H. 2003. "Demography, Identity, Space: Defining American Muslims." In *Muslims in the United States*, edited by Philippa Strum and Danielle Tarantolo. Washington, DC: Woodrow Wilson International Center for Scholars.

Bulaç, Ali. 1992. "Modern ve Mahrem." *Birikim* 33: 74–80.

2001. *Din, Devlet ve Demokrasi*. Istanbul: Zaman Kitap.

Bulliet, Richard W. 1996. "The Individual in Islamic Society." In *Religious Diversity and Human Rights*, edited by Irene Bloom, J. Paul Martin, and Wayne L. Proudfoot. New York: Columbia University Press.

Burdy, Jean-Paul. 1995. "La ville désenchantée? Sécularisation et laïcisation des espaces urbains français (XIXe–XXe siècles)." *Cahiers d'études sur la Méditerranée orientale et le monde turco-iranien* (19): 129–58.

Burdy, Jean-Paul and Jean Marcou. 1995. "Laïcité/Laiklik: Introduction." *Cahiers d'études sur la Méditerranée orientale et le monde turco-iranien* (19): 5–34.

Burgat, François. 2003. "Veils and Obscuring Lenses." In *Modernizing Islam: Religion and the Public Sphere in Europe and the Middle East*, edited by John L. Esposito and François Burgat. New Brunswick, NJ: Rutgers University Press.

Burke, Edmund. 1987 [1790]. *Reflections on the Revolution in France*. Indianapolis, IN: Hackett Publishing.

Byrnes, Timothy A. 2002. "The Challenge of Pluralism: The Catholic Church in Democratic Poland." In *Religion and Politics in Comparative Perspective: The One, the Few, and the Many*, edited by Ted Gerard Jelen and Clyde Wilcox. New York: Cambridge University Press.

Cabanel, Patrick. 2004. "1905: Une loi d'apaisement?" *L'Histoire* (289): 68–71.

———. 2005a. "La laïcité scolaire face aux religions: de quelques accommodements sous la IIIe République." In *Des maîtres et des dieux: écoles et religions en Europe*, edited by Jean-Paul Willaime and Séverine Mathieu. n.p.: Belin.

———. 2005b. "Le Combisme et l'antitotalitarisme prophétique de Péguy." In *Les Entretiens d'Auxerre: De la séparation des Églises et de l'État à l'avenir de la laïcité*, edited by Jean Baubérot and Michel Wieviorka. n.p.: L'aube.

Cabanel, Patrick and Jean-Dominique Durand, eds. 2005. *Le Grand Exil: Des Congrégations Religieuses Françaises 1901–1914*. Paris: Cerf.

Caeiro, Alexandre. 2006. "Religious Authorities or Political Actors? The Muslim Leaders of the French Representative Body of Islam." In *European Muslims and the Secular State*, edited by Jocelyne Cesari. Burlington, VT: Ashgate.

Cainkar, Louise. 2008. "Thinking Outside the Box: Arabs and Race in the United States." In *Race and Arab Americans before and after 9/11: From Invisible Citizens to Visible Subjects*, edited by Amaney Jamal and Nadine Naber. Syracuse, NY: Syracuse University Press.

Çakır, Ruşen and İrfan Bozan. 2005. *Sivil, Şeffaf ve Demokratik Bir Diyanet İşleri Başkanlığı Mümkün mü?* Istanbul: TESEV.

Canatan, Kadir. 1997. *Din ve Laiklik*. Istanbul: İnsan.

Capoccia, Giovanni and R. Daniel Kelemen. 2007. "The Study of Critical Junctures: Theory, Narrative, and Counterfactuals in Historical Institutionalism." *World Politics* 59 (3): 341–69.

Carens, Joseph H. and Melissa S. Williams. 1999. "Muslim Minorities in Liberal Democracies: The Politics of Misrecognition." In *Secularism and Its Critics*, edited by Rajeev Bhargava. Delhi, India: Oxford University Press.

Çarkoğlu, Ali. 2004. "Religiosity, Support for Şeriat and Evaluations of Secularist Public Policies in Turkey." *Middle Eastern Studies* 40 (2): 111–36.

Çarkoğlu, Ali and Binnaz Toprak. 2000. *Türkiye'de Din, Toplum ve Siyaset*. Istanbul: TESEV.

———. 2006. *Değişen Türkiye'de Din, Toplum ve Siyaset*. Istanbul: TESEV.

Carter, Stephen L. 1993. *The Culture of Disbelief: How American Law and Politics Trivialize Religious Devotion.* New York: Basic Books.

Casanova, Jose. 1994. *Public Religions in the Modern World.* Chicago: University of Chicago Press.

———. 2001. "Civil Society and Religion: Retrospective Reflections on Catholicism and Prospective Reflections on Islam." *Social Research* 68 (4): 1041–80.

Çavdar, Gamze. 2006. "Islamist New Thinking in Turkey: A Model for Political Learning." *Political Science Quarterly* 121 (3): 477–97.

Çayır, Kenan. 2007. "Tensions and Dilemmas in Human Rights Education." In *Human Rights in Turkey*, edited by Zehra F. Kabasakal. Philadelphia: University of Pennsylvania Press.

Cesari, Jocelyne. 1995. "Demande d'islam en banlieue: Un défi a la citoyenneté?" *Cahiers d'études sur la Méditerranée orientale et le monde turco-iranien* (19): 167–81.

———. 2001. "L'unité républicaine menace par les idéologies multiculturelles." In *La laïcité, une valeur d'aujourd'hui ? Contestations et renégociations du modèle français*, edited by Jean Baudouin and Philippe Portier. Rennes, France: Presses Universitaires de Rennes.

———. 2002. "L'islam en europe: L'incorporation d'une religion." *Cahiers d'études sur la Méditerranée orientale et le monde turco-iranien* (33): 7–20.

———. 2006a. "Islam, Secularism and Multiculturalism in after 9/11: A Transatlantic Comparison." In *European Muslims and the Secular State*, edited by Jocelyne Cesari. Burlington, VT: Ashgate.

———. 2006b. *When Islam and Democracy Meet: Muslims in Europe and in the United States.* New York: Palgrave Macmillian.

Çetinkaya, Tuncer. 2005. *En Uzun Şubat: Belge ve Şahitlerle Bir Dönemin Trajik Hikayeleri.* Izmir: Kaynak.

Cetinsaya, Gokhan. 1999. "Rethinking Nationalism and Islam: Some Preliminary Notes on the Roots of 'Turkish-Islamic Synthesis' in Modern Turkish Thought." *Muslim World* 89 (3–4): 350–76.

Chadwick, Kay. 2000a. "Introduction." In *Catholicism, Politics and Soicety in Twentieth-Century France*, edited by Kay Chadwick. Liverpool: Liverpool University Press.

———. 2000b. "Accueillir l'étranger: Immigration, Integration and the French Catholic Church." In *Catholicism, Politics and Soicety in Twentieth-Century France*, edited by Kay Chadwick. Liverpool: Liverpool University Press.

Chambers, Richard L. 1964. "The Civil Bureaucracy: Turkey." In *Political Modernization in Japan and Turkey*, edited by Robert E. Ward and Dankwart A. Rustow. Princeton, NJ: Princeton University Press.

Chanet, Jean-Francois. 2004. "Le Choix de Ferry." *L'Histoire* (289): 58–63.

Chaves, Mark and David E. Cann. 1992. "Regulation, Pluralism, and Religious Market Structure." *Rationality and Society* 4 (3): 272–90.

Chehabi, Houchang. 2004. "Dress Codes for Men in Turkey and in Iran." In *Men of Order: Authoritarian Modernization under Atatürk and Reza Shah*, edited by Touraj and Erik Jan Zürcher Atabaki. New York: I. B. Tauris.

Çınar, Menderes. 2004. "Modified Orientalism: The Case of Hakan Yavuz's Islamic Political Identity in Turkey." *New Perspectives on Turkey* 30: 155–68.

Çınar, Menderes and Burhanettin Duran. 2007. "The Specific Evolution of Contemporary Political Islam in Turkey and Its 'Difference.'" In *Secular and Islamic Politics in Turkey: The Making of the Justice and Development Party*. Abingdon, UK: Routledge.

Cirtautas, Arista Maria. 2000. "France." In *Comparative Politics: Interests, Identities, and Institutions in a Changing Global Order*, edited by Jeffrey Kopstein and Mark Lichbach. New York: Cambridge University Press.

Çıtak-Aytürk, Zana. 2005. "Laïcité et nationalisme: pour une comparaison entre la Turquie et la France." In *Les Entretiens d'Auxerre: De la séparation des Églises et de l'État à l'avenir de la laïcité*, edited by Jean Baubérot and Michel Wieviorka. n.p.: L'aube.

Çıtak, Zana. 2004. "Nationalism and Religion: A Comparative Study of the Development of Secularism in France and Turkey." PhD diss. Boston University.

Cizre, Ümit. 1999. *Muktedirlerin Siyaseti: Merkez Sağ-Ordu-İslamcılık*. Istanbul: İletişim.

Clayton, Cornell W. and Howard Gillman, eds. 1999. *Supreme Court Decision-Making: New Institutionalist Approaches*. Chicago: University of Chicago Press.

Cochran, Clarke E. 1998. "Introduction." In *A Wall of Separation? Debating the Public Role of Religion*, edited by Mary C. Segers and Ted G. Jelen. Lanham, MD: Rowman and Littlefield.

Cole, Juan. 2007. "Islamophobia as a Social Problem." *MESA Bulletein* 41 (1): 3–7.

Collier, David. 1991. "The Comparative Method: Two Decades of Change." In *Comparative Dynamics: Global Research Perspectives*, edited by Dankwart A. Rustow and Kenneth Paul. New York: HarperCollins.

Collier, David and Steven Levitsky. 1997. "Democracy with Adjectives: Conceptual Innovation in Comparative Research." *World Politics* 49 (3): 430–51.

Collier, David and James E. Mahon. 1993. "Conceptual 'Stretching' Revisited: Adapting Categories in Comparative Analysis." *American Political Science Review* 87 (4): 845–55.

Collier, Ruth Berins and David Collier. 1991. *Shaping the Political Arena: Critical Junctures, the Labor Movement, and Regime Dynamics in Latin America*. Princeton, NJ: Princeton University Press.

Conseil d'Etat. 2004. "Rapport public: Réflexions sur la laïcité." http://lesrapports.ladocumentationfrancaise.fr/BRP/044000121/0001.pdf, accessed on March 20, 2008.

Constant, Benjamin. 1988 [1819]. "The Liberty of the Ancients Compared with that of the Moderns." In *Political Writings*, edited by Benjamin Constant. Translated by Biancamaria Fontana. Cambridge: Cambridge University Press.

Coq, Guy. 2004. "Les Batailles de l'école." *L'Histoire* (289): 100–1.

Costa, Jean-Paul. 1995. "Interview with Jean Marceau. Le Conseil d'Etat, le droit public français et le 'foulard.'" *Cahiers d'études sur la Méditerranée orientale et le monde turco-iranien* (19): 79–84.

Curry, Thomas J. 1986. *The First Freedoms: Church and State in America to the Passage of the First Amendment*. New York: Oxford University Press.

Dağı, İhsan D. 1998. *Kimlik, Söylem ve Siyaset: Doğu-Batı Ayrımında Refah Partisi Geleneği*. Ankara: İmge.

——— 2004. "Rethinking Human Rights, Democracy, and the West: Post-Islamist Intellectuals in Turkey." *Critique: Critical Middle Eastern Studies* 13: 135–51.

Daver, Bülent. 1955. *Türkiye Cumhuriyetinde Layiklik*. Ankara: A. Ü. Siyasal Bilgiler Fakültesi.

Davis, Derek H. 1998. "Equal Treatment: A Christian Separationist Perspective." In *Equal Treatment of Religion in a Pluralistic Society*, edited by Stephen V. Monsma and J. Christopher Soper. Grand Rapids, MI: Eerdmans.

——— 2004. "Reacting to France's Ban: Headscarves and Other Religious Attire in American Public Schools." *Journal of Church and State* 46 (2): 221–35.

Davison, Andrew. 2003. "Turkey, a 'Secular' State? The Challenge of Description." *The South Atlantic Quarterly* 102 (2–3): 333–50.

Davison, Roderick H. 1964. "Environmental and Foreign Contributions: Turkey." In *Political Modernization in Japan and Turkey*, edited by Robert E. Ward and Dankwart A. Rustow. Princeton, NJ: Princeton University Press.

Davutoğlu, Ahmet. 1994. *Alternative Paradigms: The Impact of Islamic and Western Weltanschauungs on Political Theory*. Lanham, MD: University Press of America.

Debray, Regis. 1992. *Contretemps: Eloges des idéaux perdus*. Paris: Gallimard.

——— 2002. *L'Enseignement du fait religieux dans l'école laïque*. Paris: Odile Jacob.

Debré, Jean-Louis. 2004. *La laïcité à l'école: Un principe républicain à réaffirmer. Rapport de la mission d'information de l'Assemblée nationale*. Paris: Odile Jacob.

Dekker, Henk and Jolanda Van Der Noll. 2007. "Islamophobia and Its Origins." Paper presented at the Fourth European Consortium for Political Research Conference, Pisa, Italy, September 6–8.

Dekker, Paul and Peter Ester. 1996. "Depillarization, Deconfessionalization, and De-Ideologization: Empirical Trends in Dutch Society 1958–1992." *Review of Religious Research* 37 (4): 325–41.

Delasselle, Claude. 2005. "Les sociétés de libre pensée de l'Yonne, 1880–1914." In *Les Entretiens d'Auxerre: De la séparation des Églises et de l'État à l'avenir de la laïcité*, edited by Jean Baubérot and Michel Wieviorka. n.p.: L'aube.

Demerath, N. J. and H. Williams. 1987. "A Mythical Past and Uncertain Future." In *Church-State Relations: Tensions and Transitions*, edited by Thomas Robbins and Ronald Robertson. New Brunswick, NJ: Transaction Books.

Dereymez, Jean-William. 1995. "Les Socialistes français et la laïcité." *Cahiers d'études sur la Méditerranée orientale et le monde turco-iranien* (19): 235–53.

Deringil, Selim. 1993. "The Ottoman Origins of Kemalist Nationalism: Namik Kemal to Mustafa Kemal." *European History Quarterly* 23 (2): 165–92.

Deverell, William F. 1987. "Church-State Issues in the Period of the Civil War." In *Church and State in America: A Bibliographical Guide. The Civil War to the Present Day*, edited by John F. Wilson. New York: Greenwood Press.

Dienstang, Joshua Foa. 1996. "Serving God and Mammon: The Lockean Sympathy in Early American Political Thought." *American Political Science Review* 90 (3): 497–511.

Dilipak, Abdurrahman. 1995. *Bu Din Benim Dinim Değil: "Resmi Din" Öğretisine Eleştirel Bir Yaklaşım*. Istanbul: Risale.

Dillon, Michele. 2002. "Catholicism, Politics, and Culture in the Republic of Ireland." In *Religion and Politics in Comparative Perspective: The One, the Few, and the Many*, edited by Ted Gerard Jelen and Clyde Wilcox. New York: Cambridge University Press.

Dilulio, John J. 2007. *Godly Republic: A Centrist Blueprint for America's Faith-Based Future*. Berkeley: University of California Press.

Dionne, E. J. 2002. "Foreword." In *Religion Returns to the Public Square: Faith and Policy in America*, edited by Hugh Heclo and Wilfred M. McClay. Baltimore, MD: The Johns Hopkins University Press.

Dombrowski, Daniel A. 2001. *Rawls and Religion: The Case for Political Liberalism*. Albany: State University of New York Press.

Dreisbach, Daniel L. 2002. *Thomas Jefferson and the Wall of Separation between Church and State*. New York: New York University Press.

Ducomte, Jean Michel. 2001. *La laïcité*. Toulouse, France: Editions Milan.

Durand-Prinborgne, Claude. 2004. *La laïcité*. n.p.: Dalloz.

Durham, W. Cole, Jr. 1996. "Perspectives on Religious Liberty: A Comparative Framework." In *Religious Human Rights in Global Perspective: Legal Perspectives*, edited by Johan D. van der Vyver and John Witte Jr. The Hague: Martinus Nijhoff.

Eastman, John C. 2000. "'We Are a Religious People Whose Institutions Presuppose a Supreme Being.'" *Nexus: A Journal of Opinion* 5: 13–23.

Eickelman, Dale F. and James P. Piscatori. 1996. *Muslim Politics*. Princeton, NJ: Princeton University Press.

El Fadl, Khaled Abou. 2003. *The Place of Tolerance in Islam*. Boston: Beacon Press.

Elias, Norbert. 2000. *The Civilizing Process*. Translated by Edmund Jephcott. Malden, MA: Blackwell.

Englund, Steven. 1992. "Church and State in France since the Revolution." *Journal of Church and State* 34 (2): 325–60.

Epstein, Lee and Jack Knight. 1998. *The Choices Justices Make*. Washington, DC: CQ Press.

Epstein, Lee and Jeffrey A. Segal. 2005. *Advice and Consent: The Politics of Judicial Appointments*. New York: Oxford University Press.

Erdoğan, Mustafa. 1997. *Rejim Sorunu*. Ankara: Vadi.

    1998. "Anayasa Mahkemesi Nasıl Karar Veriyor: Başörtüsü Kararı." *Liberal Düşünce* 3 (9): 5–16.

    1999. "Religious Freedom in the Turkish Constitution." *The Muslim World* 89: 377–88.

Erdoğan, Recep Tayyip. 2004. "Keynote Speech." In *International Symposium on Conservatism and Democracy*. n.p.: AK Parti.

Esbeck, Carl H. 1986. "Five Views of Church-State Relations in Contemporary American Thought." *BYU Law Review* (2): 371–404.

    2004. "Dissent and Disestablishment: The Church-State Settlement in the Early American Republic." *BYU Law Review* (4): 1385–1492.

Esposito, John L. 2000. "Introduction: Islam and Secularism in the Twenty-First Century." In *Islam and Secularism in the Middle East*, edited by John L. Esposito and Azzam Tamimi. London: Hurst and Company.

EUMC, European Monitoring Centre on Racism and Xenophobia. 2006. "Muslims in the European Union: Discrimination and Islamophobia." http://fra.europa.eu/fra/material/pub/muslim/Manifestations_EN.pdf, accessed on June 25, 2008.

European Stability Initiative. 2007. "Sex and Power in Turkey: Feminism, Islam and the Maturing of Turkish Democracy." Berlin, June 2, www.esiweb.org/pdf/esi_document_id_90.pdf.

Fautre, Willy, Alain Garay, and Yves Nidegger. 2004. "The Sect Issue in the European Francophone Sphere." In *Facilitating Freedom of Religion or Belief: A Deskbook*, edited by Tore Lindholm, W. Cole Durham Jr., and Bahia G. Tahzib-Lie. Leiden, the Netherlands: Martinus Nijhoff.

Fehér, Ferenc. 1990. "The Cult of Supreme Being and the Limits of the Secularization of the Political." In *The French Revolution and the Birth of Modernity*, edited by Ferenc Fehér. Berkeley: University of California Press.

Feldman, Noah. 2002a. "The Intellectual Origins of the Establishment Clause." *New York University Law Review* 77: 346–428.

    2002b. "From Liberty to Equality: The Transformation of the Establishment Clause." *California Law Review* 90 (3): 673–731.

    2005. *Divided by God: America's Church-State Problem and What We Should Do about It*. New York: Farrar, Straus and Giroux.

Fernando, Mayanthi L. 2006. "'French Citizens of Muslim Faith': Islam, Secularism, and the Politics of Difference in Contemporary France." PhD Diss., The University of Chicago.

Feroze, Muhammad Rashid. 1976. *Islam and Secularism in Post-Kemalist Turkey*. Islamabad: Islamic Research Institute.

Fetzer, Joel S. and J. Christopher Soper. 2003. "The Roots of Public Attitudes towards State Accommodation of European Muslims' Religious Practices Before and After September 11." *Journal for the Scientific Study of Religion* 42 (2): 247–58.

    2005. *Muslims and the State in Britain, France, and Germany*. New York: Cambridge University Press.

Filiztekin, Alpay and İnsan Tunalı. 1999. "Anatolian Tigers: Are They for Real?" *New Perspectives on Turkey* 20: 77–106.

Findley, Carter V. 1980. *Bureaucratic Reform in the Ottoman Empire: The Sublime Port, 1789–1922*. Princeton, NJ: Princeton University Press.

Finke, Roger. 1990. "Religious Deregulation: Origins and Consequences." *Journal of Church and State* 32 (3): 609–26.

Fiorina, Morris P. 2005. *Culture War? The Myth of Polarized America*. New York: Pearson Longman.

Fisher, Louis. 2005. *American Constitutional Law: Constitutional Structures. Separated Powers and Federalism*. Durham, NC: Carolina Academic Press.

Flory, Richard W. 2003. "Promoting a Secular Standard: Secularization and Modern Journalism, 1870–1930." In *The Secular Revolution: Power, Interests, and Conflict in the Secularization of American Public Life*, edited by Christian Smith. Berkeley: University of California Press.

Flowers, Ronald B. 2005. *That Godless Court? Supreme Court Decisions on Church-State Relationships*. Louisville, KY: Westminster John Knox Press.

Fortna, Benjamin C. 2000. "Islamic Morality in Late Ottoman 'Secular' Schools." *International Journal of Middle East Studies* 32 (3): 369–93.

    2002. *Imperial Classroom: Islam, the State, and Education in the Late Ottoman Empire*. New York: Oxford University Press.

Fowler, Robert Booth, Allen D. Hertzke, Laura R. Olson, and Kevin R. Den Dulk. 2004. *Religion and Politics in America: Faith, Culture, and Strategic Choices*. Boulder, CO: Westview.

Fox, Jonathan. 2006. "World Separation of Religion and State into the 21st Century." *Comparative Political Studies* 39 (5): 537–69.

    2008. *A World Survey of Religion and the State*. New York: Cambridge University Press.

Franchi, Anne-Marie. 1994. "La franc-maçonnerie en Europe." In *Religions et laïcité dans l'Europe des douze*, edited by Jean Baubérot. Paris: Syros.

Francis, John G. 1992. "The Evolving Regulatory Structure of European Church-State Relationships." *Journal of Church and State* 34 (4): 775–804.

Fraser, James W. 1999. *Between Church and State: Religion and Public Education in a Multicultural America.* New York: St. Martin's Griffin.

Fraser, Nancy. 1997. *Justice Interruptus: Critical Reflections on the "Postsocialist" Condition.* New York: Routledge.

Frégosi, Frank. 2008. *Penser l'islam dans la laïcité.* n.p.: Fayard.

Frey, Frederick W. 1964. "Education: Turkey." In *Political Modernization in Japan and Turkey,* edited by Robert E. Ward and Dankwart A. Rustow. Princeton, NJ: Princeton University Press.

Furet, François. 1992. *Revolutionary France 1770–1880.* Translated by Antonia Nevill. Cambridge, MA: Blackwell.

Gaillard, Jean-Michel. 2004. "L'Europe sera laïque ou ne sera pas!" *L'Histoire* (289): 102–8.

Garroutte, Eva Marie. 2003. "The Positivist Attack on Baconian Science and Religious Knowledge in the 1870s." In *The Secular Revolution: Power, Interests, and Conflict in the Secularization of American Public Life,* edited by Christian Smith. Berkeley: University of California Press.

Garry, Patrick M. 2005. "The Cultural Hostility to Religion." *Modern Age* 47 (2): 121–31.

Gaspard, Françoise and Farhad Khosrokhavar. 1995. *Le Foulard et al République.* Paris: La Découverte.

———. 2003. "The Headscarf and the Republic." In *Beyond French Feminisms: Debates on Women, Politics, and Culture in France, 1981–2001,* edited by Roger Célestin, Eliane DalMolin, and Isabelle de Courtivron. New York: Palgrave Macmillian.

Gastaut, Yvan. 2004. "L'islam français: est-il soluble dans la laïcité?" *L'Histoire* (289): 92–7.

Gauchet, Marcel. 1998. *La religion dans la démocratie.* n.p.: Foli.

Gaustad, Edwin S. 2004. *Faith of the Founders: Religion and the New Nation 1776–1826.* Waco, TX: Baylor University Press.

Gazeteciler ve Yazarlar Vakfı. 1998. *İslam ve Laiklik.* Istanbul: Gazeteciler ve Yazarlar Vakfı.

———. 1999. *Din, Devlet, Toplum.* Istanbul: Gazeteciler ve Yazarlar Vakfı.

Gedicks, Frederick Mark. 1995. *The Rhetoric of Church and State.* Durham, NC: Duke University Press.

———. 2005. "The Permissible Scope of Legal Limitations on the Freedom of Religion or Belief in the United States." *Emory International Law Review* 19 (2): 1187–274.

Gellner, Ernest. 1983a. *Nations and Nationalism.* Ithaca, NY: Cornell University Press.

———. 1983b. *Muslim Society.* Cambridge: Cambridge University Press.

———. 1992. *Postmodernism, Reason and Religion.* New York: Routledge.

———. 1997. "The Turkish Option in Comparative Perspective." In *Rethinking Modernity and National Identity in Turkey,* edited by Sibel Bozdoğan and Reşat Kasaba. Seattle: University of Washington Press.

Gencer, Mustafa. 2003. *Jöntürk Modernizmi ve "Alman Ruhu": 1908–1918 Dönemi Türk-Alman İlişkileri ve Eğitim.* Istanbul: İletişim.

Genel Kurmay Başkanlığı. 1983. *Atatürkçülük I-III*. Ankara: Genel Kurmay Başkanlığı.

George, Alexander L. and Andrew Bennett. 2005. *Case Studies and Theory Development in the Social Sciences*. Cambridge, MA: MIT Press.

Gill, Anthony. 1998. *Rendering unto Caesar: The Catholic Church and State in Latin America*. Chicago: University of Chicago Press.

1999. "Government Regulation, Social Anomie, and Protestant Growth in Latin America: A Cross-National Analysis." *Rationality and Society* 11 (3): 287–316.

2005. "The Political Origins of Religious Liberty: A Theoretical Outline." *Interdisciplinary Journal of Research on Religion* 1 (1): 1–33.

2007. *The Political Origins of Religious Liberty*. New York: Cambridge University Press.

Gill, Anthony and Arang Keshavarzian. 1999. "State Building and Religious Resources: An Institutional Theory of Church-State Relations in Iran and Mexico." *Politics and Society* 27 (3): 430–64.

Giry, Stéphanie. 2006. "France and Its Muslims." *Foreign Affairs* 85 (5): 87–104.

Glenn, Charles. 2002. "Public Education Changes Partners." In *Religion Returns to the Public Square: Faith and Policy in America*, edited by Hugh Heclo and Wilfred M. McClay. Baltimore, MD: The Johns Hopkins University Press.

Goertz, Gary. 2006. *Social Science Concepts: A User's Guide*. Princeton, NJ: Princeton University Press.

Göle, Nilüfer. 1995. "Laïcité, modernisme et islamisme en Turquie." *Cahiers d'études sur la Méditerranée orientale et le monde turco-iranien* (19): 85–96.

1996. *The Forbidden Modern: Civilization and Veiling*. Ann Arbor: University of Michigan Press.

1997. "Secularism and Islamism in Turkey: The Making of Elites and Counter-Elites." *Middle East Journal* 51 (1): 46–58.

2000. *İslam ve Modernlik Üzerine Melez Desenler*. Istanbul: Metis.

2002. "Islam in Public: New Visibilities and New Imaginaries." *Public Culture* 14 (1): 173–90.

2004. "Islam as Ideology." In *Modest Claims: Dialogues and Essays on Tolerance and Tradition*, edited by Adam B. Seligman. Notre Dame, IN: University of Notre Dame Press.

2005. *Interpénétrations: L'Islam et l'Europe*. Paris: Galaade Editions.

Gould, Andrew C. 1999. *Origins of Liberal Dominance: State, Church, and Party in Nineteenth-Century Europe*. Ann Arbor: University of Michigan Press.

Gramsci, Antonio. 1991. *Prison Notebooks, Vol. 1*, edited by Joseph A. Buttigieg. New York: Columbia University Press.

Green, Donald and Ian Shapiro. 1996. *Pathologies of Rational Choice Theory: A Critique of Applications in Political Science*. New Haven, CT: Yale University Press.

Green, John and Mark Silk. 2003. "The New Religion Gap." *Religion in the News* 6 (3): 1–15.

Greenawalt, Kent. 2004. *Does God Belong in Public Schools?* Princeton, NJ: Princeton University Press.

Grunberg, Slawomir and Ben Crane. 1999. *School Prayer: A Community at War*. Spencer, NY: Log In Productions.

Gülalp, Haldun. 2001. "Globalization and Political Islam: The Social Base of Turkey's Welfare Party." *International Journal of Middle East Studies* 33 (3): 433–48.

Gülen, Fethullah. 2001. "A Comparative Approach to Islam and Democracy." *SAIS Review* 21: 133–8.

Gürbüz, Mustafa. 2007. "Performing Moral Opposition: Musings on the Strategy and Identity in the Gülen Movement." In *Muslim World in Transition: Contributions of the Gülen Movement* (Conference Proceedings). London: Leeds Metropolitan University Press.

Guerlac, Othon. 1908. "The Separation of Church and State in France." *Political Science Quarterly* 23 (2): 259–96.

Gunn, T. Jeremy. 2004. "Religious Freedom and Laïcité: A Comparison of the United States and France." *Brigham Young University Law Review* 24 (2): 419–506.

2005a. "French Secularism as Utopia and Myth." *Houston Law Review* 42 (1): 81–102.

2005b. "Fearful Symbols: The Islamic Headscarf and the European Court of Human Rights." Acessed on the Web site of the Strasbourg Conference: A Forum on Freedom of Religion or Belief at http://www .strasbourgconference.org/papers/Sahin%20by%20Gunn%2021%20 by%20T.%20Jeremy%20Gunn.pdf, accessed March 1, 2006.

Gusfield, Joseph R. 1986. *Symbolic Crusade: Status Politics and the American Temperance Movement*. Urbana: University of Illinois Press.

Haarscher, Guy. 2004. *La laïcité*. Paris: PUF, Que sais-je?

Habermas, Jürgen. 1998. *The Inclusion of the Other: Studies in Political Theory*. Cambridge, MA: MIT Press.

1999. *The Structural Transformation of the Public Sphere: An Inquiry into a Category of Bourgeois Society*. Translated by Thomas Berger. Cambridge, MA: MIT Press.

2004. "Religious Tolerance – The Pacemaker for Cultural Rights." *Philosophy* (79): 5–18.

2006. "Religion in the Public Sphere." *European Journal of Philosophy* 14 (1): 1–25.

Hall, Mark David. 2006. "Jeffersonian Walls and Madisonian Lines: The Supreme Court's Use of History in Religion Clause Cases." *Oregon Law Review* 85 (2): 563–614.

Hall, Peter A. 2005. "Preference Formation as a Political Process: The Case of Monetary Union in Europe." In *Preferences and Situations: Points of Intersection between Historical and Rational Choice Institutionalism*, edited by Ira Katznelson and Barry R. Weingast. New York: Russell Sage Foundation.

Hamburger, Philip. 2004. *Separation of Church and State.* Cambridge, MA: Harvard University Press.

Hamilton, Carolyn. 1995. *Family, Law and Religion.* London: Sweet and Maxwell.

Hammond, Phillip E. 1987. "The Courts and Secular Humanism." In *Church-State Relations: Tensions and Transitions*, edited by Thomas Robbins and Ronald Robertson. New Brunswick, NJ: Transaction Books.

Handy, Robert T. 1991. *Undermined Establishment: Church-State Relations in America 1880–1920.* Princeton, NJ: Princeton University Press.

Hanioğlu, M. Şükrü. 1985. *Bir Siyasal Örgüt Olarak Osmanlı İttihad ve Terakki Cemiyeti ve Jön Türklük (1889–1902).* Istanbul: İletişim.

1990. "Jön Türkler ve Fransız Düşünce Akımları." In *De la Révolution Française a la Turquie D'Atatürk*, edited by Jean-Louis Bacqué-Grammont and Edhem Eldem. Paris: Editions ISIS.

1997. "Garbcılar: Their Attitudes toward Religion and Their Impact on the Official Ideology of the Turkish Republic." *Studia Islamica* 86 (2): 133–58.

2000. *Preparation for a Revolution: The Young Turks, 1902–1908.* New York: Oxford University Press.

2005. "Blueprints for a Future Society: Late Ottoman Materialists on Science, Religion, and Art." In *Late Ottoman Society: The Intellectual Legacy*, edited by Elisabeth Özdalga. New York: Routledge Curzon.

2006. *Osmanlı'dan Cumhuriyet'e Zihniyet, Siyaset ve Tarih.* Ankara: Bağlam.

2008. *A Brief History of the Late Ottoman Empire.* Princeton, NJ: Princeton University Press.

Hanson, Stephen E. 1997. *Time and Revolution: Marxism and the Design of Soviet Institutions.* Chapel Hill: University of North Carolina Press.

2003. "Review Article: From Culture to Ideology in Comparative Politics." *Comparative Politics* 35 (3): 355–76.

Hartz, Louis. 1991 [1955]. *The Liberal Tradition in America.* San Diego: Harcourt Brace and Company.

Haut conseil à l'intégration. 2001. *L'Islam dans la République.* Paris: La documentation Française.

Healey, Robert M. 1968. "Protestantism and Contemporary French Education Laws." *Journal of Church and State* 10 (1): 29–36.

Heclo, Hugh. 2007. "Is America a Christian Nation?" *Political Science Quarterly* 122 (1): 59–87.

Hefner, Robert W., ed. 2005. *Remaking Muslim Politics: Pluralism, Contestation, Democratization.* Princeton, NJ: Princeton University Press.

Henkel, Reinhard. 2006. "State-Church Relationship in Germany: Past and Present." *GeoJournal* 67 (4): 307–16.

Heper, Metin. 2000. "The Ottoman Legacy and Turkish Politics." *Journal of International Affairs* 54 (1): 63–82.

Heper, Metin and Şule Toktaş. 2003. "Islam, Modernity, and Democracy in Contemporary Turkey: The Case of Recep Tayyip Erdoğan." *Muslim World* 93 (2): 157–85.

Hertzke, Allen D. 1988. *Representing God in Washington: The Role of Religious Lobbies in the American Polity*. Knoxville: University of Tennessee Press.

Himmelfarb, Gertrude. 2003. *The Roads to Modernity: The British, French, and American Enlightenments*. New York: Vintage Books.

Hirschman, Albert O. 1972. *Exit, Voice and Loyalty: Responses to Declines in Firms, Organizations and States*. Cambridge, MA: Harvard University Press.

Hunter, James Davison. 1991. *Culture Wars: The Struggle to Define America*. New York: Basic Books.

Huntington, Samuel P. 1993. "The Clash of Civilizations?" *Foreign Affairs* 72 (3): 22–49.

1996. *The Clash of Civilizations and the Remaking of World Order*. New York: Simon and Schuster.

2005. *Who Are We? The Challenges to America's National Identity*. New York: Simon and Schuster.

Hurd, Elisabeth Shakman. 2007. *The Politics of Secularism in International Relations*. Princeton, NJ: Princeton University Press.

Hutson, James H. 1998. *Religion and the Founding of the American Republic*. Washington, DC: Library of Congress.

2008. *Church and State in America: The First Two Centuries*. New York: Cambridge University Press.

Iannaccone, Laurence R. 1996. "Rational Choice: Framework for the Social Scientific Study of Religion." In *Rational Choice Theory and Religion: Summary and Assessment*, edited by Lawrence A. Young. New York: Routledge.

İnalcık, Halil. 1964. "The Nature of Traditional Society: Turkey." In *Political Modernization in Japan and Turkey*, edited by Robert E. Ward and Dankwart A. Rustow. Princeton, NJ: Princeton University Press.

1998. "Turkey between Europe and the Middle East." *Perceptions* 3 (1): 5–18.

Inkeles, Alex and David Horton Smith. 1976. *Becoming Modern: Individual Change in Six Developing Countries*. Cambridge, MA: Harvard University Press.

Jacobsohn, Gary Jeffrey. 2003. *The Wheel of Law: India's Secularism in Comparative Constitutional Context*. Princeton, NJ: Princeton University Press.

Jacoby, Susan. 2004. *Freethinkers: A History of American Secularism*. New York: Metropolitan Books.

Jeanneney, Jean-Noël. 2004. "Les présidents peuvent-ils aller à la messe?" *L'Histoire* (289): 72–3.

Jeffries, John C., Jr. and James E. Ryan. 2001. "A Political History of the Establishment Clause." *Michigan Law Review* 100 (2): 279–370.

Jelen, Ted G. 1998. "In Defense of Religious Minimalism." In *A Wall of Separation? Debating the Public Role of Religion*, edited by Mary C. Segers and Ted G. Jelen. Lanham, MD: Rowman and Littlefield.

2000. *To Serve God and Mammon: Church-State Relations in American Politics*. Boulder, CO: Westview.

Jelen, Ted G. and Clyde Wilcox. 1995. *Public Attitudes toward Church and State*. Armonk, NY: M. E. Sharpe.

Jenkins, Gareth. 2004. "Non-Muslim Minorities in Turkey: Progress and Challenges on the Road to EU Accession." *Turkish Policy Quarterly* 3 (1): 53–61.

Kadıoğlu, Ayşe. 1998. "Republican Epistemology and Islamic Discourses in Turkey in the 1990s." *Muslim World* 88 (1): 1–21.

Kahn, Pierre. 2005. *La Laïcité*. Paris: Le Cavalier Bleu.

Kaltenbach, Jeanne-Helene and Michele Tribalat. 2002. *La République et l'islam: Entre crainte et aveuglement*. n.p.: Gallimard.

Kalyoncu, Mehmet. 2008. *A Civilian Response to Ethno-religious Conflict: The Gulen Movement in Southeast Turkey*. Somerset, NJ: Light.

Kalyvas, Stathis N. 1996. *The Rise of Christian Democracy in Europe*. Ithaca, NY: Cornell University Press.

Kandiyoti, Deniz. 1991. "End of Empire: Islam, Nationalism and Women in Turkey." In *Women, Islam and the State*, edited by Deniz Kandiyoti. London: Macmillan.

Kansu, Aykut. 1997. *The Revolution of 1908 in Turkey*. New York: Brill.

Kaplan, İsmail. 1999. *Türkiye'de Milli Eğitim İdeolojisi*. Istanbul: İletişim.

Kaplan, Sam. 2006. *The Pedagogical State: Education and the Politics of National Culture in Post-1980 Turkey*. Stanford, CA: Stanford University Press.

Kara, İsmail. 2003. "Türkiye'de Laiklik Uygulamaları Açısından Diyanet İşleri Başkanlığı." In *Devlet ve Din İlişkileri-Farklı Modeller, Konseptler ve Tecrübeler*. Ankara: Konrad Adenauer Vakfı.

Karabelias, Gerassimos. 1999. "The Evolution of Civil-Military Relations in Post-war Turkey, 1980–95." *Middle Eastern Studies* 35 (4): 130–51.

Karpat, Kemal. 1973. *An Inquiry into the Social Foundations of Nationalism in the Ottoman Empire: From Social Estates to Classes, from Millets to Nations*. Princeton, NJ: Princeton University.

1988. "The Ottoman Ethnic and Confessional Legacy in the Middle East." In *Ethnicity, Pluralism, and the State in the Middle East*, edited by Milton J. Esman and Itamar Rabinovich. Ithaca, NY: Cornell University Press.

2001. *The Politization of Islam: Reconcstructing Identity, State, Faith, and Community in the Late Ottoman State*. New York: Oxford University Press.

Kasaba, Reşat. 1993. "Populism and Democracy in Turkey: 1946–1961." In *Rules and Rights in the Middle East: Democracy, Law, and Society*, edited by Reşat Kasaba, Ellis Goldberg, and Joel S. Migdal. Seattle: University of Washington Press.

1997. "Kemalist Certainties and Modern Ambiguities." In *Rethinking Modernity and National Identity in Turkey*, edited by Sibel Bozdoğan and Reşat Kasaba. Seattle: University of Washington Press.

Katznelson, Ira and Barry W. Weingast, eds. 2005. *Preferences and Situations: Points of Intersection between Historical and Rational Choice Institutionalism*. New York: Russell Sage Foundation.

Kavakçı, Merve. 2004. "Headscarf Heresy." *Foreign Policy* (142): 66–7.

Kayalı, Hasan. 1997. *Arabs and Young Turks: Ottomanism, Arabism, and Islamism in the Ottoman Empire, 1908–1918*. Berkeley: University of California Press.

Keaton, Trica Danielle. 2006. *Muslim Girls and the Other France: Race, Identity Politics, and Social Exclusion*. Bloomington: Indiana University Press.

Keddie, Nikki R. 1997. "Secularism and the State: Towards Clarity and Global Comparison." *New Left Review* (226): 21–40.

Kelley, Dean M. 1963. "Beyond Separation of Church and State." *Journal of Church and State* 5 (2): 181–98.

Kemeny, P.C. 2003. "Power, Ridicule, and Destruction of Religious Moral Reform Politics in the 1920s." In *The Secular Revolution: Power, Interests, and Conflict in the Secularization of American Public Life*, edited by Christian Smith. Berkeley: University of California Press.

Kengor, Paul. 2004. *God and Ronald Reagan*. New York: Regan Books.

Kepel, Gilles. 1994. *A l'Ouest d'Allah*. Paris: Editions du Seuil.

Kernell, Samuel and Gary C. Jacobson. 1999. *The Logic of American Politics*. Washington, DC: CQ Press.

Keyder, Çağlar. 2004. "The Turkish Bell Jar." *New Left Review* (28): 65–84.

Khosrokhavar, Farhad. 1997. *L'islam des jeunes*. n.p.: Flammarion.

2004. "La Laïcité française à l'épreuve de l'islam." In *La Laïcité à l'épreuve: Religions et libertés dans le monde*, edited by Jean Baubérot. n.p.: Universalis.

Killian, Caitlin. 2003. "The Other Side of the Veil: North African Women in France Respond to the Headscarf Affair." *Gender and Society* 17 (4): 567–90.

Kindopp, Jason and Carol Lee Hamrin, eds. 2004. *God and Caesar in China: Policy Implications of Church-State Tensions*. Washington, DC: Brookings Institution Press.

King, Gary, Robert O. Keohane, and Sidney Verba. 1994. *Designing Social Inquiry: Scientific Inference in Qualitative Research*. Princeton, NJ: Princeton University Press.

Klausen, Jytte. 2005. *The Islamic Challenge: Politics and Religion in Western Europe*. New York: Oxford University Press.

Knippenberg, Hans. 2006. "The Changing Relationship between State and Church/Religion in the Netherlands." *GeoJournal* 67 (4): 317–30.

Kobylka, Joseph F. 1995. "The Mysterious Case of Establishment Clause Litigation: How Organized Litigants Foiled Legal Change." In *Contemplating Courts*, edited by Lee Epstein. Washington, DC: CQ Press.

Kogacioglu, Dicle. 2004. "Progress, Unity, and Democracy: Dissolving Political Parties in Turkey." *Law and Society Review* 38 (3): 433–61.

Kohut, Andrew et al. 2000. *The Diminishing Divide: Religions' Changing Role in American Politics.* Washington, DC: Brookings Institution Press.

Kokosalakis, Nikos. 1987. "Religion and Modernization in 19th Century Greece." *Social Compass* 34 (2–3): 223–41.

Kösebalaban, Hasan. 2003. "The Making of Enemy and Friend: Fethullah Gülen's National Security Identity." In *Turkish Islam and the Secular State: The Gülen Movement*, edited by M. Hakan Yavuz and John L. Esposito. Syracuse, NY: Syracuse University Press.

——— 2005. "The Impact of Globalization on Islamic Political Identity." *World Affairs* 168 (1): 27–37.

Kosmin, Barry A., Egon Mayer, and Ariela Keysar. 2001. "American Religious Identification Survey 2001." http://www.gc.cuny.edu/faculty/research_studies/aris.pdf, accessed on June 13, 2008.

Kramer, Lloyd S. 1994. "The French Revolution and the Creation of American Political Culture." In *The Global Ramifications of the French Revolution*, edited by Joseph Klaits and Michael H. Haltzel. New York: Cambridge University Press.

Kramnick, Isaac and R. Laurence Moore. 2005. *The Godless Constitution: A Moral Defense of the Secular State.* New York: W. W. Norton.

Krindatch, Alexey D. 2006. "Changing Relationships between Religion, the State, and Society in Russia." *GeoJournal* 67 (4): 267–82.

Küçükcan, Talip. 2003. "State, Islam, and Religious Liberty in Modern Turkey: Reconfiguration of Religion in the Public Sphere." *BYU Law Review* (2): 475–506.

Küçükömer, İdris. 2002. *"Batılılaşma": Düzenin Yabancılaşması.* Ankara: Bağlam.

Kuo, David. 2006. *Tempting Faith: An Inside Story of Political Seduction.* New York: Free Press.

Kuru, Ahmet T. 2003. "Fethullah Gülen's Search for a Middle Way between Modernity and Muslim Tradition." In *Turkish Islam and the Secular State: The Gülen Movement*, edited by M. Hakan Yavuz and John L. Esposito. Syracuse, NY: Syracuse University Press.

——— 2005a. "Globalization and Diversification of Islamic Movements: Three Turkish Cases." *Political Science Quarterly* 120 (2): 253–74.

——— 2005b. "Review of *Sacred and Secular: Religion and Politics Worldwide*." *Comparative Political Studies* 38 (10): 1300–4.

——— 2007. "Passive and Assertive Secularism: Historical Conditions, Ideological Struggles, and State Policies towards Religion." *World Politics* 59 (4): 568–94.

——— 2008. "Secularism, State Policies, and Muslims in Europe: Analyzing French Exceptionalism." *Comparative Politics* 41 (1): 1–19.

Kuru, Zeynep Akbulut and Ahmet T. Kuru. 2008. "Apolitical Interpretation of Islam: Said Nursi's Faith-Based Activism in Comparison with Political Islamism and Sufism." *Islam and Christian-Muslim Relations* 19 (1): 99–111.

Kuyucu, Ali Tuna. 2005. "Ethno-Religious 'Unmixing' of Turkey: 6–7 September Riots as a Case in Turkish Nationalism." *Nations and Nationalism* 11 (3): 361–80.

Lacorne, Denis. 2003. "La séparation de l'Eglise et de l'Etat aux États-Unis. Les paradoxes d'une laïcité philo-cléricale." *Le Débat* (127): 63–79.

2007. *De la Religion en Amérique: Essai d'histoire politique.* n.p.: Gallimard.

Lalouette, Jaqueline. 2004. "Portrait d'un anticlérical." *L'Histoire* (289): 64–7.

Laot, Laurent. 1998. *La laïcité, un défi mondial.* Paris: Les éditions de l'atelier.

Lapidus, Ira M. 1975. "The Separation of State and Religion in the Development of Early Islamic Society." *International Journal of Middle East Studies* 6 (4): 363–85.

Larkin, Maurice. 1973. *Church and State after the Dreyfus Affair: The Separation Issue in France.* New York: Barnes and Noble.

2002. *Religion, Politics and Preferment in France since 1890.* New York: Cambridge University Press.

Larson, Edward J. 2006. *Summer for the Gods: The Scopes Trial and America's Continuing Debate over Science and Religion.* New York: Basic Books.

Laurence, Jonathan. 2005. "From the Elysée Salon to the Table of the Republic: State-Islam Relations and the Integration of Muslims in France." *French Politics, Culture and Society* 23 (1): 36–63.

Laurence, Jonathan and Justin Vaisse. 2006. *Integrating Islam: Political and Religious Challenges in Contemporary France.* Washington, DC: Brookings Institution Press.

Laurens, Henry. 2004. "La projection chrétienne de l'Europe industrielle sur les provinces arabes de l'Empire ottoman." Paper presented at the conference "Colonisation, laïcité et sécularisation," Paris, November 22–25.

Layman, Geoffrey. 2001. *The Great Divide: Religious and Cultural Conflict in American Politics.* New York: Columbia University Press.

Le Tourneau, Dominique. 2000. *L'Eglise et l'Etat en France.* Paris: PUF.

Leege, David C. and Lyman A. Kellstedt, eds. 1993. *Rediscovering the Religious Factor in American Politics.* Armonk, NY: M. E. Sharpe.

Lewis, Bernard. 1968. *The Emergence of Modern Turkey.* London: Oxford University Press.

1990. "The Roots of Muslim Rage." *The Atlantic Monthly* (266): 47–60.

1991a. *The Political Language of Islam.* Chicago: University of Chicago Press.

1991b. *Secularism in the Middle East.* Rehovot, Israel: Chaim Weizmann Lecture.

1996. "Islam and Liberal Democracy: A Historical Overview." *Journal of Democracy* 7 (2): 52–63.

2003. *What Went Wrong? The Clash between Islam and Modernity in the Middle East.* New York: Perennial.

Libération, Les Dossiers de. 2004. *La laïcité dévoilée: Quinze années de débat en quarante rebonds.* n.p.: *Libération* and éditions de l'Aube.

Lieberson, Stanley. 1992. "Small N's and Big Conclusions." In *What Is a Case?*, edited by Charles Ragin and Howard Becker. Cambridge: Cambridge University Press.

Liederman, Lina Molokotos. 2000. "Religious Diversity in Schools: the Muslim Headscarf Controversy and Beyond." *Social Compass* 47 (3): 367–81.

——— 2003. "Identity Crisis: Greece, Orthodoxy, and the European Union." *Journal of Contemporary Religion* 18 (3): 291–315.

Lindner, Eileen W., ed. 2007. *Yearbook of American and Canadian Churches 2007*. Nashville, TN: Abingdon Press.

Lindsay, Thomas. 1991. "James Madison on Religion and Politics: Rhetoric and Reality." *American Political Science Review* 85 (4): 1321–37.

Lipset, Seymour M. and Stein Rokkan. 1967. "Cleavage Structures, Party Systems, and Voter Alignments: An Introduction." In *Party Systems and Voter Alignments: Cross-National Perspectives*, edited by Seymour M. Lipset and Stein Rokkan. New York: The Free Press.

Luizard, Pierre-Jean, ed. 2006. *Le choc colonial et l'islam: Les politiques religieuses des puissances coloniales en terres d'islam*. Paris: La Découverte.

Lyon, David and Marguerite Van Die, eds. 2000. *Rethinking Church, State, and Modernity: Canada between Europe and America*. Toronto: University of Toronto Press.

Macedo, Stephen. 2000. *Diversity and Distrust: Civic Education in a Multicultural Democracy*. Cambridge, MA: Harvard University Press.

Macneill, Dominique. 2000. "Religious Education and National Identity." *Social Compass* 47 (3): 343–51.

Madeley, John T.S. 2003a. "European Liberal Democracy and the Principle of State Religious Neutrality." *West European Politics* 26 (1): 1–20.

——— 2003b. "A Framework for the Comparative Analysis of Church-State Relations in Europe." *West European Politics* 26 (1): 23–50.

Mahoney, James. 2000a. "Path Dependence in Historical Sociology." *Theory and Society* 29 (4): 507–48.

——— 2000b. "Strategies of Causal Inference in Small-N Analysis." *Sociological Method and Research* 28 (4): 387–424.

——— 2001. *The Legacies of Liberalism: Path Dependence and Political Regimes in Central America*. Baltimore, MD: The Johns Hopkins University Press.

Mahoney, James and Dietrich Rueschemeyer. 2003. *Comparative Historical Analysis in the Social Sciences*. New York: Cambridge University Press.

Maigre, Marie-Elisabeth. 2005. "L'émergence d'une 'éthique musulmane' dans le monde des affaires turc: Réflexions autour de l'évolution du MÜSIAD et des communautés religieuses." *Religioscope: Etudes et analyses* (7): 1–25.

Mansfield, Stephen. 2004. *The Faith of George W. Bush*. New York: Tarcher Penguin.

Manuel, Paul Christopher. 2002. "Religion and Politics in Iberia: Clericalism, Anticlericalism, and Democratization in Portugal and Spain." In *Religion and Politics in Comparative Perspective: The One, the Few, and the Many*, edited by Ted Gerard Jelen and Clyde Wilcox. New York: Cambridge University Press.

Mapp, Alf J., Jr. 2003. *The Faiths of Our Fathers: What America's Founders Really Believed*. Lanham, MD: Rowman and Littlefield.

March, Andrew F. 2007. "Islamic Foundations for a Social Contract in non-Muslim Liberal Democracies." *American Political Science Review* 101 (2): 235–52.

Mardin, Şerif. 1961. "Some Explanatory Notes on the Origins of the Mecelle (Medjelle)." *Muslim World* 51 (3–4): 189–96, 274–9.

1973. "Center Periphery Relations: A Key to Turkish Politics?" *Daedalus* 102: 169–90.

1982. "Turkey: Islam and Westernization." In *Religions and Societies: Asia and the Middle East*, edited by Carlo Caldarola. Berlin: Mouton.

1989. *Religion and Social Change in Modern Turkey: The Case of Bediüzzaman Said Nursi*. New York: State University of New York Press.

1991. "The Just and the Unjust." *Daedalus* 120 (3): 113–29.

1994. "Islam in Mass Society: Harmony versus Polarization." In *The Politics in the Third Turkish Republic*, edited by Metin Heper and Ahmet Evin. Boulder, CO: Westview.

1995. "Laïcité en Turquie et en France: Propositions pour une meilleure compréhension." *Cahiers d'études sur la Méditerranée orientale et le monde turco-iranien* (19): 5–34.

1997a. "Projects as Methodology: Some Thoughts on Modern Turkish Social Science." In *Rethinking Modernity and National Identity in Turkey*, edited by Sibel Bozdoğan and Reşat Kasaba. Seattle: University of Washington Press.

1997b. "Religion and Secularism in Turkey." In *Atatürk: Founder of a Modern State*, edited by Ergun Özbudun and Ali Kazacıgil. London: Hurst and Company.

1997c. "The Ottoman Empire." In *After Empire: Multiethnic Societies and Nation-Building*, edited by Karen Barkey and Mark von Hagen. Boulder, CO: Westview.

1997d. *Türkiyede Toplum ve Siyaset*. Istanbul: İletişim.

2000 [1962]. *The Genesis of Young Ottoman Thought: A Study in the Modernization of Turkish Political Ideas*. Syracuse, NY: Syracuse University Press.

Marr, Timothy. 2006. *The Cultural Roots of American Islamicism*. New York: Cambridge University Press.

Marshall, Paul, ed. 2000. *Religious Freedom in the World: A Global Report on Freedom and Persecution*. Nashville, TN: Broadman and Holman.

Martin, Jean-Paul. 2005. "La Ligue de l'enseignement, le combisme et la loi de 1905." In *Les Entretiens d'Auxerre: De la séparation des Églises et de l'État à l'avenir de la laïcité*, edited by Jean Baubérot and Michel Wieviorka. n.p.: L'aube.

Martin, William. 2002. "With God on Their Side: Religion and U.S. Foreign Policy." In *Religion Returns to the Public Square: Faith and Policy in*

America, edited by Hugh Heclo and Wilfred M. McClay. Baltimore, MD: The Johns Hopkins University Press.

Marx, Karl. 1994. *Selected Writings*, edited by Lawrence H. Simon. Indianapolis, IN: Hackett Publishing.

Massicard, Elise. 2005. *L'autre Turquie: Le mouvement aléviste et ses territoires*. Paris: PUF.

Massignon, Bérengère. 2000. "Laïcité et gestion de la diversité religieuse à l'école publique en France." *Social Compass* 47 (3): 353–66.

Mathieu, Séverine. 2005. "Conclusion: Synthèse des contributions." In *Des maîtres et des dieux: écoles et religions en Europe*, edited by Jean-Paul Willaime and Séverine Mathieu. n.p.: Belin.

Mathy, Jean-Philippe. 2000. *French Resistance: The French-American Culture Wars*. Minneapolis: University of Minnesota Press.

Mavrogordatos, George Th. 2003. "Orthodoxy and Nationalism in the Greek Case." *West European Politics* 26 (1): 117–36.

Mayeur, Françoise. 2004. *Histoire de l'enseignement et de l'éducation III: 1789–1930*. Paris: Tempus.

McCarthy, Justin. 2004. *Death and Exile: The Ethnic Cleansing of Ottoman Muslims, 1821–1922*. Princeton, NJ: The Darwin Press.

McClay, Wilfred M. 2002. "Two Concepts of Secularism." In *Religion Returns to the Public Square: Faith and Policy in America*, edited by Hugh Heclo and Wilfred M. McClay. Baltimore, MD: The Johns Hopkins University Press.

McConnell, Michael W. 1990. "The Origins and Historical Understanding of Free Exercise of Religion." *Harvard Law Review* 103 (7): 1409–517.

1992. "Accommodation of Religion: An Update and a Response to the Critics." *George Washington Law Review* 60 (3): 685–742.

1998. "Equal Treatment and Religious Discrimination." In *Equal Treatment of Religion in a Pluralistic Society*, edited by Stephen V. Monsma and J. Christopher Soper. Grand Rapids, MI: Eerdmans.

1999. "Governments, Families, and Power: A Defense of Educational Choice." *Connecticut Law Review* 31 (3): 847–59.

McGarvie, Mark Douglas. 2004. *One Nation under Law: America's Early National Struggles to Separate Church and State*. DeKalb: Northern Illinois University Press.

McGoldrick, Dominic. 2006. *Human Rights and Religion: The Islamic Headscarf Debate in Europe*. Portland, OR: Hart Publishing.

McGraw, Barbara A. 2003. *Rediscovering America's Sacred Ground: Public Religion and Pursuit of the Good in a Pluralistic America*. Albany: State University of New York Press.

Meacham, Jon. 2007. *American Gospel: God, the Founding Fathers, and the Making of a Nation*. New York: Random House.

Mecham, R. Quinn. 2004. "From the Ashes of Virtues, a Promise of Light: The Transformation of Political Islam in Turkey." *Third World Quarterly* 25 (2): 339–58.

Mehmedoğlu, Yurdagül. 2001. *Tanzimat Sonrasında Okullarda Din Eğitimi (1838–1920)*. Istanbul: M. Ü. İlahiyat Fakültesi Vakfı.

Merle, Gabriel. 2005. "Emile Combes et la loi de séparation." In *Les Entretiens d'Auxerre: De la séparation des Églises et de l'État à l'avenir de la laïcité*, edited by Jean Baubérot and Michel Wieviorka. n.p.: L'aube.

Merrick, Jeffrey. 1990. *The Desacralization of the French Monarchy in the Eighteenth Century*. Baton Rouge: Louisiana State University.

Messick, Brinkley. 1988. "Kissing Hands and Knees: Hegemony and Hierarchy in Shari'a Discourse." *Law and Society Review* 22 (4): 637–59.

Messner, Francis, Pierre-Henri Prélot, and Jean-Marie Woehrling., eds. 2003. *Traité de droit français des religions*. Paris: Litec.

Michaelien, Robert S. 1987. "Civil Rights, Indian Rites." In *Church-State Relations: Tensions and Transitions*, edited by Thomas Robbins and Ronald Robertson. New Brunswick, NJ: Transaction Books.

Migdal, Joel S. 2001. *State in Society: Studying How State and Societies Transform and Constitute One Another*. Cambridge: Cambridge University Press.

Migdal, Joel S., Atul Kohli, and Vivienne Shue. 1994. *State Power and Social Forces: Domination and Transformation in the Third World*. Cambridge: Cambridge University Press.

Mill, John Stuart. 1961. *A System of Logic*. New York: Longmans.

Miller, Robert T. and Ronald B. Flowers. 1996. *Toward Benevolent Neutrality: Church, State, and the Supreme Court. Vol I*. Waco, TX: Baylor University Press.

Modood, Tariq and Riva Kastoryano. 2006. "Secularism and the Accommodation of Muslims in Europe." In *Multiculturalism, Muslims and Citizenship: A European Approach*, edited by Tariq Modood, Anna Triandafyllidou, and Ricard Zapata-Barrero. New York: Routledge.

Monsma, Stephen V. 1995. *Positive Neutrality: Letting Religious Freedom Ring*. Grand Rapids, MI: Baker Books.

1996. *When Sacred and Secular Mix: Religious Nonprofit Organizations and Public Money*. Lanham, MD: Rowman and Littlefield.

Monsma, Stephen V., ed. 2002a. *Church-State Relations in Crisis*. Lanham, MD: Rowman and Littlefield.

2002b. "Working Faith: How Religious Organizations Provide Welfare-to-Work Services," http://publicpolicy.pepperdine.edu/davenportinstitute/reports/workingfaith/working1.html, accessed on July 1, 2006.

Monsma, Stephen V. and J. Christopher Soper. 1997. *The Challenge of Pluralism: Church and State in Five Democracies*. Lanham, MD: Rowman and Littlefield.

Moruzzi, Norma Claire. 1994. "A Problem with Headscarves: Contemporary Complexities of Political and Social Identity." *Political Theory* 22 (4): 653–72.

Mouritsen, Per. 2006. "The Particular Universalism of a Nordic Civic Nation: Common Values, State Religion and Islam in Danish Politial Culture." In *Multiculturalism, Muslims and Citizenship: A European Approach*, edited by Tariq Modood, Anna Triandafyllidou, and Ricard Zapata-Barrero. New York: Routledge.

Muhammad, Zakiyyah. 2003. "Islamic Schools in the United States: Perspectives of Identity, Relevance and Governance." In *Muslims in the United States*, edited by Philippa Strum and Danielle Tarantolo. Washington, DC: Woodrow Wilson International Center for Scholars.

Munoz, Vincent Phillip. 2003a. "James Madison's Principle of Religious Liberty." *American Political Science Review* 97 (1): 17–32.

　2003b. "George Washington on Religious Liberty." *The Review of Politics* 65 (1): 11–33.

　2006. "The Original Meaning of the Establishment Clause and the Impossibility of Its Incorporation." *University of Pennsylvania Journal of Constitutional Law* 8 (4): 585–639.

Murrin, John M. 2007. "Religion and Politics in America from the First Settlements to the Civil War." In *Religion and American Politics: From the Colonial Period to the Present*, edited by Mark A. Noll and Luke E. Harlow. New York: Oxford University Press.

Mutlu, Kayhan. 1996. "Examining Religious Beliefs among University Students in Ankara." *British Journal of Sociology* 47 (2): 353–9.

National Center of Education Statistics. 2002. *Private Schools: A Brief Portrait*. Washington, DC: National Center of Eduction Statistics.

Navaro-Yashin, Yael. 2002. *Faces of the State: Secularism and Public Life in Turkey*. Princeton, NJ: Princeton University Press.

Neuhaus, Richard John. 1986. *The Naked Public Square: Religion and Democracy in America*. Grand Rapids, MI: Eerdmans.

Neyzi, Leyla. 2002. "Remembering to Forget: Sabbateanism, National Identity, and Subjectivity in Turkey." *Comparative Study of Society and History* 44 (1): 137–58.

Nicolet, Claude. 1982. *L'ideé républicaine en France (1789–1924)*. Paris: Gallimard.

Nord, Philip. 1995. *The Republican Moment: Struggles for Democracy in Nineteenth-Century France*. Cambridge, MA: Harvard University Press.

Nord, Warren A. 1994. *Religion and American Education: Rethinking a National Dilemma*. Chapel Hill: University of North Carolina Press.

Nordmann, Charlotte, ed. 2004. *Le foulard islamique en questions*. Paris: Editions Amsterdam.

Norris, Pippa and Ronald Inglehart. 2004. *Sacred and Secular: Religion and Politics Worldwide*. Cambridge: Cambridge University Press.

Ocak, Ahmet Yaşar. 1997. "Türkiye'de Kemalizm-İslam (Yahut Şeriat) Kavgası." In *İslam'ın Bugünkü Meseleleri*. Ankara: Türk Yurdu.

　1999. *Türkler, Türkiye ve İslam: Yaklaşım, Yöntem ve Yorum Denemeleri*. Istanbul: İletişim.

Ognier, Pierre. 1994. "La laïcité scolaire dans son histoire (1880–1945)." In *Histoire de la laïcité*, edited by Jean Baubérot et al. n.p.: CRDP.

Öktem, Niyazi. 2002. "Religion in Turkey." *BYU Law Review* (2): 371–404.

Okumuş, Ejder. 1999. *Türkiye'nin Laikleşme Serüveninde Tanzimat*. Istanbul: İnsan.

Olson, Mancur. 1984. *The Rise and Decline of Nations: Economic Growth, Stagflation, and Social Rigidities.* New Haven, CT: Yale University Press.

Onar, S. Sami. 1955. "The Majalla." In *Law in the Middle East, Vol. I: Origin and Development of Islamic Law,* edited by Majid Khadduri and Herbert J. Liebesny. Washigton, DC: The Middle East Institute.

Öniş, Ziya. 2001. "Political Islam at the Crossroads: From Hegemony to Co-existence." *Contemporary Politics* 7 (4): 281–98.

Opp, Karl-Dieter. 1999. "Contending Conceptions of the Theory of Rational Action." *Journal of Theoretical Politics* 11 (2): 171–202.

Oran, Baskın. 2007. "The Minority Concept and Rights in Turkey: The Lausanne Peace Treaty and Current Issues." In *Human Rights in Turkey,* edited by Zehra F. Kabasakal. Philadelphia: University of Pennsylvania Press.

Ortaylı, İlber. 1983. *İmparatorluğun En Uzun Yüzyılı.* Istanbul: Hil.

2006. *Osmanlı İmparatorluğu'nda Alman Nüfuzu.* Istanbul: Alkım.

Owen, J. Judd. 2007. "The Struggle between 'Religion and Nonreligion': Jefferson, Backus, and the Dissonance of America's Founding Principles." *American Political Science Review* 101 (3): 493–503.

Özdalga, Elisabeth. 1999. "Education in the Name of 'Order and Progress': Reflections on the Recent Eight Year Obligatory School Reform in Turkey." *Muslim World* 89 (3–4): 414–38.

Özek, Çetin. 1962. *Türkiye'de Laiklik: Gelişim ve Koruyucu Ceza Hükümleri.* Istanbul: İ. Ü. Hukuk Fakültesi.

Özervarlı, M. Sait. 2007. "Alternative Approaches to Modernization in the Late Ottoman Period: İzmirli İsmail Hakkı's Religious Thought against Materialist Scientism." *International Journal of Middle East Studies* 39: 77–102.

Ozouf, Mona. 1982. *L'Ecole, l'Eglise et la République: 1871–1914.* Paris: Editions Cana.

Özyürek, Esra. 2006. *Nostalgia for the Modern: State Secularism and Everyday Politics in Turkey.* Durham, NC: Duke University Press.

Paçacı, Mehmet and Yasin Aktay. 1999. "75 Years of Higher Religous Education in Modern Turkey." *Muslim World* 89 (3–4): 389–413.

Page, Scott E. 2005. "The Types and Causes of Path Dependence." http://www.bramson.net/academ/public/Page-Path%20Dependence.pdf, accessed on September 1, 2005: 1–29.

Pak, Soon-Yong. 2004. "Cultural Politics and Vocational Religious Education: The Case of Turkey." *Comparative Education* 40 (3): 321–41.

Palau, Yves. 2001. "La Ligue de l'enseignement depuis les années 1980: nouvelle réflexion sur la laïcité et position dans l'espace politique." In *La laïcité, une valeur d'aujourd'hui? Contestations et renégociations du modèle français,* edited by Jean Baudouin and Philippe Portier. Rennes, France: Presses Universitaires de Rennes.

Pals, Daniel L. 1996. *Seven Theories of Religion.* New York: Oxford University Press.

Pantham, Thomas. 1999. "Indian Secularism and Its Critics: Some Reflections." In *Border Crossings: Toward a Comparative Political Theory*, edited by Fred Dallmayr. Lexington, KY: Lanham Books.

Papkov, Irina Andre. 2006. "Orthodoxy and Democracy in Russia: New Interpretations." PhD diss., Georgetown University.

Papp, Julien, ed. 1998. *Laïcité et séperation des Eglises et de l'Etat: Tome II – De la loi de 1905 à nos jours*. n.p.: CRDP.

Peiser, Gustave. 1995. "Ecole publique, école privée et laïcité en France." *Cahiers d'études sur la Mediterranée orientale et le monde turco-iranien* (19).

Pena-Ruiz, Henri. 1999. "La Laïcité, ou la différence entre le 'collectif' et le 'public.'" *Hommes and Migrations* (1218): 59–63.

———. 2003. *Qu'est-ce que la laïcité?* n.p.: Folio.

Pfaff, Steven and Anthony J. Gill. 2006. "Will a Million Muslims March? Muslim Interest Organizations and Political Integration in Europe." *Comparative Political Studies* 39 (7): 803–28.

Pierson, Paul. 2000a. "Increasing Returns, Path Dependence, and the Study of Politics." *American Political Science Review* 94 (2): 251–67.

———. 2000b. "Not Just What, But When: Timing and Sequence in Political Processes." *Studies in Comparative Political Development* 14 (1): 72–92.

Pietri, Gaston. 1998. *La laïcité est une idée neuve en Europe: Le cas franco-allemand*. Paris: Salvator.

Portier, Philippe. 2002. "De la séparation a la reconnaissance: l'évolution du régime français de laïcité." In *Les mutations contemporaines du religieux*, edited by Jean-Robert Armogathe and Jean-Paul Willaime. n.p.: Brepols.

———. 2005. "L'Eglise catholique face au modèle français de laïcité: histoire d'un ralliement." *Archives de sciences sociales des religions* (129): 97–113.

Poulat, Emile. 1987. *Liberté, laïcité: La guerre des deux France et le principe de la modernité*. Paris: Cerf.

———. 2000. "La laïcité en France au vingtième siècle." In *Catholicism, Politics and Society in Twentieth-Century France*, edited by Kay Chadwick. Liverpool: Liverpool University Press.

———. 2003. *Notre laïcité publique*. Paris: Berg Internationale Éditeurs.

———. 2004. "L'intégrisme." In *La Laïcité à l'épreuve: Religions et libertés dans le monde*, edited by Jean Baubérot. n.p.: Universalis.

Putnam, Robert D. 1994. *Making Democracy Work: Civic Traditions in Modern Italy*. Princeton, NJ: Princeton University Press.

———. 2001. *Bowling Alone: The Collapse and Revival of American Community*. New York: Simon and Schuster.

Rahman, Fazlur. 1982. *Islam and Modernity: Transformation of an Intellectual Tradition*. Chicago: University of Chicago Press.

Ramadan, Tariq. 2003a. "Les Musulmans et la mondialisation." *Pouvoirs* (104): 97–109.

———. 2003b. "Les évolutions de la pensée musulmane contemporaine." In *L'Avenir de l'islam en France et en Europe*, edited by Michel Wieviorka. Paris: Editions Balland.

2005. *Western Muslims and the Future of Islam.* New York: Oxford University Press.

Ramet, Sabrina P. 1999. *Nihil Obstat: Religion, Politics, and Social Change in East-Central Europe and Russia.* Durham, NC: Duke University Press.

Ravitch, Frank S. 1999. *School Prayer and Discrimination: The Civil Rights of Religious Minorities and Dissenters.* Boston: Northeastern University Press.

Rawls, John. 1971. *A Theory of Justice.* Cambridge, MA: Belknap Press of Harvard University Press.

1996. *Political Liberalism.* New York: Columbia University Press.

Rebérioux, Madeleine. 1975. *La République radicale? 1898–1914.* Paris: Editions du seuil.

Reed, Howard A. 1955. "The Religious Life of Modern Turkish Muslims." In *Islam and the West,* edited by Richard N. Frye. The Hague: Mouton and Co.

Reichley, A. James. 2002. "Faith in Politics." In *Religion Returns to the Public Square: Faith and Policy in America,* edited by Hugh Heclo and Wilfred M. McClay. Baltimore, MD: The Johns Hopkins University Press.

Reid, Charles J., Jr. 2002. "The Religious Conscience and the State in U.S. Constitutional Law, 1789–2001." In *Religion Returns to the Public Square: Faith and Policy in America,* edited by Hugh Heclo and Wilfred M. McClay. Baltimore, MD: The Johns Hopkins University Press.

Remond, Rene. 1995. "La Laïcité et ses contraires." *Pouvoirs* (75): 7–16.

Renaut, Alain and Alain Touraine. 2005. *Un débat sur la laïcité.* Paris: Éditions Stock.

Ricoeur, Paul 1998. *Critique and Conviction: Conversations with François Azouvi and Marc de Launay.* Translated by Kathleen Blamey. New York: Columbia University Press.

Robbins, Thomas. 1987. "Church-State Tension in the United States." In *Church-State Relations: Tensions and Transitions,* edited by Thomas Robbins and Ronald Robertson. New Brunswick, NJ: Transaction Books.

Robert, Jacques. 2003. "Religious Liberty and French Secularism." *BYU Law Review* (2): 637–60.

Roberts, Colin. 2000. "Secularization and the (Re)formulation of French Catholic Identity." In *Catholicism, Politics and Society in Twentieth-Century France,* edited by Kay Chadwick. Liverpool: Liverpool University Press.

Roy, Olivier. 1999. *Vers un islam européen.* Paris: Esprit.

2007. *Secularism Confronts Islam.* Translated by George Holoch. New York: Columbia University Press.

Rustow, Dankwart A. 1959. "The Army and the Founding of the Turkish Republic." *World Politics* 11 (4): 511–52.

Saeed, Agha. 2003. "Muslim-American Politics: Developments, Debates and Directions." In *Muslims in the United States,* edited by Philippa Strum and Danielle Tarantolo. Washington, DC: Woodrow Wilson International Center for Scholars.

Safran, William. 2003a. "Pluralism and Multiculturalism in France: Post-Jacobin Transformations." *Political Science Quarterly* 118 (3): 437–65.

2003b. "Religion and Laïcité in a Jacobin Republic: The Case of France." In *The Secular and the Sacred: Nation, Religion, and Politics*, edited by William Safran. Portland, OR: Frank CASS.

Sahu, Sunil K. 2002. "Religion and Politics in India: The Emergence of Hindu Nationalism and the Bharatiya Janata Party (BJP)." In *Religion and Politics in Comparative Perspective: The One, the Few, and the Many*, edited by Ted Gerard Jelen and Clyde Wilcox. New York: Cambridge University Press.

Said, Edward W. 1979. *Orientalism*. New York: Vintage Books.

1997. *Covering Islam: How the Media and the Experts Determine How We See the Rest of the World*. New York: Vintage Books.

Sandel, Michael. 1999. "Religious Liberty: Freedom of Choice or Freedom of Conscience?" In *Secularism and Its Critics*, edited by Rajeev Bhargava. Delhi, India: Oxford University Press.

Santorum, Rick. 1997. "But Are They Catholic?" *National Review* 49 (10): 42–5.

Sarıtoprak, Zeki, ed. 2008. "Special Issue on Bediüzzaman Said Nursi." *Islam and Christian-Muslim Relations* 19 (1): 1–147.

Sarkozy, Nicolas. 2004. *La République, les religions, l'espérance*. Paris: Cerf.

Sarna, Jonathan D. and David G. Dalin. 1997. *Religion and State in the American Jewish Experience*. Notre Dame, IN: University of Notre Dame Press.

Sartori, Giovanni. 1970. "Concept Misformation in Comparative Politics." *American Political Science Review* 64 (4): 1033–53.

Sayyid, S. 2003. *A Fundamental Fear: Eurocentrism and the Emergence of Islamism*. New York: Zed Books.

Schlesinger, Arthur M., Jr. 1998. *The Disuniting of America: Reflections on a Multicultural Society*. New York: W. W. Norton.

Scott, James. 1985. *Weapons of the Weak: Everyday Forms of Peasant Resistance*. New Haven, CT: Yale University Press.

1999. *Seeing Like a State: How Certain Schemes to Improve the Human Condition Have Failed*. New Haven, CT: Yale University Press.

Scott, Joan Wallach. 2007. *The Politics of the Veil*. Princeton, NJ: Princeton University Press.

Segal, A. Jeffrey and Harold J. Spaeth. 2002. *The Supreme Court and the Attitudinal Model Revisited*. New York: Cambridge University Press.

Segal, Jeffrey A. n.d. "Perceived Qualifications and Ideology of Supreme Court Nominees, 1937–2005." http://ws.cc.stonybrook.edu/polsci/jsegal/qualtable.pdf, accessed on June 4, 2006.

Segal, Jeffery A. and Albert D. Cover. 1989. "Ideological Values and the Votes of U.S. Supreme Court Justices." *American Political Science Review* 83 (2): 557–65.

Segers, Mary C. 1998. "In Defense of Religious Freedom." In *A Wall of Separation? Debating the Public Role of Religion*, edited by Mary C. Segers and Ted G. Jelen. Lanham, MD: Rowman and Littlefield.

Seksig, Alain, Patrick Kessel, and Jean-Marc Roirant. 1999. "Ni Plurielle ni de combat: La laïcité." *Hommes and Migrations* (1218): 64–75.

Selçuk, Sami. 1999. "Laiklik ve Demokrasi." *Türkiye Günlüğü* (56): 45–9.

Sewell, William H., Jr. 1985. "Ideologies and Social Revolutions: Reflections on the French Case." *The Journal of Modern History* 57 (1): 57–85.

Sezgin, Yüksel. 2003. "Can the Israeli Status Quo Model Help Post–February 28 Turkey Solve Its Problems?" *Turkish Studies* 4 (3): 47–70.

    2007. "The State's Response to Legal Pluralism: The Case of Religious Law and Courts in Israel, Egypt and India." PhD diss. University of Washington, Seattle.

Shepard, Todd. 2006. *The Invention of Decolonization: The Algerian War and the Remaking of France*. Ithaca, NY: Cornell University Press.

Sikkink, David. 2003. "From Christian Civilization to Individual Civil Liberties: Framing Religion in the Legal Field." In *The Secular Revolution: Power, Interests, and Conflict in the Secularization of American Public Life*, edited by Christian Smith. Berkeley: University of California Press.

Silk, Mark. 1998. "A New Establishment?" *Religion in the News* 1 (2): 1–3.

Skocpol, Theda 1982. "Rentier State and Shi'a Islam in the Iranian Revolution." *Theory and Society* 11 (3): 265–83.

Skocpol, Theda and Meyer Kestnbaum. 1990. "Mars Unshackled: The French Revolution in World Historical Perspective." In *The French Revolution and the Birth of Modernity*, edited by Ferenc Fehér. Berkeley: University of California Press.

Smith, Christian. 2002. *Christian America? What Evangelicals Really Want*. New York: Cambridge University Press.

Smith, Christian, ed. 2003a. *The Secular Revolution: Power, Interests, and Conflict in the Secularization of American Public Life*. Berkeley: University of California Press.

    2003b. "Preface." In *The Secular Revolution: Power, Interests, and Conflict in the Secularization of American Public Life*, edited by Christian Smith. Berkeley: University of California Press.

    2003c. "Introduction." In *The Secular Revolution: Power, Interests, and Conflict in the Secularization of American Public Life*, edited by Christian Smith. Berkeley: University of California Press.

    2003d. "Secularizing American Higher Education: The Case of Early American Sociology." In *The Secular Revolution: Power, Interests, and Conflict in the Secularization of American Public Life*, edited by Christian Smith. Berkeley: University of California Press.

Smith, D. E. 1999. "India as a Secular State." In *Secularism and Its Critics*, edited by Rajeev Bhargava. Delhi, India: Oxford University Press.

Smith, Gary Scott. 2006. *Faith and the Presidency: From George Washington to George W. Bush*. New York: Oxford University Press.

Smith, Timothy L. 1967. "Protestant Schooling and American Nationality, 1800–1850." *Journal of American History* 53 (4): 679–95.

Solnick, Steven L. 1999. *Stealing the State: Control and Collapse in Soviet Institutions*. Cambridge, MA: Harvard University Press.

Somel, Selçuk Akşin. 2001. *The Modernization of Public Education in the Ottoman Empire 1839–1908: Islamization, Autocracy and Discipline*. Boston: Brill.

Spencer, Robert F. 1958. "Culture Process and Intellectual Current: Durkheim and Atatürk." *American Anthropologist* 60 (4): 640–57.

Spurgin, Hugh. 1989. *Roger Williams and Puritan Radicalism in the English Separatist Tradition*. Lewiston, NY: The Edwin Mellen Press.

Stahnke, Tad and Robert C. Blitt. 2005a. "The Religion-State Relationship and the Right to Freedom of Religion or Belief: A Comparative Textual Analysis of the Constitutions of Predominantly Muslim Countries." http://www.uscirf.gov/countries/global/comparative_constitutions/03082005/Study0305.pdf, accessed on June 13, 2008.

   2005b. "The Religion-State Relationship and the Right to Freedom of Religion or Belief: A Comparative Textual Analysis of the Constitutions of Predominantly Muslim Countries." *Georgetown Journal of International Law* 36 (4): 947–1078.

Stark, Rodney and Roger Finke. 2000. *Acts of Faith: Explaining the Human Side of Religion*. Berkeley: University of California Press.

Stark, Rodney and Laurence R. Iannacconne. 1994. "A Supply-side Reinterpretation of the 'Secularization' of Europe." *Journal for the Scientific Study of Religion* 33 (3): 230–52.

Stasi Commission. 2003. "Rapport au président de la République, December 11," http://lesrapports.ladocumentationfrancaise.fr/brp/034000725/0000.pdf.

Stepan, Alfred. 2001. "The World's Religious Systems and Democracy: Crafting the 'Twin Tolerations.'" In *Arguing Comparative Politics*. New York: Oxford University Press.

Sugar, Peter F. 1964. "Economic and Political Modernization: Turkey." In *Political Modernization in Japan and Turkey*, edited by Robert E. Ward and Dankwart A. Rustow. Princeton, NJ: Princeton University Press.

Sunar, İlkay. 2004. *State, Society and Democracy in Turkey*. Istanbul: Bahçesaray University Publication.

Talin, Kristoff. 2001. "Les évêques français et la laïcité: entre attestation et contestation." In *La laïcité, une valeur d'aujourd'hui? Contestations et renégociations du modèle français*, edited by Jean Baudouin and Philippe Portier. Rennes, France: Presses Universitaires de Rennes.

Tanör, Bülent. 2001. "Laiklik ve Demokrasi." In *Laiklik ve Demokrasi*, edited by İbrahim Ö. Kaboğlu. Istanbul: İmge.

Tarhanlı, İştar B. 1993. *Müslüman Toplum, "Laik" Devlet: Türkiye'de Diyanet İşleri Başkanlığı*. Istanbul: AFA.

Taşpınar, Ömer. 2007. "The Old Turk's Revolt: When Radical Secularism Endangers Democracy." *Foreign Affairs* 86 (6): 114–30.

Taylor, Charles. 1999. "Modes of Secularism." In *Secularism and Its Critics*, edited by Rajeev Bhargava. Delhi, India: Oxford University Press.

2001. "Two Theories of Modernity." In *Alternative Modernities*, edited by Dilig Gaonkar. Durham, NC: Duke University Press.

2004. *Modern Social Imaginaries*. Durham, NC: Duke University Press.

2007. *A Secular Age*. Cambridge, MA: Harvard University Press.

Tepe, Sultan. 2005. "Turkey's AKP: A Model 'Muslim-Democratic' Party?" *Journal of Democracy* 16 (1): 69–82.

Tezel, Yahya Sezai. 2005. *Transformation of State and Society in Turkey: From the Ottoman Empire to the Turkish Republic*. Ankara: Roma.

Thelen, Kathleen. 2000. "Timing and Temporality in the Analysis of Institutional Evolution and Change." *Studies in Comparative Political Development* 14 (1): 102–9.

2003. "How Institutions Evolve: Insights from Comparative Historical Analysis." In *Comparative Historical Analysis in the Social Sciences*, edited by James Mahoney and Dietrich Rueschemeyer. New York: Cambridge University Press.

Thomas, George M., Lisa R. Peck, and Channin G. De Haan. 2003. "Reforming Education, Transforming Religion, 1876–1931." In *The Secular Revolution: Power, Interests, and Conflict in the Secularization of American Public Life*, edited by Christian Smith. Berkeley: University of California Press.

Timur, Taner. 1986. *Osmanlı Kimliği*. Istanbul: Hil.

Tocqueville, Alexis de. 1983 [1858]. *The Old Regime and the French Revolution*. Translated by Stuart Gilbert. n.p.: Anchor Books.

1988 [1858]. *L'ancien régime et la révolution*. Paris: GF-Flammarion.

Toprak, Binnaz. 1981. *Islam and Political Development in Turkey*. Leiden, The Netherlands: E. J. Brill.

Touraine, Alain. 1997. *Pourrons-nous vivre ensemble? Egaux et différents*. Paris: Fayard.

Troper, Michel. 2000. "Religion and Constitutional Rights: French Secularism, or Laïcité." *Cardozo Law Review* 21: 1267–84.

Turam, Berna. 2006. *Between Islam and the State: The Politics of Engagement*. Stanford, CA: Stanford University Press.

U.S. Department of State. 2006. "2006 Report on *International Religious Freedom*." http://www.state.gov/g/drl/rls/irf/2006/, accessed on May 8, 2008.

2007. "2007 Report on *International Religious Freedom*." http://www.state.gov/g/drl/rls/irf/2007/, accessed on May 8, 2008.

Üstel, Füsun. 1995. "Les partis politiques turcs, l'islamisme et la laïcité." *Cahiers d'études sur la Méditerranée orientale et le monde turco-iranien* (19): 255–64.

Uğur, Etga. 2004. "Intellectual Roots of 'Turkish Islam' and Approaches to the 'Turkish Model.'" *Journal of Muslim Minority Affairs* 24 (2): 327–45.

Ulusoy, Ali. 1999b. "Fransız ve Türk Laikliğinin Karşılaştırılması." *Liberal Düşünce* (14): 96–101.

Varisco, Daniel. 2005. *Islam Obscured: The Rhetoric of Anthropological Representation*. New York: Palgrave Macmillian.

Vergin, Nur. 2003. "Din ve Devlet İlişkileri: Düşüncenin 'Bitmeyen Senfoni'si." *Türkiye Günlüğü* (72): 23–54.

Villalon, Leonardo A. 2006. *Islamic Society and State Power in Senegal: Disciples and Citizens in Fatick*. New York: Cambridge University Press.

Wald, Kenneth D. 1996. *Religion and Politics in the United States*. New York: Congressional Quarterly.

2002. "The Religious Dimension of Israeli Political Life." In *Religion and Politics in Comparative Perspective: The One, the Few, and the Many*, edited by Ted Gerard Jelen and Clyde Wilcox. New York: Cambridge University Press.

2003. *Religion and Politics in the United States*. New York: Rowman and Littlefield.

Wald, Kenneth D. and Clyde Wilcox. 2006. "Getting Religion: Has Political Science Rediscovered the Faith Factor?" *American Political Science Review* 100 (4): 523–9.

Waldner, David. 1999. *State Building and Late Development*. Ithaca, NY: Cornell University Press.

Ward, Robert E. and Dankwart A. Rustow. 1964. "Conclusion." In *Political Modernization in Japan and Turkey*, edited by Robert E. Ward and Dankwart A. Rustow. Princeton, NJ: Princeton University Press.

Warner, Carolyn M. 2000. *Confessions of an Interest Group: The Catholic Church and Political Parties in Europe*. Princeton, NJ: Princeton University Press.

Webb, Edward. 2007. "Civilizing Religion: Jacobin Projects of Secularization in Turkey, France, Tunisia and Syria." PhD diss. University of Pennsylvania.

Weber, Eugen. 1976. *Peasants into Frenchmen: The Modernization of Rural France, 1870–1914*. Stanford, CA: Stanford University Press.

Weber, Max. 1946. "The Social Psychology of the World Religions." In *From Max Weber: Essays in Sociology*, edited by H. H. Gerth and C. Wright Mills. New York: Oxford University Press.

1949. *The Methodology of the Social Sciences*. Translated by Edward A. Shils and Henry A. Finch. New York: Free Press.

Wedeen, Lisa. 1999. *Ambiguities of Domination: Politics, Rhetoric, and Symbols in Contemporary Syria*. Chicago: University of Chicago Press.

Weil, Patrick. 2007. "La loi de 1905 et son application depuis un siècle." In *Politiques de la laïcité aux XXe siècle*, edited by Patrick Weil. Paris: Presses Universitaires de France.

Weill, Georges. 2004 [1929]. *Histoire de l'idée laïque en France au XIXe siécle*. Paris: Hachette.

Weisbrod, Carol. 2002. *Emblems of Pluralism: Cultural Differences and the State*. Princeton, NJ: Princeton University Press.

West, John G., Jr. 1991. "The Changing Battle over Religion in the Public Schools." *Wake Forest Law Review* 26 (2): 361–401.

White, Jenny B. 2003. *Islamist Mobilization in Turkey: A Study in Vernacular Politics*. Seattle: University of Washington Press.

Wieviorka, Michel. 1995. "Laïcité et démocratie." *Pouvoirs* (75): 61–71.

Wieviorka, Michel, ed. 1996. *Une société fragmentée? Le multiculturalisme en débat*. Paris: La Découverte.

Willaime, Jean-Paul. 2000. "L'enseignement religieux à l'école publique dans l'Est de la France: une tradition entre déliquescence et recomposition." *Social Compass* 47 (3): 383–95.

2004a. *Europe et religion: les enjeux du XXIe siècle*. Paris: Fayard.

2004b. "Peut-on parler de 'laïcité Européenne'?" In *La Laïcité à l'épreuve: Religions et libertés dans le monde*, edited by Jean Baubérot. n.p.: Universalis.

2004c. "The Cultural Turn in the Sociology of Religion in France." *Sociology of Religion* 65 (4): 373–89.

2005a. "Introduction." In *Des maîtres et des dieux: écoles et religions en Europe*, edited by Jean-Paul Willaime and Séverine Mathieu. n.p.: Belin.

2005b. "1905 et la pratique d'une laïcité de reconnaissance sociale des religions." *Archives de sciences sociales des religions* (129): 67–82.

2005c. "L'Union européenne est-elle laïque." In *Les Entretiens d'Auxerre: De la séparation des Églises et de l'État à l'avenir de la laïcité*, edited by Jean Baubérot and Michel Wieviorka. n.p.: L'aube.

Williams, Rhys H. 1996. "Religion as Political Resource: Culture or Ideology?" *Journal for the Scientific Study of Religion* 35 (4): 368–78.

Wills, David W. 2005. *Christianity in the United States: A Historical Survey and Interpretation*. Notre Dame, IN: University of Notre Dame Press.

Wills, Garry. 1990. *Under God: Religion and American Politics*. New York: Simon and Schuster.

Wilson, John F. and Donald L. Drakeman. 2003. *Church and State in American History: Key Documents, Decisions, and Commentary from the Past Three Centuries*. Boulder, CO: Westview.

Winock, Michel. 2004. "Comment la France a inventé la laïcité." *L'Histoire* (289): 40–9.

Witte, John, Jr. 1991. "The Theology and Politics of the First Amendment Religion Clauses: A Bicentennial Essay." *Emory Law Review* 40 (2): 489–507.

2004. *Religion and the American Constitutional Experiment*. Boulder, CO: Westview.

Witte, John, Jr. and M. Christian Green. 1996. "American Constitutional Experiment in Religious Human Rights: The Perennial Search for Principles." In *Religious Human Rights in Global Perspective: Legal Perspectives*, edited by Johan D. van der Vyver and John Witte Jr. The Hague: Martinus Nijhoff.

Wood, James E., Jr. 1985. "Preface." In *Religion and the State: Essays in the Honor of Leo Pfeffer*, edited by James E. Wood Jr. Waco, TX: Baylor University Press.

1986. "Religion and the Public Schools." *BYU Law Review* (2): 349–70.

1993. "Government Intervention in Religious Affairs: An Introduction." In *The Role of Government in Monitoring and Regulating Religion in*

Public Life, edited by James E. Wood Jr. and Derek Davis. Waco, TX: Baylor University.

1998. *Church-State Relations in the Modern World: With Historical, National, International, and Ecclesiastical Documents and an Annotated Bibliography*. Waco, TX: Baylor University Press.

WRR, Netherlands Scientific Council for Government Policy. 2004. *The European Union, Turkey and Islam*. Amsterdam: Amsterdam University Press.

Wuthnow, Robert. 1990. *The Struggle for America's Soul: Evangelicals, Liberals, and Secularism*. Grand Rapids, MI: Eerdmans.

Yalman, Nur. 1973. "Some Observations on Secularism in Islam: The Cultural Revolution in Turkey." *Daedalus* 102 (1): 139–68.

Yavuz, Hulusi. 1986. "Mecelle'nin Tedvini ve Cevdet Paşa'nın Hizmetleri." In *Ahmet Cevdet Paşa Semineri: 27–28 Mayıs 1985*. Istanbul: Edebiyat Fakültesi Basımevi.

Yavuz, M. Hakan. 2000. "Turkey's Fault Lines and the Crisis of Kemalism." *Current History* 99 (633): 33–8.

2003. *Islamic Political Identity in Turkey*. Oxford: Oxford University Press.

Yavuz, M. Hakan., ed. 2006. *The Emergence of a New Turkey: Democracy and the AK Parti*. Salt Lake City: University of Utah Press.

Yavuz, M. Hakan and John L. Esposito. 2003. "Introduction: Islam in Turkey, Retreat from the Secular Path?" In *Turkish Islam and the Secular State: The Gülen Movement*, edited by M. Hakan Yavuz and John L. Esposito. Syracuse, NY: Syracuse University Press.

Yıldız, Ahmet. 2001. *"Ne Mutlu Türküm Diyebilene": Türk Ulusal Kimliğinin Etno-Seküler Sınırları (1919–1938)*. Istanbul: İletişim.

Yılmaz, İhsan. 2002. "Secular Law and the Emergence of Unofficial Turkish Islamic Law." *Middle East Journal* 56 (1): 113–31.

2005. *Muslim Laws, Politics and Society in Modern Nation States*. Burlington, VT: Ashgate.

Young, Lawrence A., ed. 1996. *Rational Choice Theory and Religion: Summary and Assessment*. New York: Routledge.

Zald, Mayer N. 2000. "Ideologically Structured Action: An Enlarged Agenda for Social Movement Research." *Mobilization: An International Journal* 5 (1): 1–16.

Zarcone, Thierry. 2006. "Quand la laïcité des francs-maçons du Grand Orient de France vient aux Jeunes Turcs." In *Le choc colonial et l'islam: Les politiques religieuses des puissances coloniales en terres d'islam*, edited by Pierre-Jean Luizard. Paris: La Découverte.

Zeghal, Malika. 2005. "La constitution du Conseil Français du Culte Musulman: Reconnaissance politique d'un Islam français." *Archives de sciences sociales des religions* (129): 97–113.

Zoba, Wendy Murray. 2005. *The Beliefnet Guide to Evangelical Christianity*. New York: Three Leaves Press.

Zoller, Elisabeth, ed. 2005. *La conception américaine de la laïcité*. Paris: Editions Dalloz.

Zuber, Valentine. 2004. "La Commission Stasi et les paradoxes de la laïcité française." In *La Laïcité à l'épreuve: Religions et libertés dans le monde*, edited by Jean Baubérot. n.p.: Universalis.

2005. "L'idée de séparation en France et ailleurs." In *Les Entretiens d'Auxerre: De la séparation des Églises et de l'État à l'avenir de la laïcité*, edited by Jean Baubérot and Michel Wieviorka. n.p.: L'aube.

Zuckert, Michael P. 2004. "Natural Rights and Protestant Politics: A Restatement." In *Protestantism and the American Founding*, edited by Thomas S. Engeman and Michael P. Zuckert. Notre Dame, IN: University of Notre Dame Press.

Zürcher, Erik Jan. 2000. "Young Turks, Ottoman Muslims and Turkish Nationalists: Identity Politics, 1908–1938." In *Ottoman Past and Today's Turkey*, edited by Kemal H. Karpat. Leiden, The Netherlands: Brill.

2004a. *Turkey: A Modern History*. New York: I. B. Tauris.

2004b. "Institution Building in the Kemalist Republic: The Role of the People's Party." In *Men of Order: Authoritarian Modernization under Ataturk and Reza Shah*, edited by Touraj Atabaki and Erik Jan Zürcher. New York: I. B. Tauris.

2005. "Ottoman Sources of Kemalist Thought." In *Late Ottoman Society: The Intellectual Legacy*, edited by Elisabeth Özdalga. New York: Routledge Curzon.

n.d. "The Rise and Fall of 'Modern' Turkey." http://www.let.leidenuniv.nl/tcimo/tulp/Research/Lewis.htm, accessed on February 26, 2006.

Zürcher, Erik-Jan and Heleen Van Der Linden. 2004. "Searching for the Fault-Line." In *The European Union, Turkey and Islam*, edited by WRR, Netherlands Scientific Council for Government Policy. Amsterdam: Amsterdam University Press.

Zylberberg, Jacques. 1995. "Laïcité, connais pas: Allemagne, Canada, États-Unis, Royaume-Uni." *Pouvoirs* (75): 37–52.

Index